Oz Clarke's

NEW
CLASSIC
WINES

Oz Clarke's
NEW CLASSIC WINES

WEBSTERS / MITCHELL BEAZLEY

To MY MUM
WITHOUT WHOM I'D NEVER
HAVE GOT THROUGH ALL THOSE
TASTING SAMPLES

Oz Clarke's New Classic Wines

Edited and designed by Webster's Wine Price Guide Ltd,
Axe & Bottle Court, 70 Newcomen Street, London SE1 1YT,
in association with Mitchell Beazley International Ltd,
Michelin House, 81 Fulham Road, London SW3 6RB

CIP catalogue record for this book is available from the British Library.

Colour separations by Scantrans (PTE) Ltd, Singapore
Printed and bound in Hong Kong

EDITORIAL DIRECTOR Sandy Carr
ART DIRECTOR Douglas Wilson
EDITOR Fiona Wild
ART EDITOR Vanessa Courtier
DEPUTY ART EDITOR Alison Donovan
EDITORIAL ASSISTANT Siobhan Bremner
MAPS AND PICTURES RESEARCHER Wink Lorch
MAPS David Atkinson
INDEXER Naomi Good

CONTENTS

INTRODUCTION

I THINK I'VE WANTED TO WRITE this book ever since one day in the mid-seventies when I was lying on a nudist beach near Sydney with a chap who is now one of Australia's most respected winemakers. He'd promised to show me that Australia could make red wines as great as any in Europe and said the beach would do just fine. As he pulled the corks from his old bottles of Rouge Homme and Grange Hermitage, all buried in the sand to keep them cool, I was trying to swat the flies out of the plastic mugs. Red wine had never tasted so good.

And he talked about his vision. He told me that Australia had vineyard areas as good as those of the classic areas of France, as cool in climate, as well-drained in soil. They hadn't all been discovered yet, but some had flowered a century ago, before being discarded and forgotten.

And he told me that the great Burgundy grapes Chardonnay and Pinot Noir could be brilliantly successful on these cool climate sites, and that Cabernet Sauvignon, the great grape of Bordeaux, could flourish too. It simply required imagination, and commitment, and also one more thing. It required the humility and curiosity to make the long trek back to Europe, to take whatever menial jobs were available in the cellars and vineyards of Bordeaux and Burgundy, and to soak up every bit of knowledge about why some soils were better than others, why some grapes were better than others, why some wines from seemingly identical sites were delicious, and others were stale and flat. Always inquire, always observe. A traditional winemaker in France might have no idea why he did certain things. Then it was up to the inquisitive, scientific minds of travellers from new wine regions to supply the reasons and with them attempt to supply the answers.

I left Australia and crossed the Pacific to California. This wasn't a wine trip – I was acting, so we spent most of our time on the seedy side of Hollywood. One night we had a birthday party, and piled into a Chinese restaurant at the wrong end of Sunset Strip to find it was unlicensed. For a group of thirsty actors this was close to catastrophe. For me, as a budding wine fan, it was another wonderful stroke of good luck.

There was a bottle store, nothing fancy, next door. I went in, looked at the price of French Champagne, reeled back, and asked: didn't they have

something good but local? I'd asked the right man. This shop was the only Los Angeles outlet for Schramsberg, a new Napa Valley sparkling wine company. I bought an armful of the rosé and the blanc de blancs and tottered back next door. It was explosively good. There was one of those deeply satisfying moments when a whole group of people who really don't care much about the minutiae of wine – they just like it – when the whole group falls silent because the wine is so much better than they'd ever expected it could be.

In a Chinese chop suey house and on a lazy Sydney beach I'd stumbled on some of the most fundamental personality points for the new classic styles that were just feeling their way cautiously into the light – you don't have to know the ins and outs of wine talk to enjoy them; you don't have to slave away understanding the experience; these new wines are wonderful to drink young, but they'll age as well as any normal person would want them to; these new wines can be of superb quality *and* be approachable by anyone with a palate sensitive enough to tell sweet and sour sauce from a kangaroo steak.

Late that summer I was back in France, more interested in sun and romance to be honest, but we had some introductions to wine producers, one of them a grower in the hills behind Ste Maxime in Provence. His outfit was pretty recently established, but he was keen, and as we left he gave us a bottle of 'something special' he'd like us to try. We camped in an old quarry within sight of the twinkling dockside lights of Ste Maxime, cooked up a ratatouille over a fire of herb twigs and brush, and broke open our bottle. Deep dark purple, a fabulous aroma of herbs and blackcurrant storming out of the glass, and a flavour of deep ripe fruit unlike anything we'd ever tasted in the flat hard reds of Provence. Bernard Féraud was introducing his Cabernet Sauvignon to the world: that is, us, the ratatouille and the moths darting around the flames of the camp fire. The local wine regulations didn't accept Cabernet Sauvignon as a constituent for the dull Provençal reds of those days. Someone had to challenge the status quo. Within a generation there'd be people all over France challenging restrictive practices from the past. It may not require such courage now. But it required a great deal of nerve and vision then.

These weren't just coincidences in three far-flung corners of the globe. They were very definite signs that the old order of wine was being challenged, that an era when wine was dominated by the French classics of Bordeaux and Burgundy, Champagne and the Loire, was coming to an end as a new surge of confidence, ambition and daring made itself felt in the world of wine.

The groundwork had been done by a few brave pioneers from Australia and California in the 1960s. The 1970s saw a trickle of courageous enthusiasm become a flood of revolutionary zeal that is spreading still in every direction across the globe. My passion for wine was born in the 1970s.

My good fortune has been to swim in this surging tide as the old order is triumphantly replaced by the new.

But people had not simply turned up in the Napa Valley, or Coonawarra or Provence and said: right, here I am, let's make great wine. They had to have role models upon which to base their aspirations, classic flavours and styles against which to measure their efforts, and these, in almost every case – the styles of the Rhine and Mosel in Germany being the exception – came from France.

There is a deep and abiding relationship between the old classic traditions and the new, but the time has passed when producers in newer wine regions of the world needed to be in awe of the old. We are in the midst of a revolution in wine now, which will transform, not only the availability and affordability of fine wines with their grand flavours and memorable personalities, but also the provision of wine as a simple, life-enhancing drink that is cheap to buy and delicious to consume. We have certainly seen golden ages of great wine in the past, but never before have we seen a golden age which is as thrilling for the quality of its common fare as for its masterpieces. That's our age, and I'm immensely happy to be in the thick of it. Geniuses and visionaries, in America, Australia, New Zealand and various parts of Europe are combining to produce truly great wines that owe much to France's classics for their inspiration, yet are now reaching their own maturity of execution in flavour and personality. These wines have long since paid their debt to the old masters.

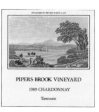

Indeed, the old masters have learned hard lessons themselves, from those very supplicants who came to learn their secrets. It was the startling success of winemakers, especially in America, introducing such ripe, exciting intensely *different* flavours to a world grown accustomed to, if not enamoured of, the leaner flavours of Europe, that sparked a revolution in the very cellars of age-old tradition. Europeans *had* to learn from the new wave just as the new wave was still striving to learn from them.

The mechanics of fine wine are now increasingly standardized throughout the world. There is an international language of wine that is understood by the leaders of all the major wine-producing nations of Europe, North and South America, South Africa and Australasia. There was a time, particularly in California, when many wine producers felt that simply to understand this language, to apply the rules of wine-making according to the book, with the latest equipment at the ready, would produce clones of Bordeaux, Burgundy and so on.

Experience has shown that there's more to wine-making than that. The technological revolution brought the possibility of control. Control in many cases brought arrogance and insensitivity, and many technically correct but unbearably characterless wines resulted. That was the first stage of our revolution. The second stage is accepting that the nuts and bolts of the winery are well understood, but the vagaries of climate, of soil, of location, and how they affect the flavours in the grapes that swell on the vine, are far from understood. Ah, but do the old classic producers understand this? Yes. They do understand it. They may not be able to tell you why, but through the generations, they have inherited lifetimes of experience of place, of style, of excellence, experience that is beyond the probing questions of a visitor from the Napa Valley, the Adelaide Hills or Hawke's Bay.

And the people I have chosen for this book realize this, too. They are the ones who are fully aware that the technological revolution *has* given them tools to employ; that the vineyard revolution *is* yielding the fruit they need; but that the modern revolution in wine is a post-technological revolution. And this is based on the efforts of men and women to understand the hearts and minds of the people who have toiled for generations in the great old winelands, to understand their inspiration, and then, not to copy the results – they'll know by now that isn't possible – but to carry back to their own vineyards a vision whose power need not be altered one jot by distance, but whose final form will be altered by every drop of rain, by every breath of wind, by every shaft of sunlight on the vines.

These people and places represent my new classics. I'm not trying to prove they are classics in the traditional sense, I am trying to show the glorious starbursts of originality and genius, of chance and determination, of eccentricity and obsession that make these people and places leaders in the new order. It's a philosophy that respects the old ways, reveres the old places, but one which can only achieve its aims through the impressive technological mastery of recent years. It is a vision that will not be denied.

My book is about dreams and dreamers. It's also a book about scientists and muddy-fingered farmers, about hillsides and valleys, sea breezes and the blazing sun, but above all it is about dreams.

The
Classic
Tradition

*There couldn't be a more 'classic' property than Château
Margaux in Bordeaux if the imposing facade is the deciding
factor. Château Margaux combines traditional qualities
with some of the most up-to-date wine-making in the region.*

The Classic Wines of France

WHAT IS THE NAME of the world's most famous fizzy wine? Which wine is a byword for sweet dessert wine? Tell me the names of the two most respected red wine styles in the world, and the most sought-after white wine style? With no desire to upset the winemakers of Germany or Italy, Spain or Portugal, they are all French. Champagne is the world's greatest sparkling wine and only comes from one small area in northern France. Sauternes is the world's top sweet wine and only comes from the Bordeaux region in south-west France. And Bordeaux is undoubtedly thought of as the home of the world's most important red wine style, except by those who support Burgundy's claims on the other side of France. White Burgundy is almost universally thought of as being the world's greatest dry white wine, although Bordeaux and even parts of the Loire Valley further north have served notice that they intend to contest this situation.

France's ability to create the great wine styles is substantially due to a happy coincidence of geography and climate. In the far north, wine grapes can hardly ripen at all. In the far south, it is almost impossible to keep them from overripeness. In between, every imaginable condition, from cool to warm, from damp to dry, can be found, and over the centuries a process of natural selection in grape types, suitable sites, and wine-making practices, has allowed wine styles to evolve of a variety unequalled so far in any other country.

It gradually became clear that the Pinot Noir and Chardonnay just ripened to perfection in Burgundy, while the Syrah reached its peak in the northern Rhône valley. The Cabernet Sauvignon, the Merlot and the white Sémillon and Sauvignon each proved that the vineyards of Bordeaux provided them with just the right amounts of moisture and warmth to ripen, not too much, not too little. The other happy coincidence is that France lies at the crossroads of Europe and is ideally placed to satisfy the thirst of the great northern trading nations. France has capitalized on this for the best part of a thousand years. There's nothing like an enthusiastic but discriminating market to persuade you to maximize your potential.

Red Bordeaux

Red Bordeaux can be majestic stuff. Dark purple, brooding, tannic, impenetrable when young, almost too rough and raw to bear, yet deep inside its soul a sweetness begins to swell with the years, the impenetrable purple retreats to garnet red, then brick, as the layers of tannin fold away. Halfway to maturity the wine can taste sturdy but powerful, the ripeness of plum and blackcurrant warring with the scouring rasp of tannin. At 10 years old, 15, maybe 20, maybe even 50, as the colour fades, the tannins seem to have melted and mingled into the cool dry scent of cedar, the sweet ripeness of blackcurrants, and just very rarely the faint-remembered perfume of violets. Red Bordeaux. Never richly indulgent, succulent or excessive, a wine that at its best can mirror a man's life in years, yet age more gracefully.

Bordeaux wine is made throughout virtually the whole department of the Gironde, but the great wines upon which the worldwide reputation rests come from three regions: the Graves, to the south of the city of Bordeaux, the Médoc to the north, and the St-Émilion and Pomerol vineyards around the smaller town of Libourne on the opposite bank.

The climate is temperate in all three regions, and the Médoc in particular, a long tongue of land heading northwards from Bordeaux city towards the Bay of Biscay, benefits from the warming influence of the Gulf Stream, while also being offered protection from Atlantic rainstorms by a wide expanse of pine forests directly to the west. The result is that the summer and autumn in Bordeaux are mostly just warm and dry enough to ripen the grapes fully and allow them to develop their own individual varietal character without overripening.

The Graves region originally formed the heart of Bordeaux's fine wine production, but as the city has expanded, vineyards have been lost and it is now the Médoc that is most important. In particular, four villages – Margaux, St-Julien, Pauillac and St-Estèphe – have developed a worldwide reputation for red wines based on the Cabernet Sauvignon, blended with Merlot, Cabernet Franc and sometimes Petit Verdot.

Unlike Burgundy, where fragmented landholdings are the long-term result of breaking up large Church holdings, Bordeaux was consolidating its position of power as a great trading port during the early nineteenth century, and the wealthy merchant class developed large estates, primarily in the Médoc, where many built the grand houses we now call châteaux. These properties produced considerable amounts of wine, as against the tiny quantities produced in the different Burgundy vineyards, meaning there was more wine to go around other European markets. Bordeaux's growing fame was further enhanced in 1855 when a classification of the top properties was drawn up according to the prices the wines fetched. Of the 58 properties chosen, 57 were from the Médoc, Graves' Haut-Brion being the exception. (There are now 61 classified properties, due to division of some estates.) This exercise was intended solely as a way of categorizing a selection of wines to be shown at the 1855 Paris Exhibition, but it established a wine hierarchy which is still revered today, and its leading wines are those most frequently imitated by the Cabernet Sauvignon makers of the world's new wine regions.

Bordeaux red wines are always blends of different grapes – a factor in their personalities only gradually being understood by varietally-conscious winemakers elsewhere. Cabernet Sauvignon now generally dominates the blend in the Médoc, but Merlot is always used and there is often some Cabernet Franc, and maybe some Malbec or Petit Verdot. All add different elements to the final blend. Wines from top estates, matured in new oak barrels, can often develop for 20 to 30 years, and may last 50 years in good condition, which is why red Bordeaux has become the world's most respected and influential red wine style.

In Pomerol and St-Émilion they grow the Merlot as their main grape because it is an early ripener. The heavier, clay-dominated soils of much of the area tend to slow down the ripening process. These wines are blends too, usually using a proportion of Cabernet Franc. Until the relatively recent dramatic rise of Pomerol in fame and popularity, these wines were far less well-known than those of the Médoc, but the Pomerols in particular are now being used as models for Merlot varietal wines, especially in California.

Sweet White Bordeaux

The ugliest grapes in France make the most luscious wine, so perhaps it is fitting that, unlike many sweet wines which are intensely grapy, you rarely get even a hint of raisin or sultana sweetness in Sauternes and Barsac. Instead you get a deep mouthcoating concentration of honey, syrup, butterscotch, just occasionally heightened by the searing sugar and acid sweetness of pineapple. As the wines age they go deeper and darker until the flavour of a great old Sauternes is like the burnt caramel sweet bitterness of barley sugar and treacle.

The development of today's wine styles is littered with happy coincidences, and none was more felicitous than the accidental discovery of the beneficial effects of 'noble rot' in 1847, when Château d'Yquem allowed its crop to overripen and rot and made its first ultra-sweet wine. It must have taken quite an act of faith to set out for the first time to rot your entire crop of grapes

Château d'Yquem make what is often reckoned to be the world's greatest sweet wine in Bordeaux's Sauternes region.

deliberately, but that's exactly what the growers in Sauternes and Barsac try to do. It is the little River Ciron running up between the vineyards to the Garonne that creates special conditions in these two communes. In warm autumns the fog swirls off the river each morning and the dew evaporates, creating a muggy, humid atmosphere in which fungal diseases flourish.

Luckily this is one of the few places in the world where the balance of warmth and damp is just right to encourage a fungus called *Botrytis cinerea*, or 'noble rot'. Unlike other forms of rot, this fungus does not sour the juice of the grape, but rather feeds on the moisture and acidity inside its skin. The sugar becomes more and more concentrated while the volume of juice diminishes. Whereas a fully ripe grape might reach a sugar level that could convert to perhaps 14 degrees of alcohol, noble rot intensifies the juice to such an extent that the sugar level can easily reach a potential alcohol level of 25 degrees of which the yeasts can only convert 14 to 15 degrees into alcohol, so all the rest of the grape sugar remains unfermented in the wine. But it's an expensive business – you might only get a glass or two of wine per vine instead of the usual bottle or two.

The two main grapes used in sweet white Bordeaux are the Sémillon, which is very susceptible to noble rot and gives a luscious lanolin feel to the finished wine, and the Sauvignon Blanc which contributes more of the balance and freshness required to enable Sauternes to age for longer than any white wine in France. Muscadelle is occasionally used for its honeyed spice. When the wine is made from grapes heavily affected by noble rot and aged in oak barrels, as at properties like Climens, Guiraud, Lafaurie-Peyraguey, Rieussec or Doisy-Védrines, the result is intense richness combined with full alcoholic strength.

Dry White Bordeaux

Until the mid-1980s, the tradition of the great barrel-fermented whites of the Graves was just surviving by a thread through the few barrels produced each year at Haut-Brion and Domaine de Chevalier. But what wonderful wine those few barrels contained! The grassy bite of the Sauvignon grape was fattened up by the rich lanolin smoothness of the Sémillon, with an irresistible apricot, peaches and cream fruit salad that deepened with the years into a more serious but no less exciting nutty, honeyed splendour every bit as good as the top wines of Burgundy.

After all, Bordeaux has all the basic ingredients needed for outstanding whites – the climate, the soil and the grapes. The climate is good – kept temperate by the effects of the Gulf Stream directly to the west – and even in the poorest years it should be possible to ripen grapes for dry white adequately. Soils are also good in the Graves in general, but particularly in Pessac-Léognan. And the grape varieties are good. Both the sharp, snappy Sauvignon and the rounder, softer Sémillon are excellent varieties. All that was needed was the will to make the best of these natural advantages.

Dry white Bordeaux has for generations been dismissed as of no quality or importance. The determined efforts of châteaux like Fieuzal, Couhins-Lurton, Malartic-Lagravière, Smith-Haut-Lafitte and Rahoul ably demonstrate in the best possible way that the new classic movement is often at its most potent when rediscovering and improving upon great old classic wine styles.

Red Burgundy

Pinot Noir has the reputation for being the most fickle, most infuriating, most capricious grape variety to grow in the world. It has the reputation for being the most reluctant to yield up the perfume and the personality that your memory of precious bottles tells you must be there somewhere, but whose existence you begin to believe is as illusory as a mirage. Pinot Noir is the grape of red Burgundy, and red Burgundy has led me on more wild goose chases, cost me more high-priced disappointments, than any other wine in the world.

Until the end of the 1980s, in all Burgundy I could probably have named no more than three red wine producers of whom I could say, hand on heart – I *know* this wine will be good. Ah, but those good bottles. Even

the most poetically conceived, even the most inspired in execution of red Bordeaux cannot make your heart race and your head swim with dreams and fantasy quite like great red Burgundy can. In no other red wine can the spices swish so mischievously, the fruit seem so tantalisingly ripe yet so delicately frail, the brooding, savage scents of animal and undergrowth seem so threatening yet irresistible. The flavours of the greatest red Burgundies are sensuous, often erotic, above rational discourse and beyond the powers of measured criticism as they flout the conventions in favour of something rooted in emotions and passions too powerful to be taught, too ancient to be meddled with.

Making great red Burgundy is a tightrope walk between man and nature. Burgundy's climate is *not* perfect, and the vines are extremely vulnerable to poor autumn weather. Pinot Noir needs regular sun to ripen, but will quickly overripen if the sun gets too hot. The grape's thin skin cannot cope with much rainfall and the grapes will swell and burst and then rot if they get rained on at harvest time. And the colouring matter, flavouring extracts and tannins are so finely balanced in Pinot Noir that any overcropping is likely to produce underripe washed-out rosé in such a marginal climate as Burgundy.

So it is absolutely crucial for the winemaker to care about the quality of grapes he is using. And until the mid-1980s, this was Burgundy's biggest problem. The output of red Burgundy from the string of little villages on the Côte de Nuits and Côte de Beaune is small. The demand is considerable for the *name*, the famous name – the Gevrey-Chambertin, Nuits-St-Georges, Pommard or Volnay – it was the *name* people bought, not the taste.

But the 1980s brought change to the region. Prices soared, but so did criticism of the poor quality of much of the wine, creating a powerful backlash that persuaded many younger growers – and a few older ones – to make a move. They wanted to get out from under the thumb of the powerful merchants who traditionally controlled the region, and not only make a better living for themselves but also produce something they could be proud of. The traditional arrogance of the Burgundian merchant was replaced by the fierce pride of people who cared deeply about the land they lived and worked on. The heart of Burgundy now beats in the vineyards rather than the merchants' dining rooms, and the tussle of wills and sensitivities necessary to get the best out of

The tiny villages of Burgundy's Côte d'Or, often sporting a church spire enhanced by the local mosaic tiles, possess a timeless tranquillity. This is Pernand-Vergelesses.

Pinot Noir has made Burgundy a passionate place. Different philosophies rage through the Côte. But ten years ago communication was so poor that dispirited growers wouldn't even talk to other growers a mile up the road.

Now a sense of healthy rivalry has returned which is ushering in a golden age for red Burgundy – not only in the famous villages, but also in the previously unsung Côte Chalonnaise, a few miles to the south. Just in time, because the secrets of Pinot Noir are being unlocked in Oregon and California, in New Zealand and Australia, even in Italy and Spain by some of the most committed and inspired winemakers in the world. For the first time ever, producers of red Burgundy have some real competition on their hands.

White Burgundy

White Burgundy has been the inspiration for more winemakers around the globe than any other wine. Although the region of Burgundy technically runs from Chablis, almost on the border of Champagne to the north, way down to Beaujolais above the city of Lyon, the wines which have inspired Chardonnay producers in

Riquewihr is one of the loveliest ancient towns in Alsace, and its grand cru vineyards Schoenenburg and Sporen produce some of the region's most concentrated whites.

every corner of the world where vines will grow, have come from four small villages on the Côte de Beaune in the centre of Burgundy – Aloxe-Corton, Meursault, Chassagne-Montrachet, and above all, Puligny-Montrachet. The very dry wines of Chablis, always seeming to need just a little more richness than they can ever attain, do have a considerable reputation, and Pouilly-Fuissé in the Mâconnais region of southern Burgundy, with its full, creamy easy-going charm, can also be delicious wine. But it's only on the limey south-to east-facing slopes of these villages that the Chardonnay has traditionally achieved the astonishing balance between savoury dryness and heady lusciousness, unmasked by sweetness but enriched by oak, that has persuaded connoisseurs over the centuries to proclaim wines such as Montrachet and Corton-Charlemagne as France's greatest white wines.

These connoisseurs, primarily from Britain and the Low Countries, are important. In the nineteenth century and the first half of the twentieth, they were the arbiters of taste in fine wine. Although there were Belgian and Dutch connoisseurs knowledgeable on the subject of red Burgundy, the English-speaking fraternity were almost to a man obsessed with the red wine world of Bordeaux, and in particular, the Médoc. Dry white Bordeaux they disdained – but you have to have something to drink with the fish course, and white

Burgundy played the support role at dinners centred on red Bordeaux.

When the Californians and Australians decided not only to drink the great reds and whites of France but to emulate them in their own new vineyards, they planted Bordeaux's Cabernet Sauvignon and Burgundy's Chardonnay.

However, there's a lot more to the wines of Meursault or Puligny-Montrachet than mere grape variety. The Chardonnay ripens slowly but reliably on the Côte d'Or, keeping good acidity and attaining reasonable alcohol. But at the top estates, some special techniques transformed the wine. Firstly oak barrels, new or slightly used, were employed for fermenting the wine, not merely storing it. The acidity would be softened by encouraging the malolactic fermentation. The flavour would be further intensified by leaving the wine on its yeast deposits, and sometimes even rousing the yeasty sludge to increase the wine's soft creamy yeast character. And when the money was available, new oak barrels would be used for storage to add vanilla, toast and spice to the taste of the Chardonnay fruit.

It was only the top few estates that employed these techniques. But the incessant flow of visitors, first from America, then from every serious wine-producing country in the world, actually spread the gospel of quality throughout the lesser estates and the lesser villages of Burgundy, far more effectively than any local pressure group could have done. There is more good white Burgundy now being produced than ever before, not only in the main villages, but in the communes of the side valleys, the hills behind the main slopes, and the Côte Chalonnaise to the south – using the techniques of the top estates brought within their reach by the brilliant successes of Chardonnay producers in a dozen countries. Chardonnay has proved itself to be the most adaptable of all the great grapes, able to produce good wine under almost any conditions. Yet the variety owes its world-beating reputation to claret-loving connoisseurs of yesteryear who needed something to drink with their turbot.

Beaujolais

Beaujolais is a large area at the southern end of Burgundy and is almost entirely planted with the Gamay grape, not the Pinot Noir. It isn't a very exciting grape and is in fact banned from use in any of Burgundy's major appellations further north. But on the granite slopes of the Beaujolais hills the Gamay achieves its one moment of glory and manages to produce a red wine that at its best is sheer pleasure, all fruit and perfume and heady summer flavours, with no hard edges at all. This is almost entirely due, not to the Gamay itself, but to the method of vinification, which involves at least part of the crop not being crushed and fermentation taking place inside the grape. The process is called carbonic maceration, and it produces a very fruity, aromatic wine high in colour, but low in tannin. This technique has been copied throughout the world as a way of giving a fresh, gluggable character to wine from grapes that may possess little personality of their own. Many of the most popular quaffing reds in countries like America, Australia, South Africa and Italy are only possible thanks to use of this 'Beaujolais' method.

Loire

The Loire is often talked of as a river with a host of different wine styles. In fact it has a host of different *appellations contrôlées*, but relatively few definable wine styles, largely because its northerly position and the consequent difficulty the grapes have in ripening, seriously restrict the range of possible wine styles for the wine producer. However, the hot vintages at the end of the 1980s and beginning of the 1990s show the multiplicity of flavours of which the river *is* capable when the sun shines. If summers stay warm, on the pattern of the late 1980s, Loire styles will yield progressively more fascinating wines.

The one style that has served as a role model for other winemakers is that of the Sauvignon Blanc grown in the upper Loire villages of Sancerre and Pouilly-sur-Loire. But its rise to fame is amazingly recent. During the 1960s the wines were dismissed as green, snappy, unpretentious country wines. Spot on. That marvellous snappy green fruit of Sauvignon Blanc grown on the chalk and flint soils of the upper Loire matched the rebellious mood of the 1970s brilliantly. Made without the influence of new oak barrels, these wines can still epitomize the fresh zing of good Sauvignon, but with the advent of sensational Sauvignon Blanc from New Zealand's Marlborough vineyards, their pre-eminence is no longer assured.

Alsace

Alsace's vineyards lie along a very beautiful ribbon of land on the steep slopes of the Vosges mountains to the west of the Rhine. Between 1871 and 1918 the region was part of Germany who used it as a convenient source of cheap blending wine, and any identity and tradition it may have previously possessed was obliterated. Between the wars attempts were made to re-establish vineyards with quality wine production in mind, in line with the new *appellation contrôlée* philosophies taking shape during the 1930s, but by 1940 Alsace was in German hands again and by 1945 was once more devastated. So, another fresh start was made as vineyards were replanted and cellars rebuilt. It wasn't until 1962 that Alsace gained its *appellation contrôlée*, but the final decree showed considerable foresight. Producers decided to label all their wines according to the grape variety, the first French region to do so. In 1972 an additional rule decreed that all Alsace wines had to be bottled at source – again, the first French appellation except Champagne to do this.

The Germanic influence continues in the region, however, in that Alsace's most famous grape varieties are Riesling and Gewürztraminer, followed by Tokay Pinot Gris and Muscat, and all the wines are created to accentuate the flowery, spicy perfumes of the grapes while, except in a few cases of late-picked, noble-rotted examples, they remain basically dry.

Alsace has never had a great influence on other wine regions. The occasional attempt elsewhere with Gewürztraminer takes Alsace as its model, but Australian Riesling was developed from the old German model. The most important contribution Alsace has made is to prove that Muscat can make beautifully seductive dry white wine. Australia has already got the message, and southern France, Spain and Portugal are rapidly catching on too.

Champagne

The people in Champagne are fond of saying that it isn't the way the wine is made that matters, it's where you grow the grapes and how you blend the wines. Fair enough. Both the very particular vineyard conditions and the necessary habit of blending the wines of different grape varieties, from different villages and even of different vintages are of great importance to Champagne's own view of its own importance and uniqueness. But it is the 'Champagne method' – the way the wine is made to sparkle in the bottle – that is of enormous importance to the rest of the world's winemakers, as they strive to prove that it is not just the windswept chilly hills and valleys of this northern French region that have the ability to make great sparkling wine.

The sparkle in a wine is brought about by inducing a second fermentation through the addition of sugar and yeast to finished wine. This will in turn create alcohol and carbon dioxide. Carbon dioxide is a very soluble gas, so if you can conduct this second fermentation under pressure, the gas dissolves in the wine until such a time as the pressure is released and – whoosh, bubbles, foam and fun all over the place. Cheap sparkling wines achieve this in large pressurized tanks,

and, with modern technology, the results can be pretty good, even if the bubble doesn't last long in the wine. But *all* the best wines follow the methods pioneered more than three centuries ago of getting that second fermentation to build up the pressure and dissolve the bubbles of gas *inside* the bottle from which the wine will eventually be poured.

It's a tricky process, especially since fermentation leaves a sludgy yeast deposit which has to be removed from the bottle without wasting more than a thimbleful of the precious wine, but it is the only method that creates really fine bubbles that stay ready to burst upon your palate right to the bottom of the glass. And the influence of the yeast itself is a crucial flavour factor. The longer you can leave the bottle on its yeast during and after the second fermentation, the creamier and more mouthfilling the wine will become. That's why you need good acidity in the first place to preserve freshness in the wines as they age.

Throughout the world these methods have been followed by ever-growing numbers of companies for all of the twentieth century and much of the nineteenth too. But the results away from northern France were always heavier, stodgier, failing to combine the fullness of flavour with the magical lift of vivacity achieved by Champagne houses like Pol Roger, Laurent Perrier, Henriot, Alfred Gratien and Billecart-Salmon. And, yes, the secret does lie in the soils and grape varieties grown in Champagne.

The soils of Champagne are mostly deep chalk ridges and they produce very acid wines even in ripe years, which are not in any case all that frequent in Champagne. The weather is almost too cool here for ripening grapes, so every little nook and cranny that captures a bit more sun is sought out, and when the line between ripeness and rawness is so thin, considerable differences of flavour can be discerned between more or less favourable sites. The grapes grown for Champagne are the great grapes of Burgundy, the white Chardonnay and the red Pinot Noir – aided by the less exciting Pinot Meunier – grown at the very limit of their ripening capacity.

This has been the insoluble quandary for winemakers establishing sparkling wine projects abroad – even those working for the Champagne houses like Moët & Chandon, Deutz, Mumm and Roederer – how to get the necessary high acid in warm countries. Just picking early results in green sour tastes, because the grape is simply physiologically underdeveloped. In Champagne it might take 120 days for a berry to creep towards harvest from flowering; in warm areas of America it might take 60. And until the late 1980s, Champagne looked as though it would still repel all comers. But they're finally cracking it – in Australia, New Zealand and California, by blending widely different wines of differing ripenesses and giving the wine sufficient time on its yeast to develop creaminess. The best producers only use the original Champagne grapes. The Champagne houses are always apologizing that they can't make enough wine to go round. I hope they appreciate the competition's efforts to rectify the situation.

Rhône

If you've ever wondered where wine producers are going to search for new challenges after they grow tired of Cabernet Sauvignon, Pinot Noir and Chardonnay – just follow the road down from Burgundy, through Lyon, to the Rhône Valley and the vineyards of Hermitage and Côte-Rôtie, of Condrieu and, further south, Châteauneuf-du-Pape. There, under conditions far more similar to many recently developed wine regions than cooler Bordeaux or Burgundy, grape varieties are producing wines that vary in status from intriguing to superstar.

One of these grape varieties has in fact been proving its worth in Australia for far longer than Cabernet Sauvignon, Pinot Noir, Chardonnay or any other classic variety – the Syrah. It is thought to have come from the ancient Persian city of Shiraz, but its home for centuries has been the northern Rhône. The hill of Hermitage, planted by the Romans a good 2000 years ago, yields France's greatest Syrah wines, along with the vines on the vertiginous slopes of Côte-Rôtie. Throughout the nineteenth century, Hermitage was regarded as at least the equal of top Bordeaux and Burgundy wines, but it is only during the 1980s that worldwide renown has once again been accorded to Hermitage and Côte-Rôtie.

Although Etienne Guigal now uses new French oak barrels on his Côte-Rôtie, the Syrah doesn't need any help from the sweet spice of new oak. When fully ripe the flavours are the richest, and most complex of any French grape variety, combining a heady super-richness of blackberry and raspberry with a brooding smoky, tarry attack, sometimes tempered in a most unforgettable way with the perfume of violets.

Syrah's quality is now being recognized in the south of France too, and it is frequently blended with duller traditional varieties to provide richness and backbone. But it is only since Guigal shot to international stardom with his Côte-Rôtie that California has become interested. The grape is ideally suited to much of California and the 1990s will see some fine examples surfacing. Many of Australia's greatest reds are already made from the Shiraz, as they call it, and have been for

Champagne may be the drink of celebration, but there's a sober air of prosperity marking Bollinger's headquarters.

the last 150 years, although fashion still favours Cabernet Sauvignon and Pinot Noir.

The northern Rhône's chief white variety – although only grown in minute quantities – has also become a most unlikely celebrity. The Viognier makes the rare but lovely wines of Condrieu and Château Grillet between Côte-Rôtie and Hermitage. As wine critics began to praise the red wines, so they were amazed by the fabulously heady apricots and mayflower blossom perfume of the white Viognier wines. The vine is a pig to grow and hardly ever produces a decent crop, but this rarity and novelty value has inspired a number of the more audacious Americans to see whether this couldn't prove to be the new alternative to Chardonnay. Italy and Australia, as well as other parts of France are joining in, and there seems little doubt that Viognier is going to become a very recherché but exciting 'new wave' white in tiny patches of land all over the world.

The southern Rhône Valley spreads out in a vast delta that finally empties into the Mediterranean, and the range of grape varieties swells with the growing flood. There are at least 20 different local varieties, and I'd put money on Roussanne, Muscardin and Counoise possessing a personality far beyond their current reputations.

Other European Classics

The rest of Europe has thousands of other individual wines, but hardly any of them have been of more than local importance. Italy's influence on the international interpretation of fine wine is extremely recent. However, Spain and Portugal created the classic fortified styles copied throughout the world. And Germany, though much respected for her finely crafted Riesling wines, is in fact more important on a world stage for developing the techniques necessary to create popular white wine styles worldwide – without which the explosion of wine drinking in non-traditional wine countries might never have happened.

Germany

There's no doubt that the classic Riesling tradition has had a great effect on other countries' wine styles, varying from bone dry and florally fragrant to intensely sweet and as overpoweringly concentrated as any wine in the world. But, like it or not, Germany has pioneered another style since World War Two which has had a far greater effect on wine drinking around the world – the light, fruity, innocuous, slightly sweet style epitomized by Liebfraumilch.

Although the name Liebfraumilch was used, and to a considerable extent respected, during the nineteenth century, it was only after World War Two that technology was developed that would allow large vats of grape juice to be refrigerated and fermented slowly, preserving all the fruit and fragrance of the grape. By the 1960s, methods of centrifuging and sterile filtering had become widespread in Germany, allowing the blending back of unfermented grape juice with finished wine, adding sweetness and also the fresh fruity aroma of the grape itself. This technique is now the hallmark of inexpensive commercial white wines all over the world, and the boom in wine drinking in countries such as Britain would never have occurred without them. The standard of such wines in Germany has sunk pitifully low, but elsewhere, in particular in New York and the Pacific North-West states, in South Africa, Australia and New Zealand, the perfection of this wine style is one of the greatest but least-praised contributions Germany has made to the world of wine.

Germany's achievements with the Riesling grape are more widely recognized. The grape is grown on steep, sun-favoured, southern-facing slopes along the Mosel and Rhine rivers, and the wines vary from extremely dry to lusciously sweet when affected late in the year by sugar-intensifying 'noble rot'. The Germans are so keen on proving the impossible is attainable that some producers even wait until the winter snows to make 'ice wine' from frozen berries.

But it is the conditions of white wine-making in Germany, rather than a desire to reproduce German Rieslings in other countries that has inspired the world. Only Australia and New Zealand have imitated the drier styles with any great success, although they, along with South Africa and the United States, are producing increasingly good sweet Riesling wines.

Slowly-ripened grapes give more perfumed wines, so long as the fermentation and storage temperatures are cool, and the environment is free of bacterial contamination. Such cool conditions were natural in Germany, and the application of these principles, through refrigeration and scrupulous hygiene, transformed the possibilities of wine styles in warmer countries. Production of fresh, fruity, light whites not only attracted a vast, new wine-drinking public, but also transformed attitudes to all wine-making, and has had far-reaching effects on totally non-German styles, wines made from grapes such as Torrontes, Trebbiano, Airèn (in Argentina, Italy and Spain) as well as working wonders with the great classics of Sémillon, Sauvignon and Chardonnay.

Italy

Italy's greatest wine misfortune is being known for the most basic wines, while France has built up a reputation based on her finest creations. Partly this is due to Italy's position on the map – the immediate trading neighbours are either wine producers themselves or else do not regard wine as an integral part of their culture. France's natural trading partners were to the north, countries to whom wine was a luxury and a delight rather than an everyday commodity or forbidden fruit.

Although Italy produces long-lived red wines of great character, especially the Barolo and Barbaresco of Piedmont and Chianti Classico and Brunello in Tuscany, they have tended to be locally revered and consumed. When Italy did start exporting in a big way, America with its millions of immigrant Italians basically wanted the cheap and cheerful quaffers of their homeland. Lacking an international audience for the best traditional styles, a mixture of chaos and capricious individuality in each region allowed producers to muddle on without reference to the wider world.

With the aid of men like Antinori, de Marchi and Castelli in Tuscany, Gaja, Altare and Clerico in Piedmont, Anselmi in Soave and Schiopetto and

Gravner in Friuli, men who have used an international perspective to re-evaluate, then probe and develop the true classic qualities of their regions, we are now beginning to see, not only the development of a thrilling modernist movement in Italy, but also the revelation of how exciting many of Italy's traditional styles can be. Once appreciation of the virtues of these wines reaches a wide enough international market, Italy's next wave of exports can begin – the export of grape varieties, wine styles and philosophies to parts of the world still dependent upon France for their inspiration.

Spain and Portugal

Far too many of the so-called 'sherries', 'ports' and 'madeiras' in the Americas and the southern hemisphere are simply third-rate fortified wines, drunk for their alcohol content rather than any intrinsic quality. One or two Californian producers like Quady and Ficklin, several South African producers, and an array of 'sherry' and 'port' makers in Australia have produced wines of great style and flavour. The fortified wine producers of North-East Victoria, with their 'ports', Tokays and Muscats have adapted Portugal's methods and crafted classic wines.

All the great Spanish sherries from leading houses like Lustau, Barbadillo, Gonzalez Byass, Valdespino or

The pale chalk soil underneath a cloudless blue sky produces the grapes for the great dry fino sherries.

Hidalgo, are made dry – including the aged, deep brown and pungently-flavoured styles. They come in two basic styles: fino and oloroso. 'Fino' is the dry style copied with some success in Australia, and its unique, piercingly dry flavour derives from the action of the flor yeast, which develops on the surface of the wine. Once the wine has been fully fermented to dryness, it is then lightly fortified and this creamy yeasty flor sits on the surface of the new wine and imparts an unique flavour intensity to the wine. Oloroso wines do not develop flor but gain their richness through ageing in barrel.

Port is made along the Douro river in northern Portugal, and is normally a sweet style of fortified wine, since the fermentation is arrested by the addition of neutral spirit while about half the fruit sugar remains unconverted to alcohol. The result is strong, rich and sweet wine, and a number of years' ageing either in barrel or bottle are needed to add subtlety and smoothness to the wine. Australia and California have only recently started experimenting with traditional port grapes, but have made excellent port-style wines from such varieties as Zinfandel, Shiraz, Grenache and even Cabernet Sauvignon.

The Making of Modern Wine

Not a person in sight, either among the tanks or on the arid hills behind. But modern wine can be made to a high standard in very impersonal surroundings, such as here at the Montana winery at Blenheim in New Zealand.

Soil and Climate

YOU'RE STANDING IN A VINEYARD in Bordeaux. The narrow rows of vines, trimmed back to thin hedge shapes as close-cut and symmetrical as a soldier's haircut, march across the weed-free gravel banks in long straight lines. Cabernet Sauvignon grapes, ripening in the summer sun.

You're standing on the floor of the Napa Valley in California, the rich dark earth is clearly visible between the wide-spaced rows, and the vines, heavy with foliage and fruit, heave and sway in the early evening breeze. Cabernet Sauvignon grapes ripening in the summer sun.

So you go to Coonawarra in South Australia and find the rows of vines are like a mesh of basket work, impenetrable as jungle, yet covered on the outside with a blanket of leaves and numerous tiny bunches of grapes. To the east, at Dromana Estate near Melbourne, you wonder whether you haven't strayed into some formal decorative garden as the head-high hedges of closely trimmed foliage rear vertically into the sky. While on the rocky soil of New Zealand's South Island, the bushes sprawl and flounce like an overweight ballerina dolled up in ball-gown chiffon for a final-curtain curtsey. They're all Cabernet Sauvignon, each finding a way of ripening in the summer sun, in different conditions, in different corners of the world.

You'll find similar diversity if you look at the vineyard conditions and pruning methods for, say, Pinot Noir or Chardonnay on the cold, sun-starved chalky slopes of Champagne, on the warmer but damp limestone slopes of Burgundy and on the foggy, windy, low-lying clay soils of Carneros in California, or the torrid, irrigated semi-desert of the Riverland plantations in South Australia, as against the cool but almost rainless microclimate of Martinborough in New Zealand's North Island. In each place, even though the grape variety is the same, the soils are different, the balance between sunlight, heat and moisture is different, and indeed the aims of the grower may be different too.

In Europe, grape varieties suitable to various locations have gradually evolved over the centuries. No-one 'invented' the Pinot Noir, the Chardonnay or the Sémillon, but through a mixture of trial and error with locally planted vines, vines introduced by travellers, and with the mutations that naturally develop over the generations in a vineyard, it was possible to narrow down the varieties which best fulfilled the demands of reliability, economic yield, resistance to infection and ability to ripen. It wasn't always the best flavour that was selected. In Bordeaux the Carmenère and Petit Verdot were believed to be fine for flavour, but they weren't reliable, so the less well-regarded Cabernet Sauvignon and Merlot displaced them.

Throughout the twentieth century, the varieties suitable to the best regions in Europe have been incorporated into wine laws by numerous decrees of controlled name of origin. Specific pruning methods, generally designed to restrict yield and aid ripeness, have been prescribed, and alternative varieties have been banned from these vineyards. When the great surge of interest in fine wine began to build up during the 1970s, and winemakers from all parts of the world looked for models to emulate, the table wine styles which had most appeal were those of Bordeaux and Burgundy, possibly the Rhône and some of the German Rieslings, and definitely the sparkling wines of Champagne. So choosing the same grape varieties to plant was the first decision the would-be emulators took.

Although most of California and Australia looked a bit warm, it was reckoned that this extra heat would at least guarantee a ripe crop every year rather than the erratic results common in Europe. If the right grape varieties were planted and then the wine was made as the Europeans made it, or, more likely, was improved upon – so people hoped – by use of superior technology, then the wines should not only taste as good, they should taste better.

Blowing Hot and Cold

Of course it didn't work out like that. Quite simply, the same grape varieties grown in different conditions did not produce fruit with the same flavour, and for the most fundamental reasons. Scientists at Davis wine school in California had developed a Heat Summation scale categorizing regions from one – the coolest – to five, by measuring the average temperatures during the vine's growing season. The system was insensitive to local conditions, however, and failed to take note of such differences as the strength of the sun and the number of sunlight hours, or the difference between nighttime and daytime temperatures. Australia's Hunter Valley can only make fine wine because, despite great heat, the actual total of sunlight hours is low as a result of regular afternoon cloud cover. Dramatic shifts in temperature between nighttime and daytime enable Australia's Clare Valley to produce ripe fruit with high acid. A Californian area might look as cool as Bordeaux on paper, but with completely different soil and with a different aspect to morning or evening sun, comparisons became meaningless. In the enthusiasm to develop vineyards according to the Heat Summation scale, European theories on soil were thrown out of the window. Soil? What about it? Soil holds water, either efficiently, or too efficiently, or not efficiently enough. And that's it. Water supply is what decides whether a vine lives or dies. As for all this stuff about special flavours coming from the nutrients and minerals and chemical peculiarities of one soil versus another – that's all old hat. Rainwater or irrigation water is going to hold enough trace elements for the vine's nutrition. It's moisture that the vine wants, first and last, and, frankly, any old water will do.

That's what I'd call the mould-breaking modern view. It overstates the case, yes, but not by half as much as the European traditionalists would have us believe. They would suggest that there is a certain magic actually in the soil, a certain flavour component which some special sites do possess, and others only yards away do not. So, they would assert that Château Margaux in Bordeaux has in its very soil the ability to create a particular, unique flavour, as do Le Montrachet

The fogs have cleared for the day, but the winds still trundle the tumbleweed along between vines slowly ripening on the cool clay soils of California's Carneros.

or Richebourg in Burgundy. The truth is somewhere between the two, but, to be honest, it veers more towards the blunt modern, clued-up overstatement than towards the romance of Burgundian mystique.

There is no doubt that Le Montrachet seems to produce wine with more power and intensity and brilliant complexity than its near neighbours. But the explanation lies in a combination of factors: the physical make-up of that soil and subsoil, its capacity to hold water and warmth, and the vineyard's aspect and angle of elevation towards the sun. Whether the grapes can turn these advantages into a great crop, of course, will depend on the weather; most importantly, the number of sunlight hours and the amount of heat at the various stages of the growing season.

All through the 1970s and 1980s wine producers in Australia and California tried to edge closer to European wine styles through adopting a mixture of advanced technology and traditional methods in wine-making. But as the 1990s drew near, an increasing number of the best winemakers around the world realized that if they were ever going to achieve wines of the tantalizing and exhilarating balance of' flavours that had placed European classics at the top of the league, they were going to have to make major reappraisals about the way

they grew their grapes. It was simply not enough to plant Cabernet in order to make a Bordeaux style of red wine. The grape variety might well be the same as the European model, but a grape will reflect, in however small a way, every drop of rain that it sucks up from the earth, every shaft of sunlight that strikes its leaves, every temperature degree of warmth or cold that it experiences over its growing season. It is the totting up of all these minutiae which decides whether the grape's flavour potential is reached or not.

Most of the great European vineyards are on well-drained, relatively infertile soil. This is important when excess rainfall can be a problem. The majority of Bordeaux's good vineyards are on gravel topsoil. Bordeaux's ample rainfall sinks quickly through and as soon as the sun comes out again, the gravel pebbles rapidly warm up and some of the whiter ones in the southern Médoc may even reflect heat back on to the vine. The Burgundy sites that produce the finest wines are on perceptible slopes and the best vineyards have a pebble, clay and limestone mixture of soils at the surface. The slopes crucially ensure that the relatively frequent bouts of heavy rain largely run straight off into the roadways and gutters and down to the plain. As we go further north, to Chablis and to Champagne, the limestone becomes more evident, and the best sites need to be ever steeper, angled towards the sun, and unable to hold more water than is strictly necessary.

In most of the Australian, Californian and southern European wine regions, rainfall is in short supply. But whereas in the *appellation contrôlée* areas of France you can't irrigate, in newer vineyard areas irrigation is regarded as the ultimate grape growers' tool. If you plant on free-draining soil in a hot climate, you have to irrigate because otherwise the vine would lose so much moisture through its leaves that it wouldn't survive. If you plant on heavy fertile soils like parts of California's Napa Valley, the Yarra Valley in Australia, or around Auckland in New Zealand, holding water back is one way of controlling your crop, but when water *is* in short supply at least the vines will survive.

So most grape growers do opt to install irrigation where it is legally allowed – preferably on a drip system rather than a wasteful spray system. All young vines must have water since an overstressed young vine won't develop into a healthy plant. Most growers who irrigate will cut back after the grape's colour turns, since at this point growth stops and a grape will begin to suck in excess water and dilute the juice-to-skin ratio so crucial to deep-flavoured wine. But if the weather gets very hot – over 32° to 33°C (90° to 91°F) – the grape's ripening system will shut down for self-preservation. As water is

sucked up through the trunk, the irrigated vine will be kept cool – and the grapes will go on ripening. In torrid Cowra in New South Wales, they irrigate until just before harvest simply to keep the vines going – and the resulting wines are delicious. Garry Crittenden in Victoria isn't against watering in much cooler areas too. Josh Jensen at Calera in California just wishes he could get enough water up to his mountain vineyards to guarantee a crop in the first place.

Protecting the vine from too much hot sunshine is the next problem for many non-European wine producers. Virtually all Europe's best regions are located between 40°N and 50°N. California's vineyards are mostly between 35°N and just under 40°N. Chile's, South Africa's and almost all of Australia's vineyards are between 30°S and 40°S and only those of Tasmania and South Island in New Zealand reach down towards the Bordeaux and Burgundy southern hemisphere equivalents of around 45°S. So the sun's influence is going to be far more intense than in Europe, and factors such as wind, cloud cover and fog, all of which would

be regarded as negative factors in Europe, are positively sought out to cool down the vines and lengthen the growing season. The whole of California's fine wine industry relies upon the cooling winds that blow through gaps in the coastal range mountains to the inland valleys of Sonoma, Napa, Santa Maria, Santa Ynez and others. The vineyards of Carneros, at the southern end of the Napa and Sonoma Valleys, are blanketed with fog most mornings, and a sharp wind whistles up from San Francisco Bay in the afternoon. And whereas the Gulf Stream exerts a warming influence on the west coast of Europe, the longer sunlight hours in southern Australia and New Zealand can be tempered by the cold Antarctic currents.

In Europe, most classic vineyards are slanted towards the sun, and at no more than a reasonable 200–300 metres (650–980 feet) above sea level. In Australia, pioneers like Max Lake of Lake's Folly purposely planted his vines on land facing away from the sun, and many others have followed. And many ambitious vinegrowers, anxious to prevent grapes from being

Here in the Sonoma Valley, sea fog is sucked through gaps in the coastal ranges each day, playing a crucial role in tempering the sun's heat.

scorched by the fierce afternoon sun, have planted vineyards way up in the sky. Dunn's Howell Mountain vineyard basks in the California evening sun – but at 600 metres (1970 feet) above sea level. Brown Brothers Whitlands vineyard in Australia does the same at nearer 800 metres (2625 feet).

There's no doubt that if I had to choose the climatic problems of the New World or the Old World, I'd grab those of the New World with both hands. The whole point of growing grapes is to ripen them. There may now be a move in places like Australia and California to find cooler locations where the grapes will ripen more slowly and consequently develop a more intense flavour just as any fruit does in a cooler climate, but at least producers there start off knowing that ripening the grape is not a problem, even if ripening it gently and slowly and precisely to your requirements is.

In the Vineyard

*T*HE WINE YOU DRINK is the expression of the fruit you pick. There are all kinds of things you can do to that fruit once you've got it into your winery, all kinds of gadgets you can employ, all kinds of tricks, but the bottom line is, you've got to have decent grapes. So the choices you make in the vineyard are crucial to the eventual flavours in the wine.

The first vineyard decision is absolutely fundamental. High yield or low? France's quality wine producers have always relied upon restraint of yield as a factor that would intensify grape flavour. A small crop will also ripen faster. Where lack of sun is a problem, yield reduction does seem to make sense. But much of the best wine in America and Australia has come from vineyards where heat and sun are in plentiful supply. More heat can ripen a larger crop and therefore surely higher yields can be acceptable.

The argument rages. Most growers are inclined to believe that a restricted crop is crucial for the very top level of quality. Brian Croser of Petaluma in Australia believes there is an identifiable cut-off point below which quality dramatically improves, and this is usually between three and four tons per acre – very much in line with the appellation restrictions of France. Garry Crittenden of Dromana Estate near Melbourne might agree for the absolute peak of quality, but he maintains he can produce 'very good' wine at yields closer to nine tons to the acre, and at a lower cost too.

Next, do you graft the vine on to a particular kind of rootstock or not, and do you choose a productive or non-productive clone? A rootstock which is resistant to the vine louse phylloxera is generally necessary throughout the world. Phylloxera caused devastation in numerous vineyards in the nineteenth century, and it was eventually found that American, non-*Vitis vinifera* vines, were resistant to the louse. Almost all European vines are now grafted on to American rootstocks. However, there are substantial parts of Australia, and various areas in North America, South America, New Zealand and even Europe where phylloxera has not yet struck, meaning you can plant a vine on its own rootstock. It's cheaper, and the flow of sap through the vine is unhindered by any grafting scar tissue, but the resulting wine, it has to be said, isn't necessarily better.

Different strains of rootstock can also be useful in dealing with other vineyard problems. Some are resistant to pests like nematodes, others are able to cope with the salinity which is often a problem in very dry areas needing irrigation. And some rootstocks are very vigorous, some aren't. In the heavy soils of the Napa Valley or much of New Zealand's North Island, growers should plant de-vigorating rootstocks. On the infertile soils of somewhere like the Adelaide Hills where Yalumba have their best vineyards, a vigorous rootstock graft is the only way to guarantee a crop.

Choosing Your Vines

Every grape variety shows slight variations from one strain to the next. Some of these 'clones' may occur naturally, others may be scientifically produced. When you clone a particular strain of a grape variety, you choose a single plant which displays the qualities you desire, such as resistance to disease, and then you can propagate endlessly from it, generation after generation of theoretically identical plants from this one source. Most clones developed at laboratories are selected for resistance to disease and impressive productivity rather than flavour potential. Many of the vineyards of California, Australia and New Zealand suffer from having to try to make fine wine out of such clones. New Zealand in particular, but also Oregon, have suffered from having hot climate, high-yield clones suited to California foisted on them.

A grower establishing a vineyard *can* find high-quality, low-yielding clones if he wants to, but that depends on where his ambition lies. Numerous producers have had to resort to bending the tight quarantine rules of their countries to obtain the vine material they want. At Calera they just offer a wry smile when you repeat the rumour that cuttings came from Burgundy's great Domaine de la Romanée-Conti vineyard. Bureaucracies quite rightly try to prevent vine diseases from crossing oceans, but they do not understand the passion that grips a winemaker as he or she realizes that there are only 30 or 40 chances of trying to make great wine from scratch in a lifetime. Precious vine cuttings – say, a rare Viognier from France's Rhône Valley – may be impounded in dockside quarantine, then in an isolated laboratory, for 10 or 15 years because officials aren't quite sure they're healthy. No committed wine producer is consciously going to import disease into his vineyard. But Angelo Gaja of Italy's Piedmont is not alone when he says he doesn't want virus-free clones all the time; if the vine is struggling it can result in the natural inhibition of

Milk cartons rarely go to waste in California's wine country; they get placed around the base of young vines to stop the local animal population having them for breakfast.

excessive growth and yields. It used to be a standing joke that any wine person going to South Africa should pack his suitcase with cuttings of Pinot Noir, Chardonnay, Sauvignon Blanc – anything from a decent French vineyard – because the regulations against imports there were so severe no decent plant material ever got in.

One of the chief reasons South Africa doesn't feature in this book is not political, it is that so few wines of really exciting quality have surfaced because of poor vineyard material. Until the late 1980s there virtually wasn't any legal Sauvignon or Chardonnay in the country. Finally a leading grower was taken to court for having 'illegal' cuttings in his vineyard. The South African wine fraternity, regardless of political differences, to a man rose up and said that they either already had illegal plantings too, or would have as soon as they could get cuttings. The case was dropped. Restrictions were relaxed and South African wine at last looks as though it will start fulfilling its potential.

It's interesting that in South Australia, a phylloxera-free state with rigid quarantine regulations to protect this rare state of affairs, you'll now find growers wishing that they *had* had phylloxera, because they have such trouble getting decent clonal material. Stephen Henschke, of course, would not agree. Up in the Adelaide Hills, he's got Shiraz vines over a century old, brought out from France's Rhône Valley before phylloxera devastated those vineyards, with a bloodline running back to when Roman legionnaires established the Hermitage vineyards getting on for 2000 years ago. If South Australia remains phylloxera-free, we could see clones of his ancient vines providing the source material for great red wine all over Australia, and maybe even back in France itself.

In the meantime you've still got more decisions to make in your vineyard. Over the generations, European producers have developed systems of trellising and training vines, and habits of pruning vines that either try to maximize yield, as in various parts of Germany and northern Italy, or else try to restrict it as in most parts of France and the better parts of Italy and Spain.

In general, if the vine is in an arid, hot area, like most of the Mediterranean lands, and water is not readily available, vines are planted fairly far apart and allowed to develop floppy canopies of foliage on the understanding that wide planting gives each vine a better chance of surviving on a meagre water ration, and bush-like foliage keeps the grapes cool and restricts the overall yield.

There's some truth in that. You only have to trek northwards in France towards Germany to find vines planted closer and closer together as the conditions get wetter and wetter, in an effort to restrict the vine's vigour and yield. You provide more intense competition among the vines for that copious water supply, and you prevent the vines from being literally drowned, which, in a cool area, would produce enormous crops of unripe grapes. In Germany, clonal selection has managed to produce vines which combine astonishingly high yields with satisfactory ripeness levels. Not necessarily satisfactory *flavour* levels, otherwise there would be a greater German presence in this book to celebrate such an achievement.

Let the Sun Shine In

These European trellising and pruning systems do not suit the conditions frequently found in Californian, Australian or Southern European vineyards, where a warm climate combines with fertile soil. A vine's wood needs exposure to the sun to permit fruiting buds to form for the following year's crop. If you follow the old European idea of keeping a heavy canopy of leaves on hot-climate vines, the sun will not reach the wood, and so the plant will simply throw out more and more foliage each year and less and less fruit. Attempts to 'hedge' the vines ruthlessly, as they do in Bordeaux, won't achieve anything either because on fertile soil the vine will simply react by throwing out more shoots, diverting energy from ripening the grapes.

So, imaginative modern vineyard owners have found ways to solve the problem of over-vigorous foliage preventing ripening, not by pruning more ruthlessly, but by pruning less and adopting trellis systems for the vines which actually encourage the vine to throw a big crop and lots of foliage. To allow the sun to reach the grapes, various methods have been devised which, instead of allowing fruit to hang along a wire under its canopy of leaves, actually pull the fruiting canes upwards, often vertically, inside restraining wires. The leaves are pulled away from the fruit, which then exposes its belly to the sun.

This will ensure that the next year's crop is a good one, but, just as important, the exposure to the sun will change the flavour of the grape. Traditional wisdom was that since the leaves create the sugar in the grapes through photosynthesis, and a very hot sun will burn fruit – you must have lots of leaves, preferably shading the fruit while it ripens. But in fact, the grape only needs a certain number of leaves per bunch to ripen fully – any more is superfluous, and if you shade that fruit too much, however high the sugar goes, you'll never get rid of a green apple flavour in the finished wine, red or white. Until recently almost all New

Zealand wines had this green streak. Now, thanks to changed trellising systems, a previously unhoped-for ripeness of flavour is becoming more and more evident in both red and white wines.

Even so, a vine on fertile soil does have an enormous capacity for growth, and in order not to waste this potential, systems have been developed that split the leafy canopy, either to both sides, or else with one half going upwards and the other half going downwards. In effect this gives you two vines growing off one trunk. Yielding the equivalent of two crops? You got it.

People like Garry Crittenden of Australia, and Richard Smart of New Zealand and Australia, believe that worries about yield are misplaced. Grape production is usually expressed in tons per acre or hectare or hectolitres per hectare. But if you are pruning traditionally, what matters more is the weight of the fruit each vine is producing. If you don't have many vines per acre, but go for the same overall yield as a close-planted Burgundy vineyard, your yield per individual vine will have to be much greater, and that means the size of the grapes and their bunches in a wide-spaced vineyard will have to be much larger too. Consequently there will be more juice per grape in relation to the skin, and the character of the wine will be less intense, since flavour and colour components are held in and next to the skin of the grape. So, if you want to prune traditionally, you have no choice but to plant closely, to encourage competition between vines for nourishment and reduce the demands per vine.

Or you could take a more revolutionary approach. Some of the new trellising systems, on which the vine runs relatively free, produce enormous numbers of bunches of grapes, but of small size, with tiny grapes. Yields are very high – but the proportion of juice to skins is superb. People like Crittenden have proved that at nine tons to the acre – two to three times the ideal Bordeaux yield – he can produce dark-coloured, deeply-flavoured wines from these tiny berries growing in their profusion on his mould-breaking trellises.

The vineyard creators *had* to break the mould in Australia, in California, in New Zealand, otherwise there just wouldn't have *been* any new developments. Whereas in Europe generations of families have grown up in vineyard areas, acquiring knowledge and experience from practice, no such tradition existed in the new vineyard lands. Often – in New Zealand's South Island, in Australia's Padthaway and Coonawarra, in California's Santa Maria Valley – there simply weren't any people around to train.

Not only does there have to be a viticultural revolution to produce quality wine in an untried

Vertically trellised Chardonnay almost ready for harvesting at Dromana Estate in Australia.

environment, but there has to be a mechanical revolution to make up for the lack of traditional skills. Pruning can now be done by machine. And indeed there are many thousands of acres in Australia and New Zealand that aren't pruned at all. This goes totally against the strictures concerning limited yield being a vital part of quality control. If you don't prune a vine at all, the idea seems to be that all the sun strikes the outside of the vine – so that's where all the bunches appear, dozens and dozens, all small, all ripe, basking in the sun. All possible with a couple of machines and almost no workforce. As for picking the grapes, that used to require droves of people who would take weeks to clear a large vineyard. You can do that by machine too now, in a couple of days. But by the time we get to picking the grapes, we're talking about the wine-*making* process. That starts the moment the winemaker decides his grapes are ready to pick.

In the Winery

*T*HE AMBITIOUS TYROS of wine attempting to fashion new classics in new areas of the world, regarded Bordeaux's tragedy, Burgundy's, Champagne's, the Rhine's too, as the inability to produce a regular crop of ripe grapes. Where they were setting up vineyards – in the warm Sonoma and Napa Valleys of California, on the sunny slopes and plains of New South Wales and South Australia – they weren't expecting ripeness to be a problem.

In northern Europe it is often a case of hoping and praying for a good harvest. The planting of grapes like Cabernet Sauvignon, Pinot Noir, Chardonnay and Riesling at their northernmost limits of ripening have been enshrined in law, so by and large producers in places like Champagne or Burgundy are stuck with their inheritances. In places like New Zealand, America or Australia, it is entirely up to wine producers whether they are going to take the risk of a crop not ripening at all in the quest for grapes with greater intensity of flavour from cool, slow-ripening conditions. It's all about choice.

In general, winemakers in California or in the southern hemisphere do have this choice. Sugar levels should not be a problem, but a grape isn't ripe simply because the sugar level happens to be high. Getting the grape physiologically ripe, so that the raw green tannins have finally matured and softened without loss of acidity or sugar, is a decision that requires precision timing, and in warm climates, the peak period for a crop may only last a couple of days before the balance is lost. That's where the importance of the mechanical harvester comes in.

In traditional Europe they talk of the importance of nurturing an experienced picking crew, with the same families returning to the same vineyards over the generations. In somewhere like Australia's Coonawarra or New Zealand's Marlborough, they talk of finding a good driver for their machine. A mechanical harvester can clear in two days a vineyard that would take a big team of pickers two weeks. In Europe wines may be made from a mix of grapes picked too early, spot on, and too late – because of the time it takes teams of manual pickers to comb the vineyard. But machines enable growers to clear the vines at enormous speed – and at the point of ripeness they desire.

The grape harvesting machines rely on a good driver, because they operate by slapping or shaking the grapes off the vine and a careful operator minimizes both damage to the vines and bruising to the fruit. Styles of modern trellising which expose the fruit and concentrate on a crop of large numbers of small bunches are fine for machine picking. It would take a very patient and very hard-working crew of manual pickers to harvest fruit grown in this way.

But even though modern machines can be very gentle, they leave the stems on the vine. Some winemakers, particularly Chardonnay producers, want to press their fruit in the form of whole bunches, since the presence of stems acts as a filter and the resulting juice is naturally much clearer and free of solids. Some Pinot Noir producers want to ferment some of their grapes as whole bunches in a refinement of the method used in Beaujolais to produce a markedly fruity style of wine. They'll have to pick by hand. But in New Zealand for instance, where most of the big wineries are clustered around Auckland in the North Island, and the most attractive source of grapes is at Marlborough in the South Island, you have to harvest by machine because there just aren't enough skilled pickers around. It's a machine or no crop.

This is not a problem that occurs often in the traditional areas of Europe. Grapes get picked, and they are usually vinified within a mile or two of the vineyard. In Australia, wineries in Victoria may use grapes from Western Australia – two to three days' drive away across the baking Nullarbor Plain. Other wineries in South Australia ship in grapes from New Zealand for blending. Most large wineries in the newer wine regions of the world have to truck some of their grapes for between one and eight hours from vineyard to winery.

If you're going to do this, it's crucial to stop any bacterial action on the grapes and reduce oxidation to a minimum. Careful use of sulphur dioxide as an anti-oxidant is effective, but sulphur can change flavour and inhibit yeast action at the winery when you want to ferment the juice. The best possible way to keep your grapes in good condition is to keep them cold. Many of the best of the new vineyard areas experience very cold nighttime temperatures. So the picking machines operate at night. The first time I saw these vast monsters forging through the icy darkness in Carneros in California, searchlights blazing and their clattering picking arms making an unholy din, I thought I had got caught in the middle of some futuristic military manoeuvres. But keeping those grapes cool allows the

Anything but the traditional image, these tanks and the tangle of pipes snaking from one to another are at the ultra-modern Lindemans winery in Karadoc, Australia.

winemaker his full range of options. And options is what modern wine-making is all about.

Most traditional European areas became famous for one or two styles of wine only. The 1990s are seeing increasing specialization elsewhere in the world, as a decade of experimentation begins to yield results, but the majority of wineries still try to excel at various different types of wine. Typically a winery will make several of the following – a Cabernet Sauvignon, a Chardonnay, perhaps a Sauvignon Blanc or Riesling, maybe Pinot Noir or Shiraz, Merlot or Semillon – all under the same roof. Some will also make a sparkling wine, some a sweet wine, some will even produce their version of 'port' or 'sherry'! Yet the European homes of these grapes and wine types are in very different parts of the continent, with different natural conditions.

In particular, the ambient temperature in the winery, especially at vintage time, but also right the way through the year, is likely to be naturally much hotter in newer wine regions. Over-hot fermentation temperatures destroy the freshness and fruit flavour in wine, and can lead to problems of stuck fermentation. So the most important breakthrough in modern wine-making was understanding temperature control and in particular, the introduction of stainless steel tanks and refrigeration. As early as the 1950s, different methods of cooling grape must were being pioneered in Australia and California. Control of fermentation temperature is one of the most crucial tools the new winemaker has.

For whites it is of paramount importance if the objective is to preserve fruit flavours and fragrance, especially if the wine is to remain unoaked. When the fermentation is done in barrel, temperatures can ride up higher without detriment to the wine.

Reds are generally fermented at higher temperatures than whites, as the warmth will bring out flavour and extract from the skins, especially if followed by a period of post-fermentation maceration, when the skins and wine continue to steep together for a number of days. The temperature at which wine is then aged is also important. While in barrel, less coarse flavours will be drawn out of the wood at lower temperatures – Brian Croser at Petaluma keeps his barrel store as low as 8°C (46°F) all year round. Most winemakers would probably aim for about 15°C (59°F). A Burgundian or Bordeaux cellar would usually be somewhere between the two.

So even though you can't control the temperature out in the vineyard, you can attempt indoors to

A tank of Shiraz juice fermenting. The appetizing foam is caused by pumping over the juice and splashing it back on to the skins to try to increase tannin and colour.

duplicate the naturally cool conditions of most of the classic European cellars and wineries at harvest time. This is of enormous importance, because virtually every problem that can affect a wine during fermentation and storage can be minimized if not eradicated by keeping the winery temperature low all year round.

Most of the new classic wineries that have proved their pedigree over the last couple of decades have been involved in dry white and dry red table wines, so those are the wine-making styles we'll concentrate on here. Where sparkling wine or sweet wine is made to a particularly high standard at a winery, I discuss it in the relevant profile. And in Australia I've included two fortified wine producers and gone into detail about their wine-making, not because they demonstrate anything new – although they differ from each other in attitude – but because they demonstrate a classic tradition which is now being gloriously rejuvenated.

The main winery influences on the flavour of a wine are fourfold: the skins of the grapes themselves, the yeasts used to cause fermentation, the deposits of dead yeast cells left after fermentation and how these are utilized, and the container used in fermenting and storing the wine, nowadays usually a stainless steel tank or a wooden barrel, almost always made of oak. These influences are most obvious in the creation of white wine so let's go through the white wine process first.

Making White Wine

Most winemakers want to receive grapes fresh and unbroken, although occasionally they will accept a small proportion of grapes affected by the sugar-intensifying 'noble rot' because this can add a honeyed, glycerine effect to the wine. Wineries using hand-picked grapes will try to transport the fruit, uncrushed, in small boxes, and can chill them in a cool room if they're too warm. If

the grapes have to travel a long way to the winery, a night trip is the only way to keep them cold. This is important because some juice will inevitably flow from the grapes at the bottom of the transport trucks. If the temperature is not kept down, this juice will begin to ferment by the time the load reaches the winery, but in uncontrolled conditions. And our modern winemaker wants to be in control *all* the way.

Even so, machine-picked grapes trucked a long distance will have had some contact between skin and juice. This will alter the flavour of the juice because the aromatic and flavouring elements of a grape are contained just beneath the skin. For some grape varieties, like Riesling, a winemaker will usually want to minimize this skin contact so will crush, destem and press the juice from the grapes as soon as possible. Some Chardonnay makers also do this. But others will destem and crush the grapes and then leave them to steep together for anything up to 24 hours. This method is particularly effective in giving fruit flavour to Sauvignon Blanc and Semillon grapes, as the forward-looking white wine producers in Bordeaux are discovering. The temperature should be kept low, since anything above about 9°C (48°) will draw out oily flavours from the skins which will coarsen the wine.

If the grapes were deficient in acid, as they often can be in warm climates, this should be corrected, usually with tartaric acid, at the crusher. And if you want to protect your juice against oxidation, now is when you add sulphur dioxide. However, although most Sauvignon Blanc producers agree a sulphur addition helps preserve the sharp green fruit, many of the most talented Chardonnay makers, in California especially, are positively encouraging the juice to oxidize to the colour of cold tea before fermentation. The wine turns out lovely and clear after fermentation and with a fuller, softer flavour, and is actually less likely to spoil in bottle because there's scarcely anything left to oxidize.

Traditionally in Europe after pressing, the juice would be left for a few hours to precipitate some of the heavier grape solids before fermentation was started. However, New World winemakers with their refrigeration resources may improve upon that. The least harmful way to clarify a juice or a wine is to let it settle naturally and fall bright rather than filtering or centrifuging it. James Halliday at Coldstream Hills in Australia often lets his juice settle at around 0°C (32°F) for up to eight weeks. Brian Croser of Petaluma may store his wine for months at -2°C (28°F). The sugar-sweet juice's freezing point is lower than water's so the juices stays liquid – just – and inert, depositing tartaric crystals along with any other solids.

The decision now is – do you use wild or cultured yeasts – and do you use stainless steel or barrel. Wild yeasts – or 'native yeasts' as Josh Jensen of Calera in California insists they should be called – are present in vineyards, on grapes, even in the fabric of winery buildings. Traditionally they have always caused the sugar in grape juice to ferment in a more or less successful manner, depending upon whether the dominant yeast strains were the right kind for converting grape juice into clean-flavoured wine, or whether they were so-called 'spoilage yeasts'.

Chalone, just over the hill from Calera, believe that California's native yeasts are basically spoilage yeasts, whereas ancient European wine regions like Burgundy have developed populations of beneficial yeast strains over the centuries. So Calera Pinot Noir juice just sits and waits until the native yeasts get going, while Chalone juice gets a dose of yeast culture. Both Pinot Noirs are superb, but they are undoubtedly different. After a period in the 1980s when cultured yeasts were the only thing for a switched-on winemaker to use, many adventurous winemakers are moving back to native yeasts. For the modern winemaker, yeast is just one more tool at his disposal.

To Oak or Not to Oak?

The decision on whether to ferment and mature the wine in stainless steel or oak barrel is one of enormous stylistic importance. Stainless tanks are inert, impermeable and amenable to accurate temperature control. Oak is full of flavour, porous and you can only control the temperature of the liquid inside by cooling the outside – not an easy task. Fresh aromatic white wines – many Rieslings and Sauvignon Blancs for instance – are fermented cool – sometimes as low as 10°C (50°F), rarely above 18°C (64°F) for a period of weeks, and then stored in stainless steel and bottled early. When Californian and Australian winemakers began to imitate Burgundy and Bordeaux, they initially fermented in stainless steel, then transferred the finished wine to new oak. This is fine for red wine, but the result in whites was generally of fresh, intensely fruity wine sitting uneasily with a heavy, creamy, sometimes resinous oak overlay.

Again, it was a case of going back to the role model. The *best* white Burgundies were fermented *in* oak barrels. New or little-used oak barrels have a marvellous caramelly, vanilla coating on the inside surface drawn out by the heat applied during the bending of the staves. The finished wine will interact with the wood surface, drawing flavour into the liquid. If you actually ferment the wine in the barrel, the yeast action precipitates out a lot of the tougher, fibrous wood tannins which can make an oaked wine unbalanced. Barrel-fermented wines leave a thrilling sense of softness and richness combined. As the 1990s progress, all the best producers of Chardonnay, and many Sauvignon Blanc and Semillon producers too, are switching to fermentation in barrel.

As the wine ferments, the yeast cells die off in their billions, forming a thick creamy deposit known as lees on the bottom of the barrel or tank. The 'white coat' scientific response of the early 1980s was to remove the wine as quickly as possible from this decayed matter. And many Californian and Australian Chardonnays of this period always seemed to lack an extra dimension. Until the word spread that in Burgundy, in the village of Meursault in particular, they practised 'battonage' – must beating, rousing the lees. The Meursault producers would put an object like a golf club into the top of their barrels, and give the wine a good stir. Meursaults are renowned for a soft, creamy, hazelnut and oatmeal richness. Progressives in California and America tried the technique, and their Chardonnays were transformed, all that creamy, yeasty lusciousness became part of the wine. Nowadays, all serious Chardonnay producers leave the wine in contact with the lees in barrel, though some of them still can't quite bring themselves to put their number three wood into the bung and waggle it about.

Another thing the new winemaker whizz-kids were frightened of was the malolactic fermentation. This is a bacterial action that transforms harsh green apple malic acid into the soft, buttery, creamy lactic acid. Producers felt that the fruit quality of their wines would be spoilt, and until they isolated which sort of malolactic bacteria made the wine taste creamy as against which one made the wine taste like sauerkraut, they were understandably nervous. But if you want a young, fruity style of white, you can avoid the malolactic by adding sulphur dioxide or by centrifuging or sterile-filtering any bacteria out of the wine. If you want the lactic softness you inoculate with the good bacteria either during the alcoholic fermentation or afterwards. If you still want to preserve a strong fruit flavour, you remove the wine from the lees straight after the malolactic is finished. If you want to add the lactic butteriness to the lees creaminess – you just leave them be. The malolactic almost always happened in France, as spring weather warmed the cellar, even though it was little understood. Now it's a case of to use or not to use.

Many of the decisions in making red wine are similar – the adjustment of acid, the use of native or cultured yeasts, the need to control temperature, the use of stainless steel as against barrels for ageing the wines, the use of malolactic fermentation (almost universal in reds, but you *must* make sure it is fully complete, otherwise it may happen in the bottle!). However, there is a lot of truth in the assertion that while a white wine really does need winemaker input to mould its style, red wine at its best virtually makes itself. That is a gross oversimplification, but it is surprising how often you hear the 'non-interventionist' doctrine at the most inspiring European properties.

Making Red Wine

Again it's a question of options and control – getting the best out of the tannins, colouring and flavour elements in the grape, achieving a balance between tannin, fruit, acid and oak, making a wine with the potential to improve in bottle but able to satisfy the impatient modern market's demand for a drink that's attractive at only two or three years old.

The red winemaker will sometimes demand unbroken bunches, particularly with Pinot Noir, since he may want to ferment a proportion using a form of carbonic maceration – the technique used for Beaujolais. The uncrushed berry feeds on itself to produce life-sustaining carbon dioxide, but also produces alcohol, and at a level of three to four degrees of sugar, the fermentation within will stop as the alcohol in effect poisons the grape. This intracellular fermentation will have produced an intensely fruity, dark-coloured but soft juice. These berries will then be crushed and fermentation will proceed as normal.

With Cabernet Sauvignon, Merlot and Shiraz, the grapes will generally be destemmed and crushed. Since the pips and stems both contain harsh tannins, modern crushing and destemming machines will separate the grapes as gently as possible from the stems so as to avoid releasing unnecessary tannins. Some winemakers will then cool the juice and skins and allow them to macerate together before the temperature is raised and fermentation begins. This technique of pre-fermentation maceration is gaining increasing support among Pinot Noir producers.

The fermentation will generally take place in stainless steel tanks so that the temperature can be controlled. Some winemakers ferment reds as low as 15°C (59°F) but in general Cabernets and Shirazes will average between 25° and 30°C (77° and 86°F), while Pinot Noir may peak at 33°C (91°F) or so. 32°C (89°F) has traditionally been thought of as the danger point above which a fermentation might stall, but with greater control available, especially the ability to reduce temperature rapidly by running the juice through heat exchangers, many winemakers, like Michel Rolland in Pomerol, are risking brief periods of higher temperatures and thereby extracting greater richness from their fruit.

Red wines ferment with their skins. As the wine begins to bubble, the skins all rise to the top, which is hazardous for two reasons. The skins will dry out and become infected with vinegary bacteria, and if they're all piled up on top of the bubbling juice, you won't extract as much colour, flavour and tannin as you could. So you have to keep dunking them in the liquid. The traditional Bordeaux way is to pump juice over the skin cap at least once a day, sometimes every few hours. This is a rough, sturdy method of doing things, which rips the skins and extracts a lot of tannin.

The Burgundian method is gentler – even if it doesn't sound gentler. You either plunge down the cap by hand using a pole with a flat bit of board at the end, or you jump in and use your feet! I swear, they say that's *really* gentle and doesn't tear the skins at all. All Pinot Noir should be plunged or trodden because perfume – from the grape, not the feet – is more important than tannin. Some Cabernet producers are beginning to plunge their grapes too, as the vogue for insanely tannic wines wanes. Others use boards fixed into the tank which hold the cap under the surface of the liquid, and occasionally you see a great big circular machine like a vast cement mixer called a vinimatic which tumbles and churns everything together. But none of these beat a good old dose of Burgundian hand plunging and foot stomping.

The Australian method of ensuring a fruity wine that isn't too tannic is to run the juice off its skins when about one-third of the sugar is still unfermented and finish off the fermentation in wooden barrels. This precipitates some wood tannins and gives a lovely gentle texture to the wine, though it doesn't prevent it from ageing. But then the Australians aren't so hung up about ageability as most nations.

Young fresh red wines won't ever go into barrel – although a touch of oak taste can be added by hanging a bag of oak chips in the vat for a day or two – but any red for the long term will usually go into barrel. French 225-litre (50-gallon) oak barrels are the most in vogue, but some producers prefer American oak for its broader, sweeter flavour, and they can always moderate its effect – as they often do in Australia – by using larger barrels.

Traditionally, red wines in Bordeaux are softened and clarified by repeated rackings – the wine is drawn off its lees into a clean barrel until it is bright. The repeated exposure to oxygen also softens the wine and helps precipitate tannins. In Burgundy this is done less because Pinot Noir is a more delicate grape variety.

Shining new steel and scented new oak (here at Gaja's winery in Italy) are the two hallmarks of a modern winery.

After a decade of relying on rigorous finings – when a substance like egg white is added which then falls through the wine attracting particles – and on increasingly efficient sterile filterings, winemakers are beginning to pause and take stock. They've put all this effort into growing good grapes, all this effort into fermenting them for maximum flavour and perfume, all this money buying good oak barrels – and then they strip the heart out of the damn thing by savage filtration – simply because they didn't have the patience and the commitment to allow the wine the time and the conditions to rid itself of bacteria and fall bright, all by itself. Only when wines have residual sugar or unfinished malolactic fermentations may they need to be stabilized by filtration to stop them re-fermenting.

But these high-octane, high-tech winemakers round the world are coming full circle. They've learned every technique there is to learn, and now they're discarding them one by one and returning to the old old ways – keep the winery cool, keep it clean, and the wine will eventually make itself. A lot of learning is at last leading to a little wisdom.

Oak

CLOSE YOUR EYES. Empty your mind of the stale artificial smells of a modern urban existence. Shut out the noise. Shut out the stress. And take yourself back in time. To a forest of tall straight trees, autumn-cool in the height of summer, as the rays of the sun are filtered down to slivers of golden light by the canopy of boughs above.

I used to roam through forests like that when I was a kid. And for all the impressions of quiet serenity, there's one more memory I recall that is even more potent – the woodcutters in their smoky forest glade. I was irresistibly drawn into their clearings, seduced by the heady sweet fragrance of the timber they were cutting, sometimes so strong with the resins oozing from the wood that it felt like a blanket of invisible spiced syrup closing over the fresh country air and wrapping me round in a sweet dizzy bliss.

I'm still captivated every time I smell fresh timber. Just think of a carpenter's workshop, think of the way the air is thick with a warm, exotic perfume as all the essences built up by a tree are spilled out by the scything of a knife. Vanilla, cinnamon, cloves and nutmeg, ginger, and sometimes a melting richness like butter on warm toast. Breathing in such scents is sheer pleasure. And when we drink a carefully created, high quality wine matured in a good oak barrel, that's as near as we're going to get in this world to drinking that spicy perfume.

One feature which has characterized efforts by winemakers all round the globe to create wines accepted internationally as 'quality wines' is use of the new oak barrel to age the wine, and sometimes even as the fermentation vessel. Usually the barrel is of 225-litre (50-gallon) capacity, because that's the traditional size used in Bordeaux and Burgundy, models for quality wine in most parts of the world. And French oak, generally made by the very same coopers who sell their barrels to the cellars of Bordeaux and Burgundy, is the preferred wood. This isn't simply a case of me-too snobbery. French oak is different from any other, and most French coopers have been barrel makers through generations.

Trial and error have shown that such an oak barrel seems to allow oxygen just about the right amount of limited access to affect wine's flavours subtly, and beneficially. So long as its access to the wine is pretty restricted, the acids and tannins in the wine will be softened. Wine blanketed under gas may stay in an impermeable stainless steel tank for years, virtually unchanged, whereas the porosity of an oak barrel means gentle maturation is inevitable.

Controlling that rate of maturation is up to the winemaker. Some Australian producers consciously leave a little air gap at the top of the barrel to advance maturation. Other winemakers, especially in California, will ensure that the wine is right up to the bung at all times, to retard ageing.

For this air interchange, the wood may be old or new, the oxygen will still get in, the wine will still gradually evaporate. But the new oak barrel has the massive advantage of all that fresh, heady perfume and spice and sweetness from the timber, just waiting to be absorbed by the wine. Ah. It isn't quite as simple as that. A bar of soap may smell gorgeous, but you bite it, and it tastes horrid. It's the same with wood. You need to transfer the fragrance and flavour yet not all the resinous, fibrous harshness of the wood itself.

Going with the Grain

Oak with a tight grain will release flavours more gradually than loose-grained wood. In general, the oaks from poor ground away from rivers are best, from forests such as those of Nevers, Tronçais and Allier in the heart of France. The Limousin forests further west produce in general a more loose-grained wood, fine for Cognac, but a little too overpowering for most wines. American oak is mostly loose-grained and gives wine a strong creamy flavour, but the northern states are now beginning to produce slower-growing, tight-grained wood for barrels too. Preference now is for choosing timber from these slow-growing trees, as they are much more tightly-grained.

Only the very best oak can be used – neither the new growth nearer the bark which is too sappy, nor the dead and possibly diseased heart wood at the centre is suitable, and a 100-year-old tree may only give enough high quality, knot-free wood for two barrels. The wood is then split by hand, along the grain – rather than sawn across the grain which breaks up the wood's cell structure – to ensure maximum water tightness and minimum release of coarse-flavoured oils, and it should then be seasoned by being left in great piles in the open air for two to three years, if not more. This exposure to wind and rain and sun leaches out the hard green tannins as well as reducing the wood's natural moisture and accustoming it to differences of hot and cold, wet and dry. It cannot be hurried by hot air kiln drying.

Then the oak is ready for the cooper. He must bend those staves into the barrel shape and needs heat to do so. Although steam and hot water and gas flame can be used, the best way by far is for the staves to be worked into shape placed over a fire of oak chips. The heat is gentle and controllable, and the smoke given off comes from similar wood. You *can* bend a barrel into shape over a hot flame in ten minutes or less but the wood may split in the rush, and the inside of the barrel will be coated with soot. The magic won't be released. For best results you need half an hour, forty minutes maybe, sometimes a whole unhurried hour. Gradually the cellulose in the wood breaks down, and the sweet vanillins and aromatic essences are drawn by heat to the surface where they caramelize, ready to dissolve over a matter of months into the wine the barrel will hold. You can instruct the cooper as to how much 'toast' – high,

Bob Butler, chief cooper at Penfolds in Australia, tackles the age-old business of fashioning oak staves over a flame.

medium or low – you want and he will achieve it by adjusting the heat of the fire and the time the barrel spends over it. But in an ideal world you do what the best Bordeaux and Burgundy producers do – you tell the cooper to produce the best barrel he can at the toast which seems right to him for each batch.

One barrel maker I know near Bordeaux now has a machine to help him, so he can make three barrels a day instead of two. That means another of Pomerol's top châteaux will be able to use some of his barrels. The inside of each of his barrels glistens grey silver like polished pewter, and the heavenly scent as you poke your nose into the top is of wild raspberries, strawberries from the mountainside, bananas, cream and spice. 'It's so sweet and sensuous, it's like . . .' and I named one of Bordeaux's most expensive and sought-after red wines. My friend smiles. 'Everything you smell in the barrel, you will smell later on in the wine.'

The Modern Wine Producer

*I*N THE 1970s AND 1980s winemakers genuinely believed that everything was possible and that technology would be their slave to this end. Every minute facet of the wine-making process was studied, conclusions were drawn and then acted upon with the certainty that the right fermentation temperature, the right yeast strain, the right stainless steel tank and the right oak barrel would produce a predictable and delicious result. They did pretty well. They did manage to create the artificially cool conditions that were the basic necessity of good wine-making, through advanced methods of refrigeration and air conditioning, and they did manage to banish the unhygienic practices which were so genially tolerated in much of Europe. They learned enough to develop new wine styles that are as valid, and as exciting, and may turn out to be as classic, as the European models they set out to emulate.

But despite their belief that they could, the new winemakers still didn't recreate Bordeaux or Burgundy because they had never learned one crucial fact about the great old wine styles. It is the unpredictability of nature that gives personality to wine, even if modern scientific know-how can create an enviable consistency in standards. Every variation in the growing season will affect the flavour of the grape. And in the winery, those slow, ancient presses *did* give a different texture and flavour from the super-efficient press their technocratic obsession persuaded them would be an improvement. The unpredictable natural yeast strains resident on the grapes *might* add more flavour than the highly bred, ultra-effective cultured yeasts they had devised in their labs. A temperature of fermentation that didn't quite follow the rule book wasn't such a bad thing after all. Perhaps there wasn't one perfect wood for barrels, perhaps they didn't *all* have to be new, perhaps every barrel, in fact, was slightly different.

Through attempting to master technology, many modern winemakers had become slaves to it. As they strove harder and harder to negate the unpredictable effects of nature, a generation of 'white coat' wines emerged – often technically correct, but devoid of personality, devoid of originality as every non-conformist edge was shaved away.

Some of the blame for this can be placed on the financial pressures on all but the smallest, most 'boutique' of wineries, that make it imperative not to 'screw up'. If a million dollars of sales are riding on your Chardonnay the winemaker's first duty has to be to make sure it is at least a stable, saleable drink. Some of the blame is also laid at the door of the wine-making schools. Such criticism needs to be carefully weighed. Schools like Davis in California and Roseworthy in Australia or Montpellier in France are obliged to give their students a sound scientific grounding, so that, if nothing else, they are aware of all the pros and cons of every different stage of the wine-making process. There is no doubt at all that these schools have done remarkable work in providing a pool of scientifically competent winery personnel, without which the modern wine revolution could not have taken place at all.

However, too many graduates enter the wine industry believing that what they have learned is the sum total of everything there is to know, and that if they simply follow the rules, great wine will flow. They are not taught that to make great wine they must develop a vision of excellence and a feeling for wine far beyond that of the laboratory bench, and that their scientific grounding will come into its own in allowing they to evaluate potential risk and potential reward when they come to reach out towards excellence. Tim Mondavi in California says he tempts his new Davis graduates continually to overstep the mark, until finally they do make a mistake and Tim, instead of scolding the offenders, claps them on the back and says – 'Congratulations, you took a risk, you made a mistake – now you can start on the path of making great wine.'

Return to the Vineyard

By the mid-1980s it was clear that it was time to return to basics, go back to the land and its fruit, and then use technology simply to encourage the fruit to give of its best rather than bludgeon it into unwilling submission. Now, in the 1990s, we are seeing the concept of the modern winemaker mature as he decides to enter into partnership with nature rather than attempt to dominate it. This doesn't mean he won't try to guide events – of course he will, since many modern vineyards are situated in areas with high ambient temperatures, insufficient water supplies, lack of indigenous yeast colonies and lack of any inherited vineyard and winery knowledge among the local population – if there *is* a local population. But the modern way is one of persuasion, cajoling, subtly guiding a grape variety's natural tendency either in the arid heat of Central Australia, or the over-humid cool lushness of east coast New Zealand, and introducing conditions in the winery which ape the best of Europe and avoid the worst.

All this means that the modern wine producer is consciously recreating the best of the conditions that prevailed before there was any advanced scientific knowledge, but which occasionally gave superlative results. The *best* wines produced at the end of the nineteenth century and during the first half of the twentieth century *may* have been among the most exciting ever created. Small yields in the vineyard contributed to that, and small yields can easily be achieved so long as financial pressures don't demand a big volume of production. Gentler, maybe less efficient methods in the winery also contributed. After an era of high-tech, we're now seeing a return to low-tech – but a low-tech whose nature is now better understood in scientific terms, and more easily controlled. And often those wines were so good, simply because there was no rush, there was always time to allow the wine to sort itself out, to rid itself of leesy sulphidic overtones, to fall bright without filtration, to be sold only when its time had come.

Technological advances are only one small part of the story of the massive quality strides that we're seeing in the 'new world' of wine. Understanding of and love for the vineyard is an enduring theme among the traditional European producers and we are seeing this devotion building among even the most technologically talented producers in the New World. Brian Croser of Petaluma says his life's ambition is to get to know and love his own vineyard and let it speak through him to the limit of *its* ability. Croser led the technological surge in Australia during the 1980s. Now he's finding profounder truths lying deep in his land and its fruit.

Wine revolutions happen in vineyards. They happen in wineries. They also have to happen in the wine shops and wine bars of the world. And labelling wine according to grape variety has done more to simplify the pleasures of wine than almost any other phenomenon. Label a wine according to its grape variety and you're labelling it according to the one factor which most affects the flavour of the wine – the variety from which it was made.

So at least the wine drinker knows where he's starting from. There is a spectrum of flavours inside the bottle from which the Chardonnay taste *will* come. The Riesling or the Sauvignon Blanc will have one of relatively few fundamental flavours – none of them the same as the Chardonnay. Cabernet Sauvignon asserts itself bluntly in a way in which Pinot Noir never does, and a Merlot or Syrah will not really taste like Sangiovese or Nebbiolo.

It all seems so obvious, just a matter of common sense. But until the Californians, followed by the Australians and New Zealanders, began to label their wines according to grape variety, the vast majority of

Former accountant John Buck of Te Mata epitomizes the self-confident, determined new breed of modern winemaker.

European labels never mentioned the grape variety, and many wine titles seem more designed to satisfy local pride and parish pump politics than to enlighten the wine drinker.

Yet now even the grandest French regions are keen to label at least their less grand wines by variety. Spain and Portugal are promoting their best varieties rather than claiming ignorance of their existence. The openness and eagerness to communicate, the feeling that people have a right to know, which are so much a part of the characters of the younger nations of the world are at last persuading the old European order to treat the wine drinker with some respect.

Making the Most of It

It has become obvious that grape varieties like Cabernet and Chardonnay are remarkably easy to grow in almost any circumstances – you just have to be a bit careful with Chardonnay when it's setting its crop – and so it is possible to make progressively cheaper examples. Using less valuable land, higher yields, avoiding maturation in expensive new oak barrels – you can make wines which could appeal to a wider and wider market, yet still keep a finger-tip link with the most expensive wines on the shelves – because they are made from the same grape variety.

That's the situation today, and every new country – every Chile, every Argentina, every Bulgaria, Romania, China or Zimbabwe – feels its best shot at getting its wine noticed is to try to produce a cheap drinkable Chardonnay or Cabernet. It may soon be that Cabernet and Chardonnay become virtual generic terms for decent quality red and dry white wine. And that won't be such a bad thing because they make very decent basic wine – much better than the wine produced by the tired drab bulk-producing varieties of which most countries still have a surplus. And that will lead to an explosion of interest in *other* varieties – for the simple reason that the new breed of wine enthusiast gets bored quickly. The adventurous wine drinker can use Cabernet and Chardonnay as a base, but strike out to a different style. And the obvious way will be through the varietal, since this signals the flavour of the wine. Already Australia is rediscovering Semillon, and Shiraz, and a Riesling revival may well come from Australasia, rather than Germany.

Wine – a Brilliant Career?

The new breed of wine producer is dramatically different from the typical producer of a generation ago and the vision that impels people into the wine business often against their better financial judgement is of enormous importance. The Newtons in California are highly successful in the fields of finance and academe, yet they believe they can create a unique wine based on their visions of the best in Bordeaux. James Halliday in Australia was a high-powered lawyer and influential writer, but had a passion to create the 'Burgundian' Pinot Noir he felt Australia lacked. Former accountant John Buck of New Zealand unashamedly talks of Margaux and Montrachet when he tries to express his ambitions for his Te Mata wines.

There is a rapidly spreading internationalism manifest in all the best wineries – both in traditional Europe and iconoclastic California, Australia or New Zealand – and this wider awareness has provided the spur, the challenge, the role models, the comparisons of technique in vineyard and winery and flavours in the bottle, which are now creating new classic wine. Burgundy and Bordeaux didn't develop in a vacuum.

Bordeaux was heavily influenced by trade with northern Europe over a span of centuries. Burgundy was on the main north-south trade route between the Mediterranean and the north, and for centuries was subject to the influences of wave after wave of travellers.

Travellers still come, to Burgundy in particular, attempting to establish an almost mystical communion with the Pinot Noir and Chardonnay, but they come from Martinborough in New Zealand, Au Bon Climat in California, or Coldstream Hills in Australia, a pilgrimage from New World to Old.

And slowly but surely the Europeans from the classic regions are themselves beginning to travel. Their numbers are still few, but their influence is enormous. Miguel Torres of Spain began the revitalization of Chile when he set up a winery there in 1979 – he needed freedom to experiment and the virgin soil of Chile provided it. Christian Moueix, producer of Château Pétrus, Bordeaux's most expensive wine, studied at Davis wine school in California, while his nephew Alain went to Kumeu River of New Zealand to learn wine-making, rather than to any number of prestigious French properties. Their neighbour in Pomerol, Michel Rolland, now travels regularly to California and Argentina. If you go to Rothbury Estate or Petaluma in Australia, you'll find the scions of numerous French wine producing families knuckling under and learning the techniques and attitudes that their parents may not have thought were necessary, but which they will use, when they return to Bordeaux, Burgundy, Alsace or the Loire, to augment the natural advantages their own vineyards enjoy.

European money is on the move too. The most famous joint venture between nations in wine is Opus One. This was Robert Mondavi's inspired coup in persuading Baron Philippe de Rothschild of Château Mouton-Rothschild to create a wine in California, jointly produced, and sold with both their names and images on the same label. Others have not been slow to follow. Christian Moueix is also involved in the Napa Valley, Château Lafite-Rothschild is in Chile, négociants Joseph Drouhin of Burgundy now have land in Oregon, and the Champagne houses in particular, aware that expansion of Champagne production is restricted by rigid *appellation contrôlée* delimitation of permitted vineyard sites in France, have invested millions of francs abroad, using the Champagne grapes of Pinot Noir and Chardonnay, and the Champagne method, to make quality sparkling wine from Tasmania to Carneros.

Interestingly, we are now seeing a reverse trend beginning. Schramsberg from California are investing in sparkling wine in Portugal; Hardy's of South Australia now have properties in France and Italy. And Penfolds of Australia have bought into California, while Franciscan of the Napa Valley now make some of their best wine in Chile.

The new atmosphere of international communication has also resulted in a new role altogether in the winery – the consultant winemaker. These are skilled winemakers who advise increasing numbers of properties and producers on how to make their wine. Professor Peynaud of Bordeaux was the creator of the modern concept of red Bordeaux, with an emphasis on fruit, new oak, bacterial stability and a ruthless weeding out of lesser vats of wine in the winery. His influence on Bordeaux cannot be overstated, and by extension, his influence on every wine producer making Cabernet wines on the Bordeaux model. Go to Greece and you'll find that Professor Peynaud has been consulting at Château Carras. Go to Peru and the Tacama winery proudly tells you Peynaud is their consultant.

There is always the risk that an over-powerful consultant may impose his style upon a wine-making community and suppress individuality, but in the main men like Peynaud, and the increasingly influential

Mick Morris leans on the sides of his old concrete tank and takes a sugar reading from his fermenting Shiraz with about the most modern piece of equipment he possesses.

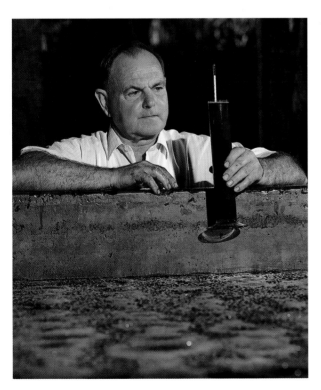

Michel Rolland in Pomerol do nothing but good. The Tuscan wine scene in Italy has been transformed by the powerful personalities of a few of its wine consultants, without question for the better. Although Giacomo Tachis has always worked with the house of Antinori, his influence has reached far beyond one company, his advice and willing help transforming the quality of the wines from numerous estates throughout the region. Men like Franco Bernabei and Maurizio Castelli do have a particular style, and properties they work with *do* reflect this, but they bring pride and passion as well as vision and technological competence to a great wine region that had lost sight of all of these.

The New Classic Style

Pride. Passion. Vision. Technological competence. These are four components that mark out the wine producers in this book. All the old clichés of what a winemaker *ought* to be don't apply any more. For a start you don't have to be the son of the son of a winemaker. And if you are born into a wine family, 'like father, like son', isn't always the way to go.

In north-western Italy, Angelo Gaja's father made the best wine in Barbaresco, they say. But Angelo saw that another generation spent making the best example of a wine nobody really wanted any more was a pretty certain road to ruin. So he planted some of his father's best Barbaresco vineyards with the heretical Cabernet Sauvignon. 'What a pity,' sighed his father. So that's what Angelo called his Cabernet – 'Darmagi: What a pity'. On the other side of the world, Ross and Bill Spence's father created some of New Zealand's most seriously undistinguished 'ports' and 'sherries' – his sons were the ones to introduce what is now New Zealand's most successful grape variety, Sauvignon Blanc, and they supply Concorde flights with their world-class Matua Valley Cabernets.

And you certainly don't need to be young to be a modern winemaker. Being young has never been a guarantee of anything except that you were born more recently. It doesn't stop you being prejudiced, it doesn't stop your vision being narrow and your mind closed to outside influences.

Bailey Carrodus' retirement hobby at Yarra Yering turns out wines regarded as pinnacles of brilliance that all other Australian winemakers aspire to. Robert Mondavi was 52 years old when he started the winery that would blaze a trail for all of California to follow. Twenty years on he was still haranguing his staff to try out the latest ideas he'd culled from his trips to Europe, Africa and Australasia. Just goes to show you don't have to be young to be young.

New Classic Wines & Winemakers

No magnificent winery buildings. No vineyards gradually evolved over the centuries. But here at Delatite in Australia, and in numerous other sites across the globe, great wines are being produced by winemakers of imagination and ambition.

UNITED STATES

*T*HE UNITED STATES OF AMERICA has achieved an astonishing amount in the world of wine in little more than a generation. I suppose we should expect nothing less. It's part of the American character to pursue a target hungrily, with greater investment of time, money and talent than any other nation on earth. And for a nation that so bravely and brashly leads from the front, along with the triumphs perhaps we should also expect America to have to undergo the lion's share of teething problems.

On balance the triumphs outweigh the tribulations, but the wine path has *not* been an easy one for the Americans to tread, perhaps because they were dealing with a craft where experience and tradition have always counted for a great deal. America had neither. There was a thin trickle of tradition and experience running through the vineyards of the Napa Valley in California, but basically, when the great surge in world wine appreciation built up during the 1960s and 1970s, little of any value had been achieved in America for almost a hundred years.

In the second half of the nineteenth century, California in particular was making quite a reputation for its wines, but the appearance of the devastating louse phylloxera which laid waste all the nation's *Vitis vinifera* grape vines (the only ones suited to fine wine production) was followed by a period of increasing anti-alcohol sentiment, culminating in the 'dry' era from 1920 to 1933 when Prohibition was in force. A whole generation grew up with no knowledge of quality wine and a close association of alcohol with bathtub gin.

Even though Prohibition was repealed, the Great Depression that followed meant nobody was in the mood to take any risks in the name of quality. Then there was World War Two, and by the time prosperity returned, another generation had grown up with little knowledge of a culture involving fine wine and food. It speaks volumes for the vision of men like Robert Mondavi that, in what must have seemed a totally inhospitable environment, they could not only detect a bright future, but also understand the achievements and learn the methods of Europe's classic areas that would bring that vision to reality in hardly more time than it took a vineyard to mature.

Of course there is a positive side to the lack of a quality wine heritage in America. It meant that there was nothing to hold back any determined pioneer. In true American style, everyone could have a go. The one great limiting factor is the relative unsuitability of most of the United States for fine wine production. In most of the north the winters are just too cold, and where the summers are hot, they are too short. As you head south, it gets hotter and hotter, but humidity becomes such

My kind of Napa: nothing brash, nothing gaudy, just the morning sun creeping up on the springtime vines and a proud old wooden water tower with a new coat of paint.

a problem that few vine varieties could ever ripen well without some of the fruit rotting first.

As a result it is the seaboards which have achieved most, east and west. California is the leading wine state, and, on its own would rank as the sixth biggest wine-producing nation in the world. Oregon and Washington to the north are both struggling to sort out what they do best and how, while Texas to the far south may yet amaze us all. On the east, New York has long been the USA's second wine-making state, but only recently has its industry become quality-minded, with the Hudson River Valley, the Finger Lakes, and in particular, Long Island showing distinct 'future classic' propensities. And from New England down to Virginia, occasional pockets of excellence do pop up against all the odds.

CALIFORNIA

If it weren't for the fog, California would not be taking the lion's share of profiles in this book. If it weren't for the fog, California might well not figure in this book at all. If it weren't for the fog this book might not exist, because the great international movement towards challenging the long European dominance of fine wine and then creating and defining a whole series of wine styles based initially on mainly French models, but in many cases deviating gloriously from the old orthodoxy along the way, would never have happened without the fog.

California is a hot state, generally scorched by the sun and with conditions that, given suitable water supplies, can provide a hothouse ripening environment for a great array of fruit and vegetables, but none of the temperate conditions needed to slowly ripen high quality grapes.

However, just off-shore is the ice-cold Humboldt Current. Just as western Europe is warmed by the Gulf Stream, California is cooled by the Humboldt. But only because of the gaps in the coastal ranges forced through by rivers heading for the ocean. Through each of these gaps – the grandest of which is the mile-wide mouth to San Francisco Bay, a turbulence of fog and chill wind roars as the sun warms up the interior, and the hot air rising inland draws cool air towards it. The gradually dwindling effect of this natural cooling can sometimes be felt a hundred miles from the sea. All California's fine wine regions are close enough to these gaps in the coastal range to feel the cooling effect.

The most famous wine areas are those clustered around San Francisco Bay itself. To the south there used to be considerable vineyard acreage in Livermore County, but urban development has gobbled most of it up. It is to the north, in Sonoma and Napa Counties, that the most important wine areas now take advantage of the cool breezes and the warm sun.

Sonoma County was where the Californian vineyard pioneer Haraszthy established his Buena Vista vineyard in 1857, and wineries like Simi and Grand Cru were famous at the end of the last century, while Hanzell was the first to import French oak barrels for maturing wines some years before Robert Mondavi. However, Sonoma as a region never fully established an identity for itself and was generally thought of as a source of high-quality blending wine until the 1970s. This is unfair, as anyone who has tasted a Simi Reserve Chardonnay, a Jordan Cabernet Sauvignon, a Dry Creek Sauvignon, a Carmenet red or Kistler white will testify. But even the top wineries have seemed to find it difficult to establish consistency of style and approach, and my favourite wines from Sonoma fruit have often been

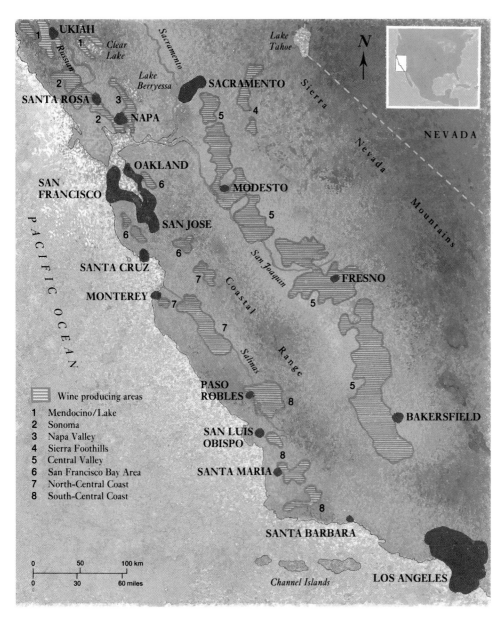

Wine producing areas
1 Mendocino/Lake
2 Sonoma
3 Napa Valley
4 Sierra Foothills
5 Central Valley
6 San Francisco Bay Area
7 North-Central Coast
8 South-Central Coast

made by wineries outside the county, like Saintsbury, Franciscan and Ridge. Even so, I still believe that Sonoma fruit is some of the best in California and Sonoma wines could be too.

Napa appears to be a solid carpet of vines from the town of Napa down in the south, right up to the head of the valley. But this is to forget two other zones which are increasingly producing exciting fruit – Carneros down by the Bay, and the numerous mountainside vineyards above the Napa Valley floor. At the south it is often so cool that even cool climate varieties like Pinot Noir struggle to ripen. At the north, the climate is more like that of the southern Rhône. In European terms you are finding the equivalent of several hundred miles difference in conditions, all inside a 30-mile stretch, because of the fog and the breeze.

If there is an orthodoxy in California fine wine, it is based in the Napa Valley. But it is a very recent orthodoxy. Although the tradition of quality wine had been kept alive by the Rutherford wineries Beaulieu and Inglenook during the 1940s and 1950s, it wasn't until the 1960s that wineries like Mondavi, Sterling, Heitz and Schramsberg began to create a new order, inspired by the progress being made in the classic areas of France. And it wasn't until 1976 that they announced to the world in the most emphatic manner possible that they had arrived in the Big Time.

On 24 May 1976 a jury of France's top palates set to work on a blind tasting in Paris. Ostensibly a Bordeaux and Burgundy tasting, it in fact pitted the old order against the young pretenders from California. Château Montelena 1973 Chardonnay and Stag's Leap 1973 Cabernet Sauvignon from the Napa Valley beat the cream of the French vineyards and a new age was ushered in. There was no more God-given right to produce the world's greatest wines on the sites hallowed by time. In less than a decade since Mondavi introduced the vision of emulating the greatest of French wines to the Napa Valley, the Californians had taken on and vanquished their role models and idols.

They had done it through a mixture of ripe fruit, expensive technology, truck-loads of the best French oak barrels, and fanatical application of the scientific diktats handed down from the wine school at nearby Davis. France took due note, and the methods of wine-making in France have been revolutionized by the adoption of many of the techniques made possible by Californian research. However, in California the brilliant inventiveness and imagination that was so thrilling in the 1970s became dogged by the demands of marketing and promotion and financial success in the face of soaring costs and ever-increasing competition. Technologically-backed guarantees of flaw-free wine became the brief for many winemakers. Often what Napa wineries produced in the late 1980s was first-class promotion but middle-of-the-road wine. Some of the trailblazers of the 1970s got left behind, unsure of their true strengths, blown from pillar to post by the buffeting winds of fashion.

In particular Napa and Sonoma wineries became increasingly entangled with the problems of being a market-led industry. This wasn't such a problem with the highly successful sparkling wine houses, both native Californian and joint venture – usually with French Champagne firms – because sparkling wine is to a considerable extent a commodity dependent upon image and presentation as much as flavour. Even so, the 1990s see several of the sparkling wine firms beginning to produce wine of a standard to rival French Champagne.

But in table wines, Chardonnay and Cabernet Sauvignon dominated winery efforts, regardless of whether or not they had sources of suitable fruit. The approval of such powerful wine critics as the wine magazine *The Wine Spectator* or writer Robert Parker became the criterion of success or failure. And political wrangles over the precise delimitations of the new Approved Viticultural Areas increasingly tainted the clear bright air of opportunity and liberty which had made the Napa Valley one of the most joyous wine regions on earth. It is the wineries that have not lost this sense of freedom and desire to excel which are included in this book; they exemplify the power and beauty of California.

And that is why I have also included the more maverick operators south of the Bay. They didn't take the easy route in their choice of vineyard sites or grape varieties. They either established entirely new areas, or revitalized old ones, or re-evaluated areas like Monterey County and Santa Maria which had been tried and found wanting simply through lack of understanding about the strengths and

Winning awards at wine shows plays an important role in spreading a winery's reputation and boosting sales.

weaknesses of the region. And these are the people who are likely to bring to the surface an unwelcome truth many in Napa and Sonoma Counties do not wish to face – that the Bordeaux and Burgundy varieties are not necessarily the most suitable grapes to grow in most of California. The Rhône varieties like Syrah, Mourvèdre, Viognier, Marsanne and Roussanne might do better, being warm climate grapes, the Spanish Tempranillo, the Portuguese Touriga Nacional and the Italian Nebbiolo, Dolcetto, Sangiovese or Barbera might ultimately produce finer wine. And it will be the mavericks on the cheaper land away from the pressures of the Napa and Sonoma marketing hothouses who have the freedom and courage to check the theories out.

PACIFIC NORTH-WEST

To the north of California you have the wine-producing states of Oregon and Washington, and Idaho is also now beginning to produce a little wine. The modern wine industries of Oregon and Washington both started virtually from scratch in the 1960s but it wasn't until the 1980s that they began to develop separate identities to any significant extent. Idaho's tiny industry only dates from the late 1980s and in any case its best wines have been vinified from Washington grapes.

Some fine wines have been made. Oregon Pinot Noir has won accolades on and off ever since Eyrie Vineyards' 1975 almost knocked Burgundy off its perch in a 1979 international tasting in Paris, but no winery, Eyrie included, has regularly produced wine of classic quality, either from Pinot Noir, or Pinot Gris, Chardonnay or Riesling — other varieties grown in Oregon to a reasonable extent.

Washington, although touted as the rainiest, mistiest, frequently the most God-forsaken state in the Union has another face. Although damp and cool on the seaboard, inland from the Cascades mountain range there is a virtually rain-free semi-desert which, with reliable climate, hot ripening conditions and unlimited

supplies of irrigation water from the Columbia River and its tributaries, provides a futuristic paradise for the grape grower.

This should be the site of that elusive beast – the consistent, high-quality, low-cost quaffing wine, and the presence of several large national companies should further ensure this. Yet the inability to match consistency with quality, marketing goals with good flavour and attractive style that dogs the giant American companies in California, is no different here, and has produced as many disappointments as successes. The thrilling wines have come from the wild and wilful band of small producers who are close enough to their soil and their fruit to see what tremendous quality you can get from these vineyards. You simply need to follow the dictates of good wine-making and avoid over-exploiting the land. Wineries like Chinook, Woodward Canyon, Blackwood Canyon, Salishan, Latah Creek and Kiona have all made small amounts of superb wines, but none have regularly repeated their success.

When they do, Washington will play an increasingly significant role in any future evaluation of 'new classic' styles, because there are strong parallels between the development of this virgin land and what is happening in Marlborough in New Zealand, the Riverland in Australia, Raimat's development in north-eastern Spain, and pockets of Southern France. All these are, in effect, artificially-created vineyard areas now supplying growing quantities of increasingly high-quality wine at eminently affordable prices.

Washington could do this too, but the wine-making philosophies of her largest groups have seemed to prefer to damp down the remarkable fruit flavours, rather than point them up. There is no doubt that the fruit quality in Washington is strong and exciting. There are now between 4500 and 4900 hectares (11,000 and 12,000 acres) of vines, mostly in the Yakima and Columbia basins, and the

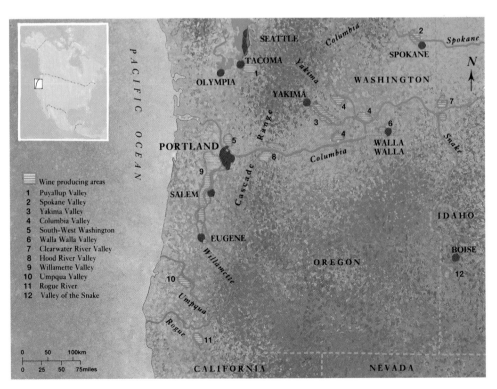

combination of long sunlight hours – up to 17 hours a day in June – high summer temperatures – up to 38°C (100°F) – and low nighttime temperatures – often 4·5° to 10°C (40° to 50°F) cooler – builds high acid and high alcohol, so long as you don't try for excessive yields.

So far there have been some excellent Chardonnays, some outstanding Rieslings and an occasional good Sauvignon Blanc. Merlot is talked of as producing lovely juicy creamy reds. Too much talk, not enough action is the problem, with the honourable exception of big outfit Columbia Crest and smaller Chinook.

Oregon is never going to be a quantity producer – its average crop of the important varieties Chardonnay and Pinot Noir was down to two tons per acre by the 1990 vintage. The theory was that it would provide Burgundian conditions for Pinot Noir and Chardonnay as against California's hotter climes. Well, it has certainly managed to emulate Burgundy's notoriously fickle early summer weather at just the time when you're hoping to set a decent crop, and its unreliable early autumn weather at harvesting time. Damp and rain are ever-present threats.

Consequently, prices and expectations are high. Oregon has the strictest quality control laws of any American state and some of the most charming and most committed winemakers. I do hope they can find a way to produce more regular yields of well-flavoured fruit, or else the new sparkling wine ventures of the French Laurent Perrier and the Australian Brian Croser may assume a greater importance than anticipated as a home for unripe grapes.

NEW YORK STATE

New York State could well surprise a lot of us in the next decade with the quality of its wines, but its first battle will be to win over the wine drinkers of New York city itself, which traditionally looks to Europe for the majority of its wine. Enormous quantities of Italian wine in particular are guzzled there each year.

But the wine producers up the Hudson River, or out on Long Island, or up on the sloping banks of the deep, thin Finger Lakes in the north of the state, can make wine to outshine most of the European stuff the New Yorkers drink, if only they were given the chance to show their paces. Yet most urban New Yorkers with any pretension to wine knowledge disdain the local produce.

The reason for this was that although New York had the second largest vineyard acreage after California, hardly any of the vines were *vinifera* varieties – virtually all the wine was made from the extremely pungently flavoured native *Vitis labrusca*, or neutral-flavoured hybrids that could withstand the freezing winters, and neither type produced wine that stood comparison with decent European wine.

However, the development of sturdy rootstocks to use as grafts for *vinifera* vines that could survive intense winter cold – one from a convent in Quebec – has resulted in a small, but impressive flow of fine Chardonnay, of dry and sweet Riesling from the Finger Lakes and the Hudson Valley. And Long Island, its climate tempered by the sea, only needed the development of efficient anti-rot sprays to combat the humid atmosphere to show that wineries like Hargrave, Pindar, Lenz, Bridgehampton and Bidwell are likely to produce supremely good Chardonnays, Merlots, Cabernet Sauvignons, Rieslings and Pinot Noirs, with a distinctly European personality and complexity, with increasing regularity over the coming years. All they need now is for their local market – the New Yorkers themselves – to develop a little pride in the produce of their own backyard.

Acacia

WINE HAS BEEN LARRY BROOKS' HOBBY since – well, before he was legally allowed, anyway; semi-sweet Rhine and Mosel whites used to disappear down his throat like soda pop. Yet until he was almost 30, he says he didn't knowingly ignore the urge to be a winemaker; it was so obviously the life he should be leading that he completely failed to see it.

For a start, he loved being wet and dirty. When his father was stationed at a naval base in San Pablo Bay, he was always out in the mudflats from breakfast until suppertime. If you don't like being wet and dirty, don't become a winemaker. He was good at science too. He ended up doing a masters degree in plant pathology and physiology at Davis – the hotbed of academic wine-making in California's Central Valley. Yet he still didn't see the career connection. He was surrounded by fledgling winemakers eager to learn from his expertise in plant physiology, but couldn't make the imaginative leap into believing he could also be a winemaker. His father was a sailor; if you wanted to be a winemaker, didn't you need an Italian grandfather sitting on a pile of old vineyards ready for you to inherit, instead of a dad with a sloop and a sextant?

So Brooks ended up selling Toyota cars and when that palled, he was about to use his knowledge of yeast behaviour by getting involved in a beer-brewing project, when a wine-loving friend – Mike Richmond – finally gave him a good shake and spelled it out in words of one syllable: 'You should be a winemaker'.

That was in 1978. Mike Richmond had been working at Freemark Abbey winery in the Napa Valley for ten years, but he had a feeling that the Carneros region was going to provide the new focus in California wine with its long, cool, growing season and suitability for Chardonnay and Pinot Noir. He'd found a site for a winery, he'd found a bunch of investors, he knew he had a fine palate and a knack for marketing, but he couldn't tell a yeast cell from a snowflake.

Larry Brooks, Toyota salesman and old friend, knew more about yeasts and plant physiology than almost anyone else in the county. Brooks gave up cars and went to work as Richmond's technical assistant. By 1981 he was partner in, and winemaker for, the big black-roofed, white-walled barn on the southern slopes of Carneros known as Acacia. And over the next ten years Larry Brooks made Acacia into one of the hottest labels available anywhere in the United States. He had come to Carneros at precisely the right time. There had been a rash of vine plantings in the late 1960s, led by the famous Winery Lake Vineyard of René di Rosa, but there were very few local wineries and the full potential of the fruit was not being explored and exploited. Brooks didn't yet own any vines but, from the porch of his barn-winery, he could see the vineyards which would provide him with his most exciting fruit, all within a few hundred yards – St Clair to the south-east, with its gnarled, stubby Pinot Noir vines heaving themselves from the dry, crumbly earth; Madonna to the west, just over the T-junction with Duhig Road, dipping to the creek then rising steeply on a long east-facing slope; and around the winery, Marina, the source of all the best Acacia Chardonnay grapes.

And in the middle distance glisten the waters of San Pablo Bay. The traditional definition of Carneros has always been that you should be able to see the water. Brooks added to that: he wanted all the vineyards he dealt with to be able to see the winery too. Even with production at 40,000 cases and with 50,000 forecast, almost every grower selling grapes to Acacia has vines within a mile of the winery.

Brooks knows that he sometimes pays over the odds for his best grapes, but then quotes John Ruskin's philosophy at you – that it is better to have paid too much and to have merely lost a little bit of money than to have paid too little and lost everything. Winemakers will often spend 10 or 15 years working out how to make the best wine from a vineyard plot – and will then lose the source of supply quibbling over the question of a few thousand dollars.

Meeting the Challenge

This seems insane to Larry Brooks. Continuity is the only way to struggle past the steep slant of the learning curve and on to the level where you finally let your creativity run free. 'Drop me anywhere at harvest time, and I'll make you a pretty good wine – that's my basic technical skill, but that last five or ten per cent to make a really great wine – that takes a whole lifetime.'

There's no doubt that the Pinot Noir from St Clair and the Chardonnay from Marina (the only vineyard Acacia actually owns) are really special. Other Pinot bottlings from the Iund, Madonna, Lee or Hudson vineyards only intermittently rise to the challenge and begin to exhibit the fragrance, the cherry-ripe fruit and wistful mellowness of great Carneros Pinot Noir.

Since Chalone bought Acacia in 1986, there has been pressure to reduce the number of single vineyard bottlings – but Brooks believes wines have to taste of their birthplace. Even if it takes 25 years to work out

Yes, I think Larry Brooks, the talented winemaker at Acacia, likes this Chardonnay.

what that taste is. If he plants a vineyard, it'll be a dozen years, and maybe more, before the vines are giving of their best, and the wine itself may then need ten years in bottle to show whether it really has the magic he's looking for. As it is, most of the Acacia Pinot Noir vines are over 20 years old.

This explains why continuity is so crucial to him. He develops pruning and training techniques with each of his growers, the use or avoidance of irrigation, the projected yields – finally, the projected *flavour*. Larry Brooks still remembers his first smell of the pungent aromas as they pressed the St Clair Pinot Noir after his first two weeks at the winery, and he remembers thinking, 'I'm going to do this until I die'.

That sensation – a remarkable crispness of fruit mingled with the perfume of a rich, deep plum and cherry sweetness, has inspired him ever since. The crispness he tries to achieve by taking enormous care over picking dates – and daily, as the sugar level mounts, he's out in the vineyards testing the grapes for that plump resistance which shows the berry is managing to contain the increasing liquid pressure inside without crumpling.

As soon as Brooks feels the grape skin soften, he'll bring the crop in, regardless of the sugar levels. He is convinced that he can judge each batch himself far more accurately than any computer could. With Pinot Noir he crushes and destems the grapes very gently, aiming to keep around a quarter of them whole for fermentation. He usually – but not always – uses cultured yeast. And some of the lighter wine is kept warm until pressing – which is giving him more colour, but isn't spoiling that fresh, crisp fruit. One of my favourite growers in Gevrey-Chambertin, Alain Burguet, is doing the same with his red Burgundy. That's where Larry got the idea.

His Chardonnays are a blend of tank-fermented and barrel-fermented wine. I smell blossom in the Marina Chardonnays – apple blossom, pear blossom – even lime blossom, but Larry says it's Chardonnay blossom – the scent of the vineyard in springtime. It's hauntingly beautiful – and he says you can't achieve it with full barrel fermentation. Which is why he mixes the two.

There's a paradox in Larry Brooks and in Acacia, the hedonist frequently at odds with the scientist. But the results can be sensationally good. Madonna is a gently fragrant Pinot which develops surprising depth with age. St Clair can be magnificent – full of brooding power; deep, strong, packed with a fiery intensity of pepper and leather, mint and black cherry and the dark flavours of fat black plums. The 1986 is still one of California's best-ever Pinots. The Marina Chardonnay holds on to a perfume of lime blossom and vine blossom and it isn't overpowered by the wine's wealth of rich apricot and honey and toasty spice or the lean lick of lemon that brings it all together. Again, the 1988 is one of California's best Chardonnays, and the '87 isn't that far behind.

Continuity. The greatest of virtues in the ancient winelands of Europe, has found an unlikely champion in Larry Brooks. My last sight of him, eyes piercing and hypnotic, sun-streaked hair swept back and an expression of inquisitive bemusement which reminded me of Keir Dullea in *2001*, was as he stood on that same Acacia porch. 'My ideal is to be buried here,' he'd said and as he gazed beyond me, across to San Pablo Bay, he was looking at those same mudflats where he'd first got wet and dirty over 30 years ago.

(Overleaf) I can feel the hot morning sun burning away the fog around the Acacia winery in the Carneros region.

CALIFORNIA

Au Bon Climat

*T*HE PAINTERS HALL is one of those terribly smart old livery halls in London. I never dream of going near such places without dusting down my one approximation of a pinstripe suit, prising the dried egg blobs off my Oxford sports club tie and at least *showing* my hair a comb. After that, I can blend in reasonably inconspicuously with the hundreds of identically attired wine buffs at the large trade tastings they hold there.

But on one occasion recently, someone broke the dress code. There was this bronzed, Big Sur surfer-type character, decked out in the very latest of tie-irrelevant, 'flounce up the silk and don't press the trousers' fashion prowling about the room. He'd repeatedly go back to sniff and slurp and spit the most expensive red and white Burgundies, his face a mask of concentration quite unexpected on a man with tumbling locks of golden hair coiled like tendrils around his open collar. Then he'd dart back to the little group of American wines at the end of the room – taste, wonder, worry, spit. After which he'd sit down well away from the action, his whole being lost in thought. Suddenly up he'd leap and elbow his way back to the Richebourg or the Charmes-Chambertin – and the whole process would start again.

This was Jim Clendenen of Au Bon Climat winery, in the Santa Maria Valley south of San Francisco, and those American wines were his own. Put into this prestigious Burgundy tasting at his request, to show the wine buffs how much he'd achieved with his Pinot Noir and Chardonnay – and to show himself how far he had yet to go. It's difficult to believe he's only been involved with wine-making for a decade, has made most of his wines in an old dairy barn and a defunct CBS record-pressing plant, and only managed to construct a winery – and that of the most basic sort – in 1988. Yet Jim Clendenen has already established himself as one of the most inspired and conscientious winemakers working in California.

Still, if he wants to check on every aspect of his progress, he'll have to put some of his wines into a red and white Bordeaux tasting as well, if not a Rhône tasting and a tasting of wines from Piedmont in northern Italy too. Sharing a winery base along with his colleagues Bob Lindquist and Adam Tolmach, Jim is prepared to tackle head-on pretty well every major European table wine style (he's also made some sweet Riesling, by the way) and to prove that the right wine-making techniques allied to the right vineyard will produce wine of exceptional flavours, even in places like the Santa Maria Valley – an area with no top class track record whatsoever up until now.

Jim Clendenen is at the apex of this trio of young turks. He and Bob Lindquist run Vita Nova – a label intent on re-defining the red and white Bordeaux styles as crafted in California so far. Au Bon Climat – literally, in Burgundian French, a toast to the good vineyard site, or *climat*, is run by Jim and Adam Tolmach and concentrates on Chardonnay and Pinot, the Burgundian styles. Qupé is run by Bob and is a highly successful Rhône varietal specialist, and Ojai produces both red Rhône and white Bordeaux styles and is Adam's baby. And of course there's Jim's Nebbiolo – under an Italian-type title – Podere Il San Olivos, and the sweet Riesling which will probably go under the Au Bon Climat label.

Working Partners

Altogether this little band produce about 16,000 cases of wine a year, and despite Qupé's Syrah, Marsanne and now Viognier being the quality trail blazers for these varieties on the West Coast – the heart of the operation is in the 7000 cases of Au Bon Climat. Given Jim Clendenen's strongly held views, I think he's found the perfect partner in Tolmach, because Clendenen is fired by a passionate and hedonistic belief in high risk wine-making from low yield vineyards, while Tolmach is the intense, bearded academic who knows all the figures and equations and can ensure that Jim's technophobic crusade doesn't career off into a sea of magnificent, undrinkable failures.

Just listen to some of this. 'High technology is an extremely effective way of making highly commercial wine in a marginal area on a large scale' – Jim particularly has the French Mâconnais, Australia's Coonawarra and much of Italy in mind – 'but in the end technology is bullshit, for people who've screwed it up all the way along and need a rescue.' Now that frame of mind by itself might be a recipe for disaster. But with Tolmach's beady eye on the basics, it actually becomes a clarion call sounding the retreat from the over-technological wines which characterized California through much of the 1980s, and the return to the basic methods and philosophies that made Burgundian wines famous in the first place.

Clendenen was aided in his search for the best vineyard sites by local knowledge and a clear idea of the low-yielding, stressed, well-drained sites he needed to produce fruit with adequate but not excessive sugar levels after a long ripening period. Wine-making trial and error has increasingly become trial and triumph thanks to his grasp of the flavour concepts he is trying to create and Tolmach's cautious finger on the throttle of invention. The best way to make Clendenen bridle is to mention that some of the Napa boys call his Chardonnays overblown. He fumes that his Napa critics traditionally pick their fruit at a whopping 14 degrees of potential alcohol, with low acid levels which need boosting, their juice is settled if not filtered before stainless steel fermentation to remove the grape flesh solids, the wines are racked straight after alcoholic fermentation to remove them from the yeast lees, and sulphur dioxide is then added to inhibit malolactic fermentation – a parade of techniques designed to put a straitjacket on the potential character of the wine – and the result is wine that somehow manages to be both clumsy and emaciated at the same time.

Then he calms down and admits that some of the go-ahead Napa winemakers are in fact beginning to make their Reserve Chardonnays at least – *his* way. Plant your Chardonnay in cooler areas, enabling you to pick at lower potential alcohol levels but higher, as well as natural, acid levels. He positively encourages the juice to oxidize – no protective sulphur gets near it – and he tries to get plenty of those grape solids into the barrels along with the juice. Fermentation temperatures can go as high as 26°C (79°F) – many Napa winemakers don't let their *reds* go that high, let alone their whites – and there's no racking off the lees or sulphuring, so that the malolactic can be completed in *every* barrel – after

That's what I call a haircut. Jim Clendenen, Au Bon Climat's exciting winemaker in contemplative mood.

which the wines will remain on their lees for up to a year, with the Reserve and Benedict vineyard bottlings altogether spending 18 months in barrel. And unless it's unavoidable, there will be no filtering of the top cuvées. If you're patient, he believes you can get the wine clear enough simply through careful racking.

His Pinot Noir attitude exhibits the same truculent anti-technological bias. He's already retaining up to 50 per cent of whole clusters of grapes, and the rest he crushes in an old and fairly coarse crusher – totally against the currently fashionable 'gently does it' philosophy, but he says that there is such a low level of bittering and colouring matter in Pinot Noir skins that a touch of rough treatment merely serves to add depth.

The mush of skins, whole grapes and juice macerates for as long as possible before fermentation, and he only adds a cultured yeast to ensure the wine ferments out fully, once the wild yeasts have become active. He does in fact usually add a little acid, but is becoming less and less concerned about perfect 'wine-school' pH acid figures. The best Burgundian red wine producers are beginning to admit that their favourite wines are rarely the ones with the most balanced figures, and as Clendenen says – 'sure, you can make a wine pH stable, but so what so what so what?' The wine school at Davis teaches that if the figures are right, the wine's right. With Tolmach valiantly manhandling the restraining leash, Clendenen is raring to prove that you just can't take this ascetic view of a hedonistic pleasure like wine. So when the Pinot does begin to ferment he'll let those temperatures ride up pretty high. But there's pretty

The grandeur of it all. Miles from anywhere, Bien Nacido provides Au Bon Climat with some of their best grapes.

high and there's pretty *high*. In 1988 the grapes came in hot from the vineyard and the fermentation spurted to boiling point in no time, suffocating the yeasts. But, as Jim says, when you've spent time in Burgundy and heard all the horror stories of stopped fermentation and ruined wines, you don't need to be told twice. As the bubbling slowed down he whacked in a 'mega-yeast' he'd obtained for just such an eventuality and the wine fermented out to dry, and he was able to leave it on the skins, start to finish, for about two weeks.

Since then, though, he's been trying to pick his grapes cold in the early morning, if necessary cool them further in a cold tank, and allow two to three days before things start to hot up. He'll punch the cap of skins down while the fermentation is going on, and then put the wine into barrel, adopting the same philosophy as for the whites – a little fining, very careful racking from barrel to barrel, and unless absolutely necessary, no filtration. Layering flavours on to fairly spare raw material is how Clendenen likes to describe his

philosophy. He is unashamed in his declaration that he makes a very considerable effort to impose his own style upon his fruit, but persuades you that his style is the one the fruit would anyway prefer if left to its own devices.

The Au Bon Climat hallmark, however, is anything but spare or raw. It is a succulence, an almost syrupy richness, and this is where Jim's and Adam's talent shows through. 'We start with lots of flavour and we don't take any flavours away' – that's their concentration on fermenting with solids in the juice, using the lees, racking carefully, not filtering. Jim uses the example of the 1981 Burgundies. He worked that vintage with the prestigious Duc de Magenta cellars in Burgundy's Côte de Beaune, after spending the early part of the year in Australia. Burgundian fruit in 1981 just wasn't fully ripe, yet the whites in particular managed to turn out remarkably well. As Clendenen says, with underripe fruit, you have to structure some flavour *in* – you can't afford to throw away any solids because they're a source of flavour. You can't rack the wine off its lees because lees are flavour and a source of nourishment. You can't block the flavour development

that's gripping your attention, it's the quality of the fruit. Sometimes almost too much so. Benedict's yield on Chardonnay can be as low as four acres to the ton. No, you didn't read it wrong – four acres to produce one ton. Pickers were traipsing along half a mile of vines and coming back with a bare half basketful of grapes! That's *too* little. An almost violent concentration of moss, and minerals, syrup and lime peel acid makes for a palate-buster right now. Five years down the line, however, and the 1987 and 1988 Benedict could be magnificent beasts. The Reserve Chardonnay is also a rich, massive wine style, but more come-hither, rich in fruit, succulent syrup, an acid of lime peel fresh-twisted, and the warm insidious spice of new French oak. These and the regular release Chardonnay are absolutely delicious from the day they hit the shelves.

Richness is the key in the Pinot Noirs. Although the Bien Nacido vines produce the driest style, there is still a sweet core of red fruits, a flicker of orange acidity and a delightful floral perfume. The flowers appear on the Rancho Viñedo fruit too, along with a really beautiful cherry perfume and a fruit that is chewy but sweet like the skin of ripe Morello cherries. As for Benedict, well, each vintage has been very different but they are all marked by a fabulous sweet fruit – more damsons in 1989, more raspberries and blackberries in '88, more plum skins and fresh pepper in '87. And the syrupy richness, the meaty intensity, finds a most delectable counterpoint in a perfume as scented as violets in 1989, something more sultry, like the scent of a favoured kid glove carelessly thrown down on a dressing table in the '88, toastier, deeper, becoming husky-voiced, dark and stately in the '87 as the years begin to tell.

I see Jim Clendenen as a prophet for the future of fine wine in California. Enthusiastically encouraged by Lindquist and Tolmach, Clendenen is a visionary whom more and more people will take seriously as the Californians critically re-examine their achievements.

His way isn't a dogmatic way, and I thought I came closest to understanding his philosophy as we stood in his glorified shed of a winery one winter evening. The coyotes were laughing out in the black fields, the mice were squeaking and mewling as they scuttled to their nests behind the barrels. And we were talking about his wife's paintings, how domineering professors at college had damped her spirit for years by swearing she couldn't draw, how Adam Tolmach's sister *did* paint but silently, with no explanation offered, no interpretation demanded. And he suddenly said, 'Anyone can paint, it just depends on their vision of things.' His mixture of courage, skill and tolerance for others' ideals and abilities is needed in California.

of the wine by piling in the sulphur dioxide, because the wine hasn't got the guts to stand the shock.

Clendenen's fruit is a bit riper than those cold, joyless 1981 offerings in Burgundy, but he does go for fruit grown at the limit of its ability to ripen – his methods might indeed prove to be too much of a good thing if applied to super-ripe Napa-style fruit. It's a rare year his fruit doesn't struggle to ripen.

The Bien Nacido and Rancho Viñedo vineyards near the winery are both in the fog-cooled Santa Maria region, very much on the cusp as far as grape-ripening is concerned. Until 1990, Clendenen also bought grapes from the Benedict vineyard, further south in Santa Ynez Valley. Richard Sanford identified it in the 1970s as possibly having the most perfect Pinot Noir conditions in California and now uses the grapes for his own winery. Clendenen agrees that this tiny micro-climate, cooled by ocean air and desperately shy of crop, is a magic Pinot Noir vineyard, though it often fails to ripen Chardonnay.

But the Au Bon Climat style shines through the Benedict vineyard wines, both Pinots and Chardonnays. Jim says a little disingenuously that it isn't his style

CALIFORNIA

Beringer

*I*T'S NOT IMMEDIATELY OBVIOUS where a great vineyard is going to spring up on the heavy, fertile flatland of the Napa Valley floor. Certainly when you turn off the Silverado Trail towards State Lane Vineyard, for about a quarter of a mile along the Yountville Cross Road, there doesn't seem to be any distinguishing feature to the land just to the south. It's close to the river, and that generally means deep, fertile loam, likely to produce heavy crops of unmemorable fruit. You sift a handful of the dark, moist earth through your fingers and find yourself saying it would be great for potatoes.

But in fact it wouldn't. As with Silver Oak's Bonny's Vineyard a couple of miles to the north, a geological quirk has created a little enclave of viticultural brilliance here at State Lane. The soil is rich, but there's very little of it. Hidden to the eye, just below the surface, is a jumble of impacted rock. Instead of the vine roots stretching languorously down, they battle to find a tortuous pathway through the fissures. Instead of six to ten tons of flavourless fruit, each acre struggles to produce as much as three tons of magnificent sweet fruit, as sticky and rich as black cherry jam.

Ed Sbragia doesn't know who it was who first identified this unlikely 5-hectare (12-acre) plot, but he now relies on that richness to provide a core of sweetness in his wine, and to bind the very different qualities of the other three vineyards he blends together to make one of California's great red wines – Beringer Private Reserve Cabernet Sauvignon. Ed Sbragia is the winemaker for Beringer, one of the Napa Valley's oldest wineries, now owned by Nestlé of Switzerland. Beringer had had glory days before, albeit a fair while back, but it wasn't until Ed arrived in 1976 that the potential of this historic company, owners then of some 285 hectares (700 acres) of excellent vineyard land (they now own nearly a thousand hectares), began to be recognized.

He didn't take over as head winemaker until 1984, but right from the start he was charged with developing a Reserve programme. They didn't tell him he had to create a classic, but that's what he's done, and he's achieved it in a manner which would be familiar to any traditional winemaker in Burgundy or Bordeaux, Tuscany or Piedmont. He has their deeply ingrained respect for the soil, the vines which grow in it, and the grapes they bear. His greatest 'innovation' has been to reintroduce to the Napa Valley the concept that the

wine producer is merely a custodian of the vineyard and its fruit, and that his wine-making philosophy should be that of caretaker, not manipulator. 'Pay attention to detail, and good grapes will make themselves. A good grape should get all the credit.'

Sbragia's grandfather once made wine in the Sonoma Valley over the hills from Napa and his father grew grapes during Prohibition. Not surprisingly perhaps, his father went bust and ended up slaving in a bottling plant in San Francisco, making just enough money to put a dollar or two on the horses. Lucky thing he did. He won the consolation prize in the 1935 Irish Sweepstakes – £100 – enough to head back to Healdsburg in Sonoma, start up a restaurant, and then, after the war – retire to the surrounding countryside to grow grapes again and make a bit of wine.

Ed can't remember a time in his life when he wasn't surrounded by vines, or watching his father make wine. Keep your cellar and your barrels clean, then leave well alone. That's how his grandfather had done it. That's how his father did it. And that's how he does it. 'My basic wine-making technique is the same as when my

March to settle. After which he'll put his Reserve batches into medium toast new French Nevers oak barrels and then he leaves them – often without racking, for between 20 and 26 months. He says the wine's been aerated enough by the time it goes into barrel not to need any more racking. He does a very loose filter just before bottling – 'to get the rocks out' and that's it.

So if there are no black arts involved in the wine-making, the memorable flavours *must* be from the vineyards. The look on Ed's generous face does rather give me the impression that he can't decide whether I'm deaf or just stupid to say this. In fact the only time I saw a glint of hardness enter his eyes was as he re-stated his vineyard philosophy. '*Everything* is site specific.'

State Lane is the sweetener, the fattener-up of the blends. But the bedrock of Private Reserve is the Chabot Vineyard. If you drive up the Silverado trail on the east side of the Napa Valley, you'll come to a Christmas tree farm just near the local hospital. And hidden back off the road, the heavily wooded hillside of Glass Mountain fades towards the flat with several smoothly rounded outcrops. Tightly terraced with vines, and skirted below by more vines, these 8 hectares (20 acres) form the Chabot vineyard. It is worth running this soil through your fingers, too, because the familiar dark loam is laced with a shiny black rock called obsidian. Near the surface the rock holds the daytime's heat well into the cool night, reflecting warmth and building up grape ripeness in the same way as the round flat stones do in France's Châteauneuf-du-Pape. And as you dig deeper the soil becomes solid with boulders, stressing the vine and reducing the crop to a mere ton or so per acre of intensely flavoured grapes.

Since it was first planted in the 1870s, Chabot has always grown Cabernet Sauvignon. Louis Martini, a grand old Napa wine producer, once used the grapes for his top-of-the-line Special Select. But Ed Sbragia showed his mettle almost as soon as he arrived at Beringer. He went to check out the Chabot Vineyard and says he felt 'the integrity of the earth' as soon as he set foot there. Back at head office he demanded: 'we must have those grapes'.

He got them. In 1977 Beringer made a Lemmon Ranch (as Chabot was briefly called) Cabernet Sauvignon Private Reserve. It was the beginning of the Private Reserve legend. 'Nearest I've ever made to Bordeaux,' says Ed. With the exception of 1979, when hot weather overstressed the vines, Chabot grapes have been at the heart of every bottling of Private Reserve. Structure, tough tannins, wrapped in a rich red fruits sweetness that slowly mellows over a decade into

The necessary, if unphotogenic, production headquarters for Beringer's Ed Sbragia and his team.

grandfather made wine. Crush, ferment, clarify, age, stabilize if you must and bottle it. Nothing's really changed, just the ability to control.' His only rule is that if he must interfere, he does so immediately. 'Do it *now*, not tomorrow.'

As well as Cabernet Sauvignon, Sbragia makes superb Reserve Chardonnay too, which he subjects to numerous experimental methods, trying to maximize the rich fruit of Napa while gaining the complexity of flavour which marks out the best French white Burgundies. But for his Cabernet Reserve it's back to the traditional way. He crushes and ferments at a fairly warm temperature, pumping the juice over three times a day for an hour to get it all really mixed up and aerated. When the wine has fermented dry he presses it off the skins in his Bucher press, which he says is so gentle that nine times out of ten, the press wine goes straight back in the blend. He induces the malolactic fermentation, then leaves the wine in stainless steel until February or

CALIFORNIA

Bonny Doon

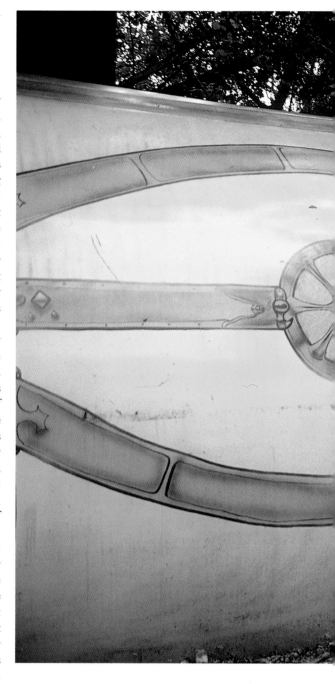

RANDALL GRAHM IS ONE of the most brilliantly original self-publicists in the wine world today. In his regular newsletter he displays a knack with words, an unfailing sense of the ridiculous which is rooted partly in Monty Python out of the Marx Brothers zaniness of S J Perelman, and partly in a free-associating stream of consciousness that often relies more on sound and rhythm than any generally accepted logical thought patterns. Ally this to an awesome ability to pastiche literary styles – Edgar Allen Poe and James Joyce would surely enjoy Grahm's parodies of *The Raven* and *Ulysses* – and it adds up to the most irreverent, entertaining but also thought-provoking document issuing, certainly from any winery, and probably from any business whatever. Wherever.

Randall Grahm is the creator and owner of Bonny Doon – a small vineyard and winery hidden among the redwoods high above the California resort town of Santa Cruz, whose fame is quite out of proportion to its volume of production or even indeed to the flavours of its wine. He is also the self-styled leader of the Rhône Rangers, a loose association of American winemakers whose chief interest is in Rhône Valley grapes rather than the Cabernet, Pinot Noir, and Chardonnay which dominate quality wine production on America's West Coast. From absolutely nowhere in the mid-1980s, Grahm has propelled Rhône varieties to a position of cult-worship that is sometimes little short of hysterical.

As for his labels, they are brilliantly bizarre – but only when they *need* to be. He makes a bit of Pinot Noir and quite a bit of Chardonnay – and these have perfectly sensible, simple labels, likely to reassure the most timid of customers. But then most people have at least heard of Chardonnay and Pinot Noir. So what about the Rhône varieties like Mourvèdre? Or Grenache, Cinsaut, Syrah, Carignane (as Carignan is known in California)? These are either totally unknown to the average wine drinker, or dismissed as junk grapes. Grahm knew that to label his wine 'Bonny Doon Mourvèdre' or 'Randall Grahm's 60 per cent Grenache, 25 per cent Syrah, 15 per cent Carignane red wine' and then stick a high price tag on it would be a certain route to the bankruptcy court.

So he took the high-risk approach and plastered the labels with the kind of inspired foolery which he hoped would act like a magnet to the whacky end of the wine world. He had a wine lying in barrel made up of Syrah, Mourvèdre and Grenache – the three most important Châteauneuf-du-Pape grapes – but no name for it. Grahm remembered reading that in 1954, the people of Châteauneuf-du-Pape had passed a law barring flying saucers from landing in their vineyards. He couldn't resist calling the wine Le Cigare Volant – that's what the French call UFOs, flying cigars – and what once had seemed a virtually unsaleable red wine was on the way to becoming a superstar. So was its maker. Grahm then labelled a 100 per cent Mourvèdre 'Old Telegram'

I think I could get to like this guy. Come to think of it, I could get fond of that water tank too. Randall Grahm of Bonny Doon leans back on his year's supply of bathwater.

(in homage to one of the great Châteauneuf-du-Pape estates, Vieux Télégraphe). The label, well, the label looks exactly like an old telegram! And along one line there is a daisy chain of dots and dashes, spelling out 'Old Telegram' in Morse code. Clos de Gilroy is his 100 per cent Grenache. Gilroy is famous for one thing only

in America – it's the nation's garlic capital. Grahm makes it seem as though Gilroy is a long-lost paradise of ancient vines.

Marketing his wines through a system of memorable labels, unforgettable newsletters and provocative public utterances has made Randall Grahm and Bonny Doon famous in little more than five years. His image is of the relentlessly exuberant eccentric. But there's a more serious side to what he has done. Grenache as a grape was believed in California to be fit for nothing but pallid pink 'blush' wine. Mourvèdre was virtually defunct and its use chiefly confined to making up the weight in shipments of grapes to home-winemakers in the East. Yet the great wines of Châteauneuf-du-Pape gained their most individual flavours from these two grape varieties in France. Syrah, despite occasionally appearing under the Phelps label, in California, was disregarded as a quality grape because an inferior grape had been titled Petite Sirah and no one had bothered to find out why it made such uninteresting wine when the real Syrah could produce the great Hermitage and Côte-Rôtie reds of France's Rhône Valley. And the Rhône whites – Marsanne and Roussanne of Hermitage, and Viognier of Condrieu were star grapes in France, but had no champion before Randall Grahm began to visualize a post-Chardonnay world.

Warming to the Theme

These are all warm climate grapes. California is naturally a warm climate state, and despite attempts to utilize mountain slopes and valleys cooled by fog and ocean breeze, most of California's vineyards are planted in warm, not cool sites. The craze to emulate the wines of Bordeaux and Burgundy was so all-consuming that no-one had really given a thought as to whether there were other equally great, but more suitable varieties available – until the Rhône Ranger rode into town.

Yet Grahm initially thought that Pinot Noir would be the route through which he could make his mark. And when he cleared the redwoods and scrub from his land at Bonny Doon, planting Pinot Noir was his top priority. But then he tasted a 1971 red wine from David Bruce, a neighbouring Santa Cruz grower – it was rich, heady, erotic wine. And it was a Grenache. He made the connection with two other 1971 wines he'd had – Rayas and Beaucastel from Châteauneuf-du-Pape – the Rayas made from 100 per cent Grenache. They were heady, too, but complex, spicy – and just as sensual in personality.

He rang up David Bruce who told him that some growers in nearby Hecker Pass, just short of garlic city Gilroy, might have a few rows of Grenache left. He went and asked around and discovered an old guy called George Besson who was eking out a living selling his Grenache for $100 a ton – if he could find a buyer. Randall offered him $250. Besson was ecstatic. Clos de Gilroy was on the way. And the idea of a full-scale Châteauneuf-du-Pape style began to look a possibility.

Except that no-one in California had ever heard of Mourvèdre, a crucial component in Châteauneuf. Luckily Grahm learned by chance from Darrell Corti, Sacramento's leading wine merchant, that Mourvèdre

was the same as Mataro, a variety that had been popular during Prohibition for shipping as whole fruit. But all his detective work to find some vines failed, until right on Sacramento's own doorstep, in the sandy soil of the river delta as it runs into San Pablo Bay, he found a small, impoverished time warp of a vineyard area, hemmed in by petrol refineries and chemical plants, still growing Mataro from 80- and 90-year-old vines, still shipping it in boxes across to the East Coast.

So that was two varieties he'd found. Syrah he initially found near Paso Robles, but now he's grafted part of his own vineyard to Syrah and persuaded the Bien Nacido vineyard in Santa Maria – also used by Au Bon Climat and Qupé – to graft over some of their vines to Syrah too. Completing the Rhône set, he has Marsanne, Roussanne and Viognier in his own vineyard, and when the gophers stop eating the shoots, and the wasps stop gorging themselves on the ripe sweet autumn-mellow juice and allow him a decent crop, he'll really start to show everyone what a post-Chardonnay world could be all about.

So far his best wines are his simplest. The Clos de Gilroy Grenache is a wonderfully juicy raspberry-ripe red, as gluggable as any I've found in California. And his blush – Vin Gris de Cigare – is a deliciously dry rosé, as fresh and clean as pebbles in a mountain stream. Yet the wines that have made him famous – his Le Cigare Volant, his Old Telegram, his Syrah and his new Marsanne/Roussanne blend, Le Sophiste – are fascinating for the fact that they exist at all rather than for their brilliant qualities of taste.

His very first Grenache from 'George's' Gilroy vineyard was 'a right screw-up'. So he blended it with a Cabernet Sauvignon he'd also screwed up, but in a different and 'complementary' fashion! Nowadays he has a still in which he produces some wonderful fruit eau de vie, but it's also very useful, he gaily admits, for distilling his mistakes. But Grahm sees wine-making as a voyage. 'For me, wine-making is a process of discovery. You have to be conscious enough to realize when you have done something right and try to understand what made it right.' But his real passion is for the vineyard – to identify the best sites, to decide which varieties are most suitable for them, to work out how to trellis and prune and protect them so that they will give him a decent crop of slowly but fully ripened grapes, and then he'll try to find a way of letting the wines virtually make themselves.

Grahm is tall, a wind-break of long, wavy black hair framing a face which is a mixture of cherubic naughtiness and eagerness to please. He seems half errant, distracted Italian orchestral conductor and half

The old bikers' café at the tiny hamlet of Bonny Doon which now serves as Randall Grahm's tasting room – with no dress code either way.

an outsized Gene Wilder. Yet his manic, punning lunacy is only evident when he commits himself to print, his passionate advocacy of the Rhône varieties as the future for California only evident when he has an audience that demands persuading. His natural personality is gentle, rather nervous, rather academic, with a mind transparently chasing after every thought that enters his head rather than concentrating on the question in hand.

Grahm was a philosophy major at Santa Cruz university. He then went to the University of California at Davis and says himself that until he finally got into the vineyard with a pair of secateurs in his fist he was a drifter, a 'brilliant under-achiever'.

At Davis he created a reputation for himself as the eccentric outsider, who, whenever the professors laid down one set of rules, would immediately frame an opposing set of arguments of much more convincing originality, just for the sake of the mental exercise. He'd flirted with medicine, flirted with philosophy, but always become bored before finishing off his projects, so wine-making, with its mixture of mystique and expertise, its annually renewable challenge must have seemed like an attractive proposition – for the time being anyway. The idea of using Rhône varieties was an inspired move which will have a major influence on California's wine future, even if it was conceived as just one more kick against the norm.

But we haven't seen the best of Grahm yet. The Rhône-style wines are now flourishing, so he's bought 65 hectares (160 acres) of land in Monterey close to Soledad Penitentiary, which he admits will make it easier to find pickers, where he has planted the top Italian varieties – Nebbiolo, Barbera, Sangiovese, Freisa. So at some date we'll see all those, as well as such brilliant oddities as Pigato, Arneis, Schioppettino. That should keep him in the limelight for a few years yet. What then? Portugal has some fabulously original warm climate varietals. Russia is probably brimful of undiscovered gems like Saperavi. No, I think those Italians will be wine challenge enough. After that he'll retire and write a novel, and it'll be a bizarre, brilliant, challenging fantasy from a shy, likeable man who just happens to love being the centre of attention.

Calera

*J*OSH JENSEN RECALLS THE SHOCK. 'I worked the 1970 vintage at Romanée-Conti. We'd bring the grapes in, punch them down, wait for the fermentation to start, press it, put it in barrels. "Is that all there is?" I asked. I was waiting for the magic, you know, where's the special process, where are the incredibly complicated steps that give you this incredibly complex wine and, really, there weren't any. And whenever I asked what it was that made these wines so special, they'd say – ah, it's the limestone soil. So . . . limestone.'

Limestone completely dominates the thinking at Calera, Jensen's winery. The very name is the Spanish for lime kiln; the Cienega Road which twists and turns along the base of the north-eastern slopes of the Gavilan mountains leads to various old limestone workings; the Calera winery itself was originally built as a rock-crushing plant. Clinging to the steep mountainside there are eight levels of winery operation, and if the bottom four exhibit a cosy, wood-beamed homeliness, the top four are some of the gauntest pieces of concrete ever put to wine-making use.

The buildings may be ugly – what rock-crushing plant isn't – but Calera's owner saw behind the daunting tangle of old weather-stained concrete and rampant weeds the possibility of something all quality-obsessed winemakers would dearly love to possess – an entirely gravity-fed winery. At the top of the eight levels he could bring in his boxes of grapes. At the bottom level he could store his bottles ready to sell. In between, each movement of grape must or wine could be by the gentlest of forces – that of gravity.

If all this sounds pretty basic stuff – that's exactly what it is. Josh Jensen and his winemaker Steve Doerner both have a vision of the perfect Pinot Noir, and a refreshingly humble attitude towards their efforts to create it. They've now added Chardonnay and Viognier to their quiver, but it's Pinot Noir which haunts their waking hours.

Jensen somehow manages to be laid-back and fired-up at the same time, with an appealing if jerky boyishness about him, which, even if it is now slightly careworn, still lets you imagine the preppy American college enthusiasm he must have exuded in his student days (Yale followed by Oxford – he even rowed in the Boat Race team). All his friends headed off to Wall Street or law school, but he decided to wander through France for a couple of years, ending up in Burgundy for

the 1970 vintage at Domaine de la Romanée-Conti, picking grapes and asking a lot of questions. He spent the whole of the following year continuing to ask a lot of questions, in Champagne and the Rhône, in Bordeaux, but most of all in Burgundy, and by the end of 1971 he knew he wanted to make wine himself.

'I thought I'd shoot the works on one big gamble. That was a time when people said Pinot Noir is no good in California and never will be. I figured, so long as I'm gambling I might as well not hedge the bets – I planted all Pinot Noir.' His obsession with limestone was seen by the bigwigs of California wine in the early 1970s as pretty quirky too. They were deeply concerned with climate in those days, saying the soil didn't matter, the sunshine hours did. But the European, especially the Burgundian, view is that the soil is of paramount importance, and Jensen pored over old geological maps from the Bureau of Mines looking for his limestone soil. It took him another three years to find his slopes – swooping up the sides of Mount Harlan, 670 metres (2200 feet) up in the Gavilan range.

Aiming for the Top

He bought 150 hectares (365 acres) of virgin scrub in 1974 – and planted 10 hectares (24 acres) with Pinot Noir. He did buy a few vines from a Napa Valley nursery, but his vision was of recreating the great red Burgundies up in his mountain vineyards, so he went out into the vineyards of Burgundy – the top vineyards; maybe even, although he gets a bit coy when you ask, the vineyards of Romanée-Conti itself – and took as many cuttings as he could carry. All of the Selleck vineyard, all of the Reed vineyard and a large part of the Jensen vineyard are planted with vines from these Burgundian cuttings. By 1978 Josh Jensen knew he was ready to make wine.

Which is where Steve Doerner came in. Jensen wanted someone technical but without any preconceived bias as to how wine should be. Doerner was a student at Davis, the centre of wine-making studies in California, but he was a biochemist not an oenologist. 'At that time Davis was teaching filtration, inoculation, centrifuging, sanitation . . .' Jensen didn't want *any* of that, and nor did Doerner. But while Jensen searched for the lowest possible tech approach, Doerner could do the chemical equations to provide more hit than miss.

All the same, Pinot Noir is a notoriously fickle grape and it is certainly having a field day testing Jensen's nerves. His first crop in 1978 was only 75 cases. His main Jensen vineyard (named after his father) gave him 2200 cases in 1987 from a crop of just over two tons to the acre. In 1988 he got 400 cases – from a crop of less

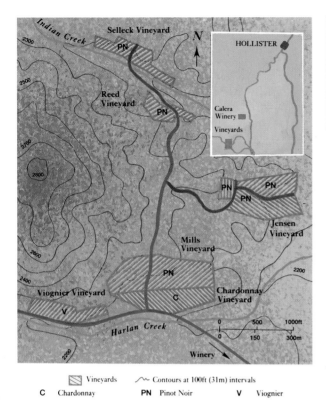

| Vineyards | ⁀ Contours at 100ft (31m) intervals |
| C Chardonnay | PN Pinot Noir | V Viognier |

than half a ton per acre! 1989 showed a return to half the 1987 level. How do you run a business with that kind of unpredictability?

With difficulty. Although he now has 20 hectares (50 acres) planted, to help cash flow Jensen buys in grapes from the Central Coast vineyards down towards Santa Barbara and up towards Gilroy to produce non-estate Chardonnay and Pinot Noir. But despite being far cheaper, they are more difficult to sell. It is the single-vineyard wines which everyone wants, and they'll pay a high price to get them.

But it wasn't until 1982 that they all started clamouring to buy. The early Calera wines had been made with alcohol levels of about 12 degrees. 'But Pinot Noir must have 13 degrees alcohol,' the Romanée-Conti people told him in 1982. To which Jensen replied, 'Why didn't you tell me that before?' – and resolved to make all his Pinot Noirs at 13 to 13.5 degrees from thenceforth. Suddenly he found the flesh, the perfume, the magnificent richness, allied with the structure and elegance which marks out the greatest Burgundies.

The Pinot Noir grapes aren't even crushed, and the whites are pressed still on their stems, and from then on it's 'real dirty wine-making' says Steve with a grin. Lots of lees contact, grape solids left with the wine in barrel, an absolute minimum of fining, racking or filtration – and wild yeasts. 'Native yeasts, please' Jensen corrects

me, 'Americans are so apprehensive about using native yeasts they even call them wild.' And suddenly the wines got noticed. This combination of low yields and a let-well-alone attitude produce great wine. The whites are terrific, the Viognier packed with the flavours of orange and cream and the leafy-edged richness of dried apricots, and is already better than all but the top French examples. The Mount Harlan Chardonnay smells a little earthy, but is outstandingly rich, full of cream and honey and peach, just scoured in a most original way by a savage sweet-sourness from all those native yeasts.

But Calera's fame still rests on the Pinot Noirs. Jensen is the most open, with deliciously accessible flavours of strawberry and honey, sometimes developing an almost candied sweetness which ages to a thrilling combination of raspberry sauce richness, swished with the rasping perfume of leather. Reed has a less dense style – combining the savoury fumes of roast coffee and earth with a fruit of blackberry and strawberry and a perfume of exotic wild raspberries and the herbal aromas of sassafras. Selleck is denser in every way. More tannic, slower to evolve, but magnificently perfumed, full of the classic Burgundian entangled mysteries of cherry and plum, wild raspberry, toast and cinnamon spice. The vines of Mills Vineyard were only planted in 1984 but already the wines are exhibiting that rarest and most haunting of perfumes – that of violets.

Now for the Repeat Performance

What Calera needs to do is to get some sort of stability of crop so that a true style can emerge. The 1988s, for instance, born out of severe drought conditions yielding less than half a ton an acre, are magnificent, yet almost grotesque, still young, still packed with the dense flavours of youth and yet possessing a core so deep and old they seem like children grown old before they were ever young. The 1989s, with twice the crop, lose nothing in beauty, but gain enormously in freshness and balance. 1987 had the biggest crop so far, yet many critics hail 1987 Calera as the finest yet.

Josh Jensen says he sits and dreams of writing films. But the quality of the wines he produces should keep him at Calera for a few years yet.

Cameron

'THIS GUY SAID, "The only trouble I have with your Chardonnays is that they're so eccentric!" Which I suppose is a valid comment. In fact, I said thank you. I like being eccentric.' That was John Paul of Cameron winery talking. I tasted the 1986 Abbey Ridge Chardonnay. I could have been licking a pat of unsalted dairy butter from the end of a knife, it was *so* buttery. Too eccentric? Maybe, but just as I decide it's too rich, a distant flicker of apple and lemon acid grows into a starbright pinpoint of fresh lean fruit, to make me realize it *is* most unusual, but terribly good. The 1987 Abbey Ridge has swapped the butter for bread; cream and bread crunched up with hazelnuts, but the acidity creeps into view at the last possible moment, blending lemon with something almost like fresh orange juice. Did I like it? Yes, but I have to admit, it sure is eccentric.

John Paul is beatifically unfazed by the startled reactions to the startling wines he produces. Oregon, he says, was never meant to be mainstream. With his long wavy hair, his silk shirts and John Lennon glasses, even the odd earring dangling, Paul doesn't exactly look mainstream himself, although he is in fact a consummate winemaker, with experience on three continents, impeccable scientific credentials, and a visionary zeal to discover just how good Oregon's wine might be. And if he decides that conventional vineyard and wine-making wisdom is too limiting, I'd back his talent and imagination against a textbook any day.

He comes from a high-powered scientific background in plant physiology and microbiology which led, in the 1970s, to the world-famous Scripps Institute of Oceanography in California, where he was researching marine microbial plants. He doesn't feel that dealing with submerged yeast organisms is that different from wine-making. Except that now he can drink the product.

When John Paul decided to give wine-making a go, like so many of the most innovative American wine men, he headed for Burgundy and did his learning there. Through a friendship with Etienne Grivot he spent time with all the young turks of the red Burgundy world. He saw that they were reaching back to the old ideas which had made Burgundy great, dragging them into the glare of modern-day scrutiny, and seeing how they could be adapted to the present needs of re-establishing Burgundy's greatness. Back in California, Paul tried to put a similar philosophy into action. He worked at Carneros Creek in the Napa Valley during the early 1980s, and then went to New Zealand one year for the harvest at Coopers Creek. Then in 1984, with Pinot Noir rather than Chardonnay then uppermost in his mind, and a very small amount of money in his pocket, he made the trek north to Oregon, which, in the afterglow of the international acclaim for the wine from Eyrie Vineyards, was being talked of as America's Pinot Nirvana.

His fistful of dollars was only enough to set up business in the same dingy neighbourhood of McMinnville as the Eyrie winery. But Paul had one ace to play. In 1977 he'd made friends with another Burgundy fanatic, Bill Wayne. Bill had planted a vineyard on the Abbey Ridge, 215 metres (700 feet) up in the Dundee Hills. John Paul made him an offer he couldn't refuse – to become a partner in their own winery, with the objective of making Abbey Ridge fruit the most famous and sought after in Oregon. The investment John Paul requested? The 1984 Abbey Ridge crop. Although 1984 was a lousy year, Cameron's Pinot Noir made itself a good reputation.

The Abbey Habit

John Paul is passionate in his championing of the Abbey Ridge vineyards. He says he went all over Oregon, tasting everybody's wines, decided on the best ones, then found they had the common denominator of the Red Hills of Dundee as their grape source. Oregon is thought of as super-cool, but in fact the lower slopes of the Dundee Hills are warmer during the day than Burgundy or Bordeaux, though appreciably colder at night.

John Paul believes that Abbey Ridge is the best site in the best of the Oregon microclimates as yet discovered. But apart from knowing that the slopes should be well-drained and south-facing, he reckons that site selection in Oregon is still 'very much a crapshoot'. But the Burgundian Robert Drouhin has planted a vineyard between Abbey Ridge and Eyrie. Laurent-Perrier from Champagne have bought the property next door, and Brian Croser from Australia is a little further down the hill. A very ritzy crapshoot.

So John Paul concentrates on maximizing the quality of what he's already got. Abbey Ridge was already substantially planted by the time he arrived. And although the land had been planted, block by block, with single clones of vines, he's trying to simulate the erratic ripening rates found in Burgundian vineyards caused by the presence of numerous different strains of Pinot Noir and Chardonnay. He's sure this is a fundamental reason for the complexity of flavour in good Burgundy. So he'll pick one block at proper ripeness, but pull in a few rows on one side which aren't quite ripe, and leave a few rows to overripen on the next block, then mix them all up at the winery.

In the four acres he's got planted round his winery, he's gone the whole hog with his Pinot Noir. He obtained eight different clones and planted them in a scattergun pattern – or rather, no pattern at all. Whatever was next out of the bag went into the ground. The first full crop was in 1989. At vintage time, he swept through the vineyard, not picking and choosing which vines had done better or worse, and put the whole mish-mash into the crusher. There was only enough wine for one barrel, but he reckons it's going to be remarkable, totally unlike anything Oregon has yet produced, already reeking of dark ripe fruits and coffee beans roasting.

He's constructed his winery with those cool, damp Burgundy cellars in mind. The barrel store is below ground and whatever the weather, the temperature fluctuates very little. Again, it's those cool, damp Burgundy cellars he had in mind. I think it's that moist black mould coating the walls in the Burgundy *caves* that he's really set his heart on. He reckons that a cellar develops a certain aroma, and eventually you begin to smell the cellar in the wine. It's a perfectly valid theory. There is a magnificent autumnal, damp undergrowth quality to some great Burgundies which have spent a year or two slumbering near the mould. I would have thought it must take generations to develop that mould, yet John Paul's got mould growing in only five years. Old Burgundian trick, he confides. Shake up a bottle of beer. Spray it on the wall. Mould in no time.

Frankly, some of his wine-making ideas seem just as zany, but there's usually a potent reason for what John Paul does, be it scientifically or spiritually based. Or both. Because he believes Pinot Noir's beauty of flavour is created in the vineyard, he wants to interfere as little as possible once the must starts fermenting. He lets the temperature go up to about 32°C (90°F), then presses the wine gently into tanks for two days, and transfers it to French barrels, 20 to 30 per cent of them new, just as dirty as it wants to be. No sulphur anywhere along the track. In fact, he says he's happy if he gets a few barrels showing some sulphide, it'll add complexity.

And he won't filter Pinot Noir. He tried it in 1984, and he says the wine was pretty, but lacked complexity. But he still has to get his wine to fall bright. It takes the Reserve and Abbey Ridge two years in barrel before they're star bright. His ordinary Pinot couldn't cope with so long in barrel. But he remembered one of his Burgundian friends chiding him for dismissing the

phases of the moon in a winemaker's calculations. He went back to his records. Every barrel he'd racked on the waxing moon was showing far more sediment than those he'd done as the moon waned. It's all to do with air pressure if you're being strictly scientific – but it was the proving of an age-old folk wisdom that appealed to John Paul. Now all his Pinot Noir is racked – and bottled – without filtration, on the waning of the moon.

And that stuff tastes. Pinot Noir's most important claim to fame is its silky softness and heavenly perfume. That's not enough for John Paul. There's a darker, more savage, more uncontrolled side to Pinot Noir's personality, not quite acceptable in polite society, nervously shunned by the timid taster. And wildly unpredictable. His 1986 Abbey Ridge has on occasion seemed to me skinsy and tough, sullen, intense, the fruit frightened to cry. Only days later it has seemed hot and jam-rich, shining with sweat as though it's just burst out of a Turkish bath. And I've seen it tangy, chewy, with a sweet-sour curl of volatility flaring my nostrils, but such fruit, such plum and damson richness, pepper too, honey and the gradually-yielded perfume of bitter-sweet black cherry skin. Was I different? Was the wine?

His 1987 Reserve starts out reeking of linseed oil, of lanolin, the fragrant fishskin smell of unworn leather gloves. Within weeks I try it again: it's beautifully perfumed, the plums are ripe now, speckled with the fragrant silver bloom of warm autumn evenings as they weigh down the bough, somewhere nuts are grilling and . . . lavender. This lovely, deep-scented but grainy-textured wine is starting to smell of lavender.

His Chardonnays undergo similar sea-changes of flavour, but Paul doesn't let his white wine make itself as he does his Pinot Noir. Even so, he tries to coax all the barrels through malolactic fermentation and, reckoning that Oregon fruit is too delicate for more than 15 per cent new oak, he manipulates the yeast lees to create a rich texture. He doesn't believe that the lees break down and release their creamy buttery flavours until early in the summer following vintage. So all his Chardonnay spends a year on its lees.

Someone once asked him what exactly his wine-making objectives were. But how the hell can John Paul know? Whenever he's decided what target to aim for, he moves the goal posts.

Carneros

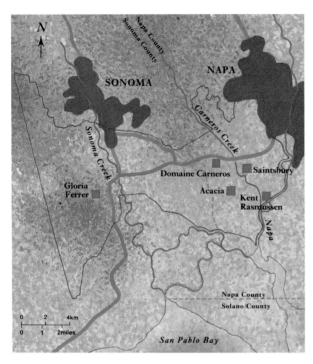

SONOMA

NAPA

Sonoma County
Napa County

Carneros Creek

Sonoma Creek

Domaine Carneros   Saintsbury

Gloria
Ferrer

Acacia

Kent
Rasmussen

Napa

Napa County
Solano County

0   2   4km
0   1   2miles

San Pablo Bay

Carneros Viticultural Area boundary

I STAND ON THE BROW of the slope just above the Acacia winery and gaze over into San Pablo Bay. Silence. The brilliant sun in midwinter tempts me to remove my coat and I'm almost dazzled by the golden carpet of mustard flowers which runs away to the glistening waters of the Bay. And this golden carpet is studded with ugly black vines, reaching like monsters' claws from the earth. There's a hut, a tired old bungalow, a dusty yard. No cars pass, no tractors growl. A rural backwater discreet in its genteel poverty.

Yes and no. I'm looking down the slopes of the St Clair vineyard, which produces one of the finest Pinot Noirs in all America. And this quiet rural backwater is the Carneros region, a viticultural area which many say is California's most exciting cool climate zone.

Carneros is a rumpled, hummocky, hillocky sprawl of land linking the Sonoma and Napa Valleys as they flatten out at their southern ends and their waters run into San Pablo Bay, itself the northern tip of San Francisco Bay. Although vines were planted here in the nineteenth century, the area reverted during the early part of this century to mixed dairy and sheep farming. The very name Carneros means 'rams' and today's

vineyards are still interspersed with pasture. Most of the vineyards themselves have no winery attached, and despite the recent construction of wine-making facilities like those of sparkling wine producers Gloria Ferrer and Domaine Carneros (respectively the California investments of Spain's Freixenet and France's Taittinger groups), this is a region still owned and worked by farmers. The parade of ostentatious architectural triumphs and follies which has transformed parts of Napa and Sonoma is absent here.

But on paper at least, the farmers of Carneros are very wealthy indeed. At the beginning of the 1990s, vineyard prices per acre were higher in Carneros than anywhere else in California. And the reason is the climate. In midwinter, the moderating influence of San Pablo Bay allows me to bask in warm sunlight. In midsummer, as I drive past the same spot above the St Clair vineyard, the early morning fog is so thick and cold I draw my coat tight around me and don't even venture from the car.

It's Cool . . .

This topsy-turvy climate is the key to Carneros. California's quality vineyards have all been developed where there is some element tempering the fierce sun of summer and the biting chill of winter. Both the Sonoma and Napa Valleys are cooled during the summer by the cold air from the Pacific. Yet in the 1960s and 1970s when California wine returned to a quality-first approach, it was California's ability to ripen grapes to bulging sugar levels which seemed important. Carneros, the first to feel the fogs and cold air currents as they were drawn up the valleys, yet the last to rid itself of fog in the late morning, seemed far too cool.

That was the 1970s. The mood in the 1990s is different. The rich, mouthfilling, blockbuster wines which thrilled a world unused to super-ripeness in the 1970s, are now seen as too bloated and unbalanced. Elegance is all, finesse, perfume and balance are the objectives – and to achieve those you need cool climate conditions, and a long growing season.

Carneros provides these. Winter and springtime temperatures are on average a few degrees warmer than areas further inland. This allows an early budbreak yet with little frost risk. Summer temperatures are appreciably cooler on average than further up the valleys. The fogs created by the collision of warm inland air and cold ocean air don't clear until mid to late morning. Then the day heats up and the grapes continue to ripen, until in the late afternoon, a breeze comes off the bay, as regular as clockwork, cooling the grapes in the torrid afternoon sun. This results in far

Vines snake across the low-slung Carneros hills while irrigation lines glow like silver in the sun.

higher natural acid levels in the grapes, although the reduced number of sunlight hours can create ripening problems. For this reason, growers in Carneros have become the most active in California in the effort to match the right grape types, and the right clones, with the right soils and aspects to the sun, and the right pruning and trellising methods to maximize both acid retention and sugar ripeness. This unique quality in the fruit enabled Carneros to gain its own appellation in 1983, based on geographical not political boundaries – amazingly, the first time this has occurred in America.

Although varieties such as Cabernet and Merlot are grown in Carneros, especially in the warmer northernmost corner, the two varieties which now cover 85 per cent of the 3000 hectares (7500 acres) of plantings are Pinot Noir and Chardonnay. Yet Winery Lake Vineyard, which created the reputation of Carneros as a wine region during the 1970s, was only planted with Chardonnay and Pinot Noir by accident. It was just that they happened to be the only disease-free vines the owner, René di Rosa, could obtain!

If it was chance that caused Pinot Noir and Chardonnay to be planted in Carneros, it is dogged determination, hard-nosed commercialism and starry-eyed idealism which have created the modern Carneros legend. The commercialism comes in the form of the sparkling wine producers. Pinot Noir and Chardonnay are the classic French Champagne grapes and they barely ripen on the chilly slopes of north-east France. Since Carneros is the coolest area close to the wine-making centres of Sonoma and Napa, and since there is a conviction on the part of many major European sparkling wine producers that America has an unquenchable thirst for sparkling wine, many of the Pinot Noir and Chardonnay vineyards are planted solely with sparkling wine production in mind.

Commercialism also shows itself in the large plantations of Chardonnay for table wine use. Chardonnay is a sure-fire seller and every winery has to make one. The more quality-conscious of the big Napa and Sonoma wineries will frequently include fresh, acid-balanced Carneros fruit in their blends. The small number of producers actually based in Carneros all admit it is Chardonnay which pays the bills.

The idealism comes with those passionate winemakers for whom Pinot Noir is the Holy Grail. The long cool growing season does seem to suit Pinot Noir and since the ZD winery bought the first Winery Lake Pinot Noir grapes back in 1969, nearly *all* the famous Pinot Noirs made north of San Francisco – have been produced from Carneros fruit.

Chalone

*I*T'S A STRANGE COINCIDENCE that two wine producers who say they owe most to André Noblet, the legendary winemaker at Domaine de la Romanée-Conti in Burgundy, should both have wound up, by quite separate paths, only a dozen miles from each other on bleak, isolated vineyard sites far from civilization – both prepared to endure the privations of wilderness wine-making in the belief that they can wrest great wines from their barren soil. Calera and Chalone, one on each side of the Gavilan mountain range; Josh Jensen of Calera and Dick Graff of Chalone are both fired with a passion for Burgundy fuelled by their lessons from André Noblet.

Or is it coincidence? Whenever Jensen or Graff probed deep into the Frenchman's wine-making methods, Noblet used to murmur the magic word 'limestone'. In fact Noblet seemed fairly content to let his wines make themselves, so long as the grapes had come from a limestone soil. First Graff, then Jensen, came back to California and set about finding a limestone soil. That is, a plantable one. There was quite a bit of limestone on the wild coastal bluffs below Monterey, but there only seemed to be one outcrop in a remotely cultivable position – on the east and west slopes of the Gavilan range that runs along the San Andreas fault south of San Francisco.

Remotely cultivable sums it up. I'm constantly amazed at the levels of ingenuity and determination an individual will demonstrate in his efforts to find a perfect vineyard site. But Graff, who'd caught the wine bug after graduating in music from Harvard, wasn't the first to prospect in these hills. In the nineteenth century, a Frenchman called Curtis Tamm planted vines here after marching up and down the California coast looking for somewhere to set up a vineyard and make sparkling wine.

Those dreams faded, but in 1919, as Prohibition descended, a man called William Silvear, obviously lacking in a sense of timing even if he knew a good vineyard site, planted Chardonnay, Pinot Noir, Pinot Blanc and Chenin Blanc at Chalone, 610 metres (2000 feet) up in the Gavilan range below the Pinnacles peaks. When Prohibition was repealed, his grapes sold for high prices to the big California wineries. His original 8 hectares (20 acres) still survive, nestling among copses of small, water-starved black oaks. And when Dick Graff struggled up the rutted mountain track in 1964 he found other vines too, that had been planted in 1946. And this was the soil he wanted. At the original vineyard sites you can see chunks of limestone chalk strewn across the landscape: they've dug down over two metres and haven't hit the bottom of the chalk yet. And where the reddish volcanic topsoil seems to dominate, you only need to put your hand into a rabbit burrow to find the chalk, a mere hand's depth from the surface.

He bought the property in 1965 and then began to discover that, whatever they think at Domaine de la Romanée-Conti, soil isn't the whole story. Water would be nice, for a start. Technically, the Chalone land would just about qualify as a desert! Average rainfall is only as high as 355mm (14in) because occasionally, in years like 1983, you'll suffer a few torrential downpours to virtually double that year's total. The following year you may get a quarter of that amount. Graff built a huge reservoir to hold the produce of Chalone's wells and the winter run-off – which was fine if there was any. Often there wasn't, and Graff had to resort to bringing water up the mountain by truck.

Quenching the Thirst

In 1987 Graff took the drastic step of drilling a well 11km (7 miles) away on the valley floor near Soledad and running a pipeline up the mountainside. Vineyard expansion was impossible without water. The vines were being stifled by salt build-up in the soil because of the absence of winter rain to wash it away. The total of 17,000 cases of wine in 1983 became 7000 in 1984 and 1985. Still, that was some improvement from Graff's starting point. In the early 1970s Graff was eking out a living in the hills, producing perhaps 500 cases of wine a year, without electricity, without a phone line even. He went into partnership with businessman Phil Woodward in 1972, but it still wasn't until 1985 that they got an electric power line up to the property. And whenever they needed to phone for supplies, they had to go to the public payphone at nearby Pinnacles National Monument. No wonder Graff and Woodward decided to establish themselves as a super-exclusive winery selling only through mail order and a few top restaurant accounts. When a Chalone Chardonnay came third in the Bicentennial Tasting Challenge held in Paris in 1976, which pitted the world's wines against the cream of France, the phone would never have stopped ringing – if they'd had one. Well, at least they've had a waiting list ever since.

Chalone began by making several hundred cases of wine a year in the Gavilan mountains. Today that figure is closer to 25,000 cases and growing, and Chalone has become Chalone Incorporated, an important, publicly-quoted company that now controls other operations – Edna Valley, Carmenet and Acacia in California, plus a joint venture with Woodward Canyon in the Columbia River Valley in Washington. The initial push to expand came in 1980, after Graff had been trying out some grapes from the Edna Valley area further south near San Luis Obispo. The result is 50,000 cases a year of 'Edna Valley' wine. And in 1989 Chalone joined forces with the Bordeaux company Domaines Barons de Rothschild – managers of Château Lafite and owners of Châteaux Duhart-Milon, La Cardonne, l'Évangile and Rieussec – in a deal which gives each company a 20 per cent stake in the other.

You might have thought Dick Graff would have wanted to join up with a Burgundy house, given his love for the wines. But I'm not sure he'd be able to find a Burgundy house sufficiently passionate to share in his dream of wresting great flavours from this ungenerous soil. Anyway, he and his winemaker, Michael Michaud, would much rather pursue their Holy Grail on their own terms.

Above all, they are great believers in *goût de terroir* – the taste of vineyard character. There's no question that the Chalone wines, particularly when young, do have a most remarkable mineral quality – a smell like wet rocks on the sea shore, an acidity like the zest from lime peel.

Michael Michaud sounds as though he should be making wine in France, but in fact he's an American making some of California's most Burgundian wines at Chalone.

It is distinctly unnerving at first, and Chalone is regularly criticized when it is first released. Are these savage flavours due to the very low yields – sometimes less than a ton per acre from the 1919 and 1946 vines – or is it really the soil? Graff planted more vines in 1970, '73 and '74 and then again, increasing plantings to about 80 hectares (200 acres) in 1984, '85, '86 and '90. The youngest plantings have benefitted from irrigation and vertical trellising systems with fruit exposed to the sun. Will the limestone still win through?

It may well, because limestone itself can form a stressful environment for vines. If your wine-making philosophy is to nurture rather than mould the character of that fruit, the vineyard character should shine through. That's very much the objective at Chalone. Wine-making is fashioned after Burgundian tradition. No sulphur is added early to protect the juice from oxidation – so the must will turn the colour of tobacco spit before precipitating out beautifully clear during fermentation. All white wine fermentation is in French oak barrels, in cellars that Michaud chills down for two weeks before harvest to simulate the autumnal conditions of a Burgundian cellar.

With chilled juice and a cool ambient temperature, the fermentation is slower, and less perfume is lost. Reserve wines from the 1919, 1946 and 1970 plots get 100 per cent new wood, the other estate wines more like 30 per cent. They all go through complete malolactic fermentation when possible – the Chenin in particular finds malolactic difficult, though – and they have

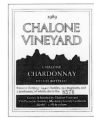

extended lees contact before being bottled after six to nine months. The Pinot Noir is increasingly picked on taste not just correct acid and sugar figures. The fruit is picked cool in the morning, and piled into tanks as whole clusters, stems and all, and given a quick tread to break up some berries. The Pinot juice stays at about 28°C (82°F) – although the cap of skins may rise to 35°C (95°F) – without refrigeration. They punch the cap down, rather than pump over, since pumping over-aerates the wine and increases Pinot Noir's already enthusiastic rate of fermentation. This takes seven to ten days – a long time for Pinot Noir – and then the wine and skins macerate for four to five days, before being pressed and put into French oak barrels. After which the wines lie undisturbed for 13 months on their lees – Michaud is sure this greatly improves the wine's perfume. There'll be one fining with egg white, and two more rackings before the wines are bottled, unfiltered, in January or February of their second winter.

The result is wines of tremendous personality. They're often criticized upon release because these Chalones are masterpieces of non-conformity. Chenin Blanc isn't my favourite grape, but Chalone's example, from those 1919 and 1946 vines, has a lovely soft, biscuit-and-honey character. Pinot Blanc isn't a top grape of mine either, but it does brilliantly here, the variety's almost milky-soft butteriness being made more exciting by a touch of toast and honey, streaked by the tang of lime peel and sea-swept stone.

Some people say they prefer the Pinot Blanc to the Chardonnay, but that's taking the easy way out. These Chardonnays are unique wines. And they are challenging, young or old. They never lose touch with their limestone birthplace, the mineral rasp and the darting perfume of lime stays in the wine as the honey and golden toast of youth gradually wraps itself in the sweet old fruit of apricots and figs, the smoke of freshly cut logs just lit.

But it is the Pinot Noirs which are Chalone's greatest achievement. That's exactly how Dick Graff wants it to be. Despite virtually all the new plantings being designed to slake the nation's thirst for Chardonnay, it is Pinot Noir that Graff grew to love in Burgundy, and in this most unlikely situation the finicky, pernickety, sulky Pinot Noir regularly produces wine of an intensity and perfume to match the best in California.

Yet there's something more. The other great California Pinot Noirs have developed a genuinely different, uniquely American style. Somehow, Chalone has managed to produce Côte de Nuits flavours thousands of miles from home. These wines would be revered in the best corners of Nuits-St-Georges and

Chalone is situated so high in the arid Gavilan mountains you can't imagine anyone starting a vineyard there, but the soil is some of the best limestone in California.

Gevrey-Chambertin. Could it be that the limestone soil makes all the difference? Certainly the Pinots from the older plantings, from the intensely chalky soil, do have a family resemblance from just a few months old. I ranged back through the 1980s, and Michaud's assertion that his wines were unfairly pilloried by critics too short-sighted and cold-hearted to judge them as wines for the long haul made more and more sense. By the time I got

to 1986, the sweet flesh of the cherry was having to accommodate the bitter, dry cherry-stone perfumes of the Côte de Nuits, the chewy skins of plums perfumed by the sun, the fragrance of soft leather hardly worn – oh, and flowers: cherry blossom, lilies, lilacs, or were they violets? It hardly mattered what they were. Michaud said 1986 was the greatest Chalone Pinot Noir yet. Yes, yes, maybe it is.

But is that fair to the 1983, with its cherries and strawberries honeyed in the mouth, its mineral streak as clear as cold steel, then its heroic fault – a high-pitched volatile sweet-sour slash of cherry and redcurrant

leaving the palate watering for more? Is that fair to the 1982, slowly finding a core of sweet damson and black cherries despite the haze of limestone dust still shrouding its perfume for a few years yet? Or the 1981, beginning to tire now, but only as a great old actor tires while he assumes his last and most memorable roles, bright perfumed youth replaced by a more ponderous but intoxicating richness of decay, the last wisps of rosehips and the strawberry fields almost engulfed by the smoky, medicinal coal tar richness of Hymettus honey? Is it fair? Does it matter? That they were made at all, that's what matters.

Cuvaison

*T*WO FACTORS EXPLAIN THE STYLE and the rapidly improving quality of Cuvaison's wines. In 1980 the owners, the Schmidheiny family, planted 110 hectares (270 acres) of prime vineyard land in Carneros, the fashionable wine area north of San Francisco, in those days only hinting at its future popularity. And in 1982 this Napa Valley winery appointed John Thacher as winemaker. He's quite the most laid-back, gentle, boyish fellow to be in charge of a major American winery, but he has a slow-burning passion for quality – and a conviction that it is control of vineyards and proper care of them which will mark out the super-achievers of California in the future. Winemakers are returning to basics – away from their technical toys, and back to the soil and to the vines. They have to be sensitive enough to cherish their land, yet must give their vines discipline and direction. Those who do, can take California to new heights, and this is John Thacher's main ambition.

Cuvaison first made something of a name for itself in the 1970s by producing blockbuster reds. Zinfandels and Cabernets were made from fruit grown in the warm northern end of the valley (where some of the winery buildings are situated), or from mountainside vineyards tracked down with Sherlock Holmes-like determination by their previous winemaker, Philip Togni. Those 1970s reds are still some of the best examples of the rip-roaring styles which shocked the world into taking California's red wines seriously.

Cuvaison continue to make Cabernet and Zinfandel, though Zin is being phased out – 'we've run out of space' – but since Thacher took over, the emphasis in the winery has shifted noticeably. With reds, there's a gradual switch of interest towards Merlot and Pinot Noir, and Cuvaison are buying their grapes further and further down towards the cooler southern end of the Napa Valley. Most of the Cabernet now comes from a rocky knoll just north of Napa city, while the Merlot and Pinot Noir wines are based on fruit from their own decidedly cool Carneros plantings.

The tremendous tannins of the Togni days have gone, but so has the super-concentrated fruit. What Thacher aims for is a round, supple gentleness which makes the wine easy to enjoy young, but also provides a balance which will allow it to age. He's crazy about fruit character in ageing red wines, and thinks that the Napa Valley obsession with tannin is totally wrong-headed.

'I'm obsessed with tannin too, but in the exact opposite way to the others – how the hell to reduce it and manage it!' A red wine which you can drink at any stage through a span of 10 to 15 years is his aim and he thinks the equable California climate is ideal for producing such wines. 'Maybe they never get the dramatic increase in character that a Bordeaux gets – but you don't have the 15-year wait either.' His 1983 and '84 Cabernets are now beautiful wines, developing a positively Pauillac-like blackcurrant and cedar fragrance. His 1984 Merlot is as juicy and plummy today as it was five years ago. Much as I love the old-style Cuvaisons, I have to admit the more subtle Thacher style makes a lot more sense.

But it is white wine which is Thacher's main preoccupation, and that means Chardonnay. Working out how to coax his Carneros grapes into producing a world-class wine takes up a lot of his time and energy. Coaxing is very much the Thacher style, because he doesn't want to force the grapes into directions of flavour they don't want to follow. He wants to discover the true character of his vineyards, and the various different clones he's planted. But subtly. 'If at any time the hand of the winemaker is evident in the wine, he's overplayed that hand.'

Control, both of the vineyard and of the winery, that's what he sees as the key to fine wine-making. In his first vintage at Cuvaison, 1982, he bought Chardonnay from 18 different growers, and the experience was just a mad scramble. There wasn't enough Chardonnay being grown, so it wasn't a matter of 'where' your Chardonnay came from – whatever you could find, you bought. Every year meant different sources, sites, qualities; it was impossible to develop a style and it was impossible to pursue a dream.

Contradictions in Terms

Thacher is definitely a man with a dream. A dream of creating his own California equivalent of great white Burgundy. As he sees it, great Burgundies are all contradiction: 'they're powerful, but they're light; they're rich but they're dry; they explode in the mouth but they're weightless'. Texture, flavour, perfume – how do you create the wine which joins these in a seamless whole?

When I asked him to describe the flavours of this great wine he was seeking, he corrected me. The flavours alone weren't the point. With the greatest wines you just go, 'Wow, I love it'. As soon as you try to analyse the flavours you're distancing yourself from the experience of greatness, he says. 'You want to know my definition of truly great wine? When they pour you

Cuvaison

Don't worry, Cuvaison does have more extensive vineyard holdings; in fact most of Cuvaison's grapes now come from the south of the Napa Valley and Carneros.

a glass and put the bottle on the table, you smell it, you taste it, and your first reaction is to look at the bottle to see how much is left because you know you're not going to be able to control yourself. You try like hell not to drink the wine too fast but you can't help it.'

I know what he means. But it's not at *all* a common phenomenon. And how is Thacher going to set out on *his* quest for this indefinable excellence? By going back to the vineyards. But you can't draw conclusions from a vineyard in just a couple of years. The French took hundreds of years to work out the best equations in the wine regions of Bordeaux, Burgundy, the Rhône. The very minimal period needed for conclusive results is to follow a vineyard through the life cycle of one planting of vines – anything up to 40 years.

John Thacher revels in the challenge, and uses all the tools available to him. He has minutely surveyed all the differing soils in his Carneros vineyards, and adapted his irrigation methods to suit them. Thacher took vine cuttings from the vineyards he liked – so he has Monticello clones, Beringer clones, and so on. With variations in flavour and rates of ripening, Thacher increases the range of variables he can work with.

When he harvests – manually, though he has experimented with machine picking in case labour should become short some time in the future – he makes as many separate lots as possible. In the 1988 vintage he had 52 different batches of grapes to process and he had a similar number in 1989, covering the early-picked, more acid grapes, right through to the glycerine-packed overripe ones. About three-quarters of the wine is fermented in barrel, and almost all gets some ageing in French oak – between three and eight months, depending on the style of the wine. Thacher tries to allow every parcel to develop its own character and he manipulates the wine as little as possible.

With the vineyards still young, his objective now is to get one main blend and perhaps one Reserve blend of Cuvaison Chardonnay up to the best possible level. But he's looking further ahead. Each year he feels he understands his numerous blocks of land a little better. Already he finds a core group of regularly superior wines which usually form the basis of the Reserve blend. He's doggedly isolating the best, pinpointing the spot in the vineyard, and then setting about understanding and enhancing the unique qualities in that parcel of vines. For the present it all adds up to expertly blended, high-quality Cuvaison wine, but by 1995, by 2000 perhaps, Thacher reckons he may know enough to choose one or two patches of land and bottle their wines separately. Which is just how the classification system started in Meursault, in Puligny-Montrachet, and the other villages of John Thacher's promised land – Burgundy.

Dunn Vineyards

RANDY DUNN DOESN'T WELCOME VISITORS to his winery high up on the windy ridges of Howell Mountain above the Napa Valley. Even if you did arrive to seek him out, he'd probably hand you a bucket and tell you to catch the drips as he racks the wine from barrel to barrel, or hold the torch as he gets inside a tank to fork out the mush of grapeskins and pips. Because this is an all-hands-on-deck winery. Any available able-bodied person with a pair of hands is put to use wine-making, rather than pulling corks and swirling fancy wine glasses. That's the way he wants it. And having seen the invasion of privacy that many wineries endure simply to allow us to get close to them and their wines in the hope that their bonhomie will convert into cash in the till, I can't say I blame him.

But there *is* a way to get an intimate knowledge of what Randy Dunn is up to, what his wife Lori thinks about his antics, how his kids Mike, Jennifer and Kristina are getting along – even news of 'good ole Chewy, the snake dog' (getting a bit arthritic) and of the

1969 El Camino pick-up truck which clocked up 217,000 miles for him before being pensioned off (now refurbished and enjoying a new lease of life on the less arduous roads of the Napa Valley floor). What you have to do to keep up is get yourself on the mailing list. Randy Dunn may be a shy, private man, and Randy Dunn may be one of American wine's highest fliers (oh, he is a flier, by the way – he pilots a Cessna 182 Skylane up and down the valley whenever he's not making wine), but he can certainly write a folksy newsletter for his mailing list customers.

Does that sound a bit arch? If it does, I'm not being fair. The low-key, mountain man image Dunn has cultivated *is* the man. His life style, centred around his family and his wine, is the most important thing to him. And although he was the highly successful winemaker at Caymus Vineyards down in the Napa Valley for ten years between 1975 and 1985, his sights were set early on the plateaux and ridges of Howell Mountain 600 metres (2000 feet) up, where he moved in 1978. And although he paid his dues at Caymus by producing a

Randy Dunn makes great Cabernet Sauvignon high on Howell Mountain – and maybe those shades betray the fact he fancies himself as a pilot, too.

string of superb Cabernet Sauvignons – I still remember the shock and excitement the first time I tasted the 1975 and '76 – his highly individual personality was always going to lead him to establishing his own independent operation – far from the politics and horse-trading of the increasingly commercialized Napa Valley floor.

Howell Mountain, on the eastern side of the Napa Valley, was a famous vineyard area in the last century. There were 240 hectares (600 acres) of vines there in 1891, and by 1900, Cabernet and Zinfandel wines from Howell Mountain were winning gold medals at the Paris International Exhibition. Prohibition put paid to all that, but Howell Mountain's special attributes are easy to see for any expert grapegrower.

I've stood on the western side of the Napa Valley, on Spring Mountain in the evening, the sun long gone from where I stood, with Howell Mountain's slopes still basking in the gold of the warm evening sun. In the morning I've watched the fogs slowly clear from the valley and noticed that though they may rise to perhaps a thousand feet up Howell Mountain, the plateau at the top is always clear and bathed in morning sunshine. Some winemakers in the Napa Valley contend that this means the grapes get too ripe up there in a region where many winemakers are trying to reduce heat, not maximize it. Randy Dunn, after making fine wine from valley floor fruit at Caymus for ten years, isn't among the doubters.

For a start, the vineyards are at 600 metres (2000 feet) and above. So they're naturally a good deal cooler than valley floor land. You do get longer hours of sunshine, both in the morning and the evening, but you don't get elevated temperatures. The photosynthesis from the longer sunlight hours encourages the build-up of sugar in the grapes, but the lower temperatures mean the skins don't bake and thicken, avoiding a pruney, raisiny taste. On average summer days are 6° to 8°C (10° to 15°F) cooler than on the valley floor, while nights tend to be warmer.

The soil is totally different from anything you find in the Napa Valley. Crumbled, coppery-red volcanic soil, very well drained and fairly shallow is the norm, and the mountain top really can glisten like a copper cauldron when the sun catches it. This brings an average yield of up to two tons per acre which makes the intensely flavoured Howell Mountain grapes some of the most sought-after in California.

Dunn is amusedly dismissive of his peers in the valley. 'I kid with guys like Tim Mondavi. The money and effort they spend on trying to reduce the vigour of their valley floor vines. I say, hell Tim, why don't you save all that money and buy some nice low-yield hillside

ground and put that Rutherford stuff back into pasture land for cows like it should be.'

He is joking – about the world-famous Rutherford Bench vineyards – but he's also making a serious point. Valley floor soil is so deep and rich he doesn't reckon anyone has ever found the bottom of it. Vines go mad down there, they think it's Christmas seven days a week, and produce like fury. It's a recurring argument in California – whether you can ever equate high yields with high quality – but those flatland vineyards find it difficult to yield less than six tons to the acre. Dunn can't even manage two tons on Howell Mountain. And no-one makes such concentrated Cabernet as Randy Dunn from his Howell Mountain vineyards.

Committed to Cabernet

He bought his vineyards in 1978. The vines had been planted back in 1972 by an airline pilot, but they weren't exactly thriving. The crop in 1978 amounted to a meagre 30 gallons of wine. But by 1979 Dunn had licked the vineyards into better shape and had also signed a contract to manage the 2.4-hectare (6-acre) vineyard belonging to a neighbour – and this now constitutes the Howell Mountain vineyard, one hundred per cent Cabernet Sauvignon. He says he's trying to persuade the neighbour to plant three more acres of vines, and he may also plant three more himself, but then maybe he won't. 'It's a darned lot of work, growing vines,' he says. He might even need to employ someone to help him. Perhaps the neighbour can be persuaded to plant six more acres instead.

The need to employ assistance looms large in Dunn's life. At the moment he does have a chap helping him full-time in the cellar and, since the wines have become so successful, he also has someone part-time in the office. But he doesn't really want to expand his production. At present he makes about 2000 cases of the Howell Mountain Cabernet Sauvignon, and another 2000 cases of a Napa Valley blend he creates each year. In 1986 he produced enough grapes to make over 3000 cases of Dunn Vineyards Howell Mountain. Since his wine is in incredible demand and is sold at a high price, didn't this please him? No. He blended the extra 1000 cases into his cheaper Napa Valley Cuvée.

He couldn't bear the idea of getting the marketing men all het up – opening new accounts, increasing allocations – because they'd expect more wine from him every year, and he doesn't want to make more. 'The last thing I want to do is to be easily available,' he says. He knows producers who make about three times as much as they say they do – to satisfy demand – yet still swear they haven't increased production, to maintain mystique and rarity value. You won't find him doing that. Firstly, because it isn't how he likes to operate, and secondly because making more wine means 'less time to fly, less time to go horse-riding with the kids'.

That's also one of the reasons that he only makes Cabernet Sauvignon. He doesn't want to start all over again, learning to understand what makes a new variety tick, what works, what doesn't. I reckon in future years it's possible lucky visitors *might* be offered a taste of a Dunn Chardonnay, or a Pinot Noir, or a Zinfandel, but the wine would have to be phenomenally good to persuade Dunn to branch out from his Cabernet Sauvignon-only philosophy.

Still, bills are bills, and they have to be paid. Which is why you'll see him venturing back down the mountain slopes from time to time, firstly to look for grapes for his Napa Valley blend and secondly to fulfil a couple of consultancies he has taken on. If you see the name Livingston, or the name Pahlmeyer on a label – you'll be looking at a Randy Dunn wine. Pahlmeyer is a vineyard east of Napa city in an area called Coombsville. Livingston is over on the west side of the Napa Valley, just by Rutherford. Pahlmeyer, in particular, provides a high proportion of the grapes for his Napa Valley Cabernet. But the composition of the blend, which made its debut in 1982, changes every year, and trying to find the right grapes for the wine is a continuing challenge for Dunn. Some come from Rutherford, some from Spring Mountain, some from the north of the valley near Calistoga.

In Search of the Right Grapes

One of the nightmares of a winemaker's life is trying to get hold of the best grapes to achieve the end result visualized, because frequently the grapes have to be reserved as early as June – sometimes even sooner – before the fruit has even set on the vine. If the grapes don't turn out as you'd hoped, then there's a mad scramble around harvest time to try and locate grapes which will balance out the deficiencies in the crop you're committed to buying.

Some winemakers buy according to whether the acid, sugar and tannin figures seem correct, but Dunn says figures can never be more than a guide. If you've tasted wines made from the property's previous vintages, that'll be a help, but otherwise, if a grower rings and says he's got some grapes going begging – you've got to get to the vineyard, walk between the rows and taste the grapes. Right figures or wrong, a good winemaker will follow his gut reaction. In any case, the word has got around that Dunn will pay top money for top grapes, so he doesn't get bothered by bulk producers – and the

other winemakers also know that if they've got a few barrels spare of top line wine, Dunn may be interested in that too – and will pay good money if he thinks it will blend in.

The Howell Mountain Cabernet is remarkable for its consistent quality vintage after vintage. From the 660 cases of 1979, to the 2000 cases of 1989, the wines exhibit an awesome power; they're tannic and demanding in their youth, but this brutal exterior is matched by a deliciously original fruit flavour of plum and peach and blackcurrant, sharpened up by ginger and the perfume of fresh black pepper, and often showing a thrilling floral fragrance too. The wines are sturdy, massive even, but deep inside their brooding superstructure there's a sleeping beauty of blackcurrant and spice and violets. The sleep is a long one, because even the 1979 and 1980 are still not yet fully mature over ten years later, but time does calm them and coax out their magic sweetness.

The Napa Valley blend is similar in weight, but doesn't have quite the intensity or the perfume. The tannins are still fierce when the wine is young, and the fruit is piercingly direct, all black cherry and blackcurrant, sometimes sharpened by a citrus quality from Pahlmeyer's Coombsville fruit. It's another long-distance runner with the 1982 and 1983 only slowly blossoming with eight or nine years of age.

Dunn's wine-making philosophy is to let the fruit express itself. 'I don't do anything magic,' he replies when I quiz him on technique. He destems and crushes the grapes, inoculates with a Montrachet yeast and lets the the temperature rise fairly high. There's no golden rule. If he's getting short of tank space, the wine may go up to 32°C (90°F) for a few days to get things over with in time for the next batch. But he's also worked with small tanks which never got over 25°C (78°F) which he was really pleased with. He does pump the juice over the skins vigorously, usually pumping over the entire tank three times a day, before pressing, leaving the mix to settle for only a couple of days, though he'd prefer to leave it longer, and then putting the wines into a mix of new and used French oak barrels, where they stay, without fining, for about two and a half years before bottling.

The pumpover extracts a lot of tannin and colour, and many California winemakers are experimenting with a period of macerating the grape skins in the wine after fermentation is over, also intended to increase flavour and soften tannins. 'It's like follow-my-leader,' Dunn says. 'One guy starts doing a long, warm maceration, the press picks it up and starts asking everyone the same question – are you doing it? And

the winemaker says, "Oh, golly, no I'm not", but he feels perhaps he should. So next year – there he is doing a long, warm, post-fermentation maceration, without ever having thought it through at all.'

With Dunn there's no place for fads. Up until now he's done everything in such a cramped space on such a shoestring that he hasn't ever found himself in a particularly experimental frame of mind. But he has now blasted a cave from the rock behind the house, giving him space for all his barrels, and this will at last give him space to move and flexibility to experiment – if he wants to. He gets positively conspiratorial when he discusses the remote possibility of making a barrel of Chardonnay or a barrel of Zinfandel. His laughter quickens and he whispers fervently, sounding absurdly like the best bits of Marlon Brando and WC Fields all at once. But other wines would be playthings. Ever since moving to his 'way out from nowhere' mountain

The isolation and tranquillity of the Howell Mountain forests are just what Randy and Lori Dunn needed to put down roots and create great wine.

hideaway, he's been fascinated by the challenge of making California's best possible Cabernet Sauvignon and that's what he'll concentrate on.

Now he's finally got the equipment and the space and the financial security to do everything in the way he wants. I think we'll see a rising curve of excellence in the Dunn Cabernets of the 1990s before we see too many distractions like Chardonnay hitting the shops. After all, there's his plane to fly, those horse rides in the woods with his kids . . . He's even got an unfinished doctoral thesis on the hormonal problems of young mosquitoes he might polish off. A squirt or two of good Dunn Vineyards Cabernet Sauvignon would sort them out I'd have thought.

Eyrie

GOD IT WAS GOOD! After a week in Oregon tasting untold numbers of Pinot Noir, I was beginning to think I'd never find what I was after. But here it was – a mature wine with a heavenly perfume of rich, sweet plums and strawberries, a soft, voluptuous feeling of ripe glycerine coating my mouth as my palate soaked up the delicious fragrance of plums and damsons, of strawberries bulging with the summer's sun.

'Worst wine I've ever made.'

What? 'We're talking about your Eyrie Pinot Noir 1978, David. It's heavenly, it's irresistible, it's as good as any 1978 Burgundy I can think of . . .'

'I loathe the wine,' says David Lett. He only bottled 25 cases because he loathed it so much. He had a hot August, a hot September, an even hotter October. The pickers were four days late. The grapes were totally shrivelled up; he had to hose them down to get any liquid out of them at all. Bah! Humbug! He's really angry. A north-western wine expert in the group curries a little favour by muttering, 'One thing it certainly isn't is Pinot Noir'. And I'm aghast. Of course it's Pinot Noir. It's wonderful Pinot Noir, brilliantly treading the knife edge between sumptuous indulgence and embarrassing lack of manners. It's so seductive, so beautifully Burgundian. But it's exactly the style of Burgundy that David Lett is trying desperately to avoid.

David is an exile from California. Having studied viticulture rather than wine-making at the Davis wine school in 1964, he visited Europe to study their methods of wine-making and, in particular, grape-growing. Despite a flirtation with the super-hot Douro Valley in northern Portugal and, at the other extreme, the super-cool South Island of New Zealand, it was the European experience of marginal climates producing the finest grapes which impressed him most. And nowhere more so than in Burgundy.

His professors at Davis had told him that there was no region in California cool enough to grow good Pinot Noir. When the question of Oregon came up, their view was that it was too cool there to grow anything at all; that ripening would be at least six weeks later than in California, and the most one could hope for from Pinot Noir would be the possibility of crushing it into some sort of light *white* wine. But Lett had by then realized that a 'healthy grape, big yield, low cost' mentality was hardly likely to be in accord with the ambition which was taking shape in his mind – to find a marginal vineyard that would just coax its crop to ripeness as the autumn clouds closed in; and from those grapes to make America's first great Pinot Noir. Red Pinot Noir.

At the same time, it was the natural potential of Burgundy's vineyards that excited him, not the increasingly cynical exploitation of the famous names by Burgundian merchants and winemakers which was at its peak during the 1960s. He wanted to find his own mode of expression for Pinot Noir, and he wanted no one to compare his wines to the artificially sweet and limp creations which the Burgundians were so wont to tout as great wine. My praise of his 1978 had been genuine. But clearly the wine was indeed too Burgundian for him – too perfumed, too exotic, too hedonistic – and his reaction against it, excessive as I thought it, was nonetheless sincere.

So Lett headed north into the uncharted territory of Oregon, reckoning correctly that it was the risk factor – the risk of insufficient sunshine, the risk of rain during harvest – which had frightened off the California vineyard experts, yet which produced the tantalizing possibilities he needed to explore. There was already a vineyard planted in Southern Oregon, in the Umpqua Valley, but Lett decided he wanted to put more distance between himself and California. Just north of the small college town of McMinnville he found what he wanted.

The Right Site, the Right Soil

The Willamette Valley floor stretches over to the Cascade mountains, fertile and well-husbanded, just as the Saône Valley in France stretches from Burgundy to the Jura mountains. Lett briefly searched along the eastern flank of the valley, but on arriving in the little township of Dundee on the western side, and seeing the east-facing slopes of red soil rising up to forests of pines, dipping in and out to provide a range of aspects from east through south towards west, he found he was strongly reminded of the soils and shapes of Burgundy's Côte d'Or.

In 1966 he bought 8 hectares (20 acres) of hillside land just above Dundee and he and his wife planted four acres of vines that year, three the next, gradually building up, as time and money permitted, to an estate of about 12 hectares (30 acres).

From these small beginnings, Lett has led the Willamette Valley, and in particular the hillside slopes around Dundee, to the point where they are claiming to be America's answer to Burgundy's Côte d'Or. There are now over a thousand hectares of vines in the Willamette, although only a third are Pinot Noir. Even Lett only has 2.5 hectares (6 acres) of Pinot Noir as against 6.5 (16) of Pinot Gris – from which he makes what he calls a 'cash flow white'. In Oregon, unlike California, most wineries are small operations, financed and run by individuals not corporations, so cash flow matters. Lett used to have to double as a book salesman to finance his vineyard, and didn't start making a profit from Eyrie until 1983. And despite being the industry leader in the state, his winery is still situated in an unprepossessing converted turkey-processing plant, down by the railroad tracks in McMinnville.

That's not to belittle Lett. He has priorities other than investment in a glitzy showcase winery. His objective was and is to make great Pinot Noir. It didn't matter to him what his winery looked like. He just

David Lett was the first person to establish the credentials of Oregon as a major wine state and still makes some of the region's best wines at Eyrie vineyards.

wanted to learn how to make the stuff. The 1969 – crushed 'in a diaper pail' – didn't see the light of day. He was so ashamed of his 1970 he decided to label it Oregon Spring Wine rather than Pinot Noir.

Love, passion, obsession, these are the words used by all the great Pinot Noir makers. You cannot handle this fickle, wilful variety simply by waving your oenological qualifications at the vine. Lett was finding it very difficult to persuade his fellow Americans to show a little understanding towards his efforts in Oregon. But the French appreciate passion. In 1979, the Eyrie Pinot Noir 1975 was entered into the Gault Millau wine competition in Paris. It came third. Robert Drouhin, the Burgundian merchant, was incensed, and organized a re-run, significantly beefing up the quality of the Burgundian entries. The Eyrie came second, Drouhin's own 1959 Chambolle-Musigny beating it by a mere fifth

of a point. With that single flourish, David Lett and Eyrie created Oregon's reputation for Pinot Noir. Fame allowed the growers to charge high prices, and it created a fierce sense of pride in the Oregon community. Not only did Oregonians make a point of promoting their state's wines, in particular Pinot Noir, though to some extent Pinot Gris and Chardonnay as well, but Oregon's winemakers brought in America's most stringent labelling laws. Varietal wines had to contain at least 90 per cent of the stated variety (apart from Cabernet, to allow for the classic Bordeaux blend), place of origin had to be stated on the label, and so on.

But however far-reaching the legislation, Oregon has not been finding it easy to capitalize on those early successes. It will never be possible to make large amounts of cheap wine in Oregon. Neighbouring Washington and California further south can have that market and good luck to them. There are now over 70 wineries, many of whom have produced the occasional superlative wine, though none has managed it consistently. And the adulation which marked the years after the Gault Millau triumph has now turned to disappointed critiques asking what's gone wrong.

Lett remains unmoved. He knew the risks when he came to Oregon, and his sanguine views on his successes and failures confirm his position as Oregon's leading wine man. Yet shouldn't he too be making great wine more frequently? He talks with pride of his tight, dry 1981 not being ready for 40 years; of his easygoing, loose-knit '82 being a slow developer. That's Cabernet, not Pinot talk. Yet when he produces a classic in Burgundian terms, something chokes him. His 1983 really does deserve a 20-year wait – it's deep, intense, packed with dark, leathery, smoky aggression, and bitter-sweet cherry and prune juice essence scrubbed with mint and herbs, soused with black chocolate and the decaying sweetness of well-hung game – but isn't that what the top 1983 Burgundies are tasting like right now? Indeed it is. And isn't the 1978 Eyrie absolutely . . . yes, yes. Just like a really top-notch 1978 Burgundy.

The modern generation of young Burgundy makers are producing what may go down as the finest ever red wines produced on the Côte d'Or. Maybe it's time for David Lett to relax his guard a little, and allow himself to be swept up in the perfume and romance and heady excitement that is sweeping through Burgundy. And all of Oregon would follow his lead.

The views are so beautiful from the hillside vineyards in America, one wonders how any grape grower could bear to stay on the valley floor. For the record, this is David Lett's Stone Ledge vineyard in Oregon's Willamette Valley.

Franciscan

AGUSTIN HUNEEUS LOOKS a lot more tired these days than when I first met him. Still handsome, still elegant, still casting a welcome aura of South American passion and charm about him at his headquarters in the Napa Valley, he nevertheless seems worn and drawn, drained by tribulation. The reason? He's trying to make a business out of offering the wine drinker high quality at a low price.

That really shouldn't be so difficult in this area. The Napa Valley floor is extensive, fertile and easy to farm; the region is too far from San Francisco for land to attract any particular price premium for housing, yet close enough to have a thirsty market ready and waiting for its wine. So how come Huneeus is standing in a vineyard at Oakville which is worth $30,000 an acre, inveighing against the $20 bottle of Chardonnay?

I had always thought it was grape shortages that hiked the price of grapes, which then made land more expensive, and these two factors together contrived to produce the $20 bottle. Not so, says Huneeus. Hype creates the $20 bottle. He feels you get poorer value for money in an expensive bottle of wine from California than from anywhere else; he even excuses the gross prices charged by some top Bordeaux and Burgundies, saying they've been at it for 200 years – they've had time to prove they're special. And Napa, he says, hasn't.

If people were prepared to sell good wine for $10 – which, Huneeus fumes, they can profitably do, vineyard prices would halve, so grape prices would halve – and many more people might be persuaded that wine drinking is not an elitist activity, but an affordable, pleasurable part of life. No wonder the man looks tired.

Agustin Huneeus is Chilean, and he ran successful wineries in Chile and Argentina before coming to America in 1974. He's from a culture where wine drinking *is* an everyday, affordable, non-elitist activity – and in his various roles in the US – with Paul Masson, with Concannon, and now as president and co-owner (with the German Eckes group) of Franciscan, he has attempted to provide America with the opportunity to drink *good* wine – not merely cheap, sweet, jug wine – at a fair price.

When he took over the virtually bankrupt Franciscan, Huneeus did have one thing in his favour, something he knew was pure wineman's gold – nearly 200 hectares (500 acres) of prime vineyard land, some in Oakville in the Napa Valley, and the rest in the

Alexander Valley just over the Mayacamas mountains. He could never afford to pursue his 'good wine for a good price' policy if he had to buy that land at today's prices. And if he were reliant upon buying in grapes from contract growers to fuel what is today a 120,000-case operation and is heading higher (he is considering developing a further 260-acre plot of Napa land), he would never have been able to guarantee consistent quality. He had the concept. He had the vineyards. All he needed was a good, gutsy winemaker. And that's what he got with Greg Upton. Greg, another of Napa's floppy-haired, boy-faced wine tyros, joined Franciscan in April 1985 and his first job was to provide moral support to his president in dumping 150,000 gallons of stock. It all went for $3 to $4 a gallon – I wish I'd been around if the 1980 Estancia is anything to go by.

After the clear-out, Huneeus and Upton went back to basics. They had nearly 100 hectares (250 acres) of vineyard in the extremely prestigious Oakville area of the Napa Valley, and a similar acreage in the recently-established, but highly-rated Alexander Valley. Huneeus decided to use an existing Franciscan name – Estancia – for all his Alexander Valley wine and, since costings and reputations were less overblown outside the Napa, he'd sell the wines at around $7 a bottle. Oakville was more prestigious, so the price was a few dollars higher.

At those prices you can't rush out and buy container-loads of small new French barrels costing $350 a go; you get the best out of your existing wood. Lots of large 490-litre (130-gallon) oak puncheons were cleaned out, re-shaved and re-charred – and though they're gradually being replaced, they still give a certain vanilla touch to Estancia. The rest of the Estancia barrels are mostly American Wisconsin oak, not trendy but effective in giving a soft, creamy edge to the gentle, plum and blackcurrant Cabernet fruit.

There is an Estancia red and a white. Originally, both were from Alexander Valley grapes, but the red was always better – Alexander Valley is a wonderful area for producing soft, drinkable Cabernet, yet the Chardonnays are generally a bit lean – so Huneeus became probably the only person in California to rip out valuable Chardonnay vines (he ripped out some at Oakville too) in order to replant with Cabernet. These days the Estancia Chardonnay comes from the old Paul Masson vineyards in Monterey.

Oakville Estate is supposedly the classier style, and certainly there is a more serious air to the wine, but, even though the Cabernet has won various accolades, they are having a struggle getting the wines into gear. Part of the problem lies in the heavy Oakville soil between the highway and the Napa River, which

Old water towers, old vines overshadowed by tall trees at Franciscan show the Napa Valley's more traditional side.

produces fairly tannic wine, needing a lot of time in barrel and bottle to mellow out. At only $10 a bottle, Franciscan can't afford the kind of treatment nearby winery Silver Oak, for instance, gives its wines. Even so, each year shows improvement – more fruit, more evidence of oak, some of it French – and as Huneeus says, as long as he controls the vineyard, he can give Greg Upton a totally free hand in maximizing the potential of the fruit.

This attitude shows most of all in their new prestige Chardonnay – Sauvage. The problem with making your name in the medium-price range is how to persuade people you can make top quality wine too. One way is to buy a prestigious property and Franciscan recently bought the excellent Mount Veeder winery. Another way is to risk all, to dare. Sauvage, as the name implies, does just that. 'Sauvage walks the edge,' says Upton, 'funky wine. I want people to keep returning to the glass and say – did I really taste that?' The philosophy behind it came from a visit in 1986 to one of France's greatest and most impassioned young winemakers – Dominique Lafon of Meursault, whose wines are as memorable as they are original. Greg came back, his

brain whizzing, and kept aside two barrels of 1986 Oakville Chardonnay. The grapes had been pressed straight into barrel – no sulphuring, no cultured yeast additions, no fining. Upton says there are 10 or 11 natural yeasts in the Napa Valley, each with a different speed of fermentation. He thought they'd probably all contribute. The fermentation began slowly, then took off with a roar and finished with a long drawn-out sigh. He liked it like that.

After the malolactic fermentation the wine lay in these brand new French barrels for nearly a year. And everyone loved it. In 1987 he put 20 French oak barrels through this routine, in 1988 and 1989, 160. All the same, Greg doesn't bottle them all as Sauvage. Only 14 barrels were chosen in 1988 and 50 in 1989 because you can't always predict how each barrel will turn out. Some will be merely good and those will go to beef up the Oakville Estate Chardonnay. But the chosen few – well! That 1988 Sauvage is so full and fat, it buttered up my mouth with peaches and orange flower and peel of limes. And the 1989 – that is *wicked* wine. Wonderfully rich, mmm, fresh smoky toast, butter dripping through, peaches in syrup, the orange flower is back and the lime peel too. Funky! My hips begin to wiggle, my shoulders to shake. Get me some hot sweet music, my shades and my suedes, 'cos this juice makes me want to *jive*!

The Hess Collection

*T*HE PHRASE COMES UP time and time again – tame the mountain, tame it, tame it. Tame the power, tame the savagery, and as I scrambled up the 30-degree slopes of Mount Veeder, my ears were alert for the threatening clacker-clack of the rattlesnakes, my eyes were wide open to the imagined menace of coyotes and mountain cats. Nature had unwillingly yielded up this land from the wild.

Do you need a savage terrain to produce savage wine? Not necessarily. But what the difficult mountain vineyards *will* produce is grapes starved of nutrient, thirsty from the lack of water in the sparse soil, and frequently baked by the summer sun. In the cool, damp climes of much of northern Europe, the rare, steep, sun-tilted slope may produce wonderful wine of quintessential balance and elegance. In the hot, arid climate of California you could easily achieve the exact opposite – especially if you plant the burliest of the great red wine grapes, Cabernet Sauvignon; you could end up with brooding monsters of dark tannin and glowering ferocity.

So why have winemakers since the 1860s trekked to the Mayacamas Mountains – of which Mount Veeder is the southernmost peak, near the mouth of the Napa Valley – cleared the forests, and arduously established vineyards which are impossible to mechanize and which rarely give an economically viable crop? Quality. Originality. Brilliant flavours of an intensity the valley floor vineyards simply can't match, that's the reason.

But with the traditional exponents of the mountain Cabernet art – Mayacamas winery, Diamond Creek, Mount Veeder winery – the savagery has not been tamed; indeed these wines seem to exult in the violent, passionate flavours of the mountains. The Hess Collection wines are different. Donald Hess is a highly successful businessman who, among other things, owns

Switzerland's second biggest-selling mineral water brand – Valser – but there is also a streak of romance curling in and out of the impressive balance sheets he's logged up in the last 30 years. In 1957 he sold the wine property near Lake Geneva which had been in the family for generations, regretting it almost before the ink was dry on the deal. So, by the mid-1970s he was in the mineral water business, and 1978 took him to California, intent on buying a mineral water spring. Which he might well have done if he hadn't ordered a bottle of one of Napa Valley's most famous Cabernet Sauvignons for lunch one day in a local restaurant. 1970 Beaulieu Vineyard Georges de Latour Private Reserve is a legendary wine, and Hess's dream of owning his own wine estate again was reborn as the bottle slowly emptied.

It was partly the outdoors romantic in him which took him away from the rather dull valley floor which was responsible for the memorable Beaulieu wine, but it was also because as a European, he'd inherited the idea that the best wines come from hillside sites. And the hillside whose potential attracted him most was Mount Veeder. He bought a total of 365 hectares (900 acres), some of which were already planted with Cabernet Sauvignon vines. He has since planted more vines, aiming to produce some Chardonnay but, more importantly, a mountain Cabernet which bears some of the style of the great 1970 which had inspired him. And for that, he'd have to tame the mountain.

So, along with winemaker Randle Johnson and manager Robert Craig, he set about minutely sub-dividing the upper and lower vineyards. One large site was divided into 92 separate plots, each reflecting the different soil structures, wind patterns and sunlight exposures. Each block of vines is then treated according to its needs, and numerous weather stations are dotted around the vineyards to measure wind, heat and solar radiation, both above and below the leaf canopy. These vineyards yielded grapes reflecting the primal power of the mountains. What they needed was a little modern technology to coax out their finer points too.

Above all, they needed more water. These slopes are free-draining, and lack of water tends to produce a tiny crop of small, thick-skinned berries which will in turn produce brutally tannic wine. So throughout the Hess vineyards there are field moisture stations, in particular to warn against heat stress during the torrid July days. Drip irrigation is used in the most critical areas to keep

The Hess Collection is as famous for its modern art as for its wine, but winemaker Randle Johnson only admits responsibility for the stuff in the bottle.

the vines healthy, ripen the grapes – and attempt to achieve a decent crop. They'd like to get three tons to the acre, but as yet none of their red wine vineyards have got near that figure.

In the winery, the taming process has led to rather over-sophisticated Chardonnays being released so far, but the Cabernets, occasionally mixed in with small amounts of the other Bordeaux varieties, have succeeded brilliantly. The first commercial release was the 1983 (although I have tasted earlier wines which were extremely good). 1983 was a tough, unattractive vintage in most of Napa, yet straightaway the Hess wines were on target – the beautiful sweet blackcurrant of the Cabernet easily holding its own with the tough tannins. The 1984 is remarkably like a full, ripe Bordeaux in style, but it is with the 1985, with the blending of Merlot and Cabernet Franc, and with 1987 and '88, which included for the first time the grapes from the high altitude vineyards, that we see the true extent to which the tobacco and lime peel and mineral intensity of Mount Veeder Cabernet has been fleshed out with the rich, seductive juicy sweetness of blackcurrant cassis and soft, toasty oak. All the power of Mount Veeder's tradition is there, but with far more suppleness of texture and richer, riper fruit.

The Softer Approach

The one crucial difference between Randle Johnson's wine-making technique and those of many of his Napa peers is that he does not pump the juice over the cap of skins during fermentation, since he believes this causes extraction of tough tannins; instead he uses an automatic plunger to punch the skins back into the juice. Neither does Johnson believe in steeping the skins in the wine for weeks after fermentation in an attempt to soften tannins. You soften your tannins in the vineyard by ripening your fruit properly in the first place. He takes the wine straight off the skins, after fermentation and puts it into French oak barrels for a couple of years. He usually makes 20 separate batches of Cabernet, and will generally earmark two or three for release as a Reserve Wine.

But why the Hess *Collection*? Well, Hess didn't want a vineyard and winery solely to make wine. He's got a thrilling, controversial, arresting collection of modern art too. And he wanted to show it off. Bacon, Stella, Baselitz, Franz Gertsch, Arnulf Rainer – he has hundreds of works by these and other top artists, and he's establishing a museum on the side of Mount Veeder to give the public the chance to see them. It's all deliciously unexpected and highbrow. He came to tame the mountain; perhaps he's going to educate it as well.

Laurel Glen

I HAVE A BOOK IN FRONT OF ME improbably titled *Zen and the Art of Archery*. After a hundred or so pages devoted to persuading me that the true art of shooting an arrow accurately towards its distant target is acquired when you reach the state in which the arrow looses itself from the bow, rather than through you mastering any complicated technical manoeuvres, the teacher praises a pupil whose very artlessness is the key to his success by saying, 'You need no technical training; you are already a master'. Can this approach be applied to wine-making? I think perhaps it can.

Patrick Campbell is a Harvard graduate in the philosophy of religion, and he would not now be the owner of Laurel Glen Vineyard, whose well-being is benignly watched over, incidentally, by a stone Buddha in the front garden, had he not come to Sonoma Mountain to join a community of Zen Buddhists back in the early 1970s.

His days then were composed of long hours of meditation in the morning, with evenings spent playing the viola in various local orchestras. His domestic chore for the commune was to oversee the little vineyard they owned. But several things happened. He decided his viola playing was never going to be good enough to

make a real splash in a major orchestra, with or without the Zen peace of mind. In fact he was finding that the long hours of inactivity he spent searching for the Zen truth were making him restless rather than serene. And he was getting rather interested in grapes.

The Sonoma Mountain is a beautiful, wild place, and the few dwellings that dot the slopes don't detract from its mysterious, backwoods aura. As such, it was a perfect place for a Zen commune. But when Campbell and his new wife, Faith, heard that a nearby vineyard called Laurel Glen was up for sale, they didn't realize that the sparse red loam and red gravel soils had attracted winemakers in the past, even before anyone had discovered the Napa Valley over to the east. Buena Vista, California's first winery, was established in Sonoma, and during the 1860s vineyards were planted on the mountain which rapidly achieved a reputation as some of the best in the state. The 5.3 hectares (13 acres) which were for sale in 1977 included land that had been planted with grapes as far back as 1862. The Campbells bought the property and bade goodbye to the commune.

But the philosophies of Zen have stayed with Patrick. He believes passionately in respecting and honouring his land, its life-force and its individuality and his wine-making is very much tailored to allow the fruit of the land to speak. Gentleness, utmost gentleness is his creed, and although he doesn't pamper his vines, he doesn't see that undue stress is going to help them either.

'The vine needs a lot of nutrition – it's a healthy being – you prune 98 per cent of its body away each year, and the remaining two per cent rebuilds into another 100 per cent. You have to meet minimal nutritional requirements. A plant's survival instinct is to perpetuate itself. If you withhold too much nutrient, it will simply cannibalize its own berries.' He then added with a quiet poignancy, 'Some adversity creates character, but beyond a point it will destroy you'. He should know. Since childhood, this energetic, boyish winemaker-philosopher has been completely paralysed in both legs. Yet, jauntily swinging his way on crutches through the winery and the vineyards, he works every stage of the wine-making year himself.

It is easy to feel the calm philosophical strength of the man when you're with him. He won't allow anything to make the slightest difference to his ability to drive a tractor or deal with a tank of wine, any more than he let it stop him earning his living as a professional musician. Above all, his strength is rooted

Fom Buddha to music to wine: Patrick Campbell finds challenge and reward in coaxing wines of personality from his vineyards on Sonoma Mountain.

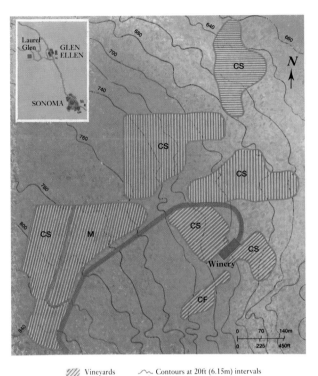

///// Vineyards   ∿ Contours at 20ft (6.15m) intervals

CF   Cabernet Franc   **CS**   Cabernet Sauvignon   **M**   Merlot (and experimental varieties)

in his belief in the special nature of the Laurel Glen land. The original 5-hectare (13-acre) estate contained a hectare or so of vineyard, replanted with Cabernet Sauvignon in 1968, which by 1977 was showing why the vineyards were so prized a hundred years ago. I've tasted a 1977 from this vineyard which was made by the Chateau St Jean winery, and the quality of the fruit is quite remarkable, the intensity of overbearing blackcurrant cassis concentration almost painfully rich in flavour and texture.

Over the next dozen years, Campbell either bought or leased more neighbouring vineyard land, some of which had also been replanted in 1968. The rest was planted in two spurts, between 1977 and 1979 and in 1987 to 1988, so that he now has nine different plots totalling 16 hectares (40 acres), just over half of them his own property.

Almost all of it is planted with Cabernet Sauvignon. The number of times I've tasted the wine and thought – it's so soft, so supple, I wonder how much Merlot he's got? Patrick is used to this by now, but he says there's simply no need for Merlot – the fruit off the estate has always had this delicious, soft, blackcurrant-pastille sweetness to it. 'Merlot is a pain to grow, a miserable grape.' I was as surprised as anyone to see he'd planted a few hectares of it in 1987. But it's Cabernet Sauvignon that made the reputation of Sonoma Mountain, and,

except for an acre or so of Cabernet Franc and a few acres of various experimental oddities, Campbell is absolutely convinced that his future lies with Cabernet Sauvignon. He has planted a variety of different clones on half a dozen different rootstocks, with varied spacings and three different trellising systems. In fact he believes that Sonoma Cabernet Sauvignon is poised to overtake the more famous Napa in quality, and he isn't short of arguments to support his view.

As so often in northern California, discussion turns immediately to the insistent glare of the Pacific sun. How to milk it of its energy while at the same time avoiding its excesses? The most powerful sunlight comes in the afternoon. I have stood in the Laurel Glen vineyards, looking east across the wide Sonoma Valley to the Mayacamas Mountains, and the view is thrilling. Way across the valley, the early evening sun turns those west-facing slopes a wild, raging, reddened gold. I could almost feel the sunburn on the distant parched earth and any grapes facing this daily onslaught of rays could not help but develop thick, tough skins, resulting in harsh, tannic wines. But at Laurel Glen the evening sun is just tinging the vine leaves with a gentle silvery gold, as the cool of a long drawn-out dusk descends on these north-east-facing slopes.

As Campbell has expanded his vineyard holdings he has always looked for the same exposure – north-east – away from the blazing afternoon sun, and angled obliquely away from the midday sun too. It's only the wrong kind of intense heat that Campbell is trying to avoid. Sonoma provides heat in subtle form. The Laurel Glen property is between 190 and 250 metres (620 and 820 feet) above sea level. The vineyard is warmed by morning sun, and this temperature is maintained rather than increased in the afternoon. As the fogs from the Pacific fill the valley floor, chilling even the midsummer nights, the displaced warm air rises up the mountain slopes to keep the evenings and nights temperate too. Consequently the daytime highs are lower than average, while nighttime lows are higher. The soft, juicy character of Sonoma Mountain fruit, if anything a little deficient in acidity and tannin, is a direct result of this 'compressed' moderate temperature during the growing season. The satisfying complexity of that fruit is

Robert Mondavi

I ALWAYS KNOW when the Mondavis are in town. I get to taste Château Lafite-Rothschild, Château Margaux, Château Latour and Domaine de la Romanée-Conti. You know, *the* best French wines, *the* most expensive. Mind you, I get to taste Mondavi wine too. It's just that while most wine producers will invite you to a tasting of their own wines and hope to persuade you how exciting they are without anything else diverting attention from them, the Mondavis like to put their wines on display next to others absolutely guaranteed to make the Francophile British drool.

Ah – but there is one qualification. At a Mondavi tasting all the wines are masked. 'I just want to prove that our wines belong on the same table as France's greatest wines. I'm not trying to compete, to say which is best or worst'.

Robert Mondavi swears that he is not competitive, yet his whole life has been one long competition. And he has emerged the winner from most of his battles. When he does his France versus Mondavi, sorry, France arm-in-arm with Mondavi tastings, he wins these too. The absolute top wine may indeed be a Lafite or a La Tâche, but if two of the top four places aren't taken by Mondavi wines, I'd be very surprised.

Robert Mondavi is a tough man. Now in his late 70s, he came from a tough Italian background, firstly among the open cast iron mines of Minnesota, then in the Californian horticultural heartland of Lodi in the Central Valley, where his father Cesare ran a fresh grape shipping business. To listen to Robert Mondavi joshing with guests in his elegant dining room, sipping splendid wine, dallying with dainty cuisine, surrounded by magnificent works of art and all the trappings of sophisticated life style, you could be seduced into thinking of the man as merely an affable, open-handed patriarch of the Napa Valley, epitomizing all that is admirable and enviable about the modern world of wine and its enjoyment.

But, catch him unawares around the winery, dealing with some problem in the works. Suddenly you can see the fighter. A short man with a long body, his legs slightly bowed but as firmly planted as tree trunks, and his magnificent powerful head, all broadacres forehead and patrician nose. Power. Passion. And a determination to prove himself that is of such intensity that he seems to have worn out his voice doing it – and all he has left is the rasping rush of breath scratching against the raw

nerves of his vocal cords. Mondavi *is* affable, and he *is* generous. But it was passion and sheer determination which got him to a position where he could finally enjoy such indulgences.

There was no time for indulgence when he came home from Stanford University in 1936, with a degree in economics mixed in with chemistry and some spare time oenology lessons. Prohibition had been over for two years and Robert's father had not only taken on a local winery near Lodi, but also a majority share in Sunny St Helena, a Napa Valley winery. He needed help. Whatever academic ambitions he may have harboured, Robert found he had no choice but to knuckle under in the family business.

Discovering Napa

There was a boom in wine after Prohibition, despite the fact that most of the stuff available was pretty frightful because, although grapes were being grown right through Prohibition, most wineries and their equipment had been left to rot. And no new talent had come into the business for a generation. But in 1936 Robert Mondavi became a winemaker. It was the beginning of a pioneering trail to make the Napa Valley the focal point for California's quality wines and, as Mondavi would have you agree, by inference a focal point for the world.

The Mondavis increased the sales at their first Napa winery by 600 per cent between 1936 and 1943 – but virtually the entire output of valley grapes was still used for cheap bulk wines. Yet Robert could taste the difference in quality between Napa grapes and Central Valley grapes, and with a foot in both camps, he also knew the difference in production costs. If Napa didn't try to upgrade its image, large quantities of cheap Central Valley grapes would swamp the market as soon as there was a glut of wine.

The chance came when the well-respected but near-derelict Charles Krug winery came on the market in 1943. The family bought the business, along with a hundred acres of vineyard. Robert ripped out the tired old vines and at last got the chance to put his quality-first philosophy into action – he planted Cabernet Sauvignon, Pinot Noir, Chardonnay and Riesling among other varieties – just so long as they had proven in Europe they could make classic wines.

He taught himself about methods of cold-fermenting white wines to retain fruitiness, he pioneered the use of sterile conditions to combat oxidation and began to experiment with ageing wine in oak barrels. He took on the internationally-regarded winemaker André Tchelistcheff as his consultant. Robert was aiming as high as he knew how. Except that neither the market

Bob Mondavi doesn't make the wine and shift the barrels these days, but his efforts are largely responsible for the Napa Valley's current success.

nor the rest of the Mondavi family were that interested in his obsession with making world class wines in Napa. The Charles Krug winery was chugging along profitably enough, selling a mix of cheap jug wine and some of Robert's new varietals, and outside California itself, the rest of America still refused to accept that Californian wine could be better than mere quaffing stuff. New York was as close to Europe as to California. French wines were dirt cheap. Why Californian? Why indeed.

I think 1962 was the year that did it. Robert was approaching 50. And he made his first trip to the vineyards of Europe. The importance of vineyard sites, of mature vines, of controlled yields, and of good oak for ageing the wine all hit home, as well as the blunt evidence that the flavours of the wines he was producing at Charles Krug were still a million miles

away from displaying the perfume and elegance of the French originals. Robert Mondavi came back to Napa with a crystal-clear idea for the first time of what he wanted to achieve – and a realization that he'd never do it at Charles Krug: he'd have to go out on his own.

Italian family break-ups are passionate affairs, and the Mondavi crisis was no exception. In 1965 when Robert was told by his mother Rosa that there was no place at Krug for his son Michael and that he'd better take six months leave of absence himself to cool his temper, Robert Mondavi, 52 years old, finally broke away from the family business.

Let's not underestimate his courage. He had to borrow the first $100,000 and for the next ten years trod the financial high wire as he strove to expand on the one hand, and to keep family control on the other. At one time he owned as little as 18 per cent of his own company as he gambled on the growth of volume and reputation. Today the initial sales of 20,000 cases have grown to two and a half million. And although the company is once more in family hands, the treadmill is still turning. You don't grow that fast just by making better wine. You have to know how to sell it too.

The difference between the Charles Krug wines of the early 1960s and Mondavi's very first Cabernet Sauvignon in 1966 is dramatic – a sea-change from a rich, overripe Californian style to something more restrained, already yearning to be French. But Mondavi's greatest skill has been to sniff the wind of change, and then concentrate fanatically on a small but complementary range of wines.

His trip to France in 1962 convinced him that the Bordeaux Cabernet style *was* attainable in Napa, with grapes grown under the right conditions and vinified correctly. He was convinced that Rutherford and Oakville provided the right sites. His new understanding of Bordeaux fermentation methods and the use of new French oak barrels to age the wine made him sure he could do it. The brilliant 1961 vintage in Bordeaux had once again made the Médoc a key talking point after a long depressed period. By emphasizing a Bordeaux pedigree he'd be able to sell his wine too.

That 1966 Mondavi Cabernet Sauvignon was a remarkably successful wine, tasting like a ripe but distinctly Bordeaux-based red when I first tried it in the 1970s, achieving balance without sacrificing fruit. It immediately set a new standard for California Cabernet,

Mondavi's mission-inspired winery was a revolutionary design when built in 1966 and is still impressive for its blend of tradition and innovation.

and despite the fact that the Mondavi winery now produces 100,000 cases of Napa Valley Cabernet Sauvignon every year, it is *still* regarded as the benchmark style.

That's when those comparative tastings started. The crucial East Coast American market still wouldn't touch expensive Californian wine. So Mondavi would book into a city's smarter restaurants, order a bottle of top Bordeaux, then pull out a bottle of his own wine and invite the owner to taste. He got a lot of listings, frequently making Mondavi Cabernet Sauvignon the only quality wine from California on sale.

Mondavi's astuteness really showed in his white wine policy. There was a glut of Sauvignon Blanc around in the late 1960s, since people seemed to have a rooted aversion to the name. But they liked to drink a French Sauvignon wine from the Loire, called Pouilly Blanc Fumé. So, buy up some Sauvignon grapes, ferment them, cut the 'Pouilly' off the label and call the wine Fumé Blanc. Bob at his best – is it French or is it Californian? Many California Sauvignons are still labelled Fumé Blanc 20 years on. Mondavi's certainly is.

Success with Chardonnay and Pinot Noir has been more erratic, perhaps because California itself has not been able to settle into a natural Chardonnay style. Many of Mondavi's commercial releases of Chardonnay have been uninspired, and some even taste faulty, but when they get it right, as in their 1987 and '88 Reserve Chardonnays, the result is magnificent.

Pinot Noir, on the other hand, has reacted better to the painstaking investigation of its possibilities, perhaps

because there is less commercial pressure to produce large quantities of Pinot Noir, whereas there's a never-ending demand for Chardonnay. The other reason is that Robert, and particularly his son Tim, who now controls all the wine-making, are passionately, obsessively in love with the grape variety. Cabernet, Fumé Blanc and Chardonnay make the profits, Pinot Noir satisfies their deepest emotions.

Pinot Noir may well turn out to be their greatest achievement. I've seen their experimental programmes for Pinot Noir running right back to the 1970s and the different techniques employed seemed to veer between Châteauneuf-du-Pape, Château Latour and Rioja. The principles of Burgundy eluded them – until Tim fell under the spell of Henri Jayer. They may use Romanée-Conti in their 'we don't mind who's best, just tell us if we deserve to be on the same table – and psst – we're a quarter of the price' – gasp – tastings, but that's because they are the most famous and the most expensive. But the most glorious, joy-filled examples of Pinot Noir grown in the top vineyard sites of Vosne-Romanée and Nuits-St-Georges are those of Henri Jayer.

'Ten years ago it was inconceivable I'd say this, but I now say that nowhere in the world except parts of Burgundy can make such good Pinot Noir as California.' That's Tim talking, but what a chip off the old block, graciously allowing Burgundy on to the same table as California!

Passionate about Pinot

And I agree with him. When the Californians get Pinot Noir right, it is a thrilling wine, packed with the fruit of damsons and cherries and fat ripe plums, streaked with leather and smoke, and as it ages, smothered with chocolate and liquorice. And Tim Mondavi, exuding the breathless, word-tumbling passion of his father only when Pinot Noir is his subject, is only too happy to take up the challenge.

He looks for low yields from small-berried clones, preferably off dry farmed acres, except in sandy Santa Maria where you need to irrigate. Care in the vineyard, protection in the cellar; 'you can wipe out the gentleness of Pinot in a moment by traditional production-led methods'. He has abandoned stem retention because Jayer says that although stems give spice, they also dry the wine out as it ages. Instead he follows Jayer's principle of extending the alcoholic fermentation to about seven days, followed by long skin contact to maximize fruit and perfume – up to 28 days in all, punching the cap of skins down with the gentlest of juice pumpovers, just sufficient to wet the surface layer. 'Structure is easy to get in a wine. Subtleness, perfume,

richness, they're the difficult things.' He hasn't filtered the Reserve Pinot Noir since 1985, and when I wondered whether its success had influenced the decision not to filter the '87 *Cabernet* Reserve, he said 'sure; we learn through the Pinot Noir then apply it to Cabernet'. Thinking of the delicious flavours of that 1987 at only three years old, I began to ask whether ageability isn't a prerequisite for greatness in a wine. Tim wasn't having that. 'Greatness has to do with what it tastes like. Sweetness, fragrance, richness are all continually traded off in the quest for a wine's ageability. I won't pickle my wine just to ensure its ageability.'

So far, Pinot Noir is an indulgence for father and son, which has to be paid for by the other, more popular wines. There's no shortage of these. As the last wine boom in America began taking off, Robert Mondavi calculated that there was a gap in the market between the 'half gallon jug' wines he had once produced at Lodi, and the smart 'varietal' wines he now produced at Oakville. So he went back to his roots in Lodi, and created a second Mondavi label at the Woodbridge winery, in 1979. Mondavi calculated that the echoes of his good Napa name would draw new drinkers to these wines without affecting his quality image. He was absolutely right. By 1990 two million cases of Woodbridge wine had left the cellars, and his Napa Valley reputation didn't even falter.

But Mondavi's greatest marketing coup was to persuade Baron Philippe de Rothschild of Bordeaux's great Château Mouton-Rothschild to enter into a joint venture, on Californian soil, and create with Mondavi a Cabernet Sauvignon wine whose label bears both their signatures and both their faces. Mondavi and Rothschild on the same label; now surely *that's* proof that his wines deserve to be on the same table as the French greats. Opus One is the name of the wine, and the 1979 vintage was released with much brouhaha for $50 a bottle. It sold like hot cakes. At the Napa Valley charity auction in 1981, the first ever case to be offered was bought for $24,000 – $2000 a bottle – by far the highest price ever paid for a bottle of American wine because the bidder knew he was buying history, not wine.

Mondavi marketing genius again. The wine *is* good, though not as yet great – but that's not the point. Mondavi had once again projected his own name and that of his company like a starburst across the world. His own company benefited, but so did the Napa Valley in general. It took the Médoc hundreds of years to reach its present pre-eminence, it took Burgundy a thousand. Bob didn't even have a lifetime to spare. The modern Napa Valley is the fulfilment of his vision. And all that from a standing start at 52 years of age.

CALIFORNIA

Napa Valley

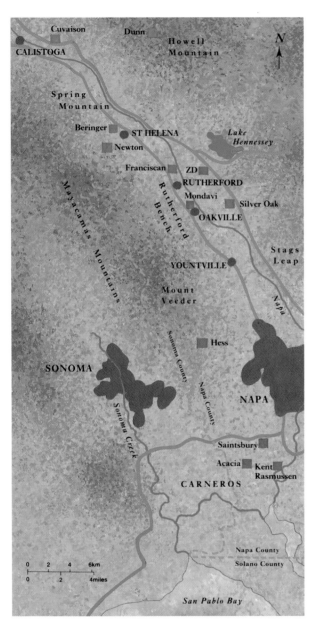

ASK A WINEMAKER ANYWHERE in the world what makes his particular vineyard stand out from others and he will almost certainly start straight in with a lecture about his soil. Except in California's Napa Valley. If a Napa winemaker launches into the question of soil, he isn't telling you the half of it, because much of Napa's soil would be better suited to grazing cattle and growing plums. Now if he started telling you about

fog, or about chill ocean breezes or how you'll need to take a sweater if you're going to be out in the vineyards at sundown – then you'll be getting closer to the truth.

My first visit to San Francisco was in late summer. I flung open my hotel window in the morning, ready to drink in the reviving warmth of the sunlight. Ugh. Damp, clinging fog swirled menacingly around the building. Summer? This was London in November, more like. The following morning I got into a car and drove north towards the vineyards of Napa and Sonoma, brimming with excitement as I headed for my first view of the majestic Golden Gate Bridge. With my headlights on, I crawled through the mist and the howling wind. I stopped on the far side of the road, and stood on the lookout – frozen to the bone as fog banks hurtled through the Golden Gate gap, propelled by bitter winds, and above me, out towards the ocean, white blankets of mist tumbled over the hilltops and on to the damp tarmac of Route 101.

But then I drove on. Past Sausalito, Corte Madera and Novato, the clouds lifted, the brilliant blue of the sky contrasting with the dry, parched grass and the dusty green of the tall waving eucalyptus trees. And as I headed towards Napa, around the northern shore of San Pablo Bay, I could see the blanket of fluffy cloud still creeping across the waters of the bay, its tentacles reaching up the river valley, shreds still clinging to the rumpled hummocks of Carneros. I had been bang in the middle of the phenomenon which allows the Napa Valley its claim to be one of the world's greatest vineyard areas.

California should be too hot to grow great wine grapes. And if you go, say, 100 miles inland, it *is* too hot. Yet the Pacific Ocean is particularly cold along the coastline of Northern California. Put a solid mountain range between Napa and the coast and they'd hardly affect each other. But place a gap in the mountains a mile wide at Golden Gate, leading into the enormous sump of San Francisco Bay and San Pablo Bay, fed by streams and rivers from north, east and south, and the effect is dramatic. As the hot inland air rises each morning, the cold sea air and fog is sucked inland, blanketing areas like Carneros next to the bay for much of the morning, and dramatically cooling the Napa river valley which opens into the bay just to the east of Carneros.

The Napa Valley is about 50km (30 miles) long, running approximately north to south from Calistoga to the city of Napa, after which the land to the west flattens out into Carneros and the bay. 'Napa' is the original Indian word for 'plenty' and in fact it *is* an extremely fertile valley, with rich alluvial soils able to support healthy crops of almost any fruit or vegetable.

Farmers first settled here during the 1830s, and in the next 50 years as many as 400 different grape varieties were planted, both in the heavy clay soils of the valley floor and in the better-drained sites lying at the base of the mountains.

A trend began to emerge that is even more in evidence today – the planting of Cabernet Sauvignon as the chief quality variety, and the development of Napa Valley, and in particular the central sections around Rutherford and Oakville, as the 'Bordeaux of California'. However, the title drastically understates the versatility of the Napa Valley – far greater than that of Bordeaux, and all because of those fogs.

Not All California Cabernet

For a start, Cabernet Sauvignon, and its stable mates Cabernet Franc and Merlot, are not the majority grapes in the valley. In the south, between Yountville and the city of Napa, where the fogs and breezes create substantially lower average temperatures, red Bordeaux grapes are outnumbered by white wine varieties such as Sauvignon Blanc, Chardonnay, Chenin Blanc and Gewürztraminer, and reds like Pinot Noir. In the north of the valley, between St Helena and Calistoga, where the climate is largely unaffected by the cooling Pacific influence, Cabernet shares its turf with hot-country varieties like Zinfandel. Within a space of 50km (30 miles), climate conditions can range from similar to Bordeaux in a decidedly cool vintage to more like the Rhône in an absolute scorcher – at exactly the same hour on the clock. Only around Rutherford and Oakville, in the centre of the Valley, and at Stag's Leap on the eastern rim, do you feel that Cabernet is king.

The soil isn't the same as in Bordeaux – even the famous Rutherford Bench has fairly heavy although well-drained soil, and the clay loam down towards the river sticks like thick black porridge to your shoes. Bordeaux's best Cabernet is planted on light gravel soils, although the clay soils of Pomerol, where Merlot is the chief grape, can wreck a decent pair of sneakers pretty sharpish. Even so, until recently virtually all the most famous California Cabernets came from these few square miles. They rarely tasted like Bordeaux, however, usually developing mature flavours more based on deep, ripe, plummish fruit, sometimes flecked with eucalyptus, sometimes coated in the locally revered 'Rutherford Dust'. Any wines tasting like Bordeaux tended to come from the few mountain vineyards hugging the slopes above the valley floor.

But the early winemakers not only planted Cabernet extensively during the second half of the nineteenth century, they thought of themselves as producing a Bordeaux-like wine too. Several early winemakers *were* French, and wineries would sport names like 'Nouveau Medoc', or 'Chateau Chevalier'; there were famous wines with titles like 'Miravalle Margaux', and the Inglenook winery proudly called its top Cabernet 'California Claret Medoc-type'.

Prohibition dealt a severe blow to the California wine industry, and it was left to a handful of wineries to keep the flag flying. With the end of Prohibition, however, there was no sudden revival of a wine culture, and until the late 1960s almost the only American wineries which still conscientiously pursued a quality-first approach were a small band in the Napa Valley, led by Beaulieu, Inglenook, Charles Krug and Louis Martini.

When American interest in wine *did* revive as the 1970s progressed, only the Napa Valley was immediately ready to take full advantage, with mature vineyards (even if many of the grape varieties were pretty strange) and a hold, albeit tenuous, on a wine-making tradition which a century before had created America's first great wines. During the 1970s, especially during tasting competitions against the top French red Bordeaux and white Burgundies, the rich, ripe flavours of Napa revolutionized the way people looked at wine.

Napa is no longer undisputed quality leader in America. Many wines from Sonoma County, just over the Mayacamas mountains to the west, display softer fruit and more elegant style. The cool valleys of Monterey and Santa Barbara Counties, south of San Francisco, are gaining a reputation for the exciting depth and freshness of their Pinot Noirs and Chardonnays. And Carneros, much of which is technically in the Napa Valley, has developed its own individual identity.

Inside Napa County there are now 20 different vineyard subdivisions already recognized or petitioning for recognition as separate, delimited wine areas and considerable pressure is being exerted to force these would-be autonomous subregions to include 'Napa Valley' on their labels. Why? Because despite the rise of other areas, the faddishness of other names, Napa *is* where the great traditions of American wine-making began, Napa is the one area which held to its principles through good times and bad, and Napa is the area which has provided the investment, the know-how, and finally the prestige from which the other Californian wine areas now benefit. After all that hard work, it wants to make sure it reaps at least some of the rewards.

(Overleaf) This beautiful picture of a Napa Valley farmer burning his vine prunings in the spring makes me want to be there right now, this very minute.

Newton

AS THE FOLDS of the mountains dissolve into the warm gold of the setting sun, Su Hua Newton gazes out to the west and muses – 'this reminds me of where I come from.' Just for a moment, this restless, questing woman whose whole life seems to be designed to test the theory of eternal motion, is still. Her usually animated face is quiet, sombre, solemn.

Su Hua Newton was born in the untamed wooded wilderness of northern China on the border with Siberia. A harsh, unforgiving land, which she fled as a child, trekking through the very fringes of civilization for more than a year before making her escape. And she began an odyssey criss-crossing the globe which has at last led to the steep tumbling slopes of Spring Mountain, high over the Napa Valley, where she has created a child-pure paradise full of past memories and future dreams.

Newton vineyard is quite unlike any other I have ever seen, and the Newtons are also a brilliantly unlikely pair to have created such a venture. But this is the second time they've done it. Peter Newton, an urbane, elegant English businessman with the silver thread of whimsy running refreshingly through his character, founded Sterling Vineyards in 1964. Sterling, along with the foundation of Robert Mondavi's winery in 1966, signalled the rebirth of the Napa Valley as a modern fine wine region. Newton introduced Merlot as a single varietal to California, and with Mondavi pioneered the use of Sauvignon Blanc for dry white wine. By 1977 Sterling was one of the valley's major wineries and he couldn't resist the opportunity to sell to Coca-Cola for, presumably, a pretty decent sum.

And it seems he couldn't resist the challenge of staying in the wine business, but by now his own views of what he wanted had changed. He wanted something which was more of a personal statement, something to provide more of a spiritual home. If he wanted impassioned support for those ideals, he was married to the right woman. Sterling was very much Peter's creation, but Newton Vineyards, though they run it together, is very much the brainchild of Su Hua, ex-Chanel model, ballet dancer, journalist, broadcaster, teacher, scientist – you name it, she's done it.

You have to be courageous and you have to have a remarkable imagination to scramble up the sheer slopes of Spring Mountain above St Helena, Napa's main wine town and visualize both a working winery and a world class vineyard. You're looking at pines and redwood trees undisturbed for generations, growing thick and tangled on the giddy mountain sides. You're talking of foaming spring water leaping and seething through the narrow gorges in the rock. You're envisaging the taming of a wild highland that rides the crests of ridges like a surfer's wave, then swoops into gullies, and nestles hidden in glades, only to clamber through slopes thick with timber back on to the giants' ribs of volcanic soil that sweep like avalanche trails down to the valley floor. But when you experience a deep yearning for a part of you lost in a distant land – a distant land just like this – it must do wonders for your resolve.

Nothing But the Best

Su Hua Newton's resolve is simple. She wants to make California's best Cabernet Sauvignon and Merlot from the grapes she grows on these vineyard slopes. And she wants to make California's best Chardonnays, although not from her own mountain grapes, because one of the few places Chardonnay vines can't thrive in California is in these hills – they become infected with Pierce's disease. So she intends to *grow* the best red wine grapes, and *craft* the best white from closely monitored bought-in grapes. *And*, she intends to sell them. As well as running the vineyard and the winery, she is professor in charge of the Wine Marketing Centre at the University of San Francisco. The people running some of America's most successful young wineries, like Glen Ellen, learned the hard business rules of making a winery pay at her classes. She doesn't intend to be outshone by any of her students.

I have to admit she certainly leads from the front. I wanted to see the much vaunted difference between the various soils on the Newton property. There are at least seven different volcanic rock soils, all free-draining, on slopes angled north, south, east and west to get the maximum variation in exposure to the sun. She's planted Cabernet Sauvignon, Cabernet Franc and Petit Verdot on these. There are also thick slabs of heavy Pomerol-like clay. That's where she's put her Merlot. The vines have to be terraced across the gradient, usually at differences in elevation of about 4.5 metres (15 feet) – because of the steepness of the land – so I said, let's go and see.

Well, you live and learn. After stumbling and sliding down a sheer chute of heavy wodgy clay threaded with terraces of Merlot vines, and gingerly crossing a swollen stream that looked to me as though the torrent shot straight out of the mountainside, she said 'next, Cabernet Franc'. I looked up at this, this . . . wall of shale and crumbly volcanic gravel, as steep as anything

*Perched high upon Spring Mountain, a Chinese pagoda
shares the landscape with a formal English parterre garden.
The remarkable, totally original, Newton vineyard.*

I've ever seen a vine clinging to, and a great deal steeper
than anything I've climbed in pursuit of one. 'Up we
go,' she said. *I* got rescued by a bloodhound halfway up,
which pulled me to the top. She expects people to work
on this? Excellent drainage, said Su Hua, excellent
ripening aspect to the sun. Where's the brandy, I
gasped, grappling with the hound. No brandy, bad for
the health. Let's go and see the Petit Verdot. Does she
ever pause for breath?

These volcanic soils are deep, they are free-draining,
and in general they are shielded from the direct
sunlight. Being on the eastern slopes of Spring
Mountain, the peak itself shields most of the vineyards
from the hottest of the afternoon sun, while this aspect
and the elevation of up to 488 metres (1600 feet) above
the valley floor brings not only lower average
temperatures, but also long exposure to the cooler but
equally bright rays of morning sun. The vines get all the
sunlight they need to ripen, but none of the baking
effect or heat stress that can affect valley floor fruit.

The result is a small, generally late harvest of slowly-
ripened fruit that produces wine bearing an uncanny
resemblance to the flavours of St-Julien or the Graves
in Bordeaux. In particular the Newton Petit Verdot has

a brilliantly sweet fragrance of wild raspberry,
blackberry and sloes, pepper too, the restrained intensity
of soft leather, all made unforgettably original by the
haunting scent of violets. Only tasting at great Bordeaux
châteaux like Léoville-Lascases and Pichon-Lalande
have I tasted Petit Verdot as such an exciting
component for a Bordeaux blend. 'You have to be
prepared to take an emotional bath with Petit Verdot
one year in two. Too often it just doesn't give a crop.'

But that doesn't frighten Su Hua; the effect of the
Petit Verdot on the final wine is so remarkable she's
actually expanding Petit Verdot plantings rather than
playing safe with the reliability of Cabernet Sauvignon
and Merlot. The Bordeaux producers mostly go for the
easy option and miss out on Petit Verdot altogether.
They don't have so much to prove as Su Hua Newton,
and anyway, playing safe isn't part of her vocabulary.

Since she attaches such spiritual importance to this
mountain eyrie of hers, it must have seemed almost
sacrilegious to build on a site of such unspoilt loveliness.
Certainly to clutter the place with the necessary but
charmless winery paraphernalia of storage tanks, crusher
and presses, fermentation vats, was unthinkable. So she
decided they would burrow into the mountainside. The
cellars to age the wine run in long galleries reminiscent
of the *caves* in Champagne. Very cool, very steady in
temperature and humidity. Very unobtrusive. The
cellars for fermenting the grapes were hollowed out of

the hillside – but then covered up again, not with the concrete or steel that might wreck the nobility of the landscape but with gardens. A studiedly formal parterre garden, with miniature roses, herbs and low bushes creating the geometrical divisions between its lawns provides an air of stately calm next to the line of Tuscan cypresses pointing a long finger down towards the heat-hazed valley. All the wine-making takes place under this manicured turf.

The office buildings are low, and of latticed cedar wood which is rapidly weathering to the same warm hue as the earth around. At the head of the lawn is a pagoda, again of latticed cedar, that looks like a charming Chinese folly, half way to a gazebo. And you look about, and just wonder, isn't there something missing? The crusher? The reception area? Well, that's it – that unobtrusive pagoda houses the wine-making equipment. Oh, and she designed it all herself.

Balance in All Things

The environment in which she lives and works is of paramount importance to Su Hua and reflects at every turn the tranquillity and delicacy of her Chinese heritage. Maybe she needs it to counterbalance the furious intensity with which she applies herself to the task in hand. She involves herself in every aspect of the vineyard management, and maturing of the wine, as well as the label design and marketing programmes, because she believes that it is only the vineyard owner, whose money is at stake, who can finally take the decisions which enable great wine to be made.

If, as in 1989, the whole Napa harvest is being spoiled by early rain, yet she feels that, on her high, free-draining soils, there is a chance of something superb if she waits for the grapes to dry out, as an owner she can call that shot, even if it risks a million dollars. I've tasted her 1989s. I haven't tasted better anywhere in the valley.

If the experiments with malolactic fermentation, barrel fermentation and the subsequent possibility of releasing an unfiltered Chardonnay of brilliant depth and complexity on to a market used to much safer, more uniform flavours, are causing enormous differences of opinion among the winery staff – only she can say – go for it. It's her winery's reputation that will be made or broken. And if the distributors are clamouring for more Chardonnay, more Merlot, more Cabernet Sauvignon, yet she is not convinced that enough of the crop is up to standard despite the market demand, only she can say – junk those vats, blend these, we'll be thousands of cases short, we'll be half a million dollars adrift in income, but we'll be one step nearer the acceptance of Newton

wines at the top of the quality league. In the early years of Newton she buried an entire vintage of Cabernet Sauvignon in a lake because it wasn't good enough. It's still there, and she has no intention of hauling it out.

She hasn't done badly since then. Christian Moueix of Château Pétrus has called her Merlot the best in California, and the 1982, 1984 and 1985 have regularly triumphed in competition in Europe against top Bordeaux from 1982 and 1985. Her Cabernet Sauvignon is even better, and I've even once put Newton Chardonnay into the *grand cru* Burgundy class during blind tastings. An earlier conviction that the answers to quality could always be found by scrupulous attention to the scientific minutiae, allied to whatever expenditure was necessary in terms of equipment and new oak, is giving way to a broader, but even more passionate belief. Rather than simply accepting the orthodoxy of

the wine-making school at Davis, she is now likely to be found delving and listening in the best cellars of Bordeaux and Burgundy. She talks to Christian Moueix and Michel Rolland in Pomerol about Merlot, Paul Pontallier at Margaux and Jean-Jacques Godin at Pichon-Lalande about Petit Verdot and Cabernet Sauvignon, to Robert Drouhin and Dominique Lafon about Chardonnay.

She is still driven by a dogged academic determination to understand every process down to its last fraction, but there comes a time when the sharpest brain mists over in the sheer ecstasy of revelation, when a realization about the life forces of passion and commitment brush aside mere learning, and that's what she has come face to face with in the unprepossessing cellars at Château Pétrus, in the chill and clammy deep recesses of Lafon's cellars in Meursault, and in the

These hills were all forest before the Newtons cleared them and planted them with the red Bordeaux varieties, creating some of California's most spectacular vineyards.

cottages of the artisan barrel makers in the hills behind Burgundy, where you realize how rustic and unsophisticated is the well from which great wine springs, far away from chandeliers, and jewelled gowns and brilliant chat.

And I think she *will* achieve her aims. Just so long as she's learned enough of the deeper truths about what contributes to great wine from her friends in Bordeaux and Burgundy as they pass through the limitations of logical thought and on to something far more deeply felt, less perfectly understood. Then maybe she'll slow down, relax her iron grip and remind herself of what drew her to this mountain hideaway in the first place.

Kent Rasmussen

*E*VERYONE SAID I'D HAVE DIFFICULTY finding him. So I rang first. And this great big cheery voice chortled down the line that it was as simple as falling off a log. Straight down Cuttings Wharf Road to the big bend – and I'd see the winery staring me in the face.

So I drove down Cuttings Wharf Road, slicing through sweeps of vineyard on both sides, slowed as I ducked under a group of majestic eucalyptus trees dripping their aromatic goo on to the side of the road. I saw the odd house, a chicken hutch or two, then a pale green bungalow on the right and I was at the big bend. No winery. I drove on around the corner, and came to an abrupt halt on a dingy waterfront, to see a suspension bridge towering over the sludgy inlet half a mile ahead and a clutch of bikers looking mildly threatening by the rundown bar.

But there wasn't a winery. I know what a winery looks like – stainless steel tanks, piles of barrels, notices soliciting custom at the gate. At the bend in the road there was nothing but the pale green bungalow . . . That couldn't be it – could it?

It could. This tiny suburban bungalow in need of a new coat of paint actually *hid* the winery, it was so small. The winery itself was an open-sided lean-to, a kind of outhouse where you might expect to see someone pottering about doing DIY plus a faded red shed with a sloping roof just about big enough for a couple of cars.

And standing in the driveway was this figure, grinning hugely. Portly to be sure, with a smock rolling down his contented front, a bushy dark beard, laughing eyes behind black-rimmed specs – and a straw hat. He looked like everybody's dream vision of the typical French Impressionist painter, just setting off with his easel to find some waterlilies or cornfields to paint. He did *not* bear the slightest resemblance to my image of the man I believe to be one of the brightest wine-making stars in whizzkid California.

But that's the magic of Kent Rasmussen. He doesn't want to be high profile. He *does* actually have quite a smart notice at the roadside, but he's turned it away from the oncoming traffic, because he doesn't want a driveway filled with cars and caravans. And he doesn't want approval from critics. 'I do anything I can to avoid tasting panels getting hold of my wines,' he says, even though high marks can turn a winemaker into a star, and would allow him to double his prices and jack up

his production. But that is precisely what Kent Rasmussen does *not* intend to do. 'We're not in a growth mode. We're where we want to be and we're going to stay there.'

By that Kent means that he makes about 3000 cases of wine each year – 1800 cases of Chardonnay, usually a Carneros/Napa blend, 1000 cases of Carneros Pinot Noir and, well, a few hundred cases of just about anything you can think of. There's a bit of Cabernet, a smattering of Sauvignon Blanc, some Syrah, some Dolcetto of all things, and then a couple of hundred cases comprising 16 different types of grape! He thought he could find me some Cabernet Franc, and then there was some Zinfandel he didn't like much. 'My downfall in this world is Zin. Everyone says it's the easiest wine in the world to make and I can't make it.' And if I come back in a few weeks, he says I can taste some barrel-aged Alicante Bouschet! I've never heard of *anyone* making an Alicante Bouschet by itself, but Kent says with a self-deprecating grin and a great choice of phrase, 'Sure, it's not our bailiwick, but I just find it hard to resist things, so . . .'

Basically, the whole thing is run by Kent and his wife Celia although they hire the occasional hourly worker on and off. He makes a good living because anyone who's tasted his wines can see the quality shining through, and he has virtually no expensive equipment to finance. 'So we can live a very nice life – and only really work six months of the year. From January to March there's really nothing to do, so this year we thought we'd better have a baby.' So they did. 'I'm in this for life style, not just the wine-making, and not just the money.'

Setting the Volume Control

And he proves that by telling me that actually he made 5000 cases of wine in 1989, 'but I don't want to bump up my volume, so I'm going to get rid of a lot of it. If I made more my income would go up a little bit, but my life style would go down a hell of a lot. If I had to finish off those 5000 cases and get them all into bottle, I'd be working here flat out every day until crush. If I stick to 3000, we can take two or three months off and go to Mexico.'

If his desire for a low profile is understandable, his total lack of whizzkiddery is deceptive. He used to make wine at the Robert Mondavi winery and as he himself says, he's well-trained, 'and if I need to do something, I know what to do, but I generally find if you wait a while the problem will go away'. This is a view diametrically opposed to the terror of faults which can haunt Californian wine-making, and is much more akin to the shoulder-shrugging attitude prevalent in Burgundy. With a less talented winemaker, this approach wouldn't work, but then Kent Rasmussen knows exactly what he's doing. He began to yearn for more freedom while at Mondavi, and in 1986 felt it was time to go. His father sold good grapes from his 5-hectare (12-acre) site in the Carneros region which Mondavi used in the Reserve Pinot Noir. That pale green bungalow is where his parents still live, and Kent rents the lean-to, the garage and the workshop from his father. He buys the paternal Pinot Noir grapes, too, but his father drives a hard bargain. 'I always have to pay what Mondavi pays, which is always obscenely high.' Since Kent had hardly any money in 1986, it was a case of getting a few cheap fibreglass tanks and whatever barrels he could afford, squeezing them into the space and getting going.

Lovely, I thought, nothing I'd like better than a pleasant rustic barrel-tasting *à la* Burgundy. But Kent

Kent Rasmussen looks happy. He's just put all his Pinot Noir and Chardonnay to barrel – next stop Mexico!

didn't seem so keen when I suggested it. 'We're not really big on barrel-tasting around here.' But I persisted, so he said, 'Come on, I'll show you'. And out we trooped, past the lean-to and over to the garage with the sloping roof. He pulled back the door, and I gazed in wonder at the most haphazard jumble of barrels I'd ever seen in my life. And I laughed out loud. So did he. In fact we roared. It's completely impossible to get to any of the barrels, let alone roll them until they're bung upwards so you can get a pipette in to do some tasting. 'I really would like you to taste the 1989 Pinot Noir,' he said, 'it's a lovely wine – but it'll take us several hours to get to the barrel! We've got Chardonnay from 15 different vineyards in there, and it's about a day and a half's work to find all the right barrels and lug them out for tasting!' We just stood in the rain and roared!

So we go back to the workshop to dry out and taste whatever he *can* reach. We start with his Chardonnay. This is a hell of a wine. It's totally unlike any other Chardonnay I know in California. It's got weight, and an almost syrupy viscosity, yet is totally devoid of any of the sweet tropical fruit flavours other Californian

wines of similar weight tend to exhibit. This very dry but immensely full style is more like a *grand cru* Corton from Burgundy than a California wine.

If I was hoping for some dazzling insight into new wine-making techniques used to produce this style, I was going to be disappointed. Or was I? There was more to this guileless simplicity in method than met the eye. 'We make the wine in an incredibly basic style. We're using eighteenth-century technology around here and I think it's a good thing. I pick the grapes and stand on the top of the forklift dumping them into my little crusher by hand. Then it all goes into a basket press – gets oxidized to hell – then I pump it into a cold room – gets oxidized to hell some more – it's basic crude wine-making, no fancy anything.'

This oxidation is interesting, because many wineries do everything they can to stop juice oxidizing, and the general disinfectant sulphur dioxide is often added to the grapes as they come to the crusher. Kent Rasmussen totally disagrees with this. 'The concept of sulphur dioxide on the crusher is ludicrous. The second the yeast hits it it's all going to get bound up and the only thing you're going to get is a bunch of bound SO_2 in your wine which isn't going to help anything.' Bound sulphur dioxide produces a stale papery or dull nutty taste in a wine and can completely mask a wine's personality. But it does give you clean, clear juice.

That's the last thing Kent is after. 'Virtually every drop of juice that went into that Chardonnay would have looked like Coca-Cola when it went into the barrel, virtually black. People are appalled by it. It has seven to ten days in the barrel before I do anything, by which time it smells like balsamic vinegar and looks like black tar. Three weeks later it tastes great and looks real pretty. Yeasts have a great capacity to clean things up.'

By doing nothing, Kent means he doesn't even add a cultured yeast to start the fermentation. 'Hands off' is his motto. When the fermentation is over and the black juice has magically transformed to greeny gold, he just lets the wine sit on its lees in the barrel. Does he rouse it, like many other Californian Chardonnay makers? 'I think if you pick up the barrels on the forklift now and then, that stirs them up enough.'

So the wine just sits there? Right. 'It trundles along in barrel until about May. Then I taste all the barrels, and make up my blend, usually grapes from 14 or 15 different vineyards, and if it all tastes fine and dandy, we bottle it.' Just like that? Not quite. 'The Chardonnay I sterile filter. I felt obliged to do it.' But he visibly squirmed as he said it. 'Chardonnay is what pays the bills around here, so I have to make some compromises. If we screwed up the Pinot we'd probably survive; if we

screwed up the Chardonnay we'd be out of business.' Everyone wants Kent Rasmussen's Chardonnay while only New York and California are interested in his Pinot. Yet, excellent though his Chardonnay is, it's Pinot Noir which inspires this man. And he cares passionately not just about his own Pinot Noir, but about everybody else's. This open-mindedness is as common among Californian Pinot Noir makers as it is rare among Cabernet Sauvignon makers. And the reason is that Cabernet Sauvignon is coming out of everyone's ears, while there is still a desperate shortage of good Pinot Noir. 'The drawback to Pinot Noir is that there just aren't enough good Pinot grapes.' The vineyard around Rasmussen senior's house is acknowledged to produce excellent grapes from some

Where's the winery? That's the winery? Yes, but that's also the Rasmussen vineyard, source of some of California's finest Pinot Noir grapes.

old, virtually forgotten clones of Pinot Noir. Kent says that the world and his brother now turn up each winter to take cuttings from what is rapidly becoming known as the Rasmussen clone – Mondavi were expected the week after I visited. And he gives the cuttings away. He was rather shocked when I asked if he sold them. 'If we improve the general quality of Pinot in California by cloning this vineyard it's not going to hurt us, and if it helps the others, more power to it.'

Certainly the Rasmussen Pinot Noir is special. It has a magnificent fruit flavour of cherry and plum as well as

an exciting exotic perfume, partly floral, partly like shiny, polished leather, and there's something like a handful of fresh hops there too. It's wonderful to taste young, although it will be far better with some age, and whereas his Chardonnay gains much of its personality from skill in blending the wine from different vineyards, the Pinot Noir's strength comes from those old vines around the bungalow.

As for his method of vinification – it's back to the eighteenth century again. No sulphur dioxide in the crusher for a start! 'There are no greater enemies than Pinot Noir and SO_2.' In particular it destabilizes the colour and flattens flavour components. So the grapes come in; 60 per cent are crushed and destemmed, 20 per cent are crushed but left with the stems and 20 per cent are left as whole berries.

They're thrown into plastic bins which hold about two-thirds of a ton of grapes, and then he gets a big wooden plunger and punches down the cap of skins into the juice. As often as possible. 'It's a bitch of a job, and I flake out after a few hours, but when I can get someone to help we go all night as well.'

After a couple of days the fermentation starts up quite naturally, but he goes on punching – seven, eight, nine times a day – and once the fermentation subsides he'll leave the skins and wine to steep for another week. And the whole berry bins he seals up with plastic until, as he says, he gets sick of it. After pressing, the lot goes into barrel.

What's more, 'I've never fined a Pinot anywhere in its life,' he states emphatically. He filtered his 1986 Pinot, but it taught him a sad lesson. 'It was the best Pinot I'd ever made. I coarse-filtered it before bottling and it came out about 50 per cent of what it had been. It just killed me. Since then I haven't filtered Pinot.'

I reckoned it was time to go, but I suddenly realized I hadn't seen a bottling line. 'I haven't got one.' Of course not; silly me. Where would he find room for one? So he hires a mobile line which does the job off the back of a truck. And he needs a bit of help for *that*. He rings around and people turn up on the promise of a few laughs and a good lunch. This year the Society of Jungian Psychiatrists have gone batty about his wines. One phone call and 13 PhDs turned up to bottle his Pinot Noir. 'All those years of education and it all goes into bottling my Pinot Noir!'

CALIFORNIA

Ridge Vineyards

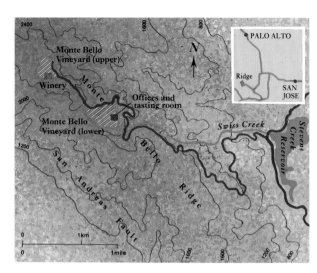

IT IS DARK WHEN we finish tasting. If you can call this dark. The pine trees throw grey silhouettes up towards an orange golden moon which rises effortlessly through a haze of smoky purple. Don't look down before you've enjoyed the silent beauty of these stars. But then look down. A couple of thousand feet down the mountains – to the glistening city of San José and the Silicon Valley. You know that activity must be seething down there, but all you can make out is one red neon sign flashing on a bed of winking gold. Up at Ridge, Paul Draper and I turn back to the mountain face on the far side of the San Andreas fault. A bird croaks. A lone light flickers briefly halfway up the wooded mountain side. Silence. Repose. Content. It's taken Draper nearly 30 years to find it, but as we stand wordless among the old Cabernet vines which straggle down through the picnic tables towards the Ridge Vineyards' tasting room, the vast night sky holds just enough light to show his look of quiet contentment.

Draper didn't start Ridge Vineyards. A winery and vineyards have perched in this setting high on the Monte Bello Ridge since the 1880s and in fact he doesn't own the place. A Japanese wine collector, Akihiko Otsuka, bought the property in 1987 and Draper seems almost relieved not to have the worries of partnership and ownership dogging him any more – but he has come to embody everything that Ridge stands for: tradition, respect for the vineyard, ceaseless striving for excellence.

The modern Ridge started in 1959 when three high-powered scientists from Stanford Research Institute bought a patch of this mountain top and some outhousing because of the view – and it is one helluva view, day and night. Still, there were Cabernet Sauvignon vines around, so they made ten gallons of wine that first year. They weren't the only ones surprised at how good it was. So were their friends and families, who did all the work over the next few years: they replanted the vines, rebuilt the housing, harvested the grapes, even collected the lion dung from San Francisco zoo to go around the vines to keep the deer off – I swear they did that – and as far as I can tell, enjoyed the kind of laid-back sixties idyll, at weekends anyway, that a lot of us just used to dream about.

And maybe that's why, when Ridge wanted to expand at the end of the 1960s, they looked for a philosopher-winemaker, an idealist winemaker, not a scientist-winemaker. Paul Draper. For him, it was like a vocation waiting to happen.

He too, lived the sixties like the songs said. He took philosophy not science at Stanford, got involved in international 'affairs' as he puts it – 'I was a free spirit, unconscious of where I was going' – until he hatched a plan with an old friend, Fritz Maytag, also a Stanford man, running aid schemes to improve living conditions in Chile – family planning clinics, soya bean plantations – and by 1967 Draper was way down in the south of the country, setting up a winery project. In Chile he discovered traditional, intuitive wine-making in a peasant community whose ways hadn't changed in a hundred years. Draper had spent some years in Europe and he'd tasted just about every Bordeaux vintage of any quality this century. He had a vision of what flavours he'd like to see in his ideal wine. And here he was down at the toe of South America learning how to make wine with equipment that would have been familiar to the Bordeaux winemakers of a century ago.

In 1969 Draper was back in California, after the political situation in Chile made it impossible for his project to continue. But Chile had one more tiny role to play. Someone held a Chilean wine tasting in Palo Alto one day – I'm sure the first, I'm sure the last. Draper went along and got talking to the man who started up Ridge, Dave Bennion. In the way of things then, Draper was offered the job of winemaker at Ridge. And he took it. He hadn't even had time to bottle the wines he made in Chile.

He didn't go to wine-making school, and still says that an oenologist is a doctor who fixes broken wines. Too many modern wineries give the oenologist the responsibility of creating fine flavours when all they've learned is how to fix bad ones, he says. All the same, Ridge probably does more wine-making research than any other winery except the Mondavi giant in Napa Valley, with the objective of making wine with as low a level of processing as possible. Draper is fascinated by science. But it's a philosopher's fascination with science that drives him on.

Employ the highest level of technology possible to enable you to use the most natural wine-making techniques, pushing the possibilities of your wine to the limits, yet remaining in absolute control. That's how it is at Ridge. The 40,000-case winery now buys in grapes from a wide area – almost entirely red, though there is a whiff of Chardonnay about the place. Since Draper believes passionately that not only is each vineyard's produce sacrosanct but the batches from each picking session must also be kept separate for their subtle differences, he could find himself with over a hundred different lots of wine each vintage in his cellar.

There'll be the Cabernets from Monte Bello itself which are the most sought-after of Ridge's wines – perhaps as many as 14 different lots, all kept separate. There'll be a dozen more from the Geyserville vineyards in Sonoma that regularly produce one of California's greatest Zinfandels. His old friend Fritz Maytag now owns a vineyard called York Creek on Spring Mountain above the Napa Valley and that's where Draper buys his Cabernet Sauvignon and Petite Sirah. Petite Sirah is not related to the great French Syrah, responsible for Hermitage and Côte-Rôtie. Yet about one year in three – 1985 for instance – Ridge Petite Sirah would put all but the greatest Syrah to shame. California wine snobs often arrogantly refuse even to taste Draper's Petite Sirah, but Gérard Jaboulet, whose family makes the most famous Hermitage in France from the real Syrah knows even better; he even carries Ridge Petite Sirah around in his suitcase to show his agents how strong the competition is.

Draper gets more pleasure, I suspect, from proving that unfashionable grapes like Zinfandel and Petite Sirah can deliver the goods than from crafting great Cabernet. After all, he has worked through the entire wine revolution of the seventies and eighties and watched from his mountain eyrie the pendulum swings of fashion. Yet he's still carrying out his wine-making as though the last hundred years hadn't happened.

But that's not so surprising. The spirit of Ridge has been moulded by a group of scientists determined to return to basics. Draper is a philosopher with the same ideals, who is aware that technological back-up will enable him to bask in the warm glow of what he calls 'no-action' wine-making. He's gradually working

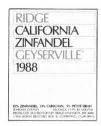

towards the same end with all his wines – to make them more accessible when young, yet with the balance to age for a generation or more. He now uses the gentlest of crusher-destemmers – but is also feeling his way towards an even milder method – removing the stems on a slatted table. That's the old nineteenth century way, and means you can control the extent to which the grapes are left whole or ripped open – increasingly he wants to leave as many as 50 per cent of his berries whole. When he does pump the juice or the finished wine, he has a machine with a pipe wide enough to take a tomato without breaking the skin – and he operates this at the slowest possible speed.

Since he wants to use naturally occurring yeasts, he'll usually pump over the juice in the tanks for the first few days to get the yeasts going, but most fermentation then takes place in stainless steel tanks, with a slatted headboard built in to keep the cap of skins submerged in liquid. The juice and skins spend anything between 14 and 25 days mixed in. Draper reckons this method avoids harshness but results in enough tannin and colouring matter to provide the structure to age. Certainly young Ridge wine is now far more approachable than it used to be. If the balance is right, that's no reason for it not to age.

The balance will partly be achieved by blending different lots of wine. These batches are all kept separate, usually in American oak casks. Draper does experiment with French oak, but he has so far seen no sign that it does Ridge wines much good. He doesn't want much new oak in his Zinfandel and Petite Sirah in any case, and the Cabernet Sauvignon from the low-yielding limestone soils of Monte Bello seems to relish the extra sweetness it gains from American oak, yet still manages to age like an old-fashioned Pauillac from Bordeaux. But then a hundred years ago in Pauillac, they thought that American wood was preferable to French in any case, so the idea isn't new.

A little early fining is done, but the objective is always to avoid filtration whenever possible. Often it is not possible, and one of Draper's tensest moments each year is when he meets up with his team to decide which wines are sufficiently clean and bright not to need any filtration at all. (They'll have been racked from barrel to barrel six or seven times by this stage.) It's a difficult decision. The chemists say that even a sterile membrane filter isn't small enough to strip a wine of any flavouring components or tannins. Paul Draper doesn't believe them. Every trial he's ever done involving varying degrees of treatment: no filtration, light filtration or sterile filtration for the same wine, has shown his tastebuds that the less you filter, the richer, the more sensuous, and – as the wine ages – the more complex the wine becomes.

It all goes back to the desire to do everything the natural way and to take the risks necessary to make great wine – not good wine, *great* wine. If Draper was just aiming to make good wine – firstly he'd find an easier place to do it than at the end of this hair-raising mountain road; and secondly his objective would be to eliminate any non-conformist or subversive elements. Trying to make great wine, he positively courts them. 'I like surprises' he says, 'the individuality is what I love.' Draper says that many wines that are truly exciting have something strange and surprising about them, not least his own. He has his own special tastes and prejudices, and given that they *are* his own, as long as he's in charge, he'll take the responsibility.

But he doesn't want vats full of unsaleable wine just because he followed a hunch. And that's why the technological back-up at Ridge is second to none. With so little processing of the wine, 'the whole world is potentially in there,' says Draper. So his high tech systems to monitor levels of bacteria, yeast, and sulphides are as advanced as any I've ever seen. Early detection of a fault allows minimal treatment. Late detection demands drastic action. Too technocratic? Not at all. Just a great support system that allows Ridge tremendous freedom to pursue their own 'no-action' style of wine-making.

Vines Worth Preserving

But not only is Ridge preserving a style of wine-making that dates back to before Prohibition in America – admittedly with the help of very sophisticated technology – but by championing Zinfandel and Petite Sirah, Draper has also done more than any other winery to preserve two of the grapes for which California was famous in the last century.

Zinfandel is thought of as America's own grape variety. It is probably related to the Italian Primitivo vine, though since the Italians themselves call the Primitivo the 'foreign' grape, no one's really sure what its genesis is. Great Zinfandels have been made in the past, but as California becomes swamped with Cabernet Sauvignon and Chardonnay mania, all over the state 100-year-old Zinfandel vines are being ripped up to be replaced by their more fashionable rivals. Indeed Draper has been fighting a battle to preserve the Geyserville Zinfandel vineyards in Sonoma from being ripped up and planted with more profitable Chardonnay. But his Geyserville Zin is great wine. Mixed in with small quantities of Carignane and Petite Sirah – 20 per cent Petite Sirah used to be the formula earlier in the century – it can exhibit a most unnervingly cloying flavour of cream and mint when young, but just a few years of age mellow the cream and mix in the tooth-aching attack of sweet raspberry sauce.

The York Creek Petite Sirah grapes can produce a wonderful wine too. Always deep red, it does sometimes keep its tannic toughness for a bit too long, but usually balances that with a remarkable array of flavours – custard, plums and pine in the 1987, pepper and mint jelly intertwined with a strange floral perfume like the sappy sweetness of lilac in the '81, or the superb juicy-sweet raspberry and pepper, custard cream biscuits and mint of the '85, which makes me realize why Gérard Jaboulet would happily show this alongside his Côte-Rôtie and Hermitage.

And then there's the Monte Bello Cabernet Sauvignon – the Bordeaux model. Of all the wines that Paul Draper muses about, going back through the 1961s, 1945s, 1928s, 1900s – all the way to the 1864s, 1865s, and 1870s – the one property whose name occurs most frequently is Château Latour – the grandest, the most unbending of the great First Growth Pauillacs in Bordeaux. Tasting his 1987, his '81, his '77, his '72 Monte Bellos, is like looking through 40 years of Pauillac compressed, concertina-like, into 20. The 1987 takes a good hour in the glass to show how the mineral, the blackcurrant and the cedar will marry over the years. The 1981 needs an hour to show the almost syrupy blackcurrant intensity of a maturing Pauillac. The 1977, still tannic, is beginning to flare up with the high-toned, sharp-tongued sweetness of blackcurrant and pure, fresh-hewn cedar that marks a great Pauillac of perhaps 30 years old. The 1972 has all the brilliant, delicious decay of liquorice and mint, blackcurrant and cream – and cedar, rich yet dry, perfumed in a most exotic yet restrained way. A 40-year-old Latour would be proud to taste like this. And to think 1972 was almost a wipe-out as a vintage for Ridge! Interesting – Château Latour is famous for the quality of its off-vintages too.

Ridge is so close to the San Andreas fault, these American oak barrels leap in the air at every earthquake. So far they've always come down again in the same place.

CALIFORNIA

Saintsbury

THE FIRST TIME I met David Graves, the bear-like bundle of irreverence who makes up one half of the Saintsbury partnership, someone aggressively challenged his insistence that he could grow Pinot Noir in California. 'So what makes you think you can make great Pinot Noir?' the inquisitor barked at Graves. From the man who is president of the Carneros Quality Alliance, who spearheads the Pinot Noir America movement, founded to persuade an unwilling public of the grape's qualities, I expected a passionate defence of American Pinot Noir. But he reacted with about as much fire as a Texas Longhorn chewing its breakfast cud. I almost think he assumed a Lone Star drawl as he replied, 'Hell, it's a free country, ain't it?'

There is fire and passion at the Saintsbury winery – from Graves or the other half of the operation, Dick Ward – Mister Ward as Graves calls him. But freedom of choice is equally important to these two men, who founded the now sizeable 35,000-case Carneros winery from scratch in 1981 with, on their own admission, barely a nickel between them. That rate of growth in the face of record-high interest rates and dwindling American wine consumption, puts tremendous pressure on the pair, and even Dick Ward's boyish good looks are now creasing with the odd line. But they stick to their guns. They offer great value for money, they offer humour when not too exhausted, and they pin their hopes on Pinot Noir finally emerging as the fashionable red wine variety of the 1990s. In any case, although both are science graduates, and both have done some – only some – study at the University of California wine school at Davis, they say 'our attitudes and work habits make us otherwise unemployable.' The two men have a belief. They'll have to sink or swim by that belief.

A major difference between Graves and virtually every other California Pinot Noir fanatic is that Graves has never been to Burgundy, hasn't got a visit on his agenda for the foreseeable future, and isn't in some kind of telepathic communication with any Burgundian eminence grise. It is Carneros he believes in. And it is only Carneros fruit that he uses, even if the buzz is that the grapes of San Luis Obispo and Santa Barbara Counties, way to the south of San Francisco, are increasingly producing wines of startling intensity from low yields of grapes grown on free-draining soils. Carneros yields are not low and Carneros soils are not well-drained. In fact Carneros is a classic example of

how California's vineyards developed on a 'climate first, soil second' philosophy. When Napa and Sonoma County vine growers wanted to produce more delicate fruit, they chose the fog-chilled, breeze-cooled Carneros acres at the edge of San Pablo Bay, because of the climate. They didn't even consider the soil. Yet Carneros had historically been an under-developed area because of water and soil problems.

Carneros' rainfall is the lowest in Napa or Sonoma Counties, and the clay, despite being water-retentive, is so dense and impenetrable that most rain simply runs off its surface. It isn't even deep clay – usually only going down three feet or so – and what root systems do develop spread laterally rather than downwards.

There are pluses and minuses here. The dense clay restricts vigorous leaf growth so, despite being a cool area, Carneros fruit rarely suffers from the green acidity that can afflict cool climate fruit grown on fertile soil. But such vines will become very susceptible to drought, and Carneros growers have to resort to regular short bursts of irrigation – if they can find the water. Some wells have had to go as deep as 244 metres (800 feet) to find a water source. And these short bursts of irrigation produce *big* yields of fruit.

Involving the Growers

There are 5 hectares (13 acres) of vineyard around the Saintsbury winery, and Graves buys in the rest of the fruit he needs from growers in Carneros. He likes to give the growers a sense of involvement by bottling the best wines separately under the grower's name, hoping to prove to them that better grapes produce better wine. But it isn't easy. Most grape growers are farmers, not wine men. Their objective is to grow a big crop of healthy fruit – and they particularly hate thinning bunches off the vine in mid season. Graves loses patience with this attitude. Saintsbury have trodden the difficult path of producing a value-for-money wine from some of the most expensive grapes in California. Graves has had to go along with soaring prices, but he wants the trade-off in return – the right to go into those vineyards in mid-season, estimate the crop, and thin it down to what he sees as a realistic volume for quality. Four tons, perhaps four and a half, to the acre for Pinot Noir, a little more for Chardonnay would be his aim.

Graves and Ward produce Pinot Noir and Chardonnay in about equal quantities (most Carneros producers usually have far more of the easy-selling Chardonnay than the quixotic Pinot Noir). Most of the Chardonnay comes from the Sonoma side of Carneros, from the flatter vineyards, trailing down towards the airport and the bay, below the town of Sonoma. As the

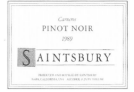

What a pair! David Graves and 'Mister Ward' – the unconventional partners at Saintsbury.

volume of production at Saintsbury has increased they've been picking riper and riper grapes, simply because their functional, barn-like winery couldn't keep up with the extra quantity and the grapes had to stay on the vine a bit longer. But that's good – many Carneros Chardonnays have too much of the lime and grapefruit tartness which has been in vogue for a while now among California winemakers. Graves and Ward have decided to make a virtue out of this acid. So they ferment their Chardonnay in barrel, put it all through malolactic fermentation (Carneros Chardonnay tends to have a higher malic acid content than Chardonnay from other vineyard areas), then age it on lees for eight months. That crisp citrus lime acid is muted but not destroyed; the buttery lactic acid is deliciously kept in check, and the toasty richness from ageing on the lees in French oak all produce a superbly attractive, buttery, toasty Chardonnay – every bit as good as a Meursault – at half the price. In the best years they'll also make a Reserve from the richest lots.

From the very beginning they've divided their Pinot Noir into a more concentrated top selection and a second label called Garnet. Virtually all the Pinot Noir for these wines comes from the Napa side of Carneros. Each year sees some refinement of technique, much of it along the lines of current Burgundian thinking, but not all. They do now allow the juice and skins to macerate before fermentation, but only because one year they forgot to inoculate with yeast and it wasn't until three days later they began to wonder why fermentation

hadn't started. The result was special, so 'cold soak' maceration was in from then on.

The fermentation runs fairly hot and, unusually for Pinot Noir, they pump the juice over the cap three times a day rather than punch the skins down. This is thought to be a rougher technique more suited to Cabernet, but Ward says they pump over using a gentle irrigation device in a closed tank, and because they only add half the yeast they used to, the fermentation is not as tumultuous as at many other Pinot Noir wineries. And then they let the wine and skins sit together for a total, start to finish, of 16 to 18 days. Saintsbury Pinot Noir is particularly marked by its delightful fresh red fruits perfume. Ward says that perfume develops during the extra five days of maceration.

It also means that the free-run juice is very clean and settled. It can be drawn off straight to barrel, with no filtration, the barrel bunged, rolled on its side and left. The only time that barrel will be disturbed is when the blends are being made up just before bottling. Gentle handling not only means virtually all the press wine is usable, but the end result keeps its fresh bright fruit character for longer. Of all the Carneros Pinot Noirs, Saintsbury's are the most likely to develop that unique flavour which California's wine guru, André Tchelistcheff has called 'the inside of a kid glove worn by a young woman'.

The Saintsbury of the winery's title was an early twentieth-century wine 'buff', gruff and sparing in his epithets. He wouldn't have approved of such fancy talk. Graves and Ward are two of America's most laid-back and attractive contemporary winemakers. They just want to know the young woman's phone number.

Sanford

YOU'LL FIND THE SANFORD WINERY between Todd's Valley Pipe Supply and Valley Automotive Services on an industrial estate just north of Buellton. Get inside those sliding doors quick, because this Santa Barbara County town is the split pea capital of the world, if not the universe. The stench of high-protein green sludge swirls thick around the jerry-built warehouse sheds, blending rather unsuccessfully with the spray paint from Valley Automotive. But get inside, slam the doors, and you're in a quiet haven of fermenting tanks, French oak barrels and the heady aromas of young Chardonnay and Pinot Noir. This is where Richard Sanford and his winemaker Bruno d'Alfonso craft their Pinots, their Chardonnays and their Sauvignons.

I'd expected Sanford, the sixties kid grown up – well, reasonably grown up – to have a ranch, some cattle grazing in the paddock, and rows of veggies thriving out the back. Where were the roots put down, the all-important life style? Just give it time, says Sanford, a hint of frustration in his voice. Sixties ideals are one thing. Nineties economic reality very much another.

His home, and the land he has been planting with vines, lie a few miles down the road. So he drives you out of grey-green downtown Buellton, and along the Santa Ynez Valley towards the Pacific Ocean. After a mile or two of sub-Steinbeck lettuce-laced valley floor, the river turns in a wide arc, first to the south, then back to the west. As if from nowhere, the casual slopes become grand majestic hills, with dry creek beds zig-zagging down between the bumps and spines, sheep looking for grass, hawks and eagles soaring high above. Time to glance at Sanford again, and now he seems ten years younger than his fortysomething, as he turns up a dirt road, ready to show me his homestead.

Three weathered clapboard shacks, no glass in the windows, and a stovepipe from the brazier jutting up through the corrugated iron roof. That's it? For now, that's it. One day, one day there'll be a beautiful adobe mission-style winery, there'll be acres of Pinot Noir and Chardonnay planted on the 308-hectare (760-acre) hillside spread Sanford bought as bare land in 1981. 'This is where I want to *be*', he states emphatically, 'and where I want my children to *be*.'

Richard Sanford has chosen this crook in the valley's arm to put down his roots. Now he needs to find a way of making the place pay, without compromise.

Uncompromising flavours are what made me first notice Sanford wines. In a dull line-up of Californian Sauvignon Blanc, suddenly there would be Sanford, gooseberry-sharp, sassy, grassy green, crisp but rounded out with cream and honey. In a line of soft, mild, nervous Chardonnays from Carneros and Napa, there'd be this snappy, lime-acid and grapefruit pith wine, plumped out magnificently with the tropical richness of guava and papaya and oozy honey. And faced with a range of Pinot Noirs which didn't seem able to decide whether they wanted to be Rambo-limbed Cabernet Sauvignons or blushing bride rosés, here was Sanford again, all *fruit* – raspberry, cherry, plum – any tannic structure swathed in rich, ripe fruit.

Challenge to Napa

And yet these are Richard Sanford's compromise wines. Despite their tremendous quality, despite the fact that he has painstakingly identified the vineyard sites that will give him fruit of a sufficiently intense flavour (from a sea of vines that won't), these are not yet the wines his ambition burns to make. Until 1990 all the grapes for his wines came from the Santa Maria Valley, an hour's drive to the north. Yet Richard Sanford was the first to identify the site of what may well become California's greatest Pinot Noir zone, its *grand cru* – the foggy, wind-cooled north-facing slopes of the Santa Ynez Valley, between 20 and 30 miles from the sea. This area, which has the potential to exceed Sonoma and Napa in quality, is exactly where he planted the valley's first Pinot Noir back in 1971, just four miles west of where his three-shack estate is now situated.

Before going on to UC Berkeley to study geography, and before spending three years in the navy, followed by a stint travelling around Europe, Sanford had studied at the university in Santa Barbara, where he'd known a botanist called Michael Benedict. In 1970 the two met up again, both sharing the conviction that the importance of specific sites and suitable grape varieties had been totally overlooked in California up until then. The mix of a geographical background and a growing interest in wine – a spell in Europe always seems to have this effect – got him started studying climatic differences right back to the beginning of the century between Burgundy, Bordeaux, and the various wine areas of California. If he was looking for a Burgundy site in the Golden West, the more he delved, the more he liked the look of Santa Barbara County.

The thing that most struck him about Santa Barbara County was that the river valleys ran east to west, whereas in the rest of California, they ran north to south. At the coast here it is so foggy you can't grow

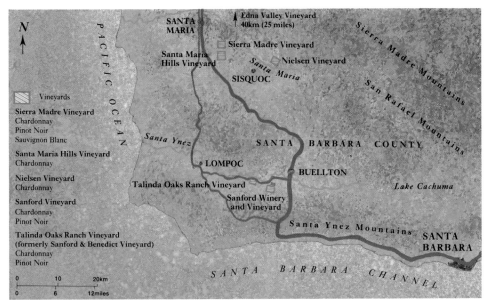

grapes at all. Forty miles inland it's too warm to grow the cool climate Burgundian grapes. But in that twenty- to thirty-mile inland stretch, the fog came up the valley at six or seven each evening, and was burned off the next morning by about ten, cooling the valley, but not freezing it out. The fierce southern California sun would have scorched the usual east- or west-facing slopes. But a north-facing slope would never be fully exposed to the sun. A ten-mile, north-facing valley slope doesn't sound much, but the climatic balance here is so delicate that the average daily heat increases by one degree for every mile you go inland. Twenty miles in from the coast, you'll have growing season heat peak approaching 27°C (80°F). Twenty miles further in it could touch 38°C (100°F) – far too hot for Pinot Noir.

So Sanford and Benedict Winery was founded, just 29km (18 miles) in from the coast, at the very limit of ripening for Pinot Noir. In 1971 and 1972 they planted a hundred acres of vines, and in 1976 they made their first Pinot Noir. I remember those early Sanford and Benedict Pinots – they had an almost shocking amount of fruit, but they often had a screeching volatility too, which, alongside other wines with volatile flavours, like Firestone, La Zaca and Zaca Mesa from further up the valley, initially made me a bit doubtful about Santa Ynez wines in general.

Sanford says the volatility certainly was there – partly caused, in the case of the other wineries, by their situation in the hotter, inland part of the valley – but at Sanford and Benedict the reasons were a little different. They were slavishly trying to do everything in the most traditional way possible without really understanding the philosophy behind the traditions or indeed the

simple day-to-day details which stop wine from turning into vinegar. Topping up barrels, for instance. Well yes, in hindsight it seems obvious, but in the excitement of finally getting to make wine, it sort of slipped his mind, and the acetic acid levels slowly rose.

And he knew it was very important to get his fermentation temperatures high and he still believes in this. But there they were in this converted barn, the two of them – no mains electricity, just a small generator to operate a small press and no cooling equipment of any sort. Even as beginners they could see when things were getting out of control but all they could lay their hands on was dry ice. They thought they were being doubly clever because adding dry ice to wine would also leave a blanket of carbon dioxide on the top to prevent oxidation. But unless my memory's going from those distant pantomimes of childhood days, when clouds of dry ice used to envelop the front rows of the theatre every time fairies or goblins or magicians attempted to make an appearance – doesn't dry ice have a petrolly smell? Sure does, said Richard. Luckily so does Riesling, so their Riesling was merely thought of as particularly pungent.

It didn't stop the wines selling, though. Tiny yields – sometimes as low as a completely absurd quarter ton to the acre, and the startling intensity of the fruit, caught the attention of the California wine world, and almost immediately Sanford and Benedict wines were available strictly on allocation. It was an exciting phase, but sadly things weren't working out between the two men. Sanford found he was doing all the admin and sales and there was no time to get his nose into a barrel. As he learned more about wine-making, there were things he wanted to change, but he didn't win the arguments and in 1980, he left.

It obviously hurt. The adventure might have been over. He might have given in to the corporate life style he'd spent so long avoiding. But he'd seen the quality of that Santa Ynez fruit. If he had to leave the valley for a while, he'd be back, and on his own terms.

First Things First

But he needed a job, quickly. Or a winery. He got the winery, well a part of one. Edna Valley Winery had some spare space and they said he could rent it while he got sorted out. Sorting himself out also meant choosing a new name, and a label. He did 107 mock-ups before it came to him to call the winery, simply, Sanford.

Next, he had to find grapes. Since the Sanford and Benedict vineyards were the only ones planted in the western Santa Ynez, and he was unlikely to be offered those by Michael Benedict, Sanford checked out certain growers he knew in the other main east-west valley, the Santa Maria. In particular he found a well-drained island of land in the middle of the flood plain called Sierra Madre. Dale Hampton, the owner, was and still is regarded as one of the valley's most conscientious growers, and has been the main source of supply for Sanford ever since, along with some growers with plots of old vines up in the Santa Maria Hills.

Richard Sanford made 2000 cases of wine in 1981 and sold them all. He did even better in 1982, and by 1983 he was seeing the light at the end of the tunnel. He'd bought an area of land just east of the Santa Ynez vineyard he'd planted in 1971, and if he was going to make those mortgage repayments, he was going to have to expand – but as economically as possible. Which is how this tall, laid-back, boyish charmer came to be squeezed into a pre-fab next to Todd's Valley Supply. Well, I thought Sanford was laid-back until I met the gaze of Bruno d'Alfonso, his full-time winemaker. With his Latin good looks and his wavy brilliantined hair he somehow manages to combine passion with insouciance, capable of being almost horizontally relaxed yet remaining combative at the same time.

But he was just what Richard Sanford was looking for. Sanford had advertised the post of winemaker when he was setting up in split pea heaven, and had met a succession of well-trained Davis wine school graduates who seemed to offer no real commitment when he explained his aspirations, and spent more time exhibiting their prejudices rather than listening to him. Bruno d'Alfonso was then the assistant winemaker at Edna Valley. He actually *wanted* to share in the adventure, and after clearing it with his bosses, the job

was his. The wine-making style is still studiously traditional. D'Alfonso uses open-top fermenting vats for his Pinot Noir, and only partially presses the grapes in order to keep some clusters whole. He doesn't add sulphur dioxide, and although he inoculates with cultured yeast, he leaves the skins and juice together first for up to 24 hours, so there is an element of wild yeast in the must too. The fermentation is warm and tumultuous, tailing off after three or four days, after which he'll let the whole lot macerate for up to two weeks. He doesn't pump over, preferring to punch the skins down with great wooden paddles. The juice is then run off into French oak barrels, some of them new, with some of the lees if they taste sweet and clean, and that's where the wine stays, for 16 to 18 months before bottling. He does filter and fine, but obviously resents the commercial pressures which make him do it.

The Sauvignon and Chardonnay both undergo barrel fermentation which he lets get as hot as it wants. No sulphur is added before or during fermentation. Both styles are put through a complete malolactic fermentation and then they have three or four months on the lees, being roused once a week before being racked off and left in barrels for eight months before bottling. Again, he now has to stabilize and filter against his inclination, although he does make a Barrel Select Chardonnay which sometimes avoids the filter pads.

What shines through in all the resulting Sanford wines is piercing fruit, with high acidity but wonderful off-the-bush freshness too, the new oak (the Sauvignon and Chardonnay are barrel-fermented too) often only noticeable as an afterthought. The Santa Maria fruit he's using is increasingly becoming sought-after throughout California for its unusual marriage of high acid and low pH with high sugar. It's enabled Sanford to win numerous gold medals. It's allowed him to increase his production to 26,000 cases, a figure which is still rising. It allowed him to make a profit in 1989 for the first time since he started. All of which brings the day closer and closer when he'll be able to return his Buellton pre-fab to the car industry, and build his adobe winery in the fold of the Santa Ynez hills.

And as for those acres of Pinot Noir he and Michael Benedict planted just to the west back in 1971, in 1990 they were sold to a British businessman. Richard Sanford has been contracted to manage the vineyard, purchase its grapes and make its wine. So it looks like a case of – over to you, Richard.

The majesty of the scenery can disguise the aridity of the dun-coloured pasture. The only green in the Santa Ynez Valley comes from the gum trees, horse paddocks – and vines.

Silver Oak

*W*HEN YOU CAN CHARGE VISITORS for the privilege of tasting your wines, and then only allow them to buy one bottle – that's what I call a successful winery. And when the winemaker admits that he had to be dragged kicking and screaming into wine-making, you begin to see some sense in the old adage that playing hard to get is the best tactic.

Yet back in the 1950s, Justin Meyer, the jovial, ruddy-faced partner and winemaker at Silver Oak, was following a completely different career, having joined the Christian Brothers monastic order, intent upon following a vocation of teaching. The last thing he wanted to be then was a winemaker. But when he was moved over into the winery side of Christian Brothers in 1964, he tackled the new subject with the same energy and commitment he had devoted to teaching.

He seems contented and relaxed enough now, as he presides over Silver Oak, one of California's hottest wineries, but the success certainly hasn't gone to his head. He still drives a less than spanking-new Buick, deriding the 'fancy automobiles' some of his fellow owners deck themselves out with, and the church is clearly still the moving force in his life. He leads the singing at his local church, though he doesn't strike up on the banjo as often as he used to, and he strives to instil some sense of proportion into the frequently one-track world of wine-making. 'I talk to the Napa Tech each year,' he says, 'and I always say to these young winemakers – you must make a list of your priorities. If you can't find three things more important than wine-making, you're all messed up.'

Maybe it's this lack of self-importance which has allowed Meyer to propel Silver Oak to its position as one of California's top Cabernet Sauvignon producers, solely based on the pleasure, the joy of the wine in the glass. We chuckled about good old-fashioned hedonism as we tasted his wines, and that was certainly my first impression of Silver Oak – sheer pleasure.

At a time when many Napa winemakers seemed determined to maximize their tannins as a talisman of some distant quality to come, the Silver Oak wines positively bulged with fruit, with coconut spice, with perfumes of ginger and violets, then leather and blackcurrant, eucalyptus too, all twining in and out of a sumptuous red wine. In an age which seemed to glorify tannins and toughness in a red wine, how did Silver Oak manage to be so utterly seductive when young, yet

age as well as any beefy, tannic California Cabernet? One of the crucial things is that Meyer has no fascination with Bordeaux, whereas many Californian winemakers are obsessed with trying to mould their Cabernets into a style similar to a Classed Growth Pauillac or St-Julien. He's never even been to Bordeaux and admits to knowing little about France. Yet he sounds merely uncomplicated rather than parochial when he says, 'I don't think that Bordeaux is better than California Cabernet. I don't even think their grapes are ripe. They say our wines are too alcoholic, too much extract, too flabby. I see their wines as thin, low alcohol, hard tannins. Bordeaux may be thought of as the world's standard for Cabernet, but if California had been the first historically, *we* would be the world's standard'. It is significant that the two Bordeaux reds he most admires are the sensuous Pichon-Lalande and the ripe, beautifully balanced Ducru-Beaucaillou.

Sweet Enough Already

The two most obvious ways of copying Bordeaux are to use a high proportion of new French oak barrels, and to blend your Cabernet with the lighter, softer Merlot and Cabernet Franc grape varieties. Meyer eschews both the barrels and the blending. He has tried French oak, but phased it out several years ago because, quite simply, he prefers the softer, sweeter taste of American oak. And he is mildly interested in Cabernet Franc, but completely dismisses the idea of Merlot. He ages his wines in barrel for almost three years – a third longer than most California wineries – and then in bottle for another two, before he releases them for sale. He reckons that gives them quite enough softness as it is.

I can see his point. Every Silver Oak wine is marked by richness and soft texture. Even the 1983, a notoriously fruitless vintage in California, has a delicious gentle creaminess and a pure, sweet blackcurrant fruit. Blending with Merlot would merely dilute the beautifully direct fruit intensity. Meyer says there are several reasons for this approachability, the first being the fruit itself.

His main source of grapes is the Alexander Valley in Sonoma. Although only planted in the 1970s, it has rapidly proved itself to be a rich source of well-flavoured but gentle-mannered Cabernet. Of Silver Oak's 22,000-case annual production, about 18,000 cases are sold under the Alexander Valley label. Three thousand cases come from Napa, and here he admits to a stroke of luck, because the vineyards are in the hot northern part between St Helena and Calistoga, and he says frankly this should be too hot for good Cabernet. In fact the Napa Cuvée is the least successful of the three labels he produces, less velvety and upfront than the Alexander Valley wine, and less memorable than Bonny's Vineyard. Bonny is Justin Meyer's wife and he named the plot of vines around their Oakville house after her. He didn't plan to sell the wine separately at first, but this little gravel patch gave wine of such depth and concentration, intensely flavoured yet blindingly direct in its personality, similar in its blackcurrant fruit structure to a great Pauillac, yet far less tannic, that Meyer felt he had to keep the wine separate. So his top-of-the-line Cabernet is Bonny's, anywhere between 500 and 1200 cases a year.

Silver Oak is a totally Cabernet Sauvignon winery. I wondered whether he didn't want to experiment with other sorts of wine. But Meyer says that in his eight years of making wine at Christian Brothers he had to produce between 35 and 40 different styles, and at Franciscan, which he ran between 1975 and '79, he made 11 different kinds of wine.

By the time he was ready to set up his own winery, he'd had enough of trying to please everybody, so Silver Oak was founded with the objective of making just a

Justin Meyer has a very gentle, rather saintly look about him. That's hardly surprising, since he trained as a monk before turning to create fine Cabernet at Silver Oak.

single wine, the one he felt California did best – Cabernet Sauvignon. 1972 was the winery's foundation date, but no wine was released until 1977 (that's why he says he needed a second job, running Franciscan – he certainly wasn't earning anything from Silver Oak). His policy of releasing wine when it's ready to drink meant that his first release was the 1972 and both it and the '73 sold quite well, but it was the '74 Silver Oak Alexander Valley which made the reputation of the winery. It won a gold medal against 80 other Cabernets at the Los Angeles County Fair in 1979, and the *Los Angeles Times* placed it second out of 75 California Cabernets in a special ranking. 'We've never had a sales problem since.' In fact the unashamed enthusiasm for Silver Oak from the influential American wine critic Robert Parker is almost too much of a good thing. To have your wine in such demand that you can only sell visitors a single bottle each doesn't exactly thrill Meyer; he has to face the disappointed customers in the tasting room far too often to be smug about it.

And it isn't just a sales pitch; there really isn't enough wine. Meyer doesn't stoop to such shallow tricks to promote his wares. 'You can sell the steak, or you can sell the sizzle,' he says, 'and in this business there's an awful lot of sizzle.' At Silver Oak, there's an awful lot of steak.

ZD

*I*WAS IN THE MIDDLE of a Classed Growth Bordeaux tasting. 1982s, '83s, '85s and '86s – pretty serious stuff – and this chap sidles up with a glass in his hand and a mischievous look on his face. I know that look. It's the 'you're never going to guess *this* one' look people give me when they're determined to catch me out in a blind tasting. And I'm an absolute sucker for it. In I dive headlong. But, wow, the smell of this one – brilliantly rich blackcurrant fruit, roughened at the edge with an earthy toughness – this was surely top-of-the-tree Pauillac or St-Julien. The taste was rich, ripe, a lime acidity insinuating itself into the indulgent, juicy, blackcurrant fruit, not much tannin, yet such balance, and freshness and power. All the things you expect from a top Bordeaux – but in a more gushing, open-handed mode. 'ZD Cab', the guy said, delighting in my dithering. 1986. Of course. ZD. Every time you find a Cabernet positively oozing with ripe, rich fruit, not quite French, not quite Australian, and certainly not a typical modern day Napa Valley style – put your money on it turning out to be ZD.

This pleasure-first principle doesn't just apply to Cabernet – ZD make exceptional Pinot Noir and Chardonnay too. The Pinot Noirs are full, rounded wines, honey and cherry and strawberry sweetness filled out with toasty oak and perfumes of mint and orange and eucalyptus. The Chardonnays have the succulent honeyed richness, the peach and passion fruit and spicy intensity, the savoury fragrance of smoking toast straight from the breakfast grill – all the sunfilled, golden delights which used to be thought of as the hallmarks of California Chardonnay, yet with none of the blowsy flab which so often caused other Chardonnays to cave in on themselves at only a year or two old. The 1981 and 1982, tasted in 1989, were rich, mature, wonderfully satisfying wines with years of life in them yet.

ZD's reputation is based on wines of unabashed hedonistic style. Yet the winery and the deLeuze family who own it are disarmingly matter-of-fact and quite devoid of any of the airs and graces which can so often make me feel uneasy in California. It's a real family affair: Norman, his wife Rosa Lee, and children Robert, Brett and Julie virtually handle the entire 20,000-case operation by themselves.

The winery was set up initially just south of Sonoma by Norman in 1969 with a partner, the late Gino Zepponi. Both men worked as aerospace engineers, and were doing little more than indulging in a bit of home wine-making in their spare time. They named their fledgling enterprise ZD – from their surnames – and whether by good fortune or sound intuition, turned up to buy some grapes from a new vineyard just offering its first crop. They'd happened on Winery Lake, destined to become the most famous of all the Carneros vineyards. They made 300 cases of wine, mostly Pinot Noir, and as Winery Lake Vineyard's fame grew, the word got about that the very first wine made from Winery Lake's fruit was the 1969 ZD.

Time to Move On

By 1977 production had grown to 2000 cases. Norman did the wine-making, Rosa Lee 'walked the streets selling it' as she gamely describes it, and the children mucked in. And ZD was becoming a success, easy to sell, winning good reviews. Norman cashed in his pension plan and started looking for a larger winery.

They found some land, anyway – half a dozen acres of it on the Silverado Trail in Napa Valley, just north of the Oakville crossroad. And in 1979 they built their own winery there – compact, homely, with sloping tiled roofs and creepers on the walls. When Norman deLeuze decided to take things a bit easier in 1983, his son Robert took over as winemaker – virtually self-trained. A year at the wine school at Davis gave him some technical background, but at ZD you always feel the flavour is the most important thing, and they'll see if they obeyed the rules once they're happy with the taste.

The ZD use of oak, in particular, goes right against current trends since, in a world dominated by enthusiasm for French oak barrels, they much prefer home-grown American oak. They want to make rich wines, yet for Chardonnay in particular they want to use cool-climate fruit. Chardonnay is their most important wine, accounting for four-fifths of production, and what Robert does is to choose grapes from up to 11 different vineyards, mostly in the cool Carneros region, and then persuade the growers to let them ripen longer than usual. This brings with it the possibility of honey-tasting noble rot, but more importantly, it means the grapes are mature, and don't have the green acidity which can plague California Chardonnay.

The grapes are pressed without preliminary crushing, then for six to eight weeks a slow fermentation in mostly American barrels takes place in a specially cooled part of the cellar, quite unlike the usual rapid warm barrel fermentation. After which they don't do other trendy things like malolactic fermentation or lees contact either. Those are all methods to increase richness; but by picking ultra-ripe grapes, then allowing

ZD winery doesn't look too trendy, but in fact this small building is stuffed to the rafters with barrels of award-winning Pinot Noir, Chardonnay and Cabernet Sauvignon.

the wines up to two months bubbling gently away in barrel, Robert says he's got all the lees contact he could need, and he's preserved all the fruit that he feels might be dissipated in a hot fermentation. It's not what the rulebook says – but it works and his magnificently rich Chardonnays are some of California's most sought-after.

I wouldn't be at all surprised in five to ten years' time to find that the ZD way has become the accepted wisdom. And I'm sure ZD will still be using it. As Brett, the younger brother, now marketing director along with Rosa Lee, said when asked for his pearls of marketing wisdom – 'Just don't change a thing'.

The approach to Pinot Noir has been modified a little by Robert, who since 1986 has been aiming at making a more perfumed style, without losing the weight of the wine. So he ferments hot, punches the cap of skins down four times a day, after which he'll just let the new wine settle – no filtering no fining – shove it into primarily American oak, and pretty well leave it alone. All the same, it's with Cabernet that the development of the ZD style really shows. They make

about 1700 cases each year, mostly from bought-in fruit, but their aim is to use the land around the winery for a single estate Cabernet – when the quality justifies it. The vines were planted in 1980-81, and they tried to produce an estate wine in 1984 but the result was dense and tough – *not* what ZD tries to stand for.

The 1985 Cabernet, blended with bought-in grapes wasn't a great success either, but, as at the Mondavi winery, Robert then found that using the gentler fermentation methods learned from Pinot Noir treatment enormously improved his Cabernet. He ferments hot and if he feels the wine is getting too tannic, he'll take the juice off the skins and finish the fermentation in another tank, or – if there isn't one free – in barrels. This is a technique commonly used in Australia, and goes some way to explaining the wonderful richness balanced by adequate, but not excessive, tannins which have made ZD Cabernets so exciting since the 1986 vintage. With the 1987, Robert finally got his estate bottling. Only 300 cases, but it's deep, deep, rich wine, sweet and almost heady with blackcurrant and mint, and there's butter oozing out at the edges, just as you'd get from a pile of pancakes. Put *that* in a blind tasting and I won't say – 'is it Pauillac or St-Julien?' I'll just say – 'that's ZD'.

AUSTRALIA

*F*OR QUALITY AT AN AFFORDABLE PRICE, for exuberant expression of fruit, for wines that give you an almost irresistible urge to order another bottle before the first is even finished – Australia currently leads the world.

Australia's greatest glory is that she has always made wine with the consumer's preferences clearly to the fore. The country's unique contribution has been less with fine wines – excellent though many of these are – but more with good everyday wines, where the everyday wine drinker pays hard-earned money for a little bit of what he fancies. The revolution in modern wine is not just about trying to rival the Margaux and the Montrachets of this world; it's about raising the standard of *all* wine which will then provide attractive, affordable avenues into the world of fine wine, which in turn may indeed lead to the expensive and rarefied heights of the great wines.

The wine revival in Australia, begun in quiet but decisive fashion by Max Schubert with Grange Hermitage in the 1950s, and continued by the large South Australian wineries, really lifted off at around the same time as California's – the end of the 1960s, and the 1970s. But whereas California set out from the start to emulate French models, the Australians had a long, proud tradition of their own to draw upon for their inspiration. Max Lake set out to recreate the 1930 Dalwood from the Hunter Valley that he described as the best wine he'd ever tasted; Len Evans determined to revive the Shiraz and Semillon that had made the Hunter Valley famous. Orlando and Yalumba set out to show how good South Australian Riesling could be while Wynns rekindled the fires of 'Coonawarra claret' with the traditional mix of Cabernet and Shiraz.

When the influence of the great Bordeaux and Burgundies became more evident with an increased commitment to Cabernet and Chardonnay during the 1980s, it was a case of integrating them with classic styles of red and white that had already proved their worth, and in the 1990s, as the wine drinker begins to hanker for a wider choice, while California has thrown itself perhaps too wholeheartedly behind the red Bordeaux and white Burgundy models, Australia has Riesling, Semillon, and Shiraz all just waiting to be asked to rejoin the party.

Australian wine styles have been able to develop freely without the deadening effects of appellation controls. At the mass production level, she has blended wines from all over the nation to achieve a taste the ordinary wine drinker would lap up. And at the top level, Australia has won international competitions hands down – in Europe, California and Australia itself – because the wines have shown that supreme quality and irresistible drinkability are not incompatible – as the top

These Hill of Grace vineyards in front of an old German church in the Adelaide Hills may hold the oldest Shiraz, or Syrah, vines in existence, older than the oldest in France.

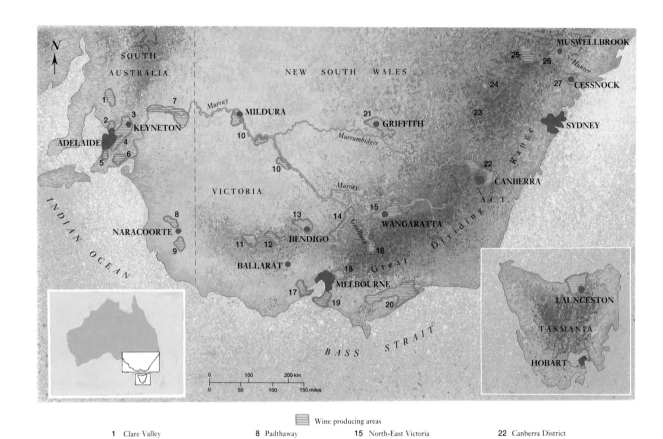

Wine producing areas

1	Clare Valley	8	Padthaway	15	North-East Victoria	22	Canberra District

1 Clare Valley
2 Adelaide Plains
3 Barossa and Eden Valleys
4 Adelaide Hills
5 Southern and McLaren Vales
6 Langhorne Creek
7 Riverland

8   Padthaway
9   Coonawarra
10 Murray River
11 Great Western
12 Pyrenees
13 Central Victoria
14 Goulburn Valley

15 North-East Victoria
16 Mansfield Hills
17 Geelong
18 Yarra Valley
19 Mornington Peninsula
20 Gippsland
21 Murrumbidgee Irrigation Area

22 Canberra District
23 Cowra
24 Orange
25 Mudgee
26 Upper Hunter
27 Lower Hunter

producers of Burgundy, of St-Émilion, or Pomerol could have told us generations ago. The wine shows in Australia provide the leadership in moulding tastes, and in the 1960s and 1970s were of inestimable importance in raising general standards as a posse of Len Evans-inspired judges dominated each state's show. But they must not become too elitist in their views. Fine wine need not be elitist. To produce truly fine wine, at an affordable price, in quantities that allow everyone who so desires to have a taste – now that's a goal worth aiming for. And Australia's far closer than any other country to achieving it.

NEW SOUTH WALES

The warm climate versus cool climate argument comes to its head in New South Wales, because some of the most forceful voices in the industry not only think that the Hunter Valley makes some of Australia's greatest wines, but actually put their money where their mouths are by producing it themselves. Max Lake of Lake's Folly, Len Evans of Rothbury, Murray Tyrrell of Tyrrells, Gerry Sissingh of Hungerford Hill and Lindemans and the boys at Rosemount have all produced some stunners, and in every single case they've done it with warm climate fruit. When Peterson's Hunter Valley Chardonnay won the trophy for Best White Wine at the National Wine Show in 1989, the grizzly old owner Ian Peterson just grinned, looked the serried ranks of trendy cool climate supporters full in the face, and said 'warm climate fruit'. The taste of that wonderful rich buttery Chardonnay made any further argument unnecessary. The cool climate fans can go on until they're blue in the face about the Hunter Valley being too hot to make great wine. Theoretically they're right. In reality they're wrong. But then the Hunter Valley is no more logical a place than its chief personalities are rational thinkers.

Indeed, no-one in their right mind would choose to make great wine in the lower Hunter Valley. Most of the decent soil was washed into the sea long ago by the torrential autumn rains. Patterns of sunshine and rainfall are the almost exact reverse of those associated with good vintage conditions in Bordeaux or Burgundy, and you have to suffer the ultimate vinegrower's torture of working in a climate that really is too hot to ripen grapes at the leisurely pace the traditionalists swear is necessary for the best flavours, yet is victim to the regular onset of autumn storms before these hothouse grapes have reached maturity.

And despite believing that Max Lake is on to something with growing Bordeaux grape Petit Verdot, the Hunter is a heartbreaker for reds – those wretched autumn rains always snatch the chalice of triumph from your lips. No, although it's the warmest of Australia's main wine-making states, I believe New South Wales is white wine country – again, contradicting conventional wine wisdom. Certainly the styles of Semillon being made by Rothbury, low in alcohol, unoaked, yet developing a unique buttery-biscuity richness flecked with lime over 10 to 20 years, are great originals. Rosemount has proved how a superb vineyard like Roxburgh transcends local weather conditions in a most magnificent manner. And way over the mountains in the heat of the interior, Cowra in the Lachlan Valley is producing perfectly balanced Chardonnay fruit of a natural lush softness at low prices and consistently high tonnage. Rothbury and Mountarrow already buy Cowra grapes. Others will follow. And we'll all be assured of a supply of fine drinkable Chardonnay at the right price well into the next millennium.

VICTORIA

Victoria is the southernmost of the mainland states in Australia and, apart from in the hot north-east corner, possesses a wide range of vine growing conditions ranging from the reasonably cool to the positively chilly. In the present hunt for cool climate sites where wines of elegance and delicate restraint, modelled on Europe may be made, Victoria has more possible candidates than any other state. Luckily, Victorian grapes also seem to be particularly adept at giving wines of tremendous intensity and individual perfume of a kind that is not at all European and not even all that similar to other states in Australia. So, in general, attempts to strip out the inherent character of the fruit have been, thank goodness, unsuccessful.

In the nineteenth century, the areas of Great Western, Geelong, Bendigo and the Yarra Valley all produced red wines deemed on a par with those of France, but Victoria is the one Australian state to have been ravaged by phylloxera, and that, added to the general loss of interest in light table wines during the early twentieth century, led to the virtual disappearance of all the old fine table wine areas, apart from small areas of vineyard that survived at Great Western.

The remaining activity centred on the Murray River irrigated vineyards, and the great Tokay and Muscat fortified wine region of North-East Victoria. But the 1960s and 1970s saw the re-awakening of interest in table wine in Australia and with it

the revival of the old original areas, and the birth of a variety of new ones, generally chosen for their ability to outchill each other! Brown Brothers' vineyard in the sky at Whitlands and Seppelt's Drumborg estate in the far south vie with each other for being the state's, and frequently Australia's, latest ripening vineyards. Delatite in Central Victoria isn't much earlier.

But the magnificent strength of the Victorian fruit personality still shines through. The Chardonnay from Nicholson River in the far south is one of the finest and most concentrated in all Australia. The Great Western Shiraz from Seppelt, Mount Langi-Ghiran or Cathcart Ridge is unbelievably intense and stuffed with flavour, and I'm sure it was this pure 'essence' of ripe fruit flavour that was winning trophies in Europe a century ago.

Victorian sparkling wine is Australia's best, with Seppelt leading the way, and the joint venture Domaine Chandon, based in the Yarra Valley, already producing outstanding sparkling wine that rivals almost anything the parent company, Champagne house Moët & Chandon, can do back in France.

WESTERN AUSTRALIA

I have to admit to a slight sense of disappointment with the wines of Western Australia. Yet when I first tasted the Vasse Felix Cabernet Sauvignon in the early 1980s I thought I had discovered an entirely new dimension in fruit intensity and piercing purity of flavour that I'd never come across in Australian wine before. When I first tasted Cullen's Sauvignon Blanc I had never experienced a southern hemisphere Sauvignon of such balance, such mouthwatering green acidity mixed with such beautifully defined fruit. And when I first tasted Moss Wood's Semillons, both wooded and unwooded – well – I remember sitting on a doorstep with a friend one midsummer's night swigging the 1977, and then walking the ten miles home as dawn came up, still heady with the sheer overwhelming pleasure of the wine.

All of these wines come from the Margaret River region about 320km (200 miles) south of Perth. Robert Mondavi of California had been interested in the area, and several other experts had pinpointed the cool, relatively damp region as likely to be good for wine. But it wasn't until Dr Cullity, a Perth doctor, founded Vasse Felix in 1967, and inspired others to follow him down and start wineries, that the region took off.

Wineries like Leeuwin Estate and Cape Mentelle have become internationally famous, and all the small wineries like Moss Wood sell out as soon as the word goes around Perth there's wine to be had. But as I taste each new vintage, I find that the winemakers seem to be trying to make leaner, less hedonistic styles that fail to make the best of the wonderful fruit, and I sneak back for a bottle of one of the early wines – a 1980 Moss Wood Cabernet, a 1982 Cape Mentelle, or even a Moss Wood Semillon 1977.

The majority of Western Australia's wines have traditionally come from the Swan Valley – except for Alice Springs, the hottest place where anyone tries to grow grapes seriously in Australia. Despite some commendable efforts by producers like Evans and Tate, the wines lack spark. Several other small areas, like the cool Great Southern area in the far south, do periodically produce good wines, but Western Australia's influence on Australian wine as a whole, has been less than perhaps it should have been. Western Australia is a very long way from the main markets of the east, in particular Sydney and Melbourne, and the smart wineries like those of Margaret River have perhaps been able to prosper thanks to a proud and loyal local following.

SOUTH AUSTRALIA

It's easy to underestimate the brilliance of much of South Australia's wine. So many of the most important vineyards are so boring to look at. You go to the Riverland, a crucially important supplier of good quality, high-yield, low-cost wine of the juicy fruit sort and you find wines that could turn a Coca-Cola drinker into a wine drinker in seconds, they're so easy to enjoy – but the landscape is just an endless hot, dry, dusty parade of irrigated vines marching over the horizon. You go way down south to Coonawarra or Padthaway to find out why these cool climate vineyards give such superb results, and the first thing that strikes you is that the landscape is just about the least inspiring you've ever seen. Where's the magic?

It's not just those vineyards. South Australia is dominated by big national and multinational companies. In every other country in the world, with the possible exception of New Zealand, this would be a recipe for mediocrity and bland, safe wine-making. Yet in South Australia these companies produce many of the finest wines in the nation – Penfolds' red wines, Lindemans' whites, reds and whites from Wynns, Orlando, Wolf Blass, Lehmann, Yalumba, Hardy – all these companies, large, market-led, nonetheless all produce some spectacular wine.

South Australia has as many high quality independent wine growers as Victoria and more than New South Wales and Western Australia – but I have to keep harping back to the large volume commercial wines, because they bring the revolution in modern wine within reach of every wine drinker, however limited their means. Lindeman's Bin 65 Chardonnay is an astonishingly come-hither, brilliantly fruity white at a low low price, yet as classy as *I* ever need on my dinner table. Yalumba's affordable and refreshing Angas Brut sparkling wines have finally broken down the barrier that made people feel they *had* to buy Champagne because cheap sparkling wine was unreliable and unpleasant. Wolf Blass showed that skilful blending, some properly seasoned American oak barrels, and an unashamed desire to please could produce vast amounts of affordable red wines that would not only sweep a cupboard-full of trophies and medals in competitions, but would be soft enough, creamy enough, fruity enough to appeal to the most timid of red wine débutantes. And it's because of such wines that I have to say that South Australia is the most impressive and, I think, the most exciting wine state in Australia.

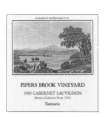

TASMANIA

Tasmania is still in the process of a long slow experiment in high quality wine-producing that began in 1972 when Andrew Pirie selected a site at Pipers Brook in the north of the island as the most suitable area in Australia for producing cool climate European-style wines. In a truly European way, both he, and the neighbouring vineyards, have produced delicious wines when ripening and vintage conditions were good, and decidedly less successful ones when the weather lets them down. I have to say, if I were going to invest *my* money in Tasmania's most exciting table wine area, I'd actually head further south, to the sheltered bays and valleys around Hobart where Moorilla Estate and Stoney Vineyard have been displaying an awesome intensity of flavour in their wines since the 1970s.

Tim Adams

*T*HE OWNER OF THE Aberfeldy vineyard was looking after Tim Adams' daughter the evening I was there. The day before, the owners of the Sheoaks vineyard, Grant and Jacky, had been round for tea. Thirty years ago Jacky's parents would have been dropping by to visit Tim's parents around teatime. And in 30 years' time, what about Tim's children and Jacky's children? 'We talk about our kids buying the grapes from their kids,' says Tim, a flush of unselfconscious emotion momentarily warming his bulldog countenance. Tim Adams is in this wine-making game for the long haul, and I could see he hoped it was more than just buying grapes that would bind the two families together.

Adams makes old-fashioned wines with no regard for what any slick marketing whizz-kid may advise, and he runs his life in a refreshingly old-fashioned way. He is passionately devoted to the community of Clare Valley, in South Australia, where he has lived since childhood. His father was a bank manager, not a grape grower and Tim began his career as cellar hand, then assistant, then winemaker for the large Stanley Leasingham winery. Leasingham were traditionally the largest purchasers of grapes in the valley, and Adams was able to observe from close quarters the delicate balance that exists between grower and winemaker in the Clare.

When he'd had enough of corporate life, on 4 July 1986 as he emphatically states, and was determined to start his own winery, he never for a moment wanted to grow the grapes as well as make the wine. He had seen big companies buy land in the Clare and plant vineyards, then cart all the grapes off to vinify elsewhere, without contributing anything to the life of the valley. 'If every winery in this district goes out and plants its own vines, where does that leave all the vineyard owners who depend on winemakers like us for their income?'

Sense of community responsibility certainly plays its part in Tim's plans. But there are other equally pressing reasons for not planting his own grapes. Money, for a start. He wasn't a member of a rich family who could bankroll his experiments. He and his wife earned the money to buy the few sheds down by the old railway track which now form their home and winery. Five years ago, he says, if he had discovered he was a few dollars overdrawn he'd have been racing down to the bank to apologize. That kind of guy won't sleep at night if he's mortgaged up to the neck. As it is, by 1989 the winery was already in profit, and not having to finance vineyard development is the chief reason he gives for the rapid success of the place.

There are other reasons, too, for the financial security. He and his wife do just about everything themselves, and Tim is a great handyman. The basket press out at the back was built by Tim from oak and steel. The large press which gently coaxed the juice out of all the 1990 reds is 117 years old, made of oak, and on sort-of permanent loan from the nearby Sevenhills monastery, so long as he maintains it. No fears about that.

Although he does now buy a little new oak, at up to A\$700 each, new oak barrels place an impossible financial burden on a young winery. So he buys used barrels, preferably of American oak – for A\$40 each, dismantles them, shaves the staves until fresh wood is revealed, then reassembles them and re-toasts each barrel over a brazier of oak shavings, until they shine like pewter and reek of vanilla and spice. Pretty well as good as new and he obviously revels in the task, as well as saving himself hundreds of dollars a barrel.

Most winemakers *do* have a passion for owning land, but Adams has just one single acre of vines in front of the winery. It's planted with Semillon, though he freely admits it's feeble vineyard land and would do better as a picnic area. Again, he uses the special characteristics of the Clare Valley to explain this lack of land lust. If he had vineyards of his own, logistically he'd need them to be in one spot, probably right by the winery. Yet within very few kilometres he can find enormous differences in ripening conditions.

Grace and Flavour

In 1990 the Riesling from the Sheoaks vineyard – 13km (8 miles) south of the town of Clare – was picked in early March. Only 7km (4 miles) closer to Clare, in a gully in the bottom of the wooded Skillogalee Valley, the chilly Waninga vineyard had barely brought its Riesling to ripeness six weeks later in April. Adams began harvesting the Sheoaks Semillon on 22 February. The last Semillon, grown north of Clare, was picked on 22 April. Thirteen kilometres (eight miles), two months' difference in ripening dates, giving him the flexibility of tremendous flavour differences within the same varieties; and the long drawn-out vintage means he can give every batch individual attention.

And those vineyards. The Aberfeldy vineyard is only a little way north of the Tim Adams winery and was planted in 1904. There's no way Tim could develop in his lifetime a vineyard capable of delivering the remarkable flavours the Aberfeldy vines give. At the Sheoaks vineyard he is actively involved in re-trellising and mechanizing the operation, meanwhile making the most of mature vines, which yield wine of remarkable complexity. Adams' close friendship with both vineyard owners, and his role as a consultant to the Waninga operation, mean he is in complete control of all sources of fruit for his vines — so why have the hassle of owning the land as well?

The one area in which Adams is not old-fashioned is in his handling of the vines themselves. He may want his kids to be making wine from the same old vines in 30 years time, but he does not want the vineyard they come from to be a viticultural museum, and he wants Grant, the owner of Sheoaks, to make enough money to stay in business. Since Grant is what he calls a 'machine' person, he's converted the Sheoaks vineyard to both mechanical pruning and mechanical harvesting. He gets dozens of tiny bunches of tiny grapes all over the outside of the vine, rather than lovely plump bunches weighing down the bough as they ripen in the sun. But the yield has doubled, and the tiny grapes actually mean darker, more highly-flavoured juice — perfect for his supremely old-fashioned wines.

Tim Adams is blunt and outspoken. So are his wines. He doesn't make a Chardonnay — he doesn't like the variety and he says he is totally disinclined to work with any grape variety that doesn't turn him on. He is playing with Cabernet Sauvignon, but although his 1990 Cabernet-Malbec is so concentrated it stains the glass, he's not sure it's quite heroic enough to release! So he sticks with what the Clare does best and he loves most — Riesling, Semillon and Shiraz.

Both the whites are remarkable for their fullness of flavour. The Riesling has a wonderful aromatic fruit of ripe Cox's apples and apple blossom all mixed up. The acidity is like a darting streak of lime, and a little maturity brings a lovely biscuit and honey richness. Yet the wine is totally dry. The blend of cooler and warmer vineyard fruit gives it the complexity of snappy acidity and mouthfilling ripeness. It sees no wood at all.

The Semillons are even better. They're based on Sheoaks fruit, grown without irrigation on a red loam soil over limestone, and ripened until the sugar levels will give a wine of between 12.5 and 13 degrees. Adams ferments an increasing amount in barrel each year, and leaves the wine on its lees for five months after fermentation, stirring it half a dozen times in the first three months. The 1988 has developed a wonderfully smooth butterscotch and kid glove leather fatness, freshened up with a twist of lime peel. The 1989 is a mixture of barrel- and tank-matured wine, and the rapier thrust of green lime acidity is already allowing itself to be coiled with the toast and honey of those

 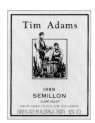

hand-shaved oak barrels. The 1990 has a wonderful richness of apricot and greengage and the musky perfume of paper-thin leather is stabbed with lime. Tim added a portion of wine he was putting through its malolactic, and the Semillon flavour was cloaked in cream until the acidity fought its way through, like the salty lime in a Margherita.

The Shiraz wines are blends of Aberfeldy and Sheoaks fruit, picked ripe to very ripe. The yields from both vineyards are low, averaging about three tons to the acre from unirrigated vines, and the flavours are a triumphant parade designed to strengthen the grape's claim to being Australia's finest variety. They are densely coloured, massively structured, and totally free of unpleasant hard edges. The quality of the vineyards is one explanation, the gentleness of the old basket press is another. He doesn't take his fermentation above 23° to 24°C (73° to 75°F) because he feels a hotter temperature might extract some bitterness. And he swears by fining the wine, one and a half to two eggs per barrel, with eggs from his own chickens. He calls egg white God's gift to winemakers, which is perhaps going a bit far. A much greater gift to Tim Adams, at least, is the availability of Aberfeldy and Sheoaks fruit.

Though he made a 1986 Shiraz that never quite settled down, and a delicious deep, dry peppery '87, it is the '88 vintage which really shows what he can do. A blend of both vineyards produces a muscular but intensely fruity red, all brambles and cherries, black plums and gooey fruitcake. The unblended Aberfeldy is shocking — all coffee grains and eucalyptus and corned beef at first, but as the wine warms, all these fade before a positive onslaught of blackcurrant and plums.

Then comes the 1989. A year ago Tim says it was so pallid he'd have sold the lot in bulk if anyone had offered him ready money. Now the wine obsesses and entrances him. The swooning fragrance of violets, brambles squashed into a boiling cauldron, handfuls of sweet fresh raspberries hurled in too, swirled about, then poured into a mould of melted chocolate, black coffee, liquorice and cream. Every time you lift the glass the flavours have changed, teasing you with improbable and brilliant combinations. If only I'd popped by with a fistful of dollars in the vintage time of 1989.

Bailey's

I BEGAN TO REALIZE what an unlikely standard bearer Steve Goodwin was in the fight for the survival of one of Australia's most tradition-soaked wine treasures when I mentioned filtration. Without thinking I started into a gloomy tirade against the winemakers who sterile-filter all their wines, in my view to the palpable detriment of their perfume, consistency and flavour. 'Prove it', said Steve, very much on the offensive. He refused to accept that there was any difference until someone had set up a totally scientific double blind experiment of identical wines both unfiltered and then filtered at all intensities right down to sterile. He held up his finger and thumb. 'If this is the size of a molecule of aroma, do you know how big the mesh in a sterile filter is by comparison?' The size of the city of Melbourne, it seems. Not for the first time I retreated blinded by the wonders of modern science.

I got another shock when I went to visit the Bailey's Vineyards at Bundarra on the western side of the Warby range of hills, three miles from Ned Kelly's hangout at Glenrowan. The first thing I was shown was the powerful pump which propels the water through all the irrigation lines on to the vines. I'd just come from Rutherglen, 50km (30 miles) to the north, the other centre for Australia's liqueur Muscats and Tokays, where filter machines are a dirty word and irrigation lines in the Muscat vineyards rarely seen and even more rarely talked about, and I expected Bailey's, which can produce wines of even greater depth and concentration than those of Rutherglen, to be a paragon of traditional practices and dry-farmed vines.

Until 1987 that's precisely what it was. And in a harsh modern world, that's what was killing the company. Steve Goodwin hasn't got any background in the old time-honoured ways of the industry and few preconceptions either; and Lindsay Corby, the vineyard expert, is as radical as anyone in the grape-growing world – and that's just what Bailey's needed.

Bailey's had been founded in the 1850s by an English family from Manchester, and by 1972 successive generations had built a strong reputation for fortified wines. The company was then bought by a conglomerate called Davis Consolidated Industries. This was the period when big business was buying up half of Australia's wine companies, often without any knowledge of the wine industry at all. But Davis struck lucky. The man they'd commissioned to find them a winery to buy was one of their corporate planners, a man called Harry Tinson. When he recommended the purchase of Bailey's, Davis bought it, and Tinson was told to go and run it until they could find a permanent winemaker. They never did, and over the next 15 years Tinson produced a series of spectacular liqueur Muscats and Tokays – as well as some pretty fearsome dry reds and some excellent vintage 'ports' – which won Bailey's huge acclaim, but never made Davis Consolidated a penny. In the 1970s they could afford to indulge Bailey's as a prestige hobby. By the late 1980s it was becoming an expensive luxury. Stocks of mature blending wine – the lifeblood of any fortified wine company – were under pressure, for the vineyard, now between 60 and 80 years old, was yielding less and less, yet there was no investment in a replanting programme. The wonderful wines sold for absurdly little, largely because, as with the great Rutherglen Muscats, the general public had decided that sweet and sticky meant cheap. There was a light white wine revolution going on in the 1970s: heavy and brown was the exact opposite of the fashion, however good the quality.

Scientist or Dreamer?

Steve Goodwin, also from Manchester as it happens, like the original Bailey family, is on the surface very much the technocrat, and his style of speech, still sprinkled with the odd bit of Manchester slang, is more that of a teacher than a hedonist. Yet the hedonist is there. His eyes blaze and his speech quickens as we talk about the great reds of Burgundy and Rhône, and the passion finally overcomes his long training as a biochemist and distillery manager for International Distillers and Vintners in Melbourne, when he talks about Australia's most treasured wines – her Muscats and Tokays. He believes that his technical know-how, his background as a national wine judge (he was just off to judge the Hobart Show in Tasmania when I last met him) and his experience of the financial realities of running a cut-throat business like a distillery is fundamental to his ability to turn Bailey's into a profitable venture without sacrificing quality. He fumes at the fact that a one-year-old Cabernet Sauvignon or Chardonnay can sell for A$20 a bottle, while he's struggling to get A$13 for his Founder label Muscat – 'hand-crafted, a style unique to this country, and a good dose of 20-year-old wine in there. People think nothing of paying twenty-five dollars for a main dish and a bowl of soup at a smart restaurant. They should pay that for my Muscat.'

This aggressive approach is already paying off. In Goodwin's first three years in charge, Bailey's made its

Steve Goodwin, the quietly determined down-to-earth career scientist, entrusted with the wine-making at Bailey's.

first three profits since Davis bought it. His Muscats and Tokays are winning trophies or gold medals at every show they enter. Can he keep it up? He reckons that with the help of Lindsay Corby and Colin Slater, his assistant winemaker, he can do just that.

The unique personality of the Bailey's wines starts with the particular soil conditions and microclimate of this small patch of land, which runs down to the spooky drowned forest of the artificially created Lake Mokoan. As happens so often with vineyard soil in Australia, it's the colour red that makes all the difference. There's a band of red granitic soil running diagonally across the Bailey's land in the lee of the Warby Range, and it's like a mix of sand with pummelled, pulverized granite. No one knows how deep it goes, though it's at least 10 metres (30 feet) in parts. It's very friable, yet does have just enough water retention to allow a massive root structure to develop for the vines.

The ability of soil to retain water is absolutely crucial in a warm climate, but Steve Goodwin refuses to accept that the soil itself actually gives any flavour to the wine. In direct contrast with the French theory that a particular soil gives a particular flavour to wines, he says there's no evidence whatsoever for their claims. I can feel the scientist getting the better of the hedonist again. Many writers *have* singled out this Warby Range soil as having unique flavour qualities. No, says Steve. Water holding capacity, yes; heat retention capacity, yes.

Otherwise flavour comes from the variety you choose to grow, the irrigation regime and the trellising and pruning methods you employ. Control is Steve Goodwin's watchword. 'I could grow any grape here,' he says. 'You have to channel the grapes to do the things you want them to do.'

However, on the oldest Muscat and Tokay vines, your options are limited. 'Tender Loving Care' is Lindsay's objective here. Lots of phosphate and manure on the roots, regular watering, none of this trendy vine stress and starvation stuff. He believes you must create a strong vine by cossetting it, not by stressing it as the French would prefer. He admits that may lead to a slightly over-vigorous vine with more foliage than you want, but at least you've got the vigour to play with. A weak vine at the start will be a weak vine at the end.

And a vine needs to be strong to support a good crop of fruit hanging long into the autumn as the sugar concentrates in the grapes. Interestingly, the Glenrowan microclimate is cooler than New South Wales' Hunter Valley, though I had thought it must be one of the most torrid parts of Australia. It's the length of the season which makes all the difference. The weather usually breaks in the Hunter Valley in February, and their white table wines often only manage 10 to 11 degrees of sugar. In Glenrowan, the break in the season doesn't come until May, by which time the grapes will have built up twice the sugar levels – 20 to 22 degrees – as they droop and shrivel on the vine.

But to get any crop at all, you must irrigate. At the moment Bailey's old blocks of vines give from two to two and a half tons to the acre, but Lindsay reckons that with more efficient irrigation and better pruning this could be increased to three and a half and then to five tons without detriment to the wine flavour. He's starting to prune differently – leaving more buds on the vine, but also trimming back the foliage so that the wood is directly exposed to sunlight, which means more fruit and less foliage. But it's a major philosophical shift from traditional pruning practice, which was always to 'prune for a drought'. In other words – don't leave too many buds, don't make them work hard, and they may just survive the year.

Simple survival is not enough for Lindsay or Steve. Making a good living means combining a good crop and high quality. For a vineyard of the size of Bailey's – 40 hectares (100 acres) with 32 (79) of those the original plantings – that calls for 260 million litres (57 million gallons) of water a year in irrigation – a staggering amount. Lindsay would actually welcome more – but in a dry continent like Australia, water is at a premium and Bailey's can only obtain a licence for that amount; 'a mixture of natural and government-induced stress' Lindsay calls it. Up until the time the grapes change colour, he'll use water from the lake and the Broken River. And each hectare can receive up to 10,000 litres a day – that's five litres of water for every vine – on top of the natural rainfall they usually get every winter!

But will the quality hold up as the yields increase? I suspect it will, because any risks will be taken with new plantations of vines for table wine and vintage 'port', rather than Muscat or Muscadelle, the grape used for Tokay. One of Steve's nightmares is to replant whole blocks of old vines and then discover that they contained some magic flavour ingredient which would then be lost for ever. And, despite the fact that Steve is a devotee of filtration, the wine-making and blending methods are kept as traditional as is feasible.

Typically they'll hedge their bets at harvest, hand-picking the Muscat and Tokay grapes in several stages – bringing in the grapes at varying stages of ripeness, until by the end of April some final blocks register 22 degrees or more. This staggered picking routine is important because the early-picked grapes will give fresh perfume and fruitiness to the wine. The last pickings will have a deep raisined caramelly richness. For a successful liqueur Tokay or Muscat, you've got to have both.

Steve will chill the fruit before roughly crushing it and letting it steep in its own juice. Usually he'll add yeast on day two, but the period of maceration may well be several days. When the yeast does begin the fermentation, he only allows it to use up about one degree of sugar, but this brief fermentation period adds immensely to the final complexity of the wine. The active yeast releases all kinds of complex organisms into the juice. When you fortify this juice by adding alcohol, the yeasts die and break up, releasing different flavours into the wine.

The fortification is done with neutral spirit, which is usually added to the juice and skins together, but sometimes just to run-off juice. You get much more intense flavours by fortifying on the skins, since the alcohol leaches out lots of flavour – but you risk astringency, which if unchecked would wreck a good Muscat. After two or three days Steve reckons the risk is unacceptable and runs the juice off its skins. In fact he puts aside all the skinsy gunge to settle in a separate tank and after about five months draws off a few hundred gallons of wine which he says is 'absolutely bloody stunning', and this is carefully stored away to provide a touch of brilliance to Bailey's top blends.

The wines are settled over the next few months, and by six months they're all in wood. The Tokays are often left initially in half-full tanks to oxidize and develop their rich caramelly character and golden brown colour as quickly as possible. The Muscat is always put into big old wood casks of between 300 and 1000 gallons, and the Tokay into smaller, 60-gallon casks. The best wines go on to a kind of mezzanine floor in the old tin shed cellar. It's at least 25°C (77°F) up there most of the time and the wines really start to cook, which makes them mature quickly as well as developing an intense dark rich fruitiness which marks out Bailey's from all the other 'stickies'.

It also helps to explain why Bailey's main wine, the Founder label Muscat, can be released with an average age of only five to eight years old, yet have such a thrilling mixture of rose petal scent, orange peel and caramel stickiness, raisin richness and another perfume, more of cigars and tea-leaves. The Founder label Tokay is also quite superb, the molasses and raisins, dry figs and dates richness balanced by an unnerving but fascinating aroma like burnt toast, fresh leather, tea-leaves and the oil from a sardine tin! They say anyone can love a Muscat, but it takes time to embrace Tokay's more wayward charms. I see what they mean!

Founder's Day

At the moment about 60 per cent of Bailey's is sold as the Founder series, with Gold Label and the rare Show blend making up a fair proportion of the rest. Steve also introduced a cheaper line – Warby Range – based on two and three-year-old wine which he'd like to see become the most popular Bailey's wines, providing the protective cash flow. The Warby Range Tokay and Muscat are perfectly pleasant, but hardly hint at the greatness of Bailey's wines at their finest. But if their introduction subsidizes the very existence of the great Bailey's 'stickies', we'll just have to grin and bear it. We'll have to pay, though. Steve's objective is to push all the other Bailey's wines further and further upmarket, and I suspect he's chosen exactly the right time to do it. But I hope not too many other producers heard his parting remark – 'I'm a great believer in pushing prices higher and higher, and it hasn't had any effect on sales yet.' He must have been taking marketing lessons from Bordeaux's Classed Growth owners.

These vineyards will produce the intensely rich fruit that goes to make Bailey's great fortified wines.

Berri Renmano

*T*HEY HOLD A SERIES of impressive agricultural shows each year in Australia. Thousands of wines are entered for them and judged by expert and critical panels. A very few entrants gain a gold medal, and only one entrant in each major class will gain the trophy for 'best wine entered'. At the New South Wales Agricultural Show in Sydney, the last in the season, all trophy-winning wines are entered for a 'Trophy of Trophies' – the 'Australian Show Wine of the Year'. In 1989 it was won by Renmano Chairman's Selection Chardonnay 1988 – a wine which broke just about every rule pertaining to the pursuit of excellence.

The best Chardonnays are supposed to come from cool climate regions, ideally, those with conditions resembling the unpredictable rain and sunshine patterns found in Burgundy's Côte d'Or. Renmano's grapes were grown in a climate so torrid that if you strayed from the main road into the bleak scrubland, I wouldn't take odds on your chances of surviving more than a day in the blistering heat.

And top Chardonnays are supposed to come from particular soil types, with limestone sloping towards the morning sun seeming to be the favourite – soil which retains some moisture while draining away most of the rain. The south-east-facing limestone slopes of Meursault or Puligny-Montrachet in Burgundy are thought of as ideal. Well, there certainly is the odd bit of limestone somewhere beneath the flat river silt and crumbly sand that form the soil of Renmano's vineyards – but none of the growers have researched its precise location yet and, anyway, what's all this about drainage? It doesn't rain for months on end at Renmano.

Well, yields should be kept low: perhaps three tons to the acre, four would be just permissible. How about ten? That's the average Chardonnay yield at Renmano. The people who grow Chardonnay for Renmano are not the kind you can easily persuade to limit their yields without pretty major financial inducements – they'd say 'why should we?'. Anyway, no one's complained about the wine – and when the wines are scooping top trophies it's difficult to argue.

These people don't sound like typical prize-winning producers – the passionate, committed winegrowers whose sacrifice and devotion lovingly draws forth magic flavours from their few precious ancestral acres. No, they're not. A haphazard selection from more than 500 fruit farmers had the business sense to realize they'd make more money growing Chardonnay grapes than avocadoes or peaches. Simple as that.

Oh dear, where's the romance, where's the idealism, the joy of achievement? Funnily enough, it's there despite the conditions. It's so hot and dry you should never really be able to grow anything up here in the outback. As it is, one-third of Australia's wine comes from these acres known as the Riverland, which ripple away on both sides of the Murray River in the heart of South Australia's wilderness. Even to visualize transforming desert into an agricultural paradise – that takes idealism. And the wine snobs who say good wine can only come from small boutique wineries could do with a bit of re-education. Because this award-winning wine producer is a 60 million-litre (13 million-gallon) capacity co-operative, formed to provide a lifeline for struggling dried fruit producers early in the century. Producing world-beating wines never crossed anyone's mind at the start.

The secret of the Riverland's success is control of water supply. The Murray River and its tributaries amble for thousands of kilometres across the parched, merciless heart of southern Australia. Yet it wasn't until 1887 that two irrigation experts from California – the Chaffey brothers – arrived to show Australia how to exploit its greatest water resource – by using Murray River water to irrigate tens of thousands of acres of otherwise worthless land along the riverbanks. Their initiative was to transform Australia's horticultural economy, but it was only after a disastrous drought in 1914 had reduced even the mighty Murray to a trickle, that the modern shape of the Riverland took place. A system of locks, dams and lakes was created to ensure that whatever the conditions, water would still flow, to be pumped into the vineyards that lined the banks of the Murray.

However, there was no thought in the early twentieth century of trying to produce great table wines in the zone. The grape varieties planted were used for drying and packing as sultanas and raisins. As enormous surpluses started to build up during World War One, growers needed to find other ways of using the fruit. Renmano was established as a co-operative distillery in 1916, with Berri following suit in 1918. For the next

You'd never expect Australians to hide their light under a bushel, and the vast Berri Estates co-operative in South Australia's Riverland obviously wouldn't dream of doing so.

half century they and the other irrigated area producers supplied the bulk needs of Australia – spirits, fortified wines, cheap table wines – without much thought for quality.

In 1982, with the Australian thirst for fortified wines and brandies withering, Berri and Renmano amalgamated and set their sights on establishing themselves in the quality wine market. By 1990 the group, along with the old Angle Vale Co-op near Adelaide, were ready to go private and develop as one of Australia's biggest wine companies: producing 12 per cent of Australia's wine, able to raise capital for investment and buy other companies and brands in open competition. It's a remarkable transformation for a co-op formed to find a use for currants and raisins.

All the same, for the Riverland to produce top quality table wine a major commitment of money and effort has been required from both management and winemakers, because large numbers of the original co-operative members were unwilling or unable to take the harsh decisions concerning replacing of poor grape varieties with good. Many also felt that a price structure based on quality would constitute unjust discrimination. The prices for Chardonnay in the late 1980s should have convinced the waverers. While their bulk varieties were fetching perhaps A$180 a ton – if they could sell them, Chardonnay in 1986 fetched A$440 a ton, in 1987, A$750 a ton; 1988 and 1989 brought A$1550 a ton and even 1990 was still bringing in A$880 a ton.

This allows Berri Renmano tremendous flexibility in providing today's most in-demand wine: Chardonnay, either light and fresh – and cheap, or Chardonnay full and sensuous, barrel-fermented, aged in new oak – and a range of price and quality points in between. But it takes money and organization. And persuasion. The winemakers like to let the Chardonnay grapes hang until they're golden and brimming with sugar. The growers prefer the grapes picked and their bills paid just as soon as the fruit touches minimum ripeness.

Heat will bring the fruit to super-ripeness – so long as the vines have sufficient water, but you need fresh acidity in the grapes too – otherwise the wines will just taste flabby. In the desert conditions of the Riverland it is the chilly nights that give medal-winning quality – the acid levels couldn't hold if the nights were warm. Also, a winery doesn't want hot grapes arriving at its door, because fermentation temperatures will be almost impossible to control and all the freshness of the fruit will be lost. So picking takes place with machines in the cool of the night – and millions of dollars are now being invested in a full-scale cooling system for all the tanks.

If this makes it look as though Berri Renmano are solely concerned with Chardonnay – of course that's not so. Chardonnay is only a small part of their production, and they make the full range of other white varieties as well as reds – their Cabernets frequently win top medals at shows. But it is the wave of easily affordable, wonderfully ripe-flavoured Chardonnays that has propelled Australia into the consciousness of the world's export markets, and almost all of these will have come from irrigated vineyards along the banks of the Murray or one of its tributaries. The name on the label may be Orlando or Penfolds or Lindemans, but the wine will be made from outback irrigated fruit. Many big companies pretend their fruit doesn't come from the Riverland. Berri Renmano proudly insist that theirs does.

Brown Brothers

*W*ELL, IT'S AS NOVEL a reason as any for deciding that a patch of dirt is just waiting for you to transform it into one of the greatest vineyards in the world. The quality of the potatoes. Every year, great big crops of plump, perfumed potatoes that stayed wonderfully firm when you boiled them, only needing a dash of butter and a sprig of mint – aaah! Pure ambrosia for a nice Irish boy like me. But would I then have made the mental leap saying the soil that grew these potatoes might be able to grow great Chardonnay, great Pinot Noir, Riesling, Gewürztraminer, you name it?

John Brown made that mental leap. He'd been making the wine and generally running things in his mild-mannered but iron-fisted way at Brown Brothers since 1934. And ever since then he'd been snooping around the state of Victoria, looking for land to plant with vines. His sons reckon he knows just about every

paddock in the northern part of the state. Brown was well placed to explore – the family company is based at Milawa in the north Victorian hinterland. The area is flat and hot, starved of rain but luckily fairly well supplied with subterranean water, so grapes grow well, but they grow fast and by the end of summer are bursting with sweet, juicy ripeness. The flavours can be unsubtle to say the least. But just to the south lie the Victorian Alps whose presence does seem to temper the fierce Milawa heat somewhat, and now and then does a lot more than that. In November 1967, the Brown Brothers Milawa vineyard was wiped out by a frost born in the lee of the Alps. John Brown credits the pioneering spirit that has marked out Brown Brothers ever since to the shock of staring ruin in the face.

They'd been ahead of the game in terms of work on getting the best out of individual grape varieties during the 1950s – in 1954 they began to develop a range of single varietal wines, when the rest of Australia was still sticking to generic descriptive names like 'burgundy', 'chablis', 'claret' and 'graves' – names which were supposed to indicate a wine style, but which in practice

could mean any kind of grape variety or blend. As John Brown said, it seemed a bit silly to enter a wine at the Melbourne Show for the 'claret' and the 'burgundy' class and see it win both. The frost crisis of 1967 provided the necessary spur to getting out of this rut.

There had been an embargo on imported vines in Australia since the early part of the century in an attempt to stop the spread of the vine louse phylloxera. This embargo was only lifted in 1965, and John Brown ordered a large consignment from Europe of whatever was available. In 1968, he bought a warm climate property called Mystic Park, on a bend of the Murray river in North-East Victoria – primarily as a buffer against any further frost devastation at Milawa. As the new European vines came out of quarantine, Brown planted them at Mystic Park, where they all grew like crazy – except for Chasselas which no one felt was any great loss. But it gradually became clear that in trying to avoid frost, he'd gone too far in the other direction – Mystic Park was far too hot for anything delicate.

Mindful of the tremendous surge of interest in light red table wines, John Brown embarked on an expansion programme southwards in the early 1970s, into the valleys of the Victorian Alps, then on to the slopes, looking for cooler and cooler vineyards, until, in 1982, stopping by for another bag of potatoes on the flat plateau of the Whitfield tableland 800 metres (2500 feet) up above the King Valley, he finally let his hunch about the potato crop sway his judgement. He bought the farm, lock, stock and barrel, and set out to transform it into the world's 'greatest vineyard'.

Brown Brothers will need another generation or two's experience to know exactly how it stacks up against the world's greats, but there's no doubt that Whitlands, as John Brown re-named it, has rapidly become one of Australia's most fascinating vineyard projects. With the current fashion for laying all the responsibility for wine quality on good vineyard management, Whitlands is textbook stuff.

Before any moves were made to transform the land, the Browns hired Jim Hardie, one of Australia's leading vine scientists, to run the whole project. He took one look at the wet, cool conditions at Whitlands and was on the next plane to Europe – somewhere they knew all about wet and cool conditions and still managed to make great wine. Not everyone was forthcoming with information, but Hardie kept his eyes peeled. In fact he reckoned some growers didn't really know why they

Brown Brothers have recently opened what they call a 'kindergarten' winery, where they can make numerous small experimental batches of wine.

were doing many of the traditional things, but several points seemed very plain to him. In a damp, cool climate your control of water was fundamental, so a high density planting pattern was necessary to provide more competition between vines for the moisture. Vertical training and running your rows towards the sun would maximize exposure to light and warmth. And to get a crop of well-flavoured, ripe grapes you had to match your yield to the climatic restraints.

Testing, Testing

Back in Australia Jim did two things. He uprooted a hundred of those Mystic Park vines from the 1968 consignment and successfully transplanted them to Whitlands. There were 15 varieties in all and it taught him that anything which ripens after Cabernet Sauvignon won't ripen at Whitlands, anything that ripens earlier will.

Then he mapped out an entire 32-hectare (80-acre) block on paper, every last detail – and began planting. (Browns have now bought the neighbouring property too, which gives them a potential vineyard area of 140 hectares (350 acres) altogether. The dark volcanic soil was amazingly homogeneous – and seemed to be at least 12 metres (40 feet) deep. Remembering those potatoes, it looked as though the chief problem was going to be developing an irrigation and pruning system that would restrain the vines' vigour.

When none of the vines had grown at the end of the first year, they discovered a quite different vigour restraint – acidity. Maybe potatoes like acid soil. Grape vines don't, their roots simply refuse to develop. They had to add tons of lime just to neutralize the acidity! The lime only penetrated to a depth of about one metre (three feet), but Jim Hardie says he is now grateful that they didn't add more. The roots stay closer to the surface and allow him to control their vigour.

But it's still a struggle, and the secret, Hardie reckons, is never to let the vines get into a vigorous cycle in the first place. This deep soil is remarkably friable and free-draining – so much so that a lot of the nutrient has been leached away over the years. And although the rainfall at Whitlands is high for Australia – about 1525mm (60in) a year – in the crucial January to February period when the grapes are in their most important growth phase, there is rarely a drop of rain. Such drought stress could reduce crops to totally uneconomic levels. So Hardie has installed a drip irrigation system along every row so that he can decide when to stress and when to pamper the vines.

The traditional planting density in Australia is under 600 vines per acre. Jim had noticed in Europe that the wetter and cooler the conditions, the denser the plantings. So he planted almost 2385 vines per acre so that in the wet spring or autumn periods when water uptake can't be controlled, there would be enough competition to restrict vine growth. The crop per vine would also be much less, although the crop per acre wouldn't, and it was too much crop per *vine*, not per acre, which hindered the ripening of the grapes.

Finally, the crop levels are shockingly high – as high as ten tons to the acre with some varieties, but Hardie is quite unashamed. The quality of the fruit is what matters. Is the flavour there at those levels or not? Well, yes it is, it certainly is. The intensity of fruit character is quite unlike anything Brown Brothers have managed before, and Hardie glows with pleasure when you say that. His objective is to maximize his crops without diluting flavour, and, like Garry Crittenden further south at Mornington Peninsula, he seems to be able to break the old rules concerning yield and quality.

Hardie takes you past his vertically-trained rows of vines inclined towards the midday sun, and shows you his minimally pruned vines. There are loads of tiny bunches of grapes all over the outside of the bush – and it is a bush, a jungle bush. These will yield ten tons to the acre, maybe more, but because the grapes are small and the bunches numerous but small, the skin to juice ratio will be extremely good and the sugar will be brought to its peak nicely by being well-exposed to the late summer sunshine. Early winter almost. April is the usual harvest time in Victoria. He may have to wait until June to pick his Cabernet Sauvignon.

So far the Brown Brothers Whitlands releases have been white wines – a straightforward but sharply defined Riesling, a very stylish barrel-fermented Chardonnay with high acidity but the capacity to age well, and a quite delightful rose petals-fragrant Gewürztraminer. But it's the Whitlands reds that are going to be the most exciting, from the results so far. When Cabernet Franc and Merlot ripen they can give an impressively deep wine, green-edged, but packed with the fruit of blackcurrant and the gumminess of eucalyptus leaves. And the Whitlands Pinot Noir, dark, almost Cabernet-dark, is thrilling stuff, again tinged with eucalyptus, and crunched together with the chewy richness of black cherries, damsons and plums.

The Whitlands vineyards are giving the fruit quality alright. Brown Brothers' winemakers now need to rise to the challenge and make the most of its potential.

Those mysterious blue mountains folding into the distance, the green of trees and vine leaves – Brown Brothers Whitlands vineyard, up in the Great Dividing Range.

Coldstream Hills

*J*AMES HALLIDAY SAYS he tends to go like the clappers, then he has to crash. 'I can survive without food, I can survive, thank God, without alcohol, but I cannot survive without sleep. It is a constant aggravation to me the time I lose in sleeping.' I can imagine! James Halliday fizzes with energy. He walks faster than anyone I know, talks faster, laughs faster, thinks faster – and despite all that stuff about needing sleep, I reckon he sleeps faster too. All very impressive. But there's one more thing. He learns faster. He soaks up knowledge like dry toast in a bowl of French onion soup. Given the speed at which he tries to perfect everything he lays his hands on, he can't waste time forgetting things or misunderstanding them.

He's . . . well, what is he? And what *has* he been? A highly successful international corporate lawyer. Australia's most informed and influential wine writer. Wine consultant to airlines and department stores. Wine judge at all the major national shows. Director of Domaine Chandon, the new Australian sparkling wine operation. Founder of Brokenwood Winery in the Hunter Valley. Founder, winemaker, managing director and majority shareholder of Coldstream Hills Winery in the Yarra Valley. And husband of Suzanne Halliday. Important point this. There's probably only one woman in Australia with enough energy and forbearance to cope with James. Between them, they urge each other forward yet just about keep each other sane.

I first met him in Melbourne in 1985. Despite a come-hither name, our meeting place turned out to be a respectable eating house, inhabited by various worthies – and one prowling, badger-busy giant, bursting with an aggressive warmth that took me a while to get used to. He was clutching bottles suitable for the classiest of dancing slippers, despite the fact that it was not going to be *that* sort of evening. Sparkling red Shiraz. A concept that had never entered my head, but James seemed to be using my reaction as a litmus test of whether or not we'd get on. Rich ripe red wine, packed with as much flavour as a fine northern Rhône Syrah – but fizzy. It was so irreverent, and I fell for it.

I fell for it in a big way. The stream of Halliday opinions and ideas and his huge involvement in and enjoyment of all sides of the wine world drew me like a moth to a flame. But how did he get involved in all this wine business in the first place? He was a young Sydney lawyer at the time of Australia's first mining boom and

he'd been flung in at the deep end, dealing with dodgy prospectuses, flotations, takeovers, anything and everything as the nation wrestled to control the explosion of fantasy and ambition, avarice and the lure of gold that mining provoked. It was a scary, exhilarating time to be a lawyer.

All the same, a man could go seriously mad without a spot of recreation. Typically, Halliday needed an interest with a compulsive edge. He was already interested in wine – especially French wine – and word that Max Lake had established the Lake's Folly vineyard in the nearby Hunter Valley was getting around. If a surgeon could do it, why not a lawyer? Halliday got together with a couple of friends, Tony Albert and John Beeston, and headed for the Hunter. After a lot of humming and hah-ing, they settled on a four-hectare (ten-acre) site just down the road from Len Evans' Rothbury Estate, bought it in 1970 and began planting vines.

Heavenly Pursuits

Halliday revelled in the sheer physical exertion of planting, pruning, cultivating and harvesting a vineyard. 'I would come back from my weekends slaving in the Hunter Valley feeling I'd had a celestial shower.' It's just as well the exercise made him feel good, because Brokenwood was pure slog right from the start. The vines were planted in the heavy pug clay soils of the Hunter, and the first five vintages combined produced fewer than 450 cases of wine! But the wine was exceptional. In 1990 the 1973 was still deep red in colour, rich and smoky thick, with sweet, tarry fruit.

The Brokenwood winery – alias the tractor shed – wasn't finished in time for their first vintage in 1973, so the three lads took their little one-ton fermenter, their trio of barrels and their crusher along to Rothbury and asked if they could borrow some space. Rothbury was discovering how meagre the Hunter yields were at the same time as Brokenwood. They had plenty of space, so Brokenwood set up in a corner.

Gerry Sissingh was Rothbury's winemaker then. He is probably the finest Hunter winemaker of the last 20 years and he created Rothbury's early reputation. Halliday will admit that Sissingh probably did the same for Brokenwood. Of course, with just three barrels, three men with good palates can give their new babies pretty well undivided attention, but the one thing Sissingh drummed into their heads was hygiene, hygiene, hygiene. Always protect your wine, even to the extent of running it into barrel before it has finished fermenting so that the carbon dioxide that still saturates the wine can protect it from oxidation and infection.

James Halliday has set out to make wine rivalling the world's finest, storing all his role models in his cellar.

The Hunter Valley was notorious for producing wines with a sweaty stink to them. Sissingh believed this was simply the development of hydrogen sulphide through poor wine-making. During the 1970s and early 1980s, Rothbury and Brokenwood produced vintage after vintage of clean, deep-flavoured wine. The old-timers huffed and puffed, but the Hunter was made to stare its own potential in the face rather than sit back in sulphidic sulks and let the world pass it by.

Halliday came face to face with *his* destiny when, during whatever annual holiday he had left after harvesting at Brokenwood, he set off to chronicle all the vineyards of Australia. Pleasant enough vacation chore. One memorable day he covered 600km (375 miles) and visited seven different wineries – but you'd expect nothing less from Halliday by now. He covered New South Wales in 1980, South Australia in 1981, and then, in 1982, he arrived in Victoria, and headed for the Yarra Valley, which a century before had produced many of Australia's most fabled table wines.

He found an agricultural paradise there, plus a fledgling wine industry so unsure of itself that the slightest breath of discouragement seemed likely to snuff it out. But he also found peace, perhaps for the first time in his life. Looking out over the ancient eucalyptus trees and grazing cattle from above Yarra Yering's vineyard, kingfishers darting through the trees, eagles soaring and swooping overhead, he'd finally found a haven for his restless spirit.

Fanciful? Maybe, but now he had a focus. He volunteered to open up a Melbourne office for his law firm, and he told his partners he'd want to retire in 1988. They didn't believe the corporate dynamo really meant it at first – what would he do with his time? But Halliday knew exactly what he'd do. He intended to make wine from Yarra Valley fruit between 1985 and 1988, but not sell any of it, so that he'd have a bank of wine ready to live off while he found a vineyard site to buy. The news that Australia's sternest wine critic was finally breaking away from his partners at Brokenwood and was going to make wine himself meant that there'd be a queue of customers ready to buy.

Our first meeting was in the middle of his first harvest. And as I wandered woozily back to my hotel after dinner, he was haring down to the Mornington Peninsula, south of the city, to see how fermentation was coming on. Some wines were doing well – the reds. The whites were a disaster. Halliday had bought five barrels of French oak on spec and put his Semillon and Chardonnay in them to ferment while he dealt with affairs up in the Yarra – and at his law office, and for his newspaper column and consultancies and entertaining visitors – just another typical week in the life of James Halliday. Well, 'the wood was crap. Awful, petrolly, dieselly flavour.' It took him two weeks to find replacement wood and by then the whites were 'irrevocably stuffed'.

In a way it shouldn't be surprising – he'd been making reds at Brokenwood since 1973, whereas this was his first attempt at white. And if you can make decent red wine through a mixture of enthusiasm, common sense and good luck – for whites, you need control. But how can you control things when there's a two hour trip – via the office – between crisis in the vineyard and crisis in the fermenting vat?

Does all this sound as though Halliday never stops to draw breath? He didn't in those days, I swear. Things seem to happen at breakneck speed when he's around. Like buying your dream house – moulded into the rock above Yarra Yering's vineyards with a view to die for – and plenty of cultivable land at a giddy gradient somewhere between 1 in 4 and 1 in 5. In July 1985, when a neighbour said the property he'd often looked at so wistfully was for sale, he could scarcely believe it was his dream house that was on the market. A month later he was proudly walking up and down the slopes of his new Coldstream property, working out how to plant one of the steepest slopes in Victoria.

Two years later, the property directly to the south came on the market. A$270,000. He didn't have the

cash. But he wanted that land. So in September 1987 he put in an offer, and told the owner he'd have his money in 90 days. He then announced that Coldstream Winemakers Ltd was going public, and invited investors to take shares. In October the stock market crashed! *Not the best of times to go public.* But Halliday did it – of course he did! Most of the money was raised through tapping large numbers of keen wine lovers for small amounts – frequently under a thousand dollars. See what I mean by not drawing breath?

But the Yarra Valley desperately needed someone like Halliday to drag it into the front line if it was ever going to be more than a community of smallholders making limited amounts of variable wine from potentially great vineyards. James Halliday believes passionately that the Yarra Valley is Australia's greatest vineyard region. Yarra styles are increasingly scooping the gold medals and trophies at wine shows, especially in the Pinot Noir and Chardonnay classes. But the vines are still so young there that it'll be the year 2000 before many vineyards really show what they're capable of. And the winemakers are mostly very inexperienced. Which is how Halliday, mixing his ability to learn techniques and interpret ideas with his undoubted talent and his formidable self-confidence, has assumed the mantle of leader and prophet in the Yarra Valley.

Halliday's own vineyards will never supply more than about a third of the fruit he needs, so he buys in grapes from different microclimates all over the valley. His beliefs become more coloured by Europe after every trip, and he is convinced that much of mainstream Australian wine-making has been heading in the wrong direction, particularly with its reds. 'I believe one of the great problems with Australian red wine is that too many are "undermade" – they're going into bottle too protected, too fruity, not structured enough.' I would only partially agree. Australia's mid-priced reds are probably without equal across the globe. But I'm interrupting. 'The average Australian ferments the wine dry – pumps it to tank, filters it star bright, induces malolactic in the tank – achieves all that by July when they're emptying the barrels and bottling the previous vintage, so it's all very neat and simple – no empty barrels. But the wine has gone into the barrel as a totally inert substance, it won't react strongly with the oak.'

Halliday puts 'dirty' wine into his barrels, and encourages some controlled oxidation in the barrel as well as leaving some of his Pinot Noir in contact with

This looks like one of those trick photos where you have to guess the mystery object. In fact it's bird-netting protecting the vines at Coldstream Hills.

the lees. He uses a mixture of crushed and uncrushed Pinot fruit from his own vineyard and other Yarra Valley sources, hand plunges and footstomps the must and runs the wine off into French oak while it is still fermenting. He'll leave it on the lees for several months and in barrel for about a year before bottling.

His Cabernet Sauvignon and Merlot grapes are all crushed, but no protective sulphur is added and some of it ferments in open-topped vessels and is hand plunged, while the rest stays in closed vats and is pumped over three times a day. The hand-plunged wine goes to barrel to finish its fermentation, the pumped-over wine macerates on its skins for up to two weeks before a 15-month spell in barrel.

Keeping It Cool

Halliday's views on white are quite different. Here he protects his fruit from oxygen all the way, even down to filling hoses with inert gas if he has to pump the wine anywhere. He crushes the grapes cool – he has a cool room to chill them down if they come in warm – he gives the juice a short skin contact and then presses the lot and returns the juice to cold tanks to settle. It may wait there as long as eight weeks before fermentation. Eighty per cent of this will be barrel-fermented very slowly in the cool room and then left on its lees – an antioxidant as well as a flavour enhancer – for about six months before bottling. Twenty per cent of the wine is tank-fermented and has some solids added back to improve flavour. Only a small amount of the wine undergoes malolactic fermentation since Halliday doesn't believe the Yarra fruit really has the intensity to cope with the extra creamy fatness.

Everything is still in the experimental stage, and Halliday takes good care to listen and learn from winemakers who have been at it far longer than he has. His Chardonnays are developing a delicious balance between the spicy toast of the oak and a relatively acid but full-flavoured fruit. His Cabernets capture the green streak and minty perfume of the Yarra fruit and coat it with a blackcurrant sweetness – demonstrating how the Yarra does struggle to ripen Cabernet fruit. And his Pinot Noirs are surely setting the pace for Australia, with their beautifully perfumed cherry and plum fruit, their soft but refreshing acidity.

Will he ever slow down and enjoy his success? Can he, even when surrounded by one of the most perfect landscapes in the world? 'There are people who elect to drift through life lying on a metaphorical beach, lurching from one crisis to another. But we . . .' he looks across at Suzanne; they both smile . . . 'yes, we elect to do what we do.'

Coonawarra

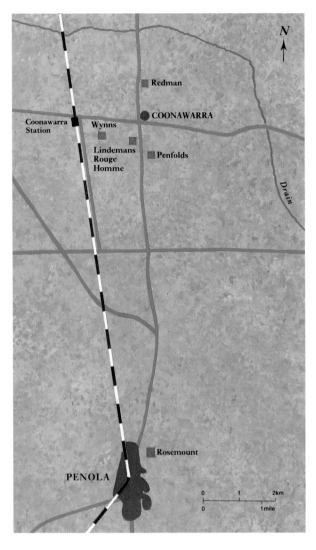

*I*T'S DEAD SIMPLE TO prove to yourself that the red terra rosa soil which runs in a thin streak up the centre of Coonawarra has special properties. But make sure you take someone beefy with you when you put it to the test. All you have to do is wait for a reasonably rainy day – half an inch or so of rain would be about right. Then you get in the car – with your beefy partner, and drive off through the vineyards from somewhere central like Wynns or Lindemans' Rouge Homme cellars towards the railway line. You'll be pleasantly surprised at how the car glides effortlessly over the firm red soil. Watch out for when the colour of the soil changes from red to white. By the railway line.

And not just that. Watch out for the puddles, the pools of water beginning to spread across your path. By the railway. And mind you don't stop.

I stopped. The railway line runs just to the west of the terra rosa across pale white clay that stretches balefully into the damp distance across a vast, featureless plain. And the rain had turned this clay into a mire. The car literally sank into the clayey mud. Luckily I was with Greg Clayfield, the decidedly beefy winemaker at Lindemans – every ounce of brawn was needed to get us out. Yet we were less than five yards off the firm terra rosa. In Coonawarra, the line between good and bad vineyard soil is often as little as five inches. The terra rosa, running for a mere 15km (9.3 miles) north-south through Coonawarra and varying from 2km (1.2 miles) to less than 200m (6.5 feet) wide, is brilliantly drained, fertile land producing some of the finest wine grapes in Australia. The white soil is little more than partially reclaimed swamp.

The Secret's in the Soil

Drainage. I've lost track of the number of times that winemakers have said that free-draining soil is the key to the quality of their wine. In the classic areas of France, where the sun's warmth is often only just sufficient to ripen the grapes, and the rainfall is normally considerable, a well-drained soil is the only way to coax the vines to ripen their crop. And Coonawarra is nothing if not cool. And nothing if not damp. In fact it's a God-forsaken corner of Australia, so flat you begin to think that perhaps the world isn't round after all. Lashed by wind and rain in its dismal winters, although spared the excessive heat of an Australian summer in most, but not all years, at best it is a dull nonentity of a place, at worst an antipodean Siberia. There's got to be a saving grace. There is. A long, slim streak of terra rosa soil, which has produced some of Australia's greatest red wines.

Coonawarra has always suffered from the total lack of a nearby thirsty populace. One wine wag, marvelling at how the Hunter Valley had gained such a reputation for its wines, despite being really rather hot for grape growing, solely because of its proximity to Sydney, once said Coonawarra's only problem is that it *isn't* within reach of Sydney. In fact it's 250 bleak miles south of Adelaide, in South Australia, without the slightest attraction for visitors, who can flock north to the welcoming Barossa Valley, or south to the convivial McLaren Vale in less than an hour.

The remarkable fertility of the land at Coonawarra was self-evident from the very first plantings of vines in 1891, yet the area never managed to notch up healthy sales, and its light, 'French-style' reds which caused the title 'Coonawarra claret' to be coined, found so few takers in the early years of this century that much of the wine was sold for distillation into brandy. A single family – the Redmans – kept the flame of quality red wine burning between the wars, when the general feeling was that the land should be turned over to sheep grazing and dairy cattle.

In 1933 Coonawarra produced a wine which took first prize in a London exhibition, and in 1935 growers made some 'claret' that found favour with Melbourne's leading wine merchant, Samuel Wynn. Many years later, Wynn's son David would at last provide the marketing flair and cosmopolitan outlook needed to force Coonawarra into the public eye and prove that Australia could make light-bodied, long-lasting red wines in the Bordeaux mould, not just the blockbusters upon which its reputation had been built for half a century. Wynns now control over 600 hectares (1500 acres) of Coonawarra vineyard. When they bought their first vines in 1981, the whole area had a mere 80 hectares (200 acres) of vines remaining, and the main winery there was about to be converted to a woolshed.

Nowadays, Coonawarra is one of the most exploited, maybe even over-exploited areas of vineyard land in Australia. In December 1981, Rosemount, the major Hunter Valley winery, issued a proud statement proclaiming: 'The Rosemount Estate has bought the last piece of the famous terra rosa land in Coonawarra'. Well they hadn't quite, but the central cigar-shaped ridge of red soil is now pretty well packed solid with vines. Yet in 1990 developments of over 400 new hectares (1000 acres) of vineyard land were somehow in progress. Informed estimates reckon that Coonawarra plantings are set to increase by a third. And I have never visited a vineyard area with such a positive gold rush feel to it.

Exploiting the Name

Unfortunately the new vines aren't being planted on the terra rosa. Yet the resulting wines will have the right to use the magic name Coonawarra, despite all the local winemakers admitting that red wine, in particular, grown on black, grey or white clay soils isn't a patch on terra rosa produce. In many people's eyes the region is in danger of becoming a 'super-Riverland'. The Riverland is the vast irrigated inland area in South Australia, whose job is to supply endless amounts of cheap bulk wine at the lowest possible price.

Coonawarra is now leading the world in devising methods of cutting costs through mechanizing vineyard tasks such as planting, pruning and harvesting. The 'industrialization' and expansion of Coonawarra's

The famous red terra rosa soil of Coonawarra that made Coonawarra reds and whites some of the most sought-after wines in Australia.

vineyards far beyond their natural frontiers does imply an interest in many cases more in high yields and utilization of the Coonawarra name than maximization of the area's tremendous quality potential.

For this reason Coonawarra's terra rosa zone may be one of the few wine regions in Australia where an *appellation contrôlée* system of delimiting the vineyard area might beneficially be applied, even though there are splatterings of the red soil well to the north and south of the main Coonawarra slab, because the soil and climate combined do make for very special vineyard possibilities.

Coonawarra's terra rosa soil *is* different from other soils – there are 58 variations on terra rosa alone in Australia for a start – but it is the subsoil and an unnaturally high water table of pure, non-saline water that create the ideal growing conditions. The reddish soil, a weathered limestone stained red over the centuries, is between a couple of centimetres and half a metre deep, and sits on a rock-hard crust of limestone up to 15cm (6in) thick. You have to break the crust up before you can plant vines, but directly below is more free-draining limestone clay and gravel and then, at a depth of only 2 to 4 metres (6 to 12 feet) is the water table. The reason most of south-east South Australia is halfway to swamp is that annual rainfall is fairly heavy, but there are virtually no natural water courses, so a

AUSTRALIA

year-round high water table has developed. A single bore sunk on these vineyards could pump up a hundred thousand gallons of good water per *hour*.

The vines, of course, love it. Free drinks all year round as their roots descend into the water table, although some growers swear that the vines don't go down that far, and that closely controlled surface irrigation provides whatever nourishment the plants require. Traditional Coonawarra reds were prized for their lightness of texture and attractive mulberry and green grass fruit. Many modern Coonawarra wines from vineyards that do not ruthlessly control the vine's crop, are dilute, and smack of overproduction.

This is particularly relevant when we look at the climate. Overall it *is* pretty cool in Coonawarra, and the harvest has been known to drag on until June. Initial attempts to classify Coonawarra's ripening conditions suggested it was as cool as Champagne, but in fact the temperature is nearer to that of Bordeaux, with much lower rainfall during the harvest months, as a rule, to threaten the crop. Even so, you can't overproduce in a cool climate and hope to ripen your fruit. Sometimes in France you can counteract this by adding sugar at fermentation. In Coonawarra, this isn't legal.

Back to the Future

Coonawarra will become increasingly important in Australian wine – especially since some of the black soils are proving reasonably suitable for early-ripening *white* varieties like Chardonnay. Still, the legend is built on Coonawarra 'claret' – despite the name initially a blend of Shiraz and Cabernet Sauvignon, but now often a pure Cabernet Sauvignon or a blend of Cabernet with the other Bordeaux varieties, Merlot and Cabernet Franc. Good examples from the past have aged brilliantly, despite their relative lack of colour and weight. But they came from fairly early-picked fruit taken from low-yielding vines.

Modern Coonawarra yields can be massive, and with all the available mechanical aids it must be tempting to use Coonawarra as a proving ground for the theory that high yield does not impinge upon quality. In the middle quality level, it probably doesn't. At the top end it surely does. I hope Coonawarra's winemakers have the will and the integrity to differentiate clearly between the two very different objectives: good wine at a fair price or great wine at whatever price it takes.

If it's isolation you want – look no further than Coonawarra, South Australia's most famous wine area. At least the train still stops here, though judging by the facilities I wouldn't want to have too long a wait.

Delatite

*T*HE BANK MANAGER RANG UP in 1983. 'We need half a million dollars from you, and you've got six weeks to find it.' The Ritchies had been on their land at Delatite for four generations and in Australia since the 1840s. But the tide of ill-fortune seemed finally to be running too strongly against them. There hadn't been a drought in Mansfield since 1881. In 1982 the Ritchies had borrowed that half million in order to put up a winery. And in 1983 the first drought for over a century meant they had almost nothing to sell so as to raise money to repay the loan. They had one priceless asset though. The bloodline running through the Ritchie livestock, as pure and powerful in 1983 as when the herds first arrived back in the 1840s. It represented their entire family history, their strength, their worth.

So Viv and Robert Ritchie called their kids home from school and university, sat them around the table and in what must have been a night of many tears and much rage against the fates, they thrashed out how to save the future by cutting themselves loose from the past. The following month they mounted their horses and drove their sheep and cattle into Mansfield. In frenzied bidding for such high-quality breeding stock, they raised their half million dollars.

A late evening at Delatite spent setting the world to rights with the family really brings home to you the cruel nature of the balance between banker and farmer. The banks had only half their pound of Ritchie flesh in the 1983 drought. In 1985, unbelievably, drought struck again. Half their land followed the cattle to the auction ring. Viv Ritchie says the two blows almost killed Robert. But by this time they had a new asset – their winemaker daughter Ros. The whole of Australia was talking about the Delatite wines, a cluster of new stars streaking brilliantly across the wine-making sky, gathering gold medals, trophies and acclaim wherever they appeared – all made by Ros.

Yet the Delatite wine operation had started by chance. The Ritchies had never touched a grape vine before 1968. They raised their animals and grew crops. They'd tried peas for freezing, beans for baking – Heinz took those – seed for the Japanese biscuit trade, but none of these had done well and they were supplying rye grass seed for lawns by the late 1960s – in fact they were the biggest producers in the southern hemisphere. Robert used to go skiing up at nearby Mount Buller, and was told one weekend by the winemaker from

Hardy's in South Australia that Mansfield was the perfect climate for growing top quality grapes. Robert must have agreed, because the following Friday, 3000 vines were dumped at the Delatite farm gate. Robert was a bit sheepish, but they cleared five acres of land for planting, and found a ready market at Brown Brothers' winery an hour or two's drive away, for what turned out to be brilliantly flavoured juice.

They knew they weren't being paid enough for the grapes – and in any case, with no irrigation those steep ironstone slopes were producing tiny crops. But it was proving a useful and enjoyable tax loss. Until 1979, when their accountant said – the sheep aren't paying any more, neither are the cattle, nor is the rye grass. Who needs a tax loss? Pull out those vines – or build your own winery and try and make more money from the vineyards. It was some risk in an area with no other wineries, and no history of wine-making.

Viv Ritchie is a determined woman – 'I'm nothing if not forward, God' – and she rang John Brown to tell him they were withdrawing the supply of his finest grapes. In the same breath she wondered, who should they ask for advice about starting a winery? Brown, to his credit, pointed them straight to the best – the top consultants Brian Croser and Tony Jordan, who quickly agreed that Delatite was a unique wine-growing locale, one which they'd never suspected existed.

The Face behind the Success

Ros Ritchie has a fierce reputation. So I was a little nervous of meeting her the first time, fearing she might eat me alive with technical jargon and fiercely-held views. Her office *is* pretty stacked with technical reviews – but she never gets around to reading them – and when you're after any specific data, she'll dig around among the squiggles in her dog-eared notebook for what you need rather than beam it up on the computer screen.

As for fiercely-held views – well, the taste of the wine is the only way she'll try to convince you of what she's doing. She's about as gentle, charming and down-to-earth a person as ever ran a winery. She works with her brother David, who runs the vineyard with pop-eyed enthusiasm, and you can sometimes feel as though you've fallen in with a couple of kids playing truant from school and revelling in the break from lessons.

Ros adopts a very carefully thought-out approach to her wine-making, and the objective is to maximize the fruit flavours the Delatite vineyards give. The striated ironstone soil streaked with copper is special, and the growing season here is very long and cool, the vines coaxed along by selective drip irrigation. Sometimes, as in 1984, and to some extent in 1989, the grapes never

Ros Ritchie combines a gentle, easy-going personality with razor-sharp, highly original wine-making talents.

quite ripen fully. The harvest in any case usually lasts from mid-March to late May. There's not much warmth left in the sun at Delatite by the end of May.

But the results are magnificent and the wines unlike any others in Australia. And interestingly, in a nation which sometimes seems besotted by Chardonnay, it is the aromatic white varieties Riesling and Gewürztraminer which won Delatite's first trophies and are in greatest demand at the chic restaurants. Chardonnay only appeared in 1987. Why so late? Robert and Viv didn't like the taste – and they were the ones planting the vineyard.

'What you see is what you get' is how Ros Ritchie describes her aromatic whites. And they are almost transparently clean, the Riesling redolent of flowers and lime, but developing a lovely apricot richness to go with the acidity as it ages. The Gewürz can be almost too light, lacking a little spice, but then you taste the 1989, orange flecked with roses, a touch of pears, a touch of peach, and you realize why it's so popular. For a grape that can be positively overblown, this is delicate stuff.

But that's what Ros wants. She picks the grapes according to intensity of flavour. She filters the juice prior to fermentation to give her greater control, and may give the Gewürztraminer some brief skin contact. She may also put some Gewürztraminer juice in a chiller for a month or two, raising the potential alcohol, and freezing out the water content as ice is shaved off the surface, slowly concentrating the flavours. The white winemakers of Bordeaux are using this technique to tremendous effect. In 1989, it made a dramatic

difference to Delatite's Gewürztraminer. The problem is time. Ros likes to ferment, bottle and sell her Riesling and Gewürztraminer as soon as possible, for cash flow. The freezing process on the Gewürz added two months to the wine-making process and created havoc with her marketing plans.

Her Chardonnay is made following more traditional production techniques, part barrel-fermented, part fermented in stainless steel, and then aged for up to nine months in a mix of new and used French oak. It's early days yet, but Ros seems to have managed to preserve the piercingly dry fruit, yet imbue it with a suggestion of apricots, and a delicious creamy oak spice.

But it is the reds which are Ros' favourite wines, and the focus is now on the Bordeaux varieties – including a juicy Malbec – and Pinot Noir. What marks them all out is their intensity of colour, their brilliantly concentrated fruit, yet their lack of intrusive tannins. The Cabernet is now blended with the other Bordeaux varieties under the Dead Man's Hill label, and has a wonderfully scented eucalyptus and mint character, a fruit of blackcurrants and plums and cherries that adds a little chocolate richness as it ages, but then, it hardly *seems* to age. All balance, no one element dominating, except perhaps the sheer pleasure of the fruit. And the Pinot Noir, ah, the Pinot. The battles I've fought for this one. It's shimmeringly soft, so soft you can hardly feel it on your tongue, but what beautiful scent, mint and eucalyptus, raspberry and cherries, and what astonishing richness for so ethereal a wine. This wine was made for romantics, not for wine judges.

'It's a magic piece of dirt, you could grow anything here,' say the Ritchies. I'm sitting out on the verandah of the house, in the still of a midsummer's night. David and Robert are dozing over their port, the only background sounds those of Viv tidying up the kitchen, and in the distant dark, a frog croaks. The sky is so bright with stars, I think I can pick out the old eucalyptus trees in the gully, I can trace the form of Dead Man's Hill, and the mountains are jagged and black against the brilliant pinpricks of silver fire. Tomorrow I return to Europe. But the Ritchies will still be here, this land will still be theirs. That was worth fighting for.

Dromana

GARRY CRITTENDEN'S PALE GREY EYES go slightly crazy when he starts talking about pruning his vines. I'm not sure his hands don't tremble a little when the subject of yield per acre and the effect on flavour comes up. Mention irrigation and it brings out beads of sweat on his brow. I had been thinking about asking him if he thought soil – you know, earth, that messy, mucky, dark-coloured stuff that seems to pop up all over the place – if he thought soil was necessary for growing vines in, or did he know of some better growing medium. Then I realized that my aeroplane back to the twentieth century left in a couple of hours and I'd better take a raincheck (or rather a nourishment stress regime management check) on any further ideas from the man who has set out to transform the face of Australia's vineyards in the next ten years, and plans to revolutionize the economics of running them.

There are other gurus in the vine-growing world who have considerable influence as consultants throughout Australia, America and Europe. Crittenden is different. As the founder of Vitinational vineyard consultancy, he has over 30 client vineyards, including such major industry forces as Seppelt, Domaine Chandon, and 200 hectares (500 acres) of newly-established vines in the Yarra Valley, Australia's trendiest new cool climate area. But he also owns his own vineyard – the Dromana Estate. All his experiments are on his own land. All the new techniques he tries out lay his own livelihood and his family's on the line. Even so, from a mere four hectares (ten acres) of vines in the holiday playground of Mornington Peninsula, an hour's drive south of Melbourne, Garry Crittenden is pioneering techniques in the vineyard – and producing wines from the grapes – which place in question many of the most dearly-held beliefs of the traditionalists, in particular the Bordelais and the Burgundians.

Crittenden was trained in biology and plant physiology, and built up his nursery business at Mount Martha – only a couple of miles from where his vines now grow at Dromana Estate. He'd always been fascinated by wine, but had never considered actually making any until, on a Tasmanian holiday in 1978, he tasted local wines of a finesse and perfume he'd never thought possible in Australia. Then the father of one of his kids' schoolmates brought round some of his own, home-grown wine one night – and here was that same piercing fruit, fragrant perfume and mouth-watering balance he'd found in Tasmania. And the grapes were growing right on his doorstep. He says he was ready for a change from the nursery. For him, it was a feeling as old as time – the desire to sit on the porch, looking out over his own land, to harvest his own fruit, and to create wine with his own label on the bottle.

Not Just a Pretty Face

You turn into Dromana Estate and everything is so manicured and correct that it seems more like a showpiece garden than a working vineyard. But it's a question of control, not cosmetics. Even if Garry decides to let a vine sprawl, he'll calculate exactly how best it should sprawl rather than leave anything to chance, and he does that by controlling the trellising, controlling the pruning and controlling the irrigation.

On the left of the vineyard, some of his vines are planted on the traditional upright French trellis, and, despite rather wider spacing than he now favours, he can still get five tons to the acre of good fruit. Over to the right, he has adapted the experimental French lyre system. You split the leafy canopy into a U-shape just above the trunk, and it's as though you have two vines growing, one metre (three feet) apart, off the same trunk. So long as you keep the leaves and shoots from meeting in the middle of the U, the sun will reach the fruit, you get excellent quality – and over six tons of grapes to the acre.

But Crittenden goes further. He's pulled the fruit-bearing canes on some of the original, traditionally trellised vines way above their normal height up to wires at 1.7 metres (5.5 feet), copying the methods used to increase yields in northern Italy. This way he can expose all the wood to sunlight, and consequently leave far more buds on the vine knowing they will fruit each year, (sunlight on wood ensures a bud produces fruit rather than just leaves and canes). And he doesn't prune them at *all*.

If you let an ordinary, low-trellised vine sprawl unpruned, it becomes a chaotic, choked-up bush, full of leaves dying for lack of sun and bunches of fruit that never see a single ray of light. But if you lay the fruiting wood along a high wire, the shoots will fan outwards and downwards during each growing season, and the fruit will naturally position itself on the outside of this leafy canopy.

I'd have thought this would still lead after a year or two to a tangle of wood and leaves. But Crittenden says no. The high number of fruiting buds left on the wood stops the vine from putting energy into throwing out too much foliage. And on his free-draining sandy loam soils, he can regulate water stress by his control of irrigation. The savings of such a system are dramatic. You plant fewer vines per acre, and the actual trellis is simple and cheap. Management costs during the season are almost halved, largely because there are no pruning costs – you just skirt the base of the vines now and then to keep them tidy. And you're producing nine tons to the acre of good fruit, instead of a more generally accepted five. Nearly double the yield, and a saving of A$2700 in maintenance costs per acre to the grower. That revolutionizes the economics of vine growing – so long as the wine's okay.

It most certainly is. I tasted the high-yield Cabernet Sauvignon amongst his other 1990s without knowing which came from which pruning system. The nine-ton wine was beautifully rich and deep, with a luscious soft plum-skin fruit. Garry worried about whether it needed more tannin. Who wants more tannin? Good exposure to the sun produces grapes with excellent colour. These young wines had a beautiful almost fluorescent colour. They also had a gorgeous juicy rich fruit balanced by a gentle lick of acid, but low tannin. So will they age? Balance is the key. The oldest Cabernet Sauvignon so far is five years old. That's ageing beautifully.

Traditionally you *had* to age a wine to allow its tannins and acids to soften. Increasingly nowadays good vine management and wine-making can produce wines of sufficiently low tannin and acid levels, but sufficiently interesting flavour from the outset, to make expensive, prolonged ageing unnecessary. Pinot Noir in particular is usually drunk just as soon as it's released for sale. Yet the conventional wisdom with Pinot Noir is that you must have mature vines, and yields must be restricted to perhaps three tons to the acre to produce interesting wine.

Keeping the yield that low, and waiting five years in theory for the vines themselves to reach a high enough quality level, has traditionally meant that Pinot Noir has been made into an extremely expensive wine – the alternative was a light, pointless brew halfway to rosé.

Crittenden has developed a system that makes it feasible for any competent farmer to make a profit right from the start, without compromising wine quality. Ideally, he'll propagate his own vines in river sand under a plastic cloche which he keeps at a high temperature. Usually the problem of 'hot bed' propagation is that the heat induces a premature bud burst and when you plant out into the vineyard at the end of winter, any frost will kill the bud. Crittenden's method keeps the bud burst delayed, so you can plant out quite safely, and he maintains he can get a crop within a year, and a big crop within two. That goes

totally against everything I've ever learned about the time it takes to establish a vine properly. But he says it's simple, and that using his methods any good farmer can get a crop immediately and a good crop *every* year from year two onwards.

'It could transform the economics of world wine' Crittenden says, not bothering to conceal his mischievous glee at the prospect. Again I was put through the blind tasting tests. Different barrels of 1990 Pinot Noir, mostly of medium colour, but with lovely delicate cherry perfume and loganberry fruit. I pick one as having a special flavour like crystallized plums with a hint of eucalyptus. Do I like that one? Absolutely. Six tons to the acre, second-year vines.

If there is one dilemma which taxes him more than any other, it is how to judge that moment when he has increased yields to the maximum point possible without compromising quality. And such a philosophy – based on the idea of more good quality fruit per vintage for the grower and, therefore, more money to be made by that grower – naturally drew the growers to him like wasps to the jam jar.

The phone was always ringing, all hours of the day and night. People kept dropping by – just to see how he did things – and, oh, you couldn't pop by my place on Sunday to show me how to do that pruning . . . Crittenden found he was spending about two days a week revolutionizing the ideas of all the local vine growers – and he wasn't being paid a cent.

So he just started saying – sure, Sunday's not that convenient, but I'll be there at ten. And it'll be seventy dollars an hour. He wanted financial security too. It would be a while before Dromana Estate would make any money, but seventy dollars an hour said his skills were obviously in demand. A viticultural consultancy might just be the answer.

He took on as a partner the local government viticultural adviser, Ian Macrae, and Vitinational was formed. Simple as that. Garry was off to Western Australia a couple of days after I last saw him. His partner was headed for New South Wales. And everywhere they go, they preach the new faith – that the right trellising system, the right pruning, the right clones of grape varieties and the right water regime can transform the vineyards of Australia – and the bank balances of the owners. Amen.

Len Evans

*T*HE FIRST TIME I MET Len Evans he stood me upon a podium in front of as many people he could muster and tricked me into pronouncing that an Australian Semillon – one of his own Rothbury Estate wines, of course – was in fact a classy French Chardonnay, Meursault at the very least. Then he told the assembled throng that I was ignorant – but a good sport, so what did it matter? Since then I've watched Evans perform his three card trick more times than I can remember, and as I shake my head at his schoolboyish triumph, I can never resist a smile.

Len Evans. Master of one-upmanship, inspirator, tall story artist, achiever supreme, coarse as rawhide, sweet as honey. Infuriating as hell too; full of generosity, yet capable of waging an impressive vendetta when need be, his language as lurid as his welcome is warm. With an eager impish grin, a face all nose and chin, and a frame squat and square as though cut from oak, he's bullied, cajoled, seduced Australia into taking pride in its wines through his unflagging enthusiasm and encouragement for Australian wines as a whole and through his magnificently partisan promotion of the Hunter Valley in particular.

He didn't come to Australia with much, it seems. Or did he? The tales proliferate. Did he get offered a place at Cambridge to study architecture, but refuse it because he was mad on golf? Did he become a golf pro? If so, why was he washing bottles within a year or two in a Sydney hotel scullery? Or was he? Wasn't he writing and producing shows at the Chevron hotel in Sydney? Wasn't he the Chevron's food and beverage manager, and running an off-licence section there so successfully that by the early 1960s it had become the leading wine retailer in Australia?

And what about his journalism, his radio shows, and how did he find the time and the energy to emerge at the beginning of the 1970s as one of Australia's best known media personalities, the embodiment of the wine revolution that was gripping the nation, and the driving force behind the renaissance of the Hunter Valley? How, how, how? Let's go back a bit.

Len Evans is a man fired by passion and ambition. These qualities have taken him all over the world, catapulted him to the heights, dragged him dangerously low, and yet, allied to a hunting dog tenacity, they have always brought him through to raise the Evans standard once again. 'I created the wine-drinking phenomenon in Australia by shrieking quality, by saying, isn't it a privilege to drink such great wine.' There weren't many people listening in the early 1960s when he worked at the Chevron hotel, but in 1962 Len had started writing what was Australia's first wine column in the Bulletin, and someone in high places must have read it, because in 1965 he took up an appointment as director of the Australian Wine Bureau. The chief function of this promotional body right then seemed to be, not to promote wine drinking, but rather merely to persuade editors to cut out specific references to wine when they reported bar room brawls.

Evans changed all that. In 1964 just 20 full-length articles on wine were published in the whole of Australia – and he'd written 14 of them himself. Three years later, in the first six months of 1967, 307 were published, and since Evans was by then using five pseudonyms, one can only assume that a good number carried the Evans hallmark of raw language, naked enthusiasm and street corner wit.

This was the hallmark of the way Australians in general communicated with each other, except that no-one was using this natural, ebullient medium to channel the Australians' undoubted enthusiasm for 'grog and tucker' into more challenging avenues than beer and beefsteak. And without a more critical and appreciative market, the wine-making revolution which was just showing its first signs of life – with Max Schubert at Grange Hermitage, Max Lake at Lake's Folly and one or two others – would never do more than sputter fitfully. Evans provided the catalyst – initially as a communicator and motivator during his two and a half years at the Wine Bureau, where he was such a success that by 1967 there was a whopping red wine boom sweeping Australia, and the Wine Bureau was instructed to stop promoting reds because the producers were running out of stock. 'Well, make some bloody more' was Evans' attitude as he grudgingly switched his energies to whites. Australia was only producing small amounts of anything decent in the way of white wine. Len didn't react well to bureaucratic restraint, and he set off to translate his nickname 'Mr Wine' into hard cash and further fame.

Without reducing his flow of newspaper, television and radio material, he became a consultant, and then a restaurateur. And in 1968 – his flow of newspaper, television and radio work, his consultancy and restaurant-running undiminished, of course – he decided to cash in on the wine boom he felt he'd created by becoming a wine producer too.

Sydney was buzzing with talk of new vineyards and new wine projects – and Evans longed to be leading the

Len Evans takes an early look at his Rothbury Chardonnay – the turbid juice is still fermenting by the look of it.

charge. His friend Murray Tyrrell, a Hunter Valley wine producer, saw all the interest in vine-growing building up and confided to Len that he was going to split up part of his land into ten-acre blocks, sell them as potential vineyards to investors and then contract to manage them. Not ambitious enough, Murray. Talk to Len. Form a syndicate. Don't just draw in thousands of dollars, be part of a million-dollar dream. You have to hand it to Len. He thinks big, and he thinks permanent. The Rothbury Estate would be Evans' grandest scheme. One syndicate, then three more, were formed to develop a total of almost 365 hectares (900 acres) of Hunter Valley land into vineyard from scratch.

Lesser men than Len might have decided that, to become a partner in – and pretty soon chairman of – the largest new wine venture in what was then Australia's most exciting wine area, was a pretty fair-sized ambition fulfilled and left it at that. Len had no choice in *not*

leaving it at that – because Rothbury has turned out to be an anguished succession of screaming nightmares, interspersed with the sweetest of dreams; more than 20 years down the track, Len can still never relax and say – I know how much wine we will produce and sell. I know we will make a profit.

The reasons then as now are the astonishing unsuitability of much of the soil in the Hunter for growing anything, let alone commercially viable crops of grapes – and the astonishing unsuitability of the Hunter's climate for top-quality wine.

Both the climate and the soil combined immediately to cause Rothbury a troubled birth. Because of the red wine boom going on at the end of the 1960s, most of the land was planted with red Shiraz grapes. But the Australian Wine Bureau had adopted Len's strategy for white wine after he left their employ in 1967. It was a tremendous success, unfortunately for Len. Just as his vast acres of red Shiraz grapes were getting ready to give a crop at Rothbury, Australians were turning from red to white by the saloon bar load. Also most of the land they'd planted with such high hopes was impenetrable pug clay that made it impossible for a vine to establish itself and produce more than a miserable yield of grapes.

But other vineyards might represent, say, half a dozen hectares of debt to their owners. Rothbury had 365 hectares (900 acres), sometimes producing less than half a ton an acre of grapes worth only a third of what it had cost to grow them. At the time Len clung to those acres despite all the evidence that most of them would just never deliver the goods. The majestic swathe of vines sweeping up on all sides to his lovely winery was part of his vision, and part of his lifeblood drained into their meagre crops. Now he admits the area around the winery has always been 'a total cowpat' in any case; today there are only 16 hectares (40 acres) of grapes left there, and 89 hectares (220 acres) at two of the other original vineyards. But with a great deal of effort put into pruning and trellising the vines to make the best use of the soil, they get adequate tonnages of grapes – when the weather is right.

Finally, in 1979, the Hunter had a perfect vintage. Rothbury made loads of superb wine – and showed a fat profit at last. By now the Rothbury Estate Society had been set up – a 30,000-strong network of wine enthusiasts, avid supporters of Rothbury's wines and regular mail order buyers. They get a strong sense of identity with the winery through endless Evans-

A cool, temperature-controlled barrel store like this one is a fundamental necessity in Australia's climate.

inspired, and frequently Evans-led events at the winery. But as Evans thumbed through the Lear jet catalogue in 1980, he was about to learn another hard truth about the Hunter.

Usually the Hunter problem is rain. It is hot throughout the ripening season, and grapes mature early here. It's a good thing they do, otherwise in most years it would be impossible to harvest a crop, because the tail-end of the monsoon anticyclones is likely to sweep down Australia's east coast in late summer and unleash drenching rain in a matter of days all over the vineyards. Some Hunter wines are made with alcohol levels no higher than eight or nine degrees – whatever the label says. The vintages of 1971, 1974, 1976, and 1984 fitted this category pretty well.

So would a little drought help? In Europe drought years are often regarded as precursors of fine quality, and one very dry season can often produce exciting, concentrated wine. But soils dry out if there is no rain at all, winter or summer. And from 1980 to 1983, the Evans fantasies of Lear jets vanished in a dustbowl. Drought hit the Hunter for four successive years. As the Rothbury Estate Society members clamoured for wine, Evans found he just couldn't produce it. It took a patch of sandy soil 457km (284 miles) from the Hunter to save Rothbury from bankruptcy.

Despite his stubborn championing of Hunter reds, which continues to this day, Evans' nose for wine trends not only sensed that the switch to white wine was long term, it also sensed that Chardonnay was going to be the hottest grape in the 1980s. He'd been agitating for some Chardonnay to be planted at Rothbury since 1976, but vines were very hard to come by, and although Evans was producing a string of sensational Rothbury Semillons under all kinds of conditions during the 1970s, Hunter Semillons traditionally take up to a decade to show how magnificent they can be, and are usually very dull and green in their early youth. A fairy godmother was needed – and quickly.

She showed up three days before the 1981 harvest. Brian Croser at Petaluma winery in South Australia, where Evans had been chairman since 1979 – that boundless energy again – had made four Chardonnays from fruit grown at Cowra, in the Lachlan Valley of central west New South Wales. The wines had shown promise, and when 40 hectares (100 acres) of Cowra land came up for sale, largely planted with Chardonnay, Evans, after an almighty battle with his board of directors who were already reeling from losses in the Hunter, gave the go-ahead to buy. The Rothbury winemaker got three days' notice to organize the picking and the transfer of 5000 cases-worth of Chardonnay grapes to the Hunter for processing into a lifeline of a wine. Cowra is *not* unique. As one Hunter man said, 'most of Australia's like that, and that's what frightens the life out of the rest of the world'. Last time I was in the region I crossed paths with Peter Sichel from Bordeaux, tramping the Cowra turf and trying to learn lessons from it that he could put to use in France. The lesson is simple. The soil is sandy and free-draining. So long as you have enough water, you can grow anything there to super-ripeness, because the sun is *hot*. But whereas climatically most of the Murray Riverland further south is similar to Cowra, the Riverland vineyards are almost all owned by smallholder grape growers whose sole objective is to pick a large healthy crop, get paid and bank the money. So they always pick early to minimize the risk of disease or bad weather, and the grapes are never left to achieve full ripeness. Rothbury was unique in owning a patch at Cowra – other wineries have since followed suit – and so they had total control over a reliable vineyard planted with the most desirable grape in the whole world: Chardonnay. This time, with the odds stacked against him, Evans had thrown the dice – and won.

Out of the woods yet? Not a bit of it. Evans' great friend and financial backer, Peter Fox, died in a car smash in December 1981. Not only had Fox supported Evans at Rothbury, he'd also entered with enormous enthusiasm into the realization of Evans' global ambitions. Evans wanted to establish a triangle of wine production in France, Australia and California. In particular he revelled in the idea of being a 'Grand Seigneur' in a French château, just as irreverent and ebullient as ever, a down-under bull in a French antique china shop – but at the same time incontrovertibly one of them, because he owned a slice of the action.

He got a property in the Napa Valley in California, and he bought small châteaux in the Graves and Sauternes regions of Bordeaux where in a few short years, with help from Brian Croser, he revolutionized local white wine-making and was doing pretty well on reds too. In 1981 Evans was even trying to buy Château Lascombes, one of the greatest properties among the Classed Growths of the Médoc. I believe, of all his projects, he really wanted this one.

Fox's death put an end to those dreams. The properties were sold off. The horizon shrank, back to Australia, back to the Hunter Valley. But it may have forced Evans to focus his mind a little more. Firstly on Australian wine in general, and secondly on his own personal contentment. By the 1980s Evans was no longer a lone voice shouting the odds for Australia around the world. As the vineyards matured and a wider experience of the alternatives available from the world's wineries percolated through Australia, a revived sense of innovation and experimentation swept across the country.

Evans saw that all this energy might be dissipated if no strong direction were provided for it. So he decided that *he* would be the arbiter of taste. Along with several other strong-minded and internationally experienced figures like Brian Croser and James Halliday, he set about establishing standards and dictating the styles that were to be successful at the annual wine shows held in each state. These are enormously important in Australia and the top medal winners gain a great deal of renown – and commercial reward – from the results. Evans has been involved with every major Australian show, and until 1990 was the chairman of the Royal Easter Show in Sydney and the National Wine Show at Canberra.

Evans personally trained up most of the younger judges who are now taking leading roles around the different states, and there is no doubt in my mind that his role was vital in educating them towards what he saw as an internationally valid concept of quality – rather than allow the winemakers to rest on the laurels of achieving success solely in their own backyard.

The Hunter and the Hunted

Evans has clung to his determination to prove that Rothbury can produce fine Hunter red, but the final conclusion I've drawn is that not only is the Hunter basically a white wine valley, but Rothbury is a white wine winery, and a great one too. Rothbury Semillons, with their astonishing ability to mix a cutting lime acidity with a marvellously rich lanolin fatness of honey and butter and nuts are probably the finest Semillons in Australia. Rothbury's Chardonnays, either from Cowra or the Hunter Valley vineyards, are some of Australia's most marvellously satisfying no-nonsense Chardonnays.

Len even makes his own Chardonnay, under the Evans Family Estate label. It's very fine, less commercial, more long-lasting, built like a top-class Meursault, certainly able to improve for a decade, maybe even two. He talks of setting up a little kiosk at the gate to his home and contentedly selling his wine by the bottle to passers-by, but then some surge of energy shakes him again and his eyes gleam with an idea for another project. He doesn't realize he doesn't need another project. He should finally take the time to draw up a chair beneath one of the old eucalyptus trees for a moment, and gaze out over his beloved valley in the brilliant light of the setting sun. And perhaps then he'll realize that the whole of the modern wine industry in Australia is his monument.

Henschke

*T*HE GRANDFATHERS REAR UP out of the brown earth, muscle bound, sinewy giants tussling and wrestling in a bizarre balletic embrace. Grandfathers of vines, not of men. Vines as old as any in Australia, older in probability than any in all of France – contorted with age, yet not wizened, their tiring limbs gaining massive girth even as their blood flow thickens to a trickle.

And these Shiraz vines are in the care of Stephen and Prue Henschke. They call them the Grandfathers because they were among the first vines planted by Stephen's great-great grandfather some time during the 1850s. Johann Henschke had emigrated from Silesia (today part of Poland) and the Shiraz cuttings he purchased from the local Barossa growers would have originated on vines from France's Hermitage vineyard during the 1840s. By the time grandfather Henschke's vines were bearing fruit, the phylloxera louse had begun to ravage the vineyards of France. The vineyards in the Rhône were ruined along with those in the rest of the country, forcing the uprooting and replanting on resistant rootstocks on a wide scale. The direct line to antiquity seemed lost for ever. Not quite. In a shallow clay dip in the hills above the Barossa Valley, that historic bloodline flows on. South Australia has never suffered phylloxera. Those gnarled Methuselahs in Henschke's Hill of Grace vineyard are the direct descendants of vines planted on the Hermitage hill in France's Rhône Valley by the Romans. Those ancient vines couldn't be in better hands today.

Stephen Henschke is a quietly intense man, with the kind of beard that prophets or German academics sport, and eyes that often twinkle with amusement, but at some philosophical conundrum rather than a bawdy gag. He has run the family business with an undeniable sense of dynastic awareness since 1979 and he intends to ensure that his son can also cast a benevolent eye over the Grandfathers in 30 years' time. The contribution of his wife Prue is going to make all the difference. She's a trained viticulturalist, and while Stephen was boning up on wine-making at Germany's Geisenheim Institute, she was becoming an expert on propagating and grafting.

Prue has a dual role: to keep the Grandfathers healthy and productive for as long as possible, while at the same time bowing to the inevitable and instituting a programme of planned replacement. At the moment the oldest vines are cosseted rather than challenged. Young, vigorous vines need competition, but not these

old boys. Only about 500 plants to the acre, regular mulching of the soil with oats and barley, some nitrogen and phosphorus, to build up soil structure, and a bit of water when the vines need it. There's a creek running through the Hill of Grace vineyard and Stephen reckons many of the vine roots probably reach down into the water table.

He has a second vineyard of 16 hectares (40 acres) a couple of miles away, called Mount Edelstone. The Shiraz vines here are venerable too – about 70 years old, but they don't have quite the look of proud, battle-scarred resilience that makes the Grandfathers so impressive. About one per cent a year of the Edelstone vines die, and it was this gradual decay which forced the Henschkes to act before it was too late.

Preserving the Heritage

Prue went through the whole Mount Edelstone vineyard, checking every vine, progressively weeding out all but the best. At bud burst, any that showed the effect of fungal infection were discarded. The success rate at flowering was checked, the subsequent number of bunches, their regularity of veraison (when the grape's colour starts to change to dark red), the different ripening rates – with the long dry autumns in the Adelaide Hills, a slow ripener is preferable because of the greater complexity of flavour its grapes will achieve. Finally Prue measures the sugar levels, the acid and pH levels of the juice, the tannin and colouring matter in the skins, and, after the secateurs have sliced away the fruit, she watches out for the tell-tale golden red burnish on the leaves which could reveal viral infection. In all, the replanting programme will take 50 years. That's some commitment.

Eventually Prue chose 150 vines which offered the characteristics she was looking for, and these she is now propagating and planting out on a new plot at Mount Edelstone. And there's one special one – her 'Supervine' she calls it – excellent acidity, low pH, marvellous colour and so sweet and ripe it regularly gives wine of 13 to 14 degrees alcohol. Exactly the characteristics that mark out the Grandfathers at the Hill of Grace vineyard.

Of course, all this reverence for a few historic vines wouldn't be worth the candle if the wine were no good. No worries on that score. Both Mount Edelstone and the Hill of Grace Shiraz are magnificent. Stephen Henschke makes a far wider range of wines than just these two – from his other vineyards near his winery at Keyneton, in the Eden Valley, and 50km (31 miles) further south towards Adelaide in the cool hillside conditions of Lenswood, he makes beautifully aromatic

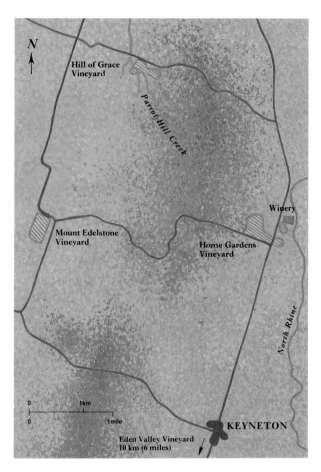

Vineyards

Hill of Grace Vineyard	Mount Edelstone Vineyard	Home Gardens Vineyard
Shiraz	Shiraz	Cabernet Sauvignon
		Riesling Semillon

Riesling, fabulously good, complex Semillon, a world-class Cabernet Sauvignon, as well as Chardonnay, Pinot Noir and goodness knows what else. But it is Henschke Shiraz which leaves me breathless with excitement.

The Henschke winery has a suitably traditional feel about it considering the big, brawny reds made there, and much of it, built in great irregular blocks of local stone, dates back to the turn of the century. In fact it's not as traditional as you might expect. Stephen gained his wine-making degree at Geisenheim in Germany and he still keeps a rather tight Germanic hold on processes like fermentation. Nothing here is allowed just to let rip. The Shiraz grapes are kept to a surprisingly low maximum of 18° to 20°C (64° to 68°F), with wooden boards inserted into the top of the tank to keep the cap of skins submerged. Henschke says this low temperature helps preserve fruit character. The juice will be pumped over the skins each day, and passed through heat exchangers to keep the temperature below 20°C (68°F). This takes six or seven days. And when between a

quarter and a third of the sugar has yet to be converted into alcohol, he runs the juice off, and at least half of it goes into new 300-litre (66-gallon) barrels of American oak. The fermentation continues for up to two more weeks, and the oak flavours have by then been drawn into the wine, integrated, in a way which he feels is not possible if you simply ferment entirely in tank, and then introduce the finished wine to new wood.

The wine will stay in this mix of new and used American oak for between 12 and 18 months, it won't be fined and the slight filtration he uses is as coarse as he dares make it. And then he'll keep the wine in bottle for another two to three years before sale.

But these Shirazes are so wonderfully rich, yet so soft-edged, you could drink them from the barrel in a jug. Ten years down the track the thrilling, heady perfume of that fruit is still the dominant feature of the wine. If anything the Mount Edelstone, from the relatively younger vines, is a little easier to approach. If Stephen wants to preserve the fruit, Mount Edelstone has it by the bucketful – rich black plums, raspberries so ripe they're turning magenta and bloated on the bush, blackberries that squirt their dark staining sweetness through your fingers at the merest touch. When the wine is young, there's an unexpected softness almost like ripe pears in cream. As it ages, the fruit sweetness has to share the limelight with mint and eucalyptus, with pepper and leather and the bitter richness of sloes steeped in brandy.

Hill of Grace has a magnificence, a brooding depth of dark and mysterious flavours exactly as you'd hope from those twisted vines born six generations ago. If the wine is opaque it nonetheless isn't impenetrable – there's a blackness of colour, a thickness of texture, filled with the scents and essence of excess. It's jam-sweet, jam-rich, sticky as cooked fruit, thick as tar and melting toffee, bitter-sweet as the blackest chocolate, herbs rubbed into the squashy juice of plums and blackberries, cherries soaked with mint, leather and pepper stewed with blackcurrants. A classic – but new? Or old? Both. The heritage of the fruit runs back to the very dawn of vineyards in France, but the expression of that fruit is brought to its peak by the distinctly modern touch of Stephen Henschke.

Lake's Folly

*I*N A LAND WHERE the four-letter word is king, Max Lake is one of the true artists. Indeed, any direct quotations from Max in this profile have probably undergone dilution for the sake of the more sensitive reader. Listening to Max in full flow is not an experience to be entered upon lightly by those of delicate disposition.

I still can't quite get used to it, though. Max Lake used to be one of Australia's most successful surgeons, specializing in the delicate filigree work of hand reconstruction. He's a man of wide-ranging artistic interests, a great intellectual who is now determinedly establishing his latest career as an expert on the psychology of scent. He's the creator of one of Australia's finest Chardonnays, as well as being the man who reintroduced Cabernet Sauvignon, the use of new oak barrels, and an awareness of the international horizons of wine to the Hunter Valley.

But along with such strengths, Max is self-indulgent on a grand scale, able to display an arrogance about his wines that is complete but irresistible and yet almost in the same moment able to wallow in self deprecation and baseless envy. He's also immersed himself in the fascinating connection between scents and sexual attraction and swears that a diet of parsley and celery washed down with old Cabernet will render me irresistible to much of the female population – here's me thinking it was my charm and wit. And he's quite unable to control his language.

With the Hunter now re-established as a major quality producer in Australia, and the small 'boutique' winery playing a crucial role in probing the quality potential of the continent, it's easy to forget the importance of what Max achieved. He did reintroduce Cabernet to the Hunter. And he gave committed, enthusiastic amateurs right across Australia the role model necessary to persuade them to 'have a go'.

I lost count of how often he said, 'I did that, I was the first one' last time we talked. Yet standing on the ridge of deep red volcanic soil at the top of his vineyard, with the Barrington Tops mountains hazy in bright noon sun behind us, the lovely calm of the Hunter Valley floor spread in front of us, a parkland of old

The original Lake's Folly winery is the little 'A' frame section on the right. The Cabernet and Chardonnay have transformed Hunter Valley wine standards.

eucalyptus trees, pasture and vines, and hearing Max say, 'I really feel very proprietorial about the whole place because I started it; there was nothing here when I came', it didn't seem so far-fetched. When he reels off the list of well-known winemakers and writers who he says learned it all at his knee, I didn't feel uneasy. And as he bent down and picked up a handful of the crumbly crimson soil, just moist, no more, after the night rains, I *can* imagine him all those years ago letting a great grin wreathe his shaggy features as he says, 'yes, this'll do'.

His longing to make wine had been aroused in 1960 when he drank a wine labelled 'Hunter River Cabernet 1930'. It was the best wine he'd ever drunk – and he'd tasted a fair few of the top French ones on his surgeon's salary by then. The Hunter River was only a hundred or so miles away from Sydney where his practice was. It took him six months to track down the wine – it had been grown at the Dalwood vineyard, a famous nineteenth-century Hunter Valley site. But only three barrels of the 1930 were made, and the following year the vines were ripped up.

Lake discovered something else – that the 'Cabernet' wasn't all Cabernet. Half the wine was Petit Verdot,

Bordeaux's most difficult, but potentially greatest grape variety. By 1960 there wasn't a single acre of Cabernet left in the Hunter Valley. There was hardly an acre of Petit Verdot left in the whole of Australia. But first things first. Lake resolved to go to the Hunter – and make *that* wine again. He could at least find cuttings of Cabernet, so that's what he'd use to start with.

He spent three years of weekends roaming the Hunter, often accompanied by his friend Max Schubert, the creator of the great Grange Hermitage. He decided most of the Hunter soil was useless – impervious pug clay hopeless for vines. Yet there were a few plots of rich red volcanic soil, on ridges and slopes that had avoided being washed away over the millennia. All the great traditional Hunter vineyards were on this crimson dirt, but they faced towards the sun. The Hunter is very hot for grape growing; grapes needed less sun, not more. Lake chose his piece of land facing south, away from the sun, on the deepest red soil thrown up during three years of digging holes. 'The most brilliant thing

Stephen Lake has taken over from his father Max at Lake's Folly and continues to make fine Cabernet Sauvignon and exceptional Chardonnay.

I've done in my life – and I've done a few!' And he planted Cabernet. Throughout 1963 he held wild parties at the weekends with friends, family and students all pitching in to help. By 1966 he'd actually got a crop – not much – but it gave him a barrel and a half of juice, which he then had to try to make into decent wine.

Lake had worked the vintages of 1960 to 1962 with local winemakers to get some practical experience, reckoning his surgeon's training gave him quite enough scientific know-how for the technical side. He knew very clearly what he wanted. He had a vision of great wine to pursue – that 1930 Dalwood red – and he'd been checking out the wines made by the famed Maurice O'Shea from grapes grown at Rosehill, just the other side of his own volcanic ridge which despite a lack of Cabernet, developed a lovely Bordeaux mellowness with age. O'Shea was notoriously secretive about how he made his wines, so was Max Schubert, but an inquisitive mind like Lake's would piece odd morsels of information together.

I've never tried the 1966 Lake's Folly Cabernet. But I've tried the subsequent wines, and by the time I tried the 1969 and '70 yet again when they were 20 years old, it had become clear that Max hadn't just reproduced an Australian model, he'd managed to create a red wine style that, given enough maturity, was redolent of the rarest and most seductive of Bordeaux perfumes – cedarwood, cigar boxes, fresh shavings from a pencil, and something of the austere dusty beauty of old books in a library. Add to that a little mint, a little toffee and blackcurrant, and you had sensational wine.

There were two reactions to his wine. The older generation of Hunter winemakers swore he was ruining the character of Hunter wine. Max provocatively named his winery Lake's Folly in response and said there wasn't much left to ruin before he came along. And the rest of Australia went batty about the wine. The mood in the country was right. An interest in table wine was reviving after half a century of slumber, and the charismatic amateur who showed how it could be done was just the tonic needed. Lake's Folly became the most sought-after and expensive wine in Australia, and a boom of plantings began which brought the Hunter Valley once again centre stage.

By the mid-1970s Max was getting fascinated, even obsessed, by Chardonnay as a still table wine. 'There's no-one in Australia who understands Chardonnay, except possibly me.' He can't bear what he calls 'Dolly Parton up-front Chardonnays with planks of wood suspended in the tanks which will be dead a few months after release'. You couldn't accuse Lake's Folly Chardonnays of that. They have a brilliant limey intensity, a mineral depth which only very slowly fattens out to a beautifully rounded hazelnuts and honey richness – yet the lime stays shining like a beacon however old and rich the wine becomes. He carts bottles of his 1981 around the world with him, and whenever any winemakers say they've got the best Chardonnay in the world, he pulls this out, opens it and waits.

I know. I've seen him do it. He's silent as he waits, and waits, until the assembled dignitaries start to mutter words like Meursault, Chevalier-Montrachet – and he's visibly relieved. He's testing you and testing himself, almost judging your palate by your response. For all his achievement, for all the accolades his wines have received it's as though he still needs one more tribute, one more paean of praise.

His son Stephen is the winemaker at Lake's Folly today, and if the 1989s are anything to go by, we could be entering a new era of brilliance. The Chardonnay is true to its limey character but has a delicious creamy finish which should bring it forward more quickly but no less successfully than earlier 'Follies'.

The Surprise in Store

Yet the red shows that Max has still got another shock up his sleeve in the vineyard. Remember the 1930? The wine that was half Petit Verdot? Brilliant though the grape is in Bordeaux, they hate its unpredictability and feeble crops. In fact Max has spent the last 11 years trying to find a way to get the capricious Petit Verdot to give him a crop. In 1989 they only got half a ton, making up a mere two per cent of the red yield – but you can smell its haunting violet perfume, the blackberry, or is it loganberry, sweetness in the 1989. 'It's the berry up there on the horizon that you can't name', says Max – and he's right – you know it is delicious, you can't quite say why. Magical wine experiences are made like that.

In 1990 I was down in the Lake's Folly vineyard and I saw this block of vines absolutely bursting with bunch after bunch of tight black berries. A big crop. A *big* crop. What are they, Max? And he's . . . he's roaring, he's helpless with mirth. They're his Petit Verdot. Over a decade after planting the vines, he's finally worked out how to grow them. And he's not telling how. If anyone asks for cuttings he says he's just burnt them. I think that before Max Lake consigns himself to the international lecture tour circuit convincing hordes of eager fans that Chardonnay has an aroma like the fresh sweat of having just made love, he's got one more date with destiny. As the man who proved that Petit Verdot could make the greatest red wine in the Hunter – and he was the man who brought it to the Valley.

Lindemans/Padthaway

*I*F IT'S 'OLD CLASSICS' from new wine regions I'm after, Lindemans have been creating them with more regularity, to more consistent standards, for longer than anyone else in Australia, and the wines made by Gerry Sissingh and Karl Stockhausen at their Hunter Valley winery during the 1970s and 1980s would certainly be recognized and applauded by the winemakers of the 1870s and 1880s.

But give them a Lindemans Bin 65 Chardonnay and the winemakers of old would gape in disbelief. It's difficult to know if they'd like it, because they'd never have tasted anything resembling it. It has wonderful cool fruit, all peaches and angelica. It has a deliciously tingly spice of cinnamon and cloves, and it has a gentle sweetness, partly honey, partly melted butter. No such wine existed a hundred years ago. And in a warm country like Australia it would have been a physical impossibility to make it, because Bin 65 is a wine which takes the full juiciness of fruit ripened under the southern sun, yet by use of ultra-hygienic winery conditions and temperature-controlled fermentation and storage, it has developed the gorgeous meadow-fresh aromatic fruit traditionally only possible in the chill conditions of Germany.

Bin 65 only exists because of modern technology. It is put together in a vast factory of a winery called Karadoc on the banks of the Murray River in outback Victoria. In the blazing heat, everything is temperature-controlled and you need to carry a sweater with you as you duck in from the broiling temperatures outside to the bone-chilling ice-box of the fermentation halls. The grapes are mainly drawn from nearby irrigated vineyards. Mainly. Until the early 1990s they were almost exclusively local and the wine was labelled as Victorian Chardonnay. Now the fruit is drawn from a much wider area and the wine has been renamed South Eastern Australian Chardonnay. And improved out of all recognition.

It's an object lesson for people obsessed with restrictive appellations of origin, that quality will out, however unlikely the location. The crucial difference in Bin 65 since the end of the 1980s has been the addition of fruit from Padthaway. Lindemans grow 900 tons of Chardonnay at Padthaway, of which only 200 tons are used for their top of the line Padthaway Chardonnay, the rest being sent to Karadoc. If Coonawarra, 400km (250 miles) down a deadbeat highway from Adelaide, is

obscure, Padthaway, 65km (40 miles) closer to Adelaide, is even more obscure. It hardly has a village. It certainly doesn't possess a winery. But it does have an awful lot of grape vines.

In the 1960s analysts calculated that Australians would have tripled their annual wine consumption to over 20 litres a head in the 1980s. For once they were right. Lindemans could see that they were going to need a lot of easy-to-grow, cheap-to-harvest grapes to fill out their bulk wine lines. For Lindemans, the Hunter Valley, their traditional base, with its erratic climate and scarcity of suitable vineyard land, offered no financially sensible solutions.

Unexplored Territory

Tulloch's winery and vineyards were on sale in the Hunter, and Lindemans had the funding, but the accountants did their sums and calculated that for the same sum as Tulloch's asking price, it would be possible to bring into production 405 hectares (1000 acres) of virgin land in the far more climatically reliable region of south-eastern South Australia.

The Department of Agriculture had discovered that a variation of Coonawarra's famous terra rosa soil made a reappearance for about ten miles at Padthaway; the soil was deep and well-drained and over limestone. The ground was mostly flat, much of it planted simply with lucerne grass; rainfall was a little lower, sunshine a bit higher than at Coonawarra, and the high water table that kept Coonawarra's yields satisfyingly healthy was present at Padthaway too, if at slightly greater depth.

Lindemans decided to create a prairie vineyard to provide cheap bulk wine. They initially purchased a 445-hectare (1100-acre) block of grazing land in 1968 and set to. As they were already increasing red wine stocks at Coonawarra, through their purchase of vineyard land and the large Rouge Homme winery in 1965, they concentrated on planting whites on the new land, and over the next dozen years Lindemans' Padthaway holdings grew into the world's biggest experimental vineyard. They didn't need to build a new winery with Coonawarra so close, so they planted everything from Riesling and Chardonnay to Sylvaner, Verdelho and Chenin Blanc.

The whole operation was planned right from the start as an employee-free environment – everything would be mechanized. There was one very immediate reason for that. There simply weren't enough workers

This view of the edge of the Lindemans Riesling plantation in Padthaway shows how close many Australian vineyards still are to the bush out of which they were carved.

to be found. And the other reason was cost. California had pioneered methods of picking grapes mechanically which drastically reduced expense. Up in the Riverland, Australia was perfecting techniques of mechanical planting, and mechanical pruning. Using automatic irrigation systems as well would mean that there would never be a time of year when you needed more than one worker per 40 hectares (100 acres) of vines. Lindemans calculated that they could produce good quality Rhine Riesling grapes at Padthaway more cheaply than the inferior Sultana grapes they were then purchasing from the Riverland area. But things worked out far better than that.

Padthaway's greater warmth than Coonawarra and more controllable water supply means that the grapes ripen two to three weeks earlier than at Coonawarra. And the nights are much colder than at Coonawarra – perhaps 6° or 7°C (11° or 13°F) colder on average. This produces grapes with much more exciting fruit acidity as well as maximum sugar ripeness. Harvesting at night means that grapes can be picked, transported the 65km (40 miles) to Coonawarra, to the Rouge Homme winery, and all be in the fermentation vats by midday – without ever having risen above 5°C (41°F) in temperature, and without having to spend a single dollar on refrigeration.

Throughout the 1970s it was becoming clear that Lindemans (along with Seppelt and Hardy, two other big firms who had taken the plunge at Padthaway) had

struck gold. Less and less fruit was diverted to bulk wine, more and more to superior regional bottlings. And reds as well as whites began to show encouraging form.

Yet it wasn't until the 1980s that the focus began to turn to the two most fashionable modern-day white grapes – Chardonnay and Sauvignon Blanc – and Padthaway assumed totally unforeseen, but deserved, star status. The Lindemans 1983 Padthaway Chardonnay won the first ever major Australian trophy awarded to the variety – amazing, when nowadays we virtually equate Australian white wine with Chardonnay. The 1984 repeated the trick, winning Best Young White Wine at the Sydney show and the 1985 won the white wine trophy at the Canberra National Show. The Sauvignon Blanc record was similarly impressive. All within five years of making the first-ever Sauvignon and Chardonnay from Padthaway soil.

What I find so encouraging about all this is that if one Padthaway can be plucked from being a stretch of insignificant grazing land and made into an area capable of making world-class wine within scarcely a decade of starting out, there are bound to be other Padthaways waiting to be discovered – in Australia, New Zealand, North and South America, Africa and Europe. And if they can all blend their cast-offs into such joyously enjoyable commercial blends as Lindemans Bin 65, there will rapidly come a time when none of us need ever drink bad white wine again.

Mitchelton

*I*F WE TRY TO UNDERSTAND Mitchelton from the viewpoint of an ordinary world of profit and loss accounts, of tonnages of grapes and marketing strategies, it may not make much sense. Mitchelton is a dream; part fantasy, part reality, a fairy tale set on a bend in the Goulburn River an hour and a half's drive north of Melbourne. At the end of a massive clearing in the eucalyptus trees stands a tower of such improbable proportions I couldn't decide whether it resembled a witch's hat set above an airport control tower, or some kind of Picasso-inspired, psychedelic toadstool.

I climbed the tower, and, coming out onto a wide terrace, I suddenly understood the majesty of the vision behind Mitchelton. The bend in the river, the waters cool and motionless, shaded by silent ranks of ancient eucalyptus trees, has a soothing tranquillity only possible in a parched land like Australia. The slight breeze carries the eerie bell-like song of magpies. Way below me, peacocks strut, lawns stretch away to lakes and high stands of trees and an amphitheatre slopes gently towards the south. Back in 1969 a Melbourne restaurateur called Shelmerdine had found this magic spot and set about turning a dream into reality.

Shelmerdine planned Mitchelton as a grand tourist 'experience'. In his magic tower he built a restaurant – and two more at and below ground level; he built a farmer's market, picnic and barbecue areas, a swimming pool, a wildlife sanctuary, an aviary – even, I am told, an underground chapel. And he also built a winery, and cleared a vast 117-hectare (290-acre) plot for vines.

If the winery sounds like an afterthought – that's how it seemed at the time. He was banking on a thousand people a day visiting his domaine, to tour and picnic, and the idea was they'd all buy Mitchelton wine on their way back home as a memento. But the visitors failed to materialize. Within five months of opening, the entire operation was in receivership, and for the next decade Mitchelton hung on to life by its fingertips.

The Mitchelton vineyards may look rather boggy, with soils of gently undulating clay loam. However, the property represents a virtual island between two rivers, and only half a metre down, the soil turns first to sandy loam, and then to river sand and gravel, to a depth of six metres and more. So drainage is actually first-class. Even so 1974 was flooded out in the region's wettest vintage for 50 years. By 1975 it was clear that the phylloxera vine louse was busily chomping its way through what vines there were, and by 1976 money was so short they couldn't even make wine – the grapes were sold unloved and uncrushed to other wineries. With a history like that, it isn't surprising that in 1980, the asking price for this white elephant was scraping rock bottom. Someone had to see the faded vision through the shrouds of failure. Someone did.

The Valmorbida family had built up a considerable empire distributing food and drink throughout Australia since arriving from Vicenza in northern Italy in 1950; but they hankered after owning the means of production rather than just the distribution. And they yearned for an estate. John Valmorbida, heir to the empire and the man who now controls Mitchelton, remembers his father brooding over the purchase, then deciding to go ahead – the price was so low they could get their money back just selling the bricks. In 1980 they bought.

'It took us only four weeks to realize we couldn't make a go of it. But we'd never failed at anything, and so it became the obsession of the family.'

Faith in the Folly

Mitchelton needed an obsessive approach. With commitments to buy the grapes from the large expanse of vineyard land around, and with a vast underground cellar area, as well as the ambitious follies above ground to finance, investment and the development of a marketing strategy had to be the priorities. So Valmorbida formed a team. Of two. Himself and Don Lewis. Lewis had been making Mitchelton wine right from the start, and, against all the odds, had managed to create quite a reputation for his efforts, winning gold medals for Riesling and Cabernet Sauvignon, and building up a following for the style that has become Mitchelton's most famous wine – their wood-aged Marsanne.

To my mind, the Marsanne is usually good rather than memorable, being full and nutty, sometimes developing a mint and cedar fragrance, sometimes white peaches and honeysuckle. The 1990 looks to be the finest so far. Estate Semillons, however, are excellent, and estate Rieslings are superb. When young they have a wonderful heady perfume of lime and honeysuckle and goldengages and as they age they go buttery and nutty, but never lose this piercing lime acidity.

That's the dry Riesling. There's also a botrytis-affected sweet wine which Don Lewis professed to find 'a real pain in the neck' to make. His 1990 has brilliant apricot and honey richness and a most original refreshing salty finish, but Lewis says, 'The only good thing about the bloody stuff is when you get it in the bottle.' Strange; all winemakers profess to hate making

The fantastical, mysterious tower of the Mitchelton winery casts its spell over the neighbouring vineyards.

sweet wine – but no amount of complaining hides the fact that he knows he made an absolute cracker in 1990.

The estate red wines are as yet less exciting – a good light Cabernet style is made, but the Shiraz needs mixing with beefier stuff. Yet Mitchelton is *not* just about estate wines. Lewis already uses Coonawarra fruit from South Australia, and has even trucked grapes across the continent from Western Australia's Mount Barker region, but it is Mitchelton's position bang in the centre of Victoria that he sees as the real advantage. It allows him to draw on neighbouring Goulburn vineyards for their rich reds, buy from the Yarra and the Mornington Peninsula when he's after finesse: the Riverland and North-East Victoria are close by for cheaper blending material. And the Strathbogie ranges are just an hour's drive to the east.

Site of the Secret

The Strathbogies hide Mitchelton's secret weapon. Valmorbida and Lewis have bought 405 hectares (1000 acres) of wind-sheltered, north-east facing land, 700 metres (2300 feet) up in the mountains, of which they've planted 8 hectares (20 acres) so far, with 120 (300) more planned if things go well. Valmorbida knows that Mitchelton lacks an 'exclusive' top-of-the-range image. These vineyards may provide it. The first Pinot Noir and Chardonnay wines from the new vineyards are

exciting, with the Pinot in particular showing deep, dry, plum and bitter chocolate flavours but attractive mint and chewy perfume too. The un-secret weapon at Mitchelton is Valmorbida's marketing flair. His most audacious coup is the development of a wine called Cab-Mac, made in Beaujolais style, which he swears can out-Gamay the Gamay, though in fact it's a blend of Shiraz, Cabernet Sauvignon and Grenache. Each year Valmorbida issues a challenge to the Beaujolais producers to a tasting competition for a 'winner takes all' prize he himself provides. A\$5000 in 1988, A\$10,000 in 1989, A\$15,000 in 1990 – but so far he's had no takers. The publicity has enabled production of Cab-Mac to grow from 500 cases to 20,000 in only five years.

If you visit Mitchelton now, you'll see another side to Valmorbida's marketing flair. The reception and tasting area, once the farmer's market, now houses a spacious art gallery. Contemporary oils and prints hang on the white walls, the work of artists who have won the increasingly prestigious Mitchelton Print Competition.

And if you'd been around in February 1990, you'd have *heard* his flair. The amphitheatre was transformed into a 15,000-strong concert arena, and Kiri Te Kanawa sang beneath the stars in the balmy evening air. I stood in the Mitchelton forecourt, and watched the pale silver beams of a new moon cast a ghostly patina on the tower, making it surreal, disturbing, brooding under the night sky. The witch's hat now topped a fairy castle holding magic spells and mystical powers for any mortal brave enough to grasp them.

Morris

MY PEN AND FINGERS were sticky with sugar, my palate was swimming in sweetness, and I was gazing at the liquid in my glass. Well, liquid is the wrong word. A black-brown gooey essence as dark as ink was clinging to the inside of my glass, too thick to slide down the sides. You could almost *see* the heady fumes of chocolate and raisins and the richest of Christmas cakes rising from the surface.

Mick Morris had stumbled on this syrup quite by chance that morning. He'd noticed a little nine-litre (two-gallon) cask stuck up near the roof. That's the smallest size of cask he's got so, curious, he climbed up and dropped a siphoning hose into the bung hole and sucked. The air he sucked in almost choked him with its steamy richness – but there was no liquid – until he got nearly to the bottom of the barrel, and suddenly he hit liquid. This was some 1976 Liqueur Tokay he'd put aside a dozen years before – and forgotten about. It had concentrated down to a couple of pints of treacle, and I must admit I found myself thinking what a waste of good wine. Until I tasted it. I virtually had to scoop it out with my finger, it was so syrupy. Even a finger-lick of it packed such a punch I felt dizzy with the richness of it all.

Mick was delighted. 'A dash or two of this'll do wonders for a young 'un.' And by a dash he literally means a tablespoon or two added to a barrique-sized cask of younger wine. So we tried it. A few drops of this essence were swirled with difficulty into a glass of young 1988 Tokay, whose thick glycerol-sweet, blackberry-syrup flavour was transformed into something so much darker, more complex, the fresh blackberry turning to a deep, old, cooked raspberry jam. The old wine in turn was broadened and lightened to a richness of coffee and raisins, and, fascinatingly, something savoury like beef tea. A memorable taste.

I asked Mick whether I could buy such a wine, and all he had to do was reach over the counter and pull out a bottle of his Show Blend. On sale to anyone who visited the cellar. He poured me a little, dark brown with a kind of luminous green edge like the spirit in a spirit level – and then came that fascinating powerhouse mix of raspberry and black chocolate, raisins and beef tea. There was some 80-year-old wine in that blend, a minute amount, but enough to transform it. 'Balancing the freshness of the young wine with the complexity of the old. If there's any secret to a good Muscat, that's

the secret.' Mick Morris is the fourth generation of a wine-making dynasty which at one time ran the largest vineyards and the largest wine cellars in the southern hemisphere. These flat prairie lands, baking under the silent, heartless sun, seem an impossible place to grow quality grapes. But visit the sherry vineyards of Jerez in Spain during the summer and this sense of stifling, searing torture by heat is just the same.

Morris is no longer an independent company – having been a part of the large Orlando group since 1970, but this loss of independence, caused, as so often, by a family rift, has probably been a blessing in disguise, because the Morris Liqueur Muscats, while being praised to the skies by every visiting wine writer who ever chanced upon them, enjoyed until recently no honour in their own land. They were sold for trifling amounts to a market which equated sweetness and high alcoholic strength with cheapness. Many other Rutherglen companies either sold out or began dipping ever more frequently into their old reserve wines which, increasingly, they could ill afford to keep. Yet it is the old reserve wines which are the heart of good fortified Muscat and Tokay.

Safety in Numbers

The financial security has meant that Mick Morris has never had to take out more wine than he puts in, and his cellar is a cobwebby treasure trove of wines going back to the last century. All of them still stored in barrel! Most modern winemakers proudly show you their old bottled wine, and then display their spanking new oak cooperage. Mick Morris leads you down rows of ancient wooden casks, their staves bulging with exhaustion, the stains of their leaking joins blackening the sagging wood, and he takes pride in saying he wouldn't let a new oak barrel near his beloved Muscats and Tokays.

Other modern winemakers will show you their temperature control systems and their pristine sterile storage conditions, with not a microbe out of place. You trudge behind Mick Morris on the moist earth floor; house martins and moths flicker and dart above your head in the warm humid air, and the sunlight throws zigzags of dust-filled beams through the pellet holes in the rusty corrugated iron roof.

Although new oak barrels are of great importance to a table wine producer, because of the richness and spice the wood will impart to his Chardonnay or his Cabernet Sauvignon, a fortified wine producer doesn't want those flavours and sees his barrels in a very different and much more personal way. 'You get to know all the casks,' says Mick. 'It's like if you've got a heap of rubbish on your desk, somehow you do know where to find everything, though occasionally you lose something for a few years in the meantime.' The different shapes and sizes mean wines mature at different rates, and while rapid oxidation is detrimental to a table wine, a fortified wine deepens its flavours and gains complexity through gentle, prolonged interaction with oxygen.

But more important is the character a barrel develops through the wines it has held before. You put the same wine in four different casks and 12 months later there'll always be one better than the others. Empty them and fill them again with different wine – and in a year the same cask will be best again. Obviously barrels do eventually wear out and newish – well, six to ten years old – barrels must be brought in to replace them. For the first few years they won't hold the best wines while Mick evaluates their personalities. As soon as one cask shows signs of influencing the wines' development particularly well it is singled out to hold the top blends. The wood will then soak up some of this top blend. When it is refilled with younger wine, some of the older wine's character will influence the new wine.

This interchange between old and new is crucial in the production of 'stickies', as these super-sweet wines are often known. Evaporation in cask amounts to about four per cent a year. The wine gradually becomes concentrated, gaining sweetness and intensity, but losing freshness and, obviously, volume. Fresh rose petal and tea-leaf perfumes are one of the joys of good Muscat, but these fade as the darker, more raisiny flavours of maturity gain ground. After ten years without being touched a cask might be only half to three-quarters full. So every few years Mick does the rounds of his older wines, to check how much they've evaporated, and if there's a particularly good young vintage – like the 1988, the '82 and the '80 he'll empty the barrel of old wine, clean it out, put the old wine back in, and top it up with the promising youngster. The young wine adds freshness to the old, while gently taking on its liquorous grandeur.

I was amazed at how rustic the actual wine-making equipment is, but Mick just grins and says that the last thing you need to make good fortified wine is brand new machinery. The grapes – Muscadelle for the Tokay and Muscat – come in from the vineyards surrounding the winery over a five week period. The land isn't irrigated and Morris reckons a good crop is two and a half to three tons to the acre. The early-picked grapes have more fruit flavour and colour, but are less sweet. The late-picked, wizened, raisiny little grapes at the end of harvest have lost their colour, and a good deal of their fruitiness, but are oozing with lusciousness. The

fruit is thrown into a crusher-destemmer which looks as though it's made out of the rusty propeller blades of a World War Two Spitfire, though I reckon that's underestimating its age. Mick likes the coarse chopping it gives the grapes, especially since the raisiny ones have the best juice but are the most difficult to split open.

Seven tons of grapes at a time are then dumped into open cement tanks coated with paraffin wax, which look more like sheep dips than vessels for creating world-beating wines. Mick adds a good dose of dried, general-purpose yeast and lets the fermentation rip. 'I don't care how hot it gets,' he says, because he only wants the yeast to convert a couple of degrees of sugar into alcohol, before he runs off the intensely sweet, bubbling juice after a day or so, and wallops in the neutral, high-strength spirit which stops any further fermentation, raising the alcohol to about 18.5 degrees.

He gives the blend a good 'rummage' – otherwise the spirit just sits on the top – and then puts it straight into big old casks. After three months he racks it, checks the 20 or so different Muscats and Tokays for quality and makes up three or four major blends at different quality levels. In years like 1988, maybe 10 to 20 per cent will be put away for reserve wine. In poor years like 1989, most of it will go to make up cheaper blends for cellar door sales. Gradually the best wines get put into smaller and smaller casks, while the rest are sold. Your father and grandfather laid down their best wines for you. You must do the same for your children and grandchildren.

As I left the winery, Mick had one more treat to share. He'd shown me the young Muscats after the Tokays. They started out full of chocolate sweetness and orange spice and strawberry freshness, getting darker and more syrupy as they aged. Then he wandered off into the jungle of his barrels and came back with a glass of liquid thick, dark and almost sludgily heavy. The weighty perfume uncoiled like a cobra, smelling first of mint and burning caramel, of cocoa, raisins and charred hazelnuts. And then the fruit was suddenly gone, the winey sweetness too, and it smelt like nothing so much as an old, old painting, the sweetness that of age and wood and oil. It was a nineteenth-century Muscat, briefly freshened up in 1960. I could see Mick thinking a dash or two of that would do wonders for his brash young 1988s.

Mountadam

Stormy, wild, threatening, the skies intensify the naked isolation of the bushland around Mountadam's vineyard development on top of the Mount Lofty Ranges.

O F DAVID AND ADAM WYNN'S Mountadam vineyard, 4.8 per cent is devoted to harvesting grapes. The other 95.2 per cent is devoted to harvesting water. Out of 1000 hectares (2500 acres), only 48 (120) are planted with vines. Such are the priorities when you decide to establish a vineyard on soil as free-draining as any in the state, miles from anywhere on one of the highest points of the Mount Lofty Ranges. Before anything else you secure your water supply. In South Australia your chances of getting any rain during spring and summer, just when the vines need nourishment, are pretty well zilch. So the Wynns harvest the winter rains instead. All across the stunning Mountadam spread, straddling the very spine of the hill tops which separate the Eden Valley from the Barossa, you'll see subtly graded banks running along the contours of the slopes, gradually working their way down to impressive dams at their base. Every winter about 865mm (34in) of rain fall on these acres. The Wynns harvest as much as they can and now own 910 million litres (200 million gallons) of rainwater – six years' supply of the lifeblood of the vine.

David Wynn knew exactly what he wanted when he bought the wild pastures of High Eden Ridge in 1972. He'd previously built up the family company of Samuel Wynn into one of Australia's most important operations. But he could see that he wouldn't be able to keep his independence for long, as bigger corporations moved in, so he decided to sell and start again.

David Wynn had always been the supreme innovator – seeing the potential of the great Coonawarra vineyards after the war, when the locals wanted to grub them up for grazing, and later pioneering the 'bag-in-box' wine cask. As the breweries closed in on Wynns, David identified a gap in the market whose existence is difficult for us nowadays to comprehend. Chardonnay. Except for a few vines in Mudgee, New South Wales, the whole of Australia had *no* Chardonnay. Ever the opportunist, David Wynn saw the gap and pounced.

The main reason South Australia had no Chardonnay was that when quarantine was imposed to guard against the vine louse phylloxera (which had destroyed the vineyards of neighbouring Victoria), the stock of available varieties was frozen at what was current at the beginning of the century. There was no Chardonnay then, so there was none now. After endless badgering of the Department of Agriculture David Wynn finally obtained the first Chardonnay vine to be allowed in

South Australia since that ban. He immediately set up a propagation system on the Adelaide Plains and began looking for a site where he could plant the vines. He realized that Australia's potential to make table wine of the highest quality lay in identifying areas of below average temperature, but if possible above average

sunlight hours and above average rainfall. He had created the cool climate vineyards of Coonawarra primarily for red grapes, because spring frosts were a real danger to early-budding white varieties like Chardonnay. The far south was cool, and had the rain, but too much of it fell in the autumn. The only solution seemed to be to head north of Coonawarra, but head high, into the mountains where the altitude would cool the air, even though the sunlight hours would be long. When David Wynn did pinpoint the place, he must have needed inspired vision to conceive of it as vineyard. Arid hilltop pasture, sandy soil full of quartz and schist, so shallow that the rocks jutted out of its slopes like fractured limbs. It could hardly support a flock of sheep, let alone a vineyard. It was parched in summer: between January and June you'd be lucky to get an inch and a half of rain. But the Mount Lofty Ranges act as magnets for all the moisture coming from the west, and Wynn's chosen spot was 600 metres (1970 feet) up; whatever winter rain came, he'd get first refusal. It would have been impossible to establish young vines here without irrigation – a single hot day and they'd just be rows of dead twigs in the sand. But that dryness suited him. 'You can always turn off the drips when the vines have had enough, but you can't stop it raining.'

When the vines are established, the soil moisture is constantly monitored and drip irrigation is used only to replace moisture lost, and then only up until veraison, when the grapes change colour. Up until that point a grape increases in size by cell division; after that point any further nourishment just pumps up the grapes with liquid – and the Wynns wanted small, intensely-flavoured berries at a maximum yield of three tons per acre. Although the first vines were planted in 1972, the Wynns didn't get a proper crop until 1979. And when I queried the fact that the spindly-looking vines were planted on wide spacings rather than in the stress-inducing narrow spacing traditional to much of Europe, Adam said that with soil as poor as this, if he planted close he probably wouldn't get any crop at all.

David planted four acres in 1972 – the biggest Chardonnay vineyard in Australia at a stroke, and he followed this with Pinot Noir, Riesling, Cabernet Sauvignon and later, Merlot. By choosing such an impoverished, well-drained site he was trying to duplicate, as far as he could, the soil conditions of the great French vineyards. In terms of selecting vines to plant, and indeed in their methods of wine-making, the Wynns are fanatically 'Burgundian'.

'You walk down a row in an old Burgundy vineyard and the vines and their grapes will all look different. They *are* different – each adding something individual to the flavour until together they make the symphonic wine.' Adam snorts in disgust at the Californian view of planting an entire vineyard with one or two clones. 'Of all the diseases we caught from America – phylloxera, downy mildew, powdery mildew – the saddest of all is clonal fixation.' He plants as many clones as he can lay his hands on. The Department of Agriculture has now appointed Mountadam as a test vineyard for new Pinot Noir clones – probably to stop Adam hassling them.

One thing worth remembering here, is that although David Wynn planted the vineyard, he never intended to make the wine as well. Mountadam was his gift to the next generation, and though he is still actively involved, the driving force in the winery is now very definitely his son, the beefy, boyish Adam Wynn.

The Wynns had made a good profit when they sold their original company, and it would have been easy simply to establish a 'state-of-the-art' vineyard and winery and run it pleasantly enough as a rich kid's plaything. Luckily Adam has a will of iron inside his rather cuddly frame. Inheriting from his father a love for the great wines of France, he attended university in Bordeaux, learning the language as he went and graduating top of his class. He then went to Burgundy and worked with leading producers Michelot and Leflaive – endlessly trying to explain to himself why what they did worked. They didn't always know. He'd ask Michelot what temperature he was fermenting his Meursault at – Michelot wouldn't know – so there would Adam be, crawling over the cobwebby barrels in the dim recesses of the cellars, clutching a thermometer in one hand and a torch in the other.

But he took everything in and even wrote a thesis for Bordeaux university on all the different factors affecting Chardonnay quality. Then he headed for California to see all the most up-to-date wine-making equipment at work – and by 1982 he was back at Mountadam, full of ideas, dying to start.

Which was all very well, but there wasn't a winery yet. So he designed one. When I first walked into this chilly barn of stainless steel and computers I was shocked. I'd been listening to Adam's passionate outpourings of belief in traditional values, yet this was the most futuristic winery I'd seen in all Australia. The reason Adam gave was simple – the key was gentleness. Despite frequently rustic conditions, all the traditional Burgundian techniques had the same final objective – the gentle coaxing of maximum flavour and fragrance from the fruit.

Simple Past, Future Perfect

'Competence, attention to detail, control,' is how Adam describes his philosophy in the winery, sounding far less impassioned than he does among his vines. His crusher-destemmer was made by the small Burgundy firm of Demoisy and is so gentle it can remove stems yet still leave a high proportion of the berries whole. His press is the most modern Willmes airbag press which massages the juice out rather than squeezing the grapes dry, though he never tests its full pressing strength on the Mountadam wines. His stainless steel tanks are all moveable and their lids can be adjusted to any level of wine inside the vessel to avoid any air contact and prevent loss of aromas. And all the tanks are computer-controlled so that they can be pre-set to a desirable fermentation temperature 24 hours a day.

That's the metal. The wood brings back the gleam to Adam's eyes. 'I love barrels,' he murmurs, and you can sense he'd happily spend all day in the dim cool vault among the casks. 'This scene hasn't changed, apart from the electric light, for a thousand years. For me as a winemaker that's a very special common thread. There ain't no substitute for growing bloody good grapes and sticking them in bloody good barrels.'

Most of his Chardonnay never sees metal again after the grapes are crushed and destemmed. The juice is run straight off, to avoid skin contact which might add bitter flavours. It settles overnight, and the next day is poured, cloudy and untreated into a mix of 225-litre (50-gallon) and 500-litre (110-gallon) French oak barrels up to three years old. (A small portion is fermented in tank just in case the final wine needs an injection of fresh fruit flavours.)

With grapes in different sections of the vineyard ripening at different times, differences in both size and age of barrel, and a varying percentage – between 15 and 40 per cent – encouraged to go through malolactic fermentation, Wynn ends up with between 12 and 18 different parcels of wine to play around with for his eventual blend. 'I'm constantly fiddling; it's bloody marvellous,' he says as any chance of us getting dinner recedes into the High Eden cool night air. And tasting alongside him, there are indeed dramatic differences between barrels, but all the wines have beautifully integrated fruit and wood flavours as well as a warm perfume of grilled cashews and hazelnuts, banana and pear, sometimes raisin, sometimes – especially from the last-picked lower vineyard block – the explosive marriage of butterscotch, banana and sarsaparilla.

And there's another feature common to all the Mountadam wines, but especially to the Chardonnays – fatness, creamy softness, what the French call 'gras'. The passion burns brighter in Adam Wynn's eyes. Low yields give tightly packed, undiluted flavours. The barrel fermentation starts at 15°C (59°F), churns up to 26°C (79°F) and then very slowly tails away, and the high temperature encourages the yeasts to produce more glycerols. The malolactic pumps up the cream – but he also leaves the wine for four months on its lees and gradually that fatness he wants seeps out of the yeasts.

That soft texture envelops his Pinot Noir too. Good Australian Pinot Noirs are still rare but Wynn thinks the problem is that many winemakers try to apply Bordeaux methods to Pinot when traditionally Bordeaux and Burgundy are poles apart. He starts with low-yield fruit – usually about three tons to the acre – and more clones than anyone else in Australia. His crusher allows him to keep up to half the berries without stems. Then he pours all the juice and fruit into stainless steel – whops in a *lot* of yeast – and lets it rip – bang. Again *very* Burgundian.

This'll froth away for four to five days at 30°C (86°F) giving all the colour, the tannin he wants. Now

he has to create the 'gras'. So he draws the semi-wine off, still hot and active, and presses it. Out shoots the juice from the whole berries, still only half-fermented and full of sugar and he then pours the juice into small barrels where fermentation continues – at about 15°C (59°F), slowly completing over two to three weeks. The yeasts, which were going like crazy in the tank, but had used up almost all their sugar and micro-nutrients, are suddenly given another dose of sugar, their temperature drops by a half and they're slapped into a small, oxygen-less barrel. Stress those yeasts. As Adam describes it, in terms of metabolic pathways detoured, even I feel stressed. Anyway, this is how the glycerol is produced, providing that essential fat texture in the wine. The Burgundians do it by adding sugar, even in the warmest years. Adam's found a better way.

Do Me a Flavour

His Pinots have a wonderful flavour – brilliantly round and gentle, bursting with the perfumed fruit of black cherries, the rough sweet caress of damson skins, the hint of soft leather. But what is just as exciting is how he has managed to moderate his Burgundian passion to encompass the Bordeaux grapes Merlot and Cabernet Sauvignon, and the Rhône grape Shiraz too.

The Merlot is absurdly good, packed with the juice of bright fresh blackcurrants, and a perfume as sweet and erotic as a handbag full of lipstick and scent. He usually blends it with his dark, gorgeously ripe yet balanced Cabernet, but I can see him agonizing about doing anything to impair the magical perfume of the Merlot. And he buys in some Shiraz to create a heady brew full of the richness of blackberries and black olives, cream and chocolate and raspberries and the slight savoury sweetness of parsley butter.

We did make dinner – just – and I finally decided that Adam Wynn does represent a crucial link between the ages-old hedonism of Burgundy and the technocratic excess which can sometimes draw Australia back from fulfilling its great potential. 'No one drinks wine for the nose,' he said. 'They drink it for the roundness, the warmth, the generosity.' He looked across at me with a sly grin. '2000 years of wine writing, and every wine those guys liked was about generosity, richness and warmth.' Right on, Adam.

Mountarrow

*I*T WAS NEVER GOING to work the way it was. Sometimes people seem to forget that the establishment of a winery and vineyards is a specialized project requiring planning and considerable expertise. At the end of the 1960s the Hunter Valley, a sleepy region with a considerable historic reputation for its wines but by then covered in more grazing land than vineyard, was convulsed with investors piling in and establishing vineyards. Almost all of them rushed in headlong, and almost all came a cropper – none more so than a place named Arrowfield.

Most of the other investment projects were centred on land which had at one time been vineyard land, but vines had never been grown on Arrowfield turf, and the

place was chiefly famous for having bred the winner of the 1920 Melbourne Cup. That didn't deter its new owners, W R Carpenter & Company, who, between 1969 and 1974, planted 485 hectares (1200 acres) of vines stretching across the hills above Jerrys Plains as far as the eye could see. Eight million vines were planted, more than half of them red Shiraz and Cabernet Sauvignon.

By 1977 Arrowfield was the largest single vineyard in Australia. At the same time it was perfectly obvious that Shiraz in particular was a completely unsuitable variety for the new vineyard and would never produce anything special. And Australians were turning in droves from red wine to white.

In the meantime the most massive winery had been constructed, an enormous, gaunt, two-level barn of a place, with stainless steel tanks ready to take 5 million litres (1 million gallons) of juice. State-of-the-art, it was thought to be, but was it? The fermenting tanks were the biggest I have ever seen – some holding 55,000 litres (12,000 gallons) of juice – and there's a battery of 16 incredibly corpulent 40,000-litre (8750-gallon) tanks. All intended for red wine. As Rob Dolan, the cheerful and talented ex-Australian-Rules-footballer, who is one of the two winemakers now coping with this jungle says – 10,000 litres (2000 gallons) is really the maximum size for making red wine. You can't control the temperature of an enormous tank, even with cooling jackets. Juice may be fermenting at 15°C (60°F) on the outside and have spots practically boiling in the middle, just where you can't get to them.

Arrowfield stayed in the game by dint of massive clearance sales of unexceptional red wine. During the 1980s, vineyards were dug up and returned to pasture, and the land under vine is now reduced to 80 hectares (200 acres). The winery limped along, making some surprisingly good wines on its own account, but paying its bills and keeping its machinery occupied by doing contract wine-making for, at the last count, nine or ten different companies. And it was this unglamorous occupation which brought about the transformation of the Arrowfield dinosaur into the go-ahead, high-profile outfit now called Mountarrow.

Andrew Simon was the owner of New South Wales' most successful wine retailing operation, Camperdown Cellars. In 1982 he went into partnership with Nick Whitlam, son of Australia's colourful ex-premier Gough, to buy a beautiful vineyard property at the western end of the lower Hunter Valley. Arrowfield wasn't far away and was touting for business as a contract winemaker, so that's where they sent their grapes. From the start the wines, sold under the label Simon Whitlam, were of exciting quality and by the end of the 1980s were winning gold medals at home and abroad. The Simon Whitlam partnership was itching to expand. The owners of Arrowfield were more than ready to offload, and the owners of an 8-hectare (17.5-acre) vineyard made a 'Jonah swallows the whale' bid for the colossal Arrowfield operation – and succeeded. They themselves have now offloaded day-to-day control to a Japanese *sake* producer.

The success can actually be put down to the shrewd professionalism and burning ambition of Andrew Simon. And this is the difference between the entrepreneurs of the sixties and those of the nineties. Andrew Simon was a very successful marketing man. He also knew what made good and bad wine. The vineyards remaining around the old Arrowfield winery

Arrowfield, now called Mountarrow, is a vast modern folly only now starting to realize its potential.

are potentially some of the best in the Upper Hunter. And the two winemakers – Rob Dolan and Simon Gilbert – had already proved they could make fine wine against considerable odds in the late 1980s.

What was needed was a brand new set of wines at different price levels – and a philosophy of wine-making which drew on whatever grape supplies were required to produce the style and quality needed – regardless of where they were grown.

Mountarrow Wines was formed by Simon and Whitlam in February 1989. They kept on the Arrowfield name, but came out with three entirely new ranges in 1989, plus the small-scale but dynamic Simon Whitlam and Simon Gilbert labels. Each line is characterized by a visually striking presentation, an aura of glamour and prestige which seems bang in line with the projected consumer self-perception.

The market for uncomplicated, everyday drinking is attacked on three different levels by the Arrowfield range – graced with original artwork by Ashleigh Manley – and the two other new names – Mountarrow Pro Hart Collection, and Carisbrook Estate. Pro Hart is a hugely popular Australian artist whose vivid colours and dynamic brushstrokes reflect raw outback life. A 'free, glossy reproduction' of a Pro Hart print is sealed inside every case of wine ordered as a bonus. I can see suburban Australia flocking to the brand. The Carisbrook Estate labels feature a unique Australian animal – the wombat embellishes the full-bodied Cabernet Sauvignon, the possum is on the Semillon, the duckbilled platypus on the Chardonnay. They aim to start making donations from each bottle purchased to the Australian Wildlife Conservation Fund. In ecologically sensitive times, this is astute marketing too.

This could all smack of nothing more than smart marketing whizzkiddery, were it not for the quality of the wines. Each line is characterized by a different personality – supremely elegant and exciting Simon Gilbert and Simon Whitlam wines, the more obviously commercial Pro Harts, the fruity, easy drinking Carisbrook Estate wines.

A lot of the best white grapes come from Mudgee and Cowra – between three and six hours' drive from the Hunter Valley. The best reds are virtually devoid of Hunter influence. Mudgee provides some, but the real class is provided by grapes from Coonawarra in southern South Australia, and Mitchelton in Central Victoria. Should we mind? Not really. Mountarrow just use the best grapes available for the styles they want to make. Good wine-making hand-in-hand with good marketing makes Mountarrow a rare example of the best of both worlds.

Petaluma

*B*RIAN CROSER IS THE MOST misunderstood winemaker in Australia. I should know. I've been doing a substantial chunk of the misunderstanding. And he wants to set the record straight. On my last trip to Australia he hauled me up to his tasting room at Piccadilly in the hills above Adelaide, lined up the samples, going from the first wines he ever made at his Petaluma winery to unfermented juice from the 1990 vintage and said, 'right, let's go through it all one more time.' The rain beat against the window panes, night was closing in, and it was a very long walk back down the mountain to Adelaide and the promise of a decent dinner. I had a distinct feeling that if I didn't concentrate I'd be getting very wet, very footsore and very hungry in the very near future.

Croser gets misunderstood because he has indeed been a passionate advocate of the use of technology – as sophisticated as you can muster – in the production of fine wine. He argues that if you are aware of every possible chemical, organic and mechanical tool, and are aware of the various applications for which these things may be suitable, it gives you enormous freedom as a winemaker – but not a freedom for you simply to interpret your own flights of fancy, rather a freedom to allow the vineyard every opportunity to express the ultimate quality of which its fruit is capable. That's where the misunderstandings occur.

In 1976 Croser, back from studying at Davis in California, set up a wine-making course in the far south-western hinterland of New South Wales at Wagga Wagga, at least partly out of a sense of dissatisfaction with the lack of 'state-of-the-art' wine-making instruction in Australia. His radical challenges to established wine-making practices in Australia encouraged many bright students to enrol, people who are now making wine all around the continent, and in New Zealand too. In 1978 Croser formed the wine consultancy Oenotec with a colleague, Tony Jordan. There is hardly a successful winery in Australia that has not availed itself of Oenotec's advice at some time, whether they admit to it publicly or not.

This was a period, running right through the 1980s, when the winemaker and his skills were seen as the most important factors in the creation of fine wine. It was felt that a bright winemaker could transform less than perfect quality fruit into great wine through high-tech wizardry in the winery. And much of the knowledge came from Croser. He was seen as the guru of high-tech during a technologically-obsessed decade.

However, in the 1990s we are in a very different kind of decade. Increasingly, wine producers are realizing

PETALUMA

1989 CHARDONNAY

750ml

PRODUCE OF AUSTRALIA BOTTLED AT PICCADILLY SA

PETALUMA

1987 COONAWARRA

750ml

PRODUCE OF AUSTRALIA BOTTLED AT PICCADILLY SA

that until they get a source of healthy, characterful grapes to work on, there is only so much they can do in the quality stakes. Many have seemed to turn against Croser, appearing to blame him for their own lack of vision, and regarding him as the ice-eyed captive of a computer-controlled stainless steel environment.

They couldn't have got him more wrong. Throughout the 1980s, Brian Croser was in fact dedicating himself to the soil, to the vines, to the fruit they produce. His views on technology have scarcely changed. Technology is his tool, not his master; he understands its capabilities probably better than any other Australian, and in so doing is aware of its shortcomings. But his views on the importance of the right land and the right grapes grown in the right way have been evolving with every vintage. And rather than any evidence of arrogance, I have noticed an increasing sense of humility as he feels confident enough to explain the shortcomings of his earlier vintages and accept the rather more hedonistic urgings of his great friend and 'agent provocateur of the palate', Len Evans. He is able to revel in the sheer beauty of his wines' flavours at the end of the 1980s rather than the impressive but slightly soulless flavours he frequently produced at the beginning of the decade.

Brian is far more a man of the soil than he is given credit for, and he is prepared to learn only as fast as his land will let him. It took him from 1979 to 1987 to produce a red wine that really satisfied his vision. It took him ten years before he produced a Chardonnay in 1988 which really thrilled him, and although he still expects people to agree with him when he calls his Riesling 1980 the best wine he's made, I have to disagree. I'm sure his 1990 Riesling will be better, and since 1988 his reds and his Chardonnays outshine his Riesling. The reason it took this long is because the vineyards he began developing in 1978 took this long to give him good enough grapes.

Croser began making wine from a variety of vineyard sources under the Petaluma label while he was teaching at Wagga Wagga, but as early as 1969, at university in Adelaide, he was researching into the feasibility of finding and developing a local cool climate site. Since his horticultural studies had convinced him of the importance of acid preservation in fruit as a precursor of quality, and a cool, humid growing climate was clearly the best way of achieving that, the damp, mist enshrouded hills above Adelaide were an immediate temptation, in particular the high Piccadilly valley

Brian Croser, one of Australia's pioneers in the table wine revolution, makes sparkling wine as well.

where his father had some land. Too cold, too rainy, said the locals, but Croser's appetite was further whetted when he did a survey of the Australian wine market and concluded that the most glaring gaps in the Australian wine-production portfolio were Chardonnay, Pinot Noir and Champagne-method sparkling wines. The classic versions of these came from Burgundy and Champagne, two of the dampest and coolest wine regions in France.

He did actually manage to plant a few vines on his father's land in 1974, but the sheep got to them before he could – except for one Traminer which even now climbs through the branches of a silver birch in the front garden. By 1979 he had managed to purchase some land of his own, and planting of Chardonnay and Pinot Noir began in earnest.

However he had bills to pay, and as well as developing Oenotec, he formed an increasingly close association with Len Evans of Rothbury Estate in the Hunter Valley. The Petaluma winery at Piccadilly was initially built to process Evans' grapes from vineyards in Clare and Coonawarra. In 1980 these vineyards were incorporated into the Petaluma operation and have provided grapes for Petaluma wines ever since. Throughout the 1980s Evans was chairman of Petaluma.

The Petaluma Riesling is made from Clare fruit and it hit its stride right from the start. The 1979 is deep and golden with soft flavours of biscuits and butter. The 1980, Croser's favourite, is leaner, higher in acid, with fresh green fruit like candied lime peel and a touch of buttered cream. Both are beautiful wines, and in each ensuing vintage, whether warmer or cooler, this marvellously incisive lime peel acid strikes through the heart of the wine, made fragrant, in years like 1987 and 1990, by the scent of flowers.

Croser keeps the yield low, and with the lightest of drip irrigations, coaxes the small crop to ripeness. The grapes are then transported in whole bunches to Piccadilly, chilled, crushed, and left to drain under cover of inert gas. This juice may remain in stainless steel at -2°C (28°F) for months before fermentation while Croser decides which yeast strain he should use for each batch. Over-technological? Croser says no. Riesling is a light-bodied, aromatic grape. He wants all that delicacy and all that aroma in the bottle. So he'll choose the yeast for fermentation with care and he'll protect the juice and wine from air and oxidation all the way. And his Rieslings last for ten years at the very least. Croser says that's because he's 'cottonwooled' the fragile fruit sufficiently to allow it the chance to bloom.

His Chardonnay juice gets the cottonwool treatment as well. He has experimented with skin contact, with

solids fermentations and with malolactic fermentation –
and bitterly regretted it every time, because it interfered
with the nature of the fruit he wished to emphasize. He
makes sure the fruit from the vineyard is totally clean,
and again subjects it to a protective regime, always
shielded from air by inert gas, always kept cold, and
after crushing he settles the juice by gravity at -2°C
(28°F) for three weeks and then racks and stores it at
-2°C (28°F) until he is ready to ferment. This can be
months later, but that juice will be naturally star-bright.
He'll begin the fermentation eventually in stainless steel,
but transfer the wine to Vosges oak barrels for the
remainder of the fermentation, which takes about a
month at 12° to 15°C (54° to 59°F), then it will be left
undisturbed on the lees in the barrel for about a year at
8°C (46°F), after which it'll be allowed to fall bright at
-2°C (28°F) again, and bottled.

Croser is using his technological skills to preserve,
not manipulate. And the dramatic improvement in
Petaluma Chardonnay during the 1980s is due to his
gradually achieving the fruit he wants. He began with
hot climate Cowra grapes. By 1982 nearly three-quarters
came from Coonawarra and the rest from Cowra. By
1986, he had cut back the Coonawarra component to 40
per cent, brought in 40 per cent Clare and 20 per cent
Piccadilly; the wine was still fairly full, yet now fell
halfway between a blowsy, tropical fruit style and
something finer.

At last in 1987, the transformation really begins. Half
the fruit is now from Piccadilly, half from Clare, and
despite the very cool year, this is a beautiful, lightly
toasted, balanced Chardonnay. 1988, from riper fruit
from the same vineyards, has a marvellous creamy
texture, an exciting lemon and apple fruit wreathed in
scent. Ah, but the 1989. All Piccadilly fruit at last.
Brian's long wait is over and the wine is wonderful – so
intense, so marvellously dry with lemon peel and peach,
already building a beautiful toasty spice richness and a
lingering savour of quince. I remember Brian saying as
long ago as 1983 that he was after the flavour of quince
in his Chardonnay. This is the first time I've seen it,
because this is the first time he's been able to use the
grapes he really wants; the grapes from Piccadilly are
ready at long last.

Petaluma reds have undergone a similar
transformation. Handling is minimal right the way
through, settling is always by sub-zero temperature and
by gravity, and he doesn't even filter the wine before
bottling. That's the mark of a truly confident
winemaker secure in the knowledge that his technology
has provided the featherbedding necessary for a totally
healthy, stable wine without safeguards like filtration.

*Carefully husbanded Riesling vineyards contrast with the
unforgiving natural conditions of the Clare Valley slopes.*

Yet the wine has only achieved the pitch of excitement
Croser seeks since 1987 and '88.

Most of the grapes for Petaluma red have always
come from the Coonawarra vineyard initially purchased
by Len Evans. Years of grafting over of varieties like
Shiraz to Merlot and Cabernet, converting the vines to
a vertical trellis, and introducing closer spacing have
paid off. In 1987 Coonawarra had a bad vintage.
Petaluma's low-yielding vines ripened about three weeks
earlier than the other vineyards, with higher sugar,
better acid and better colour. And they made a beautiful
wine with a gorgeous deep blackcurrant and raspberry
fruit and only a most attractive green leafy quality

showing that the vintage conditions had been poor. There was no leafiness in the 1988 – a triumph of perfectly balanced fruit, rich, weighty, but never cloying, the tannins in harmony, the richness of fruit coating itself with the exotic sweetness of clove and allspice. Brian's normally gentle demeanour seems to glow with pride, as, for the first time in seven years of tasting Petaluma wines, my own excitement shows that I finally understand what he's getting at.

There are now 60 hectares (150 acres) of vines planted around Piccadilly, mostly Chardonnay and Pinot Noir, and Croser has a major sparkling wine project under way in which Bollinger of France are partners. Each vintage the bubbly gets better, a little fuller, a little creamier and more tantalising. It's a challenge Croser is determined to meet, but maybe this time the technology is as important as the fruit. As he says – once you put the yeast into the bottle to start a second fermentation and slam in the cork – all you can do is sit and watch for three years and hope to hell you've got it right.

Still, he's given himself enough time to work on it. A lifetime. As we headed out into the night, he said 'the real question is – who owns the best vineyards in the right spot, growing the right grapes in the right way, and who has established the stability in business structure to enable them to sit in the same place for a lifetime, working with the same vineyards, and the same grapes, and refining things step by step. If you want my life's ambition – that's it in a flash.' And this is the guy they call a technocrat. A Burgundian twelve thousand miles from home more like.

TASMANIA

Pipers Brook

The frontiers of wine-making. Pipers Brook clears a swathe of the Tasmanian forest. The tall gums watch and wait.

*I*T'S JUST A LITTLE CREEK straggling through the last bit of dry land before you hit the Antarctic, yet the area along its banks already has the reputation of being the nearest thing in Australia to Bordeaux, and to Burgundy, *and* to Champagne. This is Pipers Brook in the north-east of Tasmania, where Pinot Noir, Chardonnay and Cabernet Sauvignon have all produced dazzling wines, if not on a regular basis, and this is where the Champagne house of Roederer has planted a 20-hectare (50-acre) plot with Pinot Noir and Chardonnay for sparkling wine.

It all started because one of Australia's foremost vineyard experts had a hunch. Andrew Pirie, who founded Pipers Brook Vineyard in 1974, had been working for several years on the hunch that Australia's burgeoning wine industry would quickly come to a point where improvement in the fruit flavour of the wines was no longer possible, and the subtleties of perfume and style that made the European cool climate classics so fascinating would seem unobtainable – because the conditions were *too* easy for the vine.

In the early 1970s the areas of New South Wales, Victoria and South Australia which were producing the most sought-after wines were all positively over-indulged with sunlight and heat during the ripening season. In a word, life for an Australian vine was cushy, but despite the fact that clever wine-making was creating some first-class flavours, they still didn't stand up against the European classics. Pirie was in the process of finishing his thesis for what would be Australia's first doctorate in viticulture, and had decided that, even if Australian wine-making know-how was already second to none, Australian vines were not delivering the right sort of fruit, for the simple reason that they were not stressed enough.

Many Australian vineyard experts tend to take a diametrically opposed view, but if you travel through the vineyards of Bordeaux, Burgundy or Champagne in France, there are several things you notice. The soil is poor, for a start, often, as in the Médoc region of Bordeaux, poor to the point of being deficient. The vines are savagely pruned, and the plants are packed far closer together than is common in Australia. Encouraging competition, this is called. And the French weather is hardly reliable and benign. Ripening the fruit enough to acquire the sugar needed to make decent wine is often a struggle right up to the moment the grapes are picked. Pirie spent 1971 touring France, noting these growing methods and these conditions time and time again in the areas which produced the wines he most admired, and he returned to Australia convinced he had to duplicate such conditions. He had to make the vines put up a struggle.

Tasmania had briefly had a wine industry in the nineteenth century – in fact the cuttings which were the basis of both the Victorian and the South Australian wine industries came from Tasmania in 1834 – but during the twentieth century, almost nothing had happened. In 1965, an official report had concluded Tasmania was simply too cold to ripen grapes.

Pirie would have agreed with this to begin with. He was based in Sydney in the early 1970s and had initially expected to find conditions similar to cool climate Europe in the high altitude areas towards Canberra. It was cool there alright. But those sites still didn't match Europe for one crucial reason – the strong sunlight

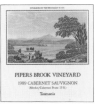 

despite being one of the most southerly vineyard areas in the world, still only straddles latitudes 41° and 43° S. In Europe that's the equivalent of the baking plains of central Spain. In Europe the long, broiling ripening season renders such land unsuitable for grapes for fine wine. The vineyards of Bordeaux and Burgundy are relatively northerly at between 45° and 47° N. However, western Europe's climate is tempered by warm ocean currents. In southern Australia, the coastal influence is cool Antarctic water. Pirie saw a double benefit here. He could get a ripening period with extended sunlight hours as long as those of Mediterranean Europe – almost eight weeks longer than the Rhine in Germany, and even a week or so longer than Bordeaux, yet the actual daily temperatures would stay low because of the humidity and Antarctic influences.

Up to a point it has worked. Some of the wines from Pipers Brook and the neighbouring Heemskerk vineyard have been exceptionally good, and some Chardonnays in particular have shown the wonderful oatmealy, buttery flavour of top Burgundy. In the south of the island, especially on mesoclimates warmed by the waters of the Derwent estuary, such as at Moorilla Estate for instance, higher temperatures for ripening have been recorded and thrilling Pinot Noirs and Cabernets have been produced.

Yet, it is still a struggle. Progress in planting has been remarkably slow, and although the late 1980s saw a spurt as not only Roederer, but also Deutz, Domaine Chandon and Yalumba all established vineyards on the island to produce sparkling wine, the entire island's production is still normally less than a single vineyard like Rosemount's Roxburgh in the Upper Hunter Valley. Roederer have found that the cooling winds, particularly those from the north-west, have more of an effect than they bargained for, and crops are depressingly erratic as a mix of poor springtime weather, uncertain vintage conditions, and flocks of grape-crazy birds make long-term planning a nightmare.

Yet when Pirie went south, he knew what he was up against. It had taken the French 2000 years to find those marginal conditions he so admired, to select the right grape types, to work out a way of cultivating them and coaxing them to ripeness. If Pirie and his colleagues get near to it in a generation, that won't be bad going.

hours during the growing season could be almost twice those of his French models. Pirie had seen how cloud cover and high humidity in the Lower Hunter Valley helped to create delicate fruit flavours despite the tremendous daytime heat. He had also seen how areas that were less hot but also less humid, often could not avoid the baked flavour of overripe fruit in their wines. Atmospheric moisture seemed to hold the key. The only place he was going to find humidity allied to gentle sunlight conditions, was south, much further south, across the Bass Strait to the island of Tasmania.

In the north-east of the island, a few miles inland along Pipers Brook, Andrew Pirie found conditions closer to cool climate France than anywhere else in Australia. Crucially, the humidity was only marginally lower than in Bordeaux, although average temperatures during the growing season were in general closer to Burgundy. In general. Some years the weather in Tasmania is so poor that temperatures are more like those of the Mosel in northern Germany. Clearly vintage quality was not going to be predictable, but then it wasn't in Bordeaux or Burgundy either. Tasmania,

Rosemount

*B*OB OATLEY IS A clackety-featured big-business bruiser, with eyes full of humour at the same time as they probe for the main chance, full of matey chat as he delves past your defences, and, when he's charmed you and beguiled you, he'll pounce. Fast, decisive, instinctive as a swooping bird of prey.

Oatley is a highly successful coffee and cocoa planter in Papua New Guinea, but he was born in Sydney, brought up within scampering distance of the boats and the beach at Manley on the edge of Sydney Harbour, and although he made his fortune in more humid, tropical climes, he's always retained a passionate need for his Sydney base, the romance of the cool breeze on his brow as he tacks to starboard, the cold beer and quiet reflection under the evening stars, as the waves lap gently over the anchor chain.

By the end of the 1960s, financially secure, he was ready to indulge the emotional side of his nature a little more – keeping a good eye on the business possibilities, of course – and he bought a broad spread of land in the Upper Hunter Valley so that he could concentrate on the gentlemanly, albeit profitable, pursuits of cattle grazing and breeding horses within easy driving distance of his Sydney home. Since there was quite a wine boom going on an hour's drive south in the Lower Hunter Valley, he planted some vines as well. That instinctive decision to plant some vines on his new property was to propel him into an international limelight he and his Rosemount winery have basked in ever since.

The move brought the discovery that Rosemount was in fact the site of the only successful nineteenth-century vineyard in the Upper Hunter. (All the famous Hunter Valley wines had until then come from the Lower Hunter, closer to Sydney, earlier ripening, and with more regular rainfall.) Rosemount made some wine in 1973 – pretty ordinary stuff by all accounts. 1974 didn't seem a great improvement, but 1975 saw them launch the first Rosemount wine into Australian shops, and suddenly this totally unknown wine company won a stream of five gold medals at the major wine shows with its decidedly unfashionable Traminer white. Overnight people began talking and drinking Rosemount.

Oatley was nothing if not sensitive to future market trends. He saw that Chardonnay was just beginning to create waves in California. Rosemount didn't have Chardonnay. But Penfolds did, at Wybong, a massive development of over 500 hectares (1235 acres), near

Rosemount, which was proving a colossal financial disaster to them. In 1977 when a Penfolds executive suggested to Oatley that they'd accept any reasonable offer for the Wybong vineyards and winery, he mortgaged everything he had, bought the whole outfit, and was set fair to make Rosemount one of the most powerful names in Australian wine.

Other Australian wineries had become famous within a decade of their birth – indeed, every year during the 1970s and 1980s saw exciting newcomers making waves. But these were all tiny weekend wineries run by people who worked as doctors or accountants during the week. Rosemount was going to be run on strictly business lines, and that meant taking on the industry giants as quickly and as efficiently as possible. The vast Wybong winery gave him the equipment and production capacity he needed. And, true, it gave him some Chardonnay. But his vineyard experts warned him that neither the Rosemount nor the Wybong vineyards would ever produce anything but good commercial wines – it was almost impossible to control the vines' vigour, and yields were high.

In the meantime, another Upper Hunter vineyard venture was getting into serious financial difficulties. Denman Estates had established a great swathe of vineyards during the early 1970s wine boom, in the middle of grazing land about 19km (12 miles) from Rosemount. Their ambitions overreached themselves at precisely the time the bottom was falling out of the wine market, and by late 1977, they had a large winery and two particularly sizeable plots of land partially planted with vines, but no customers for the wines, and not much time to run on their tax breaks.

Ugly Duckling or Swan?

Bob Oatley and his new general manager (now managing director) Chris Hancock went to have a look at the place and saw a tangle of thistles and weeds interspersed with spindly vines, some alive, some long since killed by downy mildew. The Roxburgh vineyard. Yet Hancock says it just smelled right, something just seemed . . . right. The whole property was 270 hectares (667 acres) with only a small percentage planted, including just two hectares (five acres) of Chardonnay. The price wasn't too stiff though, so they bought, and in 1980 they managed to eke 15 tons of Chardonnay from Roxburgh despite the dreadful state of the land. That was a promising yield. They mixed this with some fruit from their ex-Penfolds vines, as well as a little from Mudgee just outside the Hunter Valley and labelled it Rosemount Show Reserve. 1980 Show Reserve was a brilliant success, winning gold medals

Philip Shaw's boyish good looks belie an extremely sophisticated and market-conscious wine-making talent.

across the globe, and it confirmed several things to Oatley and Hancock. None of the big companies was ready to produce major quantities of Chardonnay. Rosemount would jump the gun and become Australia's first Chardonnay baron. More Chardonnay plantings became the top priority. They'd only had a couple of years to try to beat their Wybong and Roxburgh vineyards into some kind of shape and the Chardonnays were already producing gold medal wines. And they'd only had a couple of years' experience of how to make the wines too, yet here they were, luscious, soft, unctuous wines which had the show judges reeling in shock and wine drinkers gasping for more. And we *were* gasping for more. I remember when Rosemount Show Reserve 1980 hit the British shops, with its honeyed spice, its brazil nuts cream, its whiff of toasty smoke and an almost syrupy texture. Chardonnay was never going to be the same again.

And it showed them that Roxburgh was capable of giving fruit of an intensity far greater than any other vineyard they knew of in Australia. Roxburgh resembles a weal, an ancient scar, vivid red soil pushing up against the deep blue sky. It's the terra rosa soil, virtually the same stuff that you find in Australia's other famous terra rosa region Coonawarra. And it sits astride a limestone outcrop, while all around the vineyard knoll, the soil has eroded away. The track up the side marks the very edge. On the vineyard side the soil is warm and

red, and within the width of the track, it has become chill, brown and cloddish. At the bottom of the vineyard dark, blackish basaltic soil marks the limit of the quality land.

They've planted about 200 hectares (500 acres) of vines in Roxburgh now, and some of the new plantings are on the best soil yet – not bad going when commentators are already calling the existing land the 'Montrachet of Australia'. It's cost well over four million dollars to develop, but if the quality of the new wine is as good as the old, it'll be money well spent.

So far Roxburgh is very much a white wine vineyard – it also produces wonderful Semillon – but none of the Cabernets they've tried have succeeded. They've now committed some top land to Pinot Noir to see if that will coax out some of the Roxburgh magic into the reds.

Until it does, Roxburgh remains in everyone's mind as the vineyard yielding the most startlingly rich and luscious of Chardonnays in a country that produces its fair share. Since 1982 the wine-making has been in the hands of Philip Shaw, a boyish, shy tyro with superb technological training which he now delights in laying to one side. He experiments endlessly, in particular with different types of barrels, different uses of them, different levels of oxidation or protection for the wines. He came from a background of making some of Australia's most commercial wines at Lindeman's giant Karadoc winery and he's now in charge of the fruit from what is possibly Australia's greatest single vineyard. To the fury of his rivals, Shaw manages to produce Chardonnay of a world class which can nonetheless seduce all comers.

Commercialism and quality. That's Rosemount in a nutshell. When that 1980 Show Reserve won a Double Gold Medal at the International Wine and Spirits Competition in England in 1982, Bob Oatley and Chris Hancock travelled to London to receive their award in the House of Lords. And there they were at midnight standing on Westminster Bridge in their best bib and tucker listening to Big Ben chime twelve, still dazed by the rapid turn of events and wondering what they'd let themselves in for. Finally Bob broke the silence between the two. 'We'd better have a go at this, Chris,' he said. 'Yup,' said Chris. And they did.

Max Schubert

*H*E MUST HAVE SOME imagination, that Max Schubert. There he was, sheltering from the torrid vintage-time heat in a bodega in Jerez, the air filled with the intoxicating sweet-sour fumes of fermenting sherry – and he was beginning to formulate a first vision of what would eventually emerge as Australia's greatest red wine – Grange Hermitage. Max had been sent to Spain by the chairman of Penfolds, the company he worked for in Australia, because the feeling was that he made uncommonly good 'sherry' from Australian grapes without ever having experienced how it was really done in Spain. The chairman liked 'sherry', and certainly looked forward to Max returning to Australia full of ideas which he would then put to good use and further improve the flavour of Penfolds 'sherry'.

But there he was, in the late summer of 1949, prowling around the sherry vats and not thinking of sherry at all. He was thinking of wood. Because the air was full of another, much more exotic smell – something spicy, smoky and sweet. It was the new American oak that was being used to ferment the wine. And in all his years at Penfolds – he'd joined the company as a 16-year-old in 1931 – he'd never smelled the scent of wine fermenting in new wood. In Australia, on the rare occasions when new wood was purchased, it was used for brandy production.

New oak and its heady sweet perfume caught up with Max again a month or so later. He had managed to wheedle a few more weeks' 'study tour' out of his boss, and arrived in Bordeaux as the 1949 grape harvest was in full swing. The gradual replacement of wood ravaged by war was proceeding apace, frequently with American oak, and now Schubert could put the two different aromas together – the sweetness of wood, and the sweetness of wine from super-ripe red wine grapes. He was lucky to be in France in 1949, because Bordeaux had experienced a bakingly hot year – the temperature in the Médoc had risen to 63°C (145°F) at one point, and October was turning out to be the driest on record. If ever a Bordeaux year was bringing in fruit of comparable sugar-stuffed ripeness to the grapes Max had at his disposal in South Australia, 1949 was the one.

The thing that struck him most about the young wines was how incredibly deep and powerful they were, when Bordeaux had always had a reputation for delicacy. Schubert was lucky to have a kind and indulgent mentor in the late Christian Cruse, one of the last of the old-school grandees of the Bordeaux trade, who showed him that Bordeaux wines from ripe vintages – 1929, 1928, 1900, 1899 – could last and last, even maintaining some of their youthful structure, as well as developing their bewitching and inimitable fragrance. And Max was not overawed in the least. 'I didn't think it was any big deal. If I could get the right material I could do the same in Australia.' But would anyone want to drink the wine?

Australia in the early 1950s was not a table wine drinking society. Beer and fortified wine were the main drinks people wanted, and most red grape vineyards were planted with 'port' production in mind. Consequently Schubert returned from Europe, his mind occupied with the flavours of France, to find that there were no comparable wines at all in Australia, none whose flavours he could examine, none whose makers he could quiz about methods. So he'd have to do it the hard way. From scratch.

First Find Your Grapes

He must have kept the quality of his 'sherry' up, because the chairman was enthusiastically behind his decision to try to create a 'Bordeaux First Growth' red in Australia. Except that Max didn't have any Bordeaux grapes. And he didn't have any oak. Most red Bordeaux is based on Cabernet Sauvignon, helped out by Merlot, Cabernet Franc, Malbec and Petit Verdot. Well, Penfolds had a few sparse acres of Cabernet Sauvignon and Malbec at their Kalimna vineyard in the north of the nearby Barossa Valley, and they knew some people who had some Malbec in the Clare Valley, two or three hours' drive from Adelaide, but they knew of no sources for the other varieties. So Max decided he'd base his new wine on the Shiraz grape, known in France as Syrah, which grew in abundance all over South Australia. The Australians used to treat it as a bulk-producing grape, but that was underestimating its potential. Shiraz is the great red grape that makes Hermitage, the finest red wine of France's Rhône Valley. When Schubert's few Cabernet Sauvignon vines produced good fruit, he could add that to the blend, and he could run the Shiraz juice over the Cabernet skins to extract Cabernet flavour, but basically, Shiraz would have to do.

Because producers wanted to make port-style wines, Shiraz was planted on the hot, open plains, where the grapes ripened easily. Schubert found two areas far cooler than the norm – perhaps as cool as Bordeaux in a year like 1949 – Morphett Vale to the south of Adelaide, and the Grange vineyard around his own Magill winery, on the hillside right above Adelaide's northern

The nose that started the red wine revolution in Australia.
Max Schubert checks out a sample of his beloved Grange.

suburbs. Both plots had good plantings of mature Shiraz vines. He decided he would pick the grapes early to keep the alcohol level reasonably low and retain good acidity. Acid levels were rarely even taken into consideration in Australia at that time, but acid levels of about 7g per litre would equate pretty well with the norm in Bordeaux. Schubert's work in the Penfolds chemistry lab in his teenage days had shown him that low acid levels, the result of over-ripening the grapes, caused many of the fundamental problems with Australian efforts at red wine-making.

So Max had found his fruit. Now he needed wood. Easier said than done. Oak isn't one of Australia's strong points, eucalyptus trees are. He did try Australian oak – 'bloody terrible' – and he got some

barrels made up from Australian kauri, jarrah, stringy bark and casuarina. 'Bloody terrible' seemed to be the judgement on most of these too, and eventually he was left with a few precious casks of imported oak – partly French, partly American.

He tried the French wood, but he was pretty sure that it wasn't what he wanted. The fruit he was using was pungent and rich and he reckoned that only American oak would be aggressive enough to give as good as it got. He was right. Those French experiments never saw the light of day. But the five 300-litre (66-gallon) barrels of American oak he obtained for the 1951 vintage contained what would become the very first Grange Hermitage – named after the Grange homestead and vineyard established at Magill by the first Dr Penfold in 1844.

Schubert didn't ferment the juice in his new oak. He wanted much greater control over the fermentation

temperature than this would allow. At that time in Australia, a tumultuous uncontrolled fermentation of about three days' length was usual – get it over with as quick as possible and on to the next batch of grapes. But this had two results – a severe danger of the fermentation grinding to a halt, with acetic acid rapidly forming in the hot, still sweet juice; and a complete failure to extract all the colour, tannin and flavour that was sitting in those dark black skins just waiting to be coaxed out.

Excuse me if this is beginning to sound a bit like a wine-making lesson, but Grange Hermitage was the first concerted, scientifically-based attempt to make modern, top-quality red wine anywhere outside the classic areas of Europe. Remember, this is 1951. Before California, before New Zealand, before South Africa and South America, an obstinate, jowly-faced genius was leading the way in South Australia.

Schubert wanted every ounce of personality his grapes possessed. He crushed them, cooled down the resulting must and pumped it into open concrete tanks. He invented a system of headboards that he'd slot into slats in the concrete, below the surface of the liquid, to keep the skins submerged and each day he'd pump all of the juice over the skins – cooling it on its way through a heat exchanger. In this way, by keeping the temperature of fermentation down, he was able to limit the pace of sugar into alcohol conversion. He was getting far more rich flavour out of the skins than anyone in Australia had before, so much so that he reckoned he'd got enough extract before the fermentation was even finished. So he ran the juice off the skins and finished the fermentation in his new oak barrels. The whole process took about 12 days – four times as long as usual. But the fruit quality was already reminding him of those 1949s in Bordeaux, even if the grape variety was different. Now came the real challenge. He'd made quite a bit more than five barrels' worth of wine, so he ran the rest of it into the vast old wooden vats

The historic Penfolds winery where Grange Hermitage is still made, though the grapes now come from elsewhere.

traditionally used in Australia for maturing wine. Identical wine had been put into the two very different storage vessels. Would the new American oak he had obtained make the difference he was gambling on?

It certainly would. He was quite pleased with the 'control' wine in the big old vats, but the wine in the new oak was a revelation. After one month the raw oak and the rich fruit were producing an explosively exciting perfume and taste. After one year the intensity of fruit being displayed was far greater than Schubert had dared hope.

The wine was tough with tannin too, and traditional Australian wisdom would have left the wine in barrel to soften. But no Australian producer had ever aged a red wine in *new* oak barrels before. Once again Max harked back to what he'd learnt in France, and realized that the tannins would soften with enough time in bottle, but the fruit would be sure to tire if it stayed too long in wood, despite his insistence on keeping every barrel topped up to the bung to minimize oxidation. After 18 months, he gave the word, and the first Grange was bottled. With the 1952 vintage he got the okay from Penfolds' board of directors, and swung excitedly into commercial production.

Schubert produced increasing amounts of Grange in the ensuing vintages, but because he wanted to leave Grange for a few years to soften in bottle, it meant piling up thousands of cases of costly wine in the cellars. He was delighted at how the wines were progressing, but the Penfolds board were starting to realize that not a bottle of this noble experiment had yet earned them any money. Max marched to Penfolds headquarters in Sydney, expecting to bask in the praise that would be heaped upon his beloved Grange. But what was supposed to be a triumphal unveiling to the Sydney wine world turned into a disaster. With the exception of one of the younger members of the Penfold family, no one liked the wine.

So Schubert went back to Adelaide. But the Adelaide wine buffs' response was equally damning and the final blow came in 1957 when the Penfolds board forbade him to make another Grange, saying the public humiliation was becoming harmful to Penfolds' reputation nationwide.

But it wasn't just Max who believed in what Grange stood for. It was all the men in the cellar who felt that Grange was theirs too. So a conspiracy developed, with the help of the tacit approval of a couple of senior management members and the 1957, '58 and '59 vintages did get made – without new wood, but it was better than nothing.

And in 1960, one sympathetic board member on a visit to Magill asked to taste those original Granges. At eight and nine years old the 1951 and 1952 were finally opening up, the fruit beginning to rise above the tannin, the sweetness of the oak filling the glass with irresistible perfume. The director went back to Sydney and persuaded the board to reconsider. Just in time for the 1960 vintage the word came through – Grange is on again, new barrels and all.

In 1962, the 1955 Grange was entered in the Sydney Wine Show – one of the major wine events of the Australian year – and it won gold. The wine went on to scoop gold 50 more times; wherever it was shown it came away with awards. It had been a tortuous birth, but finally after a decade of struggle and doubt, Max Schubert and his Grange Hermitage ushered in the modern age of Australian wine.

Controversy attended Grange from the beginning, and it continues unabated. How does Grange get such depth of flavour? Is its volatile acidity level too high? Where do the grapes really come from, and what varieties are used? Is it as good as it used to be? Interestingly, it is almost as though the critics felt they had mindlessly scarred Max Schubert himself to such a degree during the years before 1960, that he has been spared personal criticism since. But his creation hasn't. Rumours abound. Do Penfolds add tannin? Do they induce a high volatile acid level? Do they pick some of their grapes super-ripe and then dilute them? Do they run the wine of various Penfolds reds off the skins, let the crush settle overnight, and then draw off the really deep black 'super-wine' that has seeped to the bottom over 12 hours – to use to thicken up Grange?

Maybe. But such discussions are secondary to the question – does Grange still have the same constituent parts? And is it as good? Well, its fruit comes from different vineyards. Morphett Vale, which provided up to 45 per cent of the early Grange fruit, is now a housing estate. And most of the historic Magill vineyard now has houses standing where vines once grew. There was a national outcry in 1982 when Penfolds sold a large part of this historic vineyard for urban development, but in fact the core of good vineyard land at Magill had always been small.

In any case, as viticultural standards have improved throughout South Australia, it has become increasingly obvious to Schubert's successors that there is much better fruit to be found elsewhere for Grange. Old low-yielding vines grown in the Kalimna vineyards, north of the Barossa Valley form the core of the wine, mostly Shiraz but with some Cabernet Sauvignon too. Kalimna fruit was first used in 1961 at a mere 15 per cent. Now it usually makes up half of the blend or more. Penfolds' wide-ranging holdings throughout South Australia, both in the Clare Valley, and through their control of Wynns and Lindemans, in Coonawarra, mean they also have first call on this fruit if any of it is seen as fitting into the Grange character.

Testing the Legend

But is the wine still as good? I wasn't legal drinking age for any of the early ones, and I've only been tasting young Granges since the late 1980s. But I've worked my way back through the Granges of the 1970s, finding that they brilliantly fulfil Max Schubert's dream of making a Bordeaux-style wine to last 20 years. They keep their colour and their trappings of youthful vigour, but develop into a rich sweet potion of toffee and fresh leather, blackberry, pine resin and the purest and sweetest of plums. Great Bordeaux? From a hot, old-fashioned year like 1959 or 1949, yes.

The modern Granges, well, *I* think they're going to be even better. These Granges are magnificent wines, sometimes, as in 1984 or '89, showing more immediate richness of fruit and swirling heady perfumes, sometimes seeming almost too savagely aggressive as in 1981 or brilliantly flawed as in 1980, but always tremendously exciting, challenging, unforgettable. And now and then, in a year like 1977, the balance is so impeccable, the flavours so rich, the cedar and blackcurrant, tar and smoke, so passionately entwined, that I found myself saying, '*This* is the great Mouton-Rothschild, *and* Hermitage La Chapelle *and* Romanée-Conti, all in one.' Impossible? Sure it is. But with flavours like this who cares what's possible? And Max Schubert had retired two years before, in 1975. Luckily, his successors at Penfolds have inherited his passion and dedication. I'm sure Max is feeling proud of how his boys are doing.

Seppelt

YOU TAKE A TON or two of the darkest, blackest Shiraz grapes you can grow. You crush them and ferment the juice with the objective of making a monster red all colour and extract and longevity, and you ruthlessly press the wine off its skins until the thick purple liquid is just a mass of powerfully tannic sludge. Then you age it for a year in big wooden vats. That's the recipe for a real gobsmacker of a traditional Aussie red, and that's exactly how Seppelt make their Great Western Hermitage – just like they always have done. Then they bottle it, add some sugar, slap on a metal crown cap and leave it for between 7 and 15 years in the cellar to mature.

Something's strange here. Add sugar? Use a metal cap? That's what they do in Champagne. It'll start fermenting again. It does. And ten to fifteen years later it'll be proudly released as Seppelt's Show Sparkling 'Burgundy'. The wine will be a frothing dark purple, reeking of home-made blackberry jam – one of the most unexpected yet intensely delicious sparkling wines in the world today.

Gold in Them Thar Vines

Seppelt don't only make sparkling wine – their fortified 'ports' and 'sherries' are some of Australia's best, and their table wines win a bevy of gold medals every year in Australia and abroad. But if there is one company which has created the Australian sparkling wine tradition, preserved it and then dramatically modernized and re-focussed it during the 1980s, it has to be Seppelt of Great Western.

Great Western is a tiny town – 200 people or so – on the main road between Melbourne and Adelaide. Not for the first time in Australia, vineyards were planted here because of the gold. Joseph Best was one of many who planted vines to supply wine for the miners, and as the gold reserves dwindled, he employed destitute miners to drive avenues of cellars deep into the granite hillsides. In fact, he had created maturing conditions almost identical to those in Champagne. When Best died in 1887, a local businessman, Hans Irvine, saw here the perfect opportunity to realize a long-cherished ambition – to create 'champagne' in Australia.

He purchased and re-equipped the cellars and brought over a winemaker from Champagne in France – the only thing he didn't do was plant the right grapes. Somehow he ended up with an obscure high-acid Cognac variety called Ondenc which was rapidly re-named Irvine's White, and until the 1980s this provided the fruit for the best of Australia's Champagne-method sparkling wine.

Seppelt's involvement with Great Western came in 1918, when they bought the business off Hans Irvine. It is typical of Seppelt that they still make a little Ondenc, though like the sparkling red 'Burgundy', it is a hopelessly uneconomic wine – it takes so long to soften, they only released the 1979 in 1990! But when Ian McKenzie arrived as chief winemaker in 1983 with a brief to revive the quality image of the company, he realized that there was nothing wrong with the method of creating Seppelt sparkling wine. The problem was that the base wines just weren't good enough and they had already reached their quality ceiling.

McKenzie quickly realized something else, too. Carl Seppelt, who headed the company until selling to South Australian Brewing in 1985, might be old-fashioned in his wine-making ideas, but he had shown astonishing foresight in his understanding of vineyards and grape varieties. In the 1960s, long before Australians realized the importance of cool climates for producing high quality wine grapes, Seppelt was patiently surveying Victoria and South Australia in the search for cool vineyard land. He discovered what he was looking for in the Keppoch/Padthaway area of South Australia just north of Coonawarra, and in the completely virgin windswept hills of Drumborg on the southern coast of Victoria. In 1964 he established vineyards which now total 278 hectares (686 acres). With another spurt of pioneering zeal, in 1982 he established a further 124 acres of cool vineyard at Partalunga high in the Adelaide Hills and recently the company has started using grapes from the Snowy Mountains in New South Wales.

Ian McKenzie saw all this cool climate vineyard, much of it planted with Chardonnay, Pinot Noir, and, remarkably, the third important Champagne variety, Pinot Meunier, and realized that no-one was maximizing its potential. Seppelt had employed a winemaker from Champagne in 1978, who had ensured the production methods were up to the mark. But there are fundamental differences between making sparkling wine in Champagne and producing it in Australia. In Champagne in most years it takes a great effort to ripen the grapes. In Australia it takes just as great an effort to stop them ripening too much. No-one at Seppelt was addressing this problem. The winemaker would simply be told when to expect a batch of grapes, like it or not.

McKenzie lost no time at all. He knew that Seppelt not only had the right grape varieties planted, they also had them in some of Australia's coolest sites. With Nick

Seppelt, the vineyard manager, McKenzie instituted a crash programme of re-trellising, re-training and, if necessary, as in Drumborg, replanting and completely altering the layout of the vineyard.

The result, since 1984, is a most astonishing and seemingly ever-expanding range of sparkling wines, which in a few short years have established Australia, and particularly Seppelt, as challengers to Champagne in quality terms at the top of the range.

The grapes for the inexpensive Great Western are, frankly, whatever's cheapest in the market. The wine gets six months on its lees and is then disgorged and re-bottled by the 'transfer' method. This is cheaper than full-scale Champagne method, since the wine is siphoned out of its bottle, yeast deposits and all, filtered under pressure, and re-bottled in one simple operation. The resulting wine is clean, and gluggable.

Queen Adelaide costs a bit more and is basically the same wine as Great Western, but with a whole year on its lees. The change in fullness and personality is considerable. But the real improvement comes with Fleur de Lys. The non vintage is still made by the transfer method, and is based on Semillon, not Chardonnay, but you'd never guess, with its delicious toasty, honeyed flavour. Good fruit, and two years on

These old date palms soften the contours of a modern tank farm at Seppelt Great Western winery, where many of Australia's best sparklers are made.

the lees, McKenzie says, gives this quality. The Fleur de Lys vintage releases are made by the traditional Champagne-method – and these are even more delicious, but McKenzie remarks with a grin that he thinks the Champagne-method is 'a damned nuisance': he'd make all the wines by transfer if he could.

That's revolutionary talk, enough to have a French Champagne maker reach for the smelling salts, but McKenzie repeats – good fruit, given enough time on its yeast will give wine with the structure to hold its bubble during the transfer method.

He didn't neglect the top wines. Neglect? He revels in them. Salinger 1984 and 1988 are two outstanding buttery, honeyed, ripe-flavoured wines with a positively creaming kind of sparkle. The 1987 is leaner – but beautifully smoky and honeyed. Top quality Chardonnay and Pinot Noir, sometimes with a little Pinot Meunier and once some Pinot Gris. And three years on the yeast. I must say I thought these Salingers would represent the peak. But McKenzie has also made a 1989 entirely from Drumborg grapes. Tasting it after a year on its yeast, it hadn't yet developed any rich creamy flavours, but the piercingly direct lemon and apple fruit, the orchard blossom perfume and the cleansing purity of the bubbles left me in no doubt that after two more years on the yeast, this will be the best Australian sparkler yet. Australian *white* sparkler, that is. Now *red* sparkling wine; he's making the best red sparkler in the world already.

Yalumba

ROB HILL SMITH WINCED. 'We were left looking like a fake art deco lamp – oh God, let's put that in the garage, it's too embarrassing to have it in the dining room'. That's how the managing director of Yalumba wines says he felt about his company at the end of the 1970s. Yet Yalumba, founded in 1849 and owned by the Smith family through six generations, had until the 1950s been a considerable and innovative force in Australian wine, and they had always managed at the same time to ride the crest of popular consumer demand. By the 1960s their name had become synonymous with good quality fortified wines and brandies, but, as Hill Smith says, they were actually producing virtually anything that was going, from cheap, sweet 'sherry' and vermouth upwards to beefy red wines and sugar-rich 'ports'. And that was a pretty fair reflection of the nation's drinking habits.

The 1970s changed all that. From being a nation of beer swillers and 'port' guzzlers, Australia embraced light table wines with fervour. Each swing of public taste was dramatic – from light, sweetish Rieslings, to strong dry reds, to four-litre boxes full of fruity white, to Cabernet, to Chardonnay – it all happened so fast – and with each swing there was good old Yalumba looking increasingly like a beached whale, each time just missing the new trend, failing to create a new image. Good old Yalumba. 'Ports' and 'sherries'. Big thick reds, a Riesling or two. Nice to have you around, but let's go and look at something more exciting, often seemed to be the mood.

It became increasingly clear to Wyndham Hill Smith, Rob's late father and company chairman, that unless Yalumba could change its image, it was doomed to takeover, if not collapse. Yet the Yalumba business was still strong, even if it was unfashionable. What they needed to do was to develop an entirely separate range of wines without using the Yalumba name. In the meantime, Yalumba could quietly modernize and transform itself and do some research into finding out just what it was the growing numbers of Australian wine drinkers wanted. Cheap, good sparkling wine has so far proved to be the most inspired of their new ideas. But if the Yalumba transformation failed, the other wines under a Hill Smith family identity wouldn't be dragged down along with it.

The key to success lay in vineyards. In 1958 Yalumba purchased Oxford Landing, a pretty large 235-hectare (580-acre) block of vines in the parched land west of Waikerie along the reaches of the Murray river. The Hill Smiths planted it with high-cropping, flavourless varieties like Doradillo, which formed the backbone of their brandy and fortified wine business. But they also planted some Cabernet Sauvignon. No-one thought much of the quality of most Oxford Landing fruit, but the Cabernet kept coming up with flavour as well as good yield. By 1980 Oxford Landing was a prime candidate for an image transplant. The vineyard had become unhealthy. Disease and increasingly saline soil – a common problem in the Murray Riverland where the salty water table was nearer the surface – were reducing efficiency. The Hill Smiths needed a supply of cheap fruit from classic varieties to provide them with 'fighting varietals', as the jargon has it – Chardonnay, Cabernet Sauvignon, Sauvignon Blanc and Riesling of good quality to sell at a sensible price. So the Hill Smiths began a massive replanting operation, concentrating on planting vines on disease- and salt-resistant rootstocks. It took a decade to turn Oxford Landing around, but the 1990s releases of Chardonnay and Cabernet show the wait was worthwhile. The wines are Yalumba products, but the name Yalumba is very small on the label and the name Oxford Landing is very large.

Rejuvenating Pewsey Vale

The name Yalumba doesn't appear at all on Pewsey Vale wines. But then it didn't really start out as a Yalumba project. In the mid-1950s, the wealthiest landowner in the area, one Geoffrey Angas Parsons, bought a 3645-hectare (9000-acre) spread in the foothills south of Angaston where Yalumba have their winery. He and Wyndham Hill Smith were great friends and as soon as Parsons discovered that one of South Australia's original vineyards – Pewsey Vale – had been located on this property, he came to Hill Smith with the idea of rejuvenating the vineyard. Ego was the driving force – the landowner loved the idea of persuading the respected Hill Smith to partner him in a vineyard venture, and was prepared to put up the money for development. That suited Hill Smith. What he didn't realize was that this unstudied approach to owning cool climate vineyards in the hills was to prove the salvation of his company.

Nor did he realize that planting a vineyard over 500 metres (1640 feet) up on wild, arid foothills was a very different challenge from the one he had taken up three years earlier in the irrigated flatlands of Oxford Landing. Yalumba planted their first Riesling vines at Pewsey Vale. They died. Quite simply because there

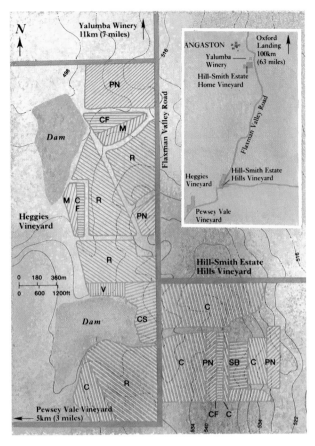

C	Chardonnay	M Merlot	R Riesling

C Chardonnay   M   Merlot   R   Riesling
CF Cabernet Franc   MN Pinot Meunier   SB Sauvignon Blanc
CS Cabernet Sauvignon PN Pinot Noir   V   Viognier

Vineyards ╱ Contours at 6m (19.5ft) intervals

was no rain between December and May when the vine should have been growing. So they replanted and pruned vigorously to keep down the demands on the vine's resources – survival pruning they call it. The result was masses of foliage and minute crops.

By the 1970s, Peter Wall, Yalumba's vineyard expert, says they were getting frustrated because nothing they tried seemed to produce bigger crops. But the wine from Pewsey Vale was delicious. First the Rieslings, then the Cabernet Sauvignons were producing juice of an intensity and character Yalumba had never before achieved from their hot, flat, valley floor vineyards. If only they could find a way to ensure a decent-sized crop each year, they'd be winning.

It took the purchase of another vineyard, and an awful lot of trial and error, before the Hill Smiths really got to grips with cool climate vineyards. The turning point came in 1971. Colin Heggie was one of the local characters – wild, argumentative – a be-whiskered bushwhacker born out of his time, whose horse probably had a clearer recollection than he did of the route home

from the village hostelries on many nights. He owned a tract of grazing land a few miles from Pewsey Vale and 'a cricket ball throw higher', all of it being over 500 metres (1640 feet). Wyndham Hill Smith loved the feel of Heggie's land and for years had joshed Colin about buying it. But Peter Wall was gripped by a more serious vision – Heggies Vineyard, as it became known, was cool and Heggies had what Pewsey Vale lacked – undulations and contours that would allow a vast dam to be built to store winter rain for use right through the parched summer.

In fact it was Peter Wall who persuaded the Hill Smiths that they *had* to head for the hills – and in 1971 Yalumba sold almost all of their Barossa valley floor vineyards to finance the purchase of 121 hectares (300 acres) from Colin Heggie. And off they went again.

The land was cleared, the vines staked out and established in the rough dry soil. And nothing happened. Once again, nature was winning hands down. Though the water resource was there, they'd gone ahead and planted before getting the irrigation sorted out. And Heggies was proving to be a mean piece of land, overgrazed for generations, all nutrient leached away and so poorly structured that the winter rains just ran off its ancient, compacted surface instead of sinking in and creating reserves for the summer drought.

This time the Yalumba team imposed a moratorium on any further vine plantings. 'Let's get the damn thing right.' For three years they went back to the drawing board. They deep-ploughed the tired old soil to break up the clay pan and allow the roots to penetrate well below the surface. They added gypsum to the earth to correct the acidity, and began to restructure it by ploughing vegetable matter back in and by crushing and ploughing in the rocks which were strewn across the surface. And they filled their dam and spread out the irrigation lines across the fields.

But the team also made a fundamental change in the way they treated the vines. South Australia's wine industry had been developed on easily-worked soils north and south of Adelaide and along the banks of the Murray river. The phylloxera vine louse was kept out of the state by rigid quarantine, and almost all vines were planted on their own roots. However, if you graft your grape-growing plant on to a different rootstock, you can dramatically alter its performance. In most parts of the world – and in neighbouring Victoria – this is done as a matter of necessity to protect against phylloxera, which destroys the roots of all quality wine varieties in the species *Vitis vinifera*, yet is tolerated by other species of grape vine. No one was doing it in South Australia.

Peter Wall reasoned that since the vines were never even getting the chance to establish a root system up in the hills, a programme of grafting their Riesling and Cabernet on to a vigorous, aggressively healthy non-vinifera rootstock might do the trick. He chose a rootstock called Ramsey and unwittingly started another profitable Yalumba sideline.

Clone and Away

Since they had a lot of vineyard they wished to plant and replant, but a virtual embargo on any decent vine material had been imposed by the government, Wall needed to find a way to propagate plants of good quality. So he now grows a vine underneath hothouse conditions, manipulating light exposure to encourage the vine into continual growth and he trains it right along a rack, the entire length of the glasshouse. Periodically he'll snip off cuttings, leave them to form a callus and then stick them in a hot bed. Within three weeks he's got growing roots, ready for potting. One vine – *one* vine – can give him 4000 plants in a year. In an area like South Australia, where new clones are almost impossible to come by and a good one is like gold dust, this system has transformed the lives of quality-conscious grape growers.

Ramsey rootstock was so successful in Heggies that their next problem became how to reduce plant vigour in a vineyard where previously nothing would grow. This they're achieving by trellising and pruning carefully, but also by re-evaluating the spacing of vines. Rob Hill Smith passionately believes in making his vines struggle – not so that they die – he'd had enough of that in the early Heggies and Pewsey Vale years – but at least so that they compete with each other. The old vineyards contained about 1100 plants per hectare. They doubled this to 2200 per hectare, then to 3000, to 5000 and the figure now stands at 10,000, so that the latest plantings are in close-packed formation.

The first wine from the revitalized Heggies vineyard was a 1979 Riesling and its steely, intensely citrus quality persuaded the Hill Smiths that they were at last getting it right. They planted Chardonnay at Heggies in 1981 – using the same clone as Adam Wynn at nearby Mountadam, following that with Cabernet Sauvignon,

Cabernet Franc and Merlot, then some Pinot Noir and Pinot Meunier for use in sparkling wine. And having really got the bit between the teeth now, they also bought the property over the road from Heggies, planted it with Chardonnay and Sauvignon Blanc and called this simply Hill-Smith Estate. Three properties, 118 hectares (290 acres) of vines, with more to be planted. The new quality identity for the Hill Smith family of Yalumba fame.

The three vineyards all produce highly individual wines, and although at one stage the wines were blended, the objective is now to allow each vineyard to express its own character. With Pewsey Vale this normally results in full-flavoured, ripe-fruited Rieslings streaked with lime intensity. And Pewsey Vale Cabernets have a deep intensity of blackcurranty fruit that is indulgently delicious.

Heggies is completely different – that mean old soil still exerts its influence on the wines. The Rieslings are brilliantly steely in a cool year like 1987, but the Cabernet-based red, called 'Cabernets', can be a bit bony and lean. In a warmer year like 1986 or 1988, the Heggies 'Cabernets' is classic stuff, less rich than Pewsey Vale but wonderfully blackcurranty with a rare and exciting scent of tobacco and mint and even ginger or cinnamon twirling in the heart of the wine.

Heggies Chardonnay shows the same wide variations from vintage to vintage. In the warmer years like 1988, there is a lusciousness of honey and figs, but also a certain green herbiness. In cooler years like 1990, the wine is positively austere when young, initially tasting more of Riesling or Sauvignon until a creamy toffee fullness slowly appears quite late in the day.

Hill-Smith Estate is hardly more than a road's width away from Heggies, but the soil is richer and the vineyards slope a little more towards the east. The vines even have to be pulled back from overcropping here, but the results, especially with Chardonnay, are exciting, with lemon acidity scything through a deep, ripe banana and pineapple fruit flecked with the fragrance of warm golden toast. And all three vineyards can produce some of Australia's best naturally botrytized sweet wines. Given that the Hill Smiths are now also producing sensationally good, low-priced sparkling wines under the Angas Brut label, I ventured to suggest to Rob he'd done a magnificent job in turning the Hill Smith company fortunes round. 'Yalumba. We're called Yalumba.' But of course. Silly me.

The Hill Smith family were among the first to establish vineyards in the dry hillside scrub above the Barossa Valley floor. This is the irrigation lake at Heggies.

Yarra Valley

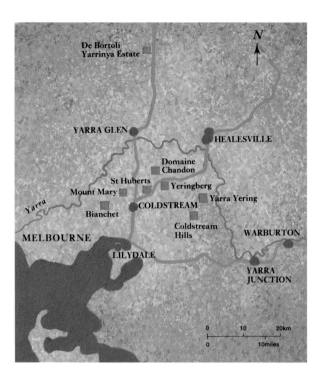

De Bortoli
Yarrinya Estate

YARRA GLEN

HEALESVILLE

Domaine
Chandon

St Huberts
Mount Mary
Yeringberg
COLDSTREAM
Yarra Yering

Bianchet

Coldstream
Hills
WARBURTON

MELBOURNE

LILYDALE

YARRA
JUNCTION

Yarra

N

0   10   20km
0   10miles

I WOULDN'T SETTLE in the Yarra Valley because of the quality of the vineyard land, the sweet ripeness of the grapes, the legendary flavours of the wines. I'd settle there because of the view.

Australia is a parched continent, and most Australian vineyard regions reflect this, but even in the dry days of late summer there is an air of calm content about the Yarra. A forty-minute drive out of Melbourne, you slip effortlessly into a bygone age. The thick jungle trees, pulsing with the cry of the bellbird, give way to the tumbled, tousled hillocks and hedgerows and dells of an English pastoral landscape from long ago. Great eucalyptus trees unfurl their magnificent fountains of cool green foliage. The cattle graze, the hills sweep up at the valley's edge. For once, it wasn't the excitement of discovering new wines, or new flavours that held me in thrall at each winery I visited. It was the thrilling, soothing, contented perfection of this lovely place.

It must have seemed like paradise to William Ryrie in 1837 when he breasted the final slopes after the exhausting overland trek from New South Wales. He settled and straightaway planted vines, which by 1845, were producing styles described as 'a red wine resembling Burgundy and a white wine resembling

Sauterne, and both very good'. The ability of the area to produce outstanding wine in the style of both Burgundy and Bordeaux, red and white, has been the keynote of the Yarra Valley ever since. But for almost half of this century, the raising of fat, tasty cattle for Melbourne's tables eclipsed the Yarra's wine-making prowess, however impressive it had been.

It had certainly been impressive. In 1849 the Yering Vineyard had been established, growing rapidly through the 1850s with the help of 20,000 cuttings, mostly from Bordeaux's famous Château Lafite-Rothschild. By 1889 the wine was good enough to win a gold medal at the Paris Exhibition. Next door to Yering, St Hubert's vineyard was established in 1864 and by 1881 a St Hubert's wine was winning the Emperor's prize at the Melbourne International Exhibition – and that wasn't just for being the best wine – there were steam engines, felt hats, cows and sheep, goodness knows what else, to beat. By the 1890s, with an annual production of 360,000 litres (79,200 gallons), St Hubert's had become Australia's biggest vineyard. And neighbouring Yeringberg was gaining plaudits for its wines in France, Belgium and England.

Yet in 1921, Yeringberg pulled out its last remaining vines, and with that act, Victoria's most flourishing vineyard of the late nineteenth century was obliterated. Not a vine remained, until at the end of the 1960s, the tentative moves of John Middleton at Mount Mary and of Guillaume de Pury at Yeringberg, along with Bailey Carrodus at Yarra Yering, set the Yarra Valley back on its path to re-establishing its claims to be Australia's leading cool climate wine area.

Its demise was simply a reflection of the changed priorities in Australian life. At the beginning of the twentieth century, milk and meat were more important to the population of Melbourne than wine, and the Yarra Valley was ideally suited to grazing. In any case, the taste in wine, which had so enthusiastically embraced light, classically structured 'European-style' wines in the 1870s and 1880s had shifted. The local populace wanted sweet, fiery fortified wines, and European wine producers, faced with vineyards ravaged by the phylloxera vine louse, wanted to import wines as heavy and thick as possible to beef up their own pallid brews. There were hot areas of Australia ideally suited to such production. The cool meadows and slopes of the Yarra Valley were not among them.

So the vine withered. It was only the upsurge of interest in table wine drinking in Australia, at the end of the 1960s, that drew attention back to the Yarra.

The common denominator that marks out all the new or resurgent wine areas of Australia, is that ripening grapes there is a knife-edge business. Delicate, perfumed wines, of the sort that an increasingly Europe-aware clientele demanded, could only originate from the marginal ripening conditions that characterize Bordeaux and Burgundy. The Yarra comes closest of all these areas to emulating both, since its average annual temperatures lie between the two – warmer than Burgundy but cooler than Bordeaux and its evenness of temperature during the ripening period is more balanced than either.

Rainfall is marginally higher than in Bordeaux and Burgundy – but much more reliable. Around the end of December the rain stops and, except for some refreshing drizzle, rarely recommences until harvest is over. In 1986 not a drop fell for three months up to harvest, although in 1989 freak weather did deluge the vintage.

There are two dramatically different soils in the Yarra, depending on which side of the valley you plant. The valley itself is divided by a ridge running along the centre in the main grape-growing area – itself barely 16km (10 miles) in length and well covered with grazing meadows as well as vines. To the north, including the north faces of the ridge itself, the soil is basically an ancient grey loam, interspersed with sand, light clay and rock. It could risk being too fertile if there were regular summer rain. As it is, the water-holding quality of the clay keeps all but the shallowest vineyards from undue drought stress during ripening, while lack of extra water naturally limits the crop. The southern side of the ridge is extremely fertile red volcanic soil of unknown depth. This is another example of Australia's famed terra rosa. The slightly cooler conditions make it more suitable for white grapes and grapes for sparkling wine than full-flavoured red table wine.

Yet red wines have caused the most excitement from the Yarra so far. Yarra Chardonnay can be excellent – usually a little lighter, more delicate than the richly exotic styles from warmer areas that have made Australia famous. The Yarra winemakers say just wait – as they age they'll get richer, deeper, toastier in the classic style of Puligny-Montrachet, and one taste of the 1988s from Yarra Yering or Coldstream Hills proves this. They're thrilling wines now, and they've got years to go before peaking. Seville Estate makes some exciting sweet wine because of positively courted regular botrytis infection in their vineyard on the south side of the valley, and St Hubert's have managed it too on the north side.

The buzz about the Yarra Valley – as about so many cool areas in Australia is that, at last, Pinot Noir will finally do its thing and produce great red wine. Well, on the north side of the valley, there's a lot of beautiful Pinot Noir fruit being grown, and some of it is being turned into great wine. The two most regularly stunning producers are Coldstream Hills and neighbouring Yarra Yering, but Mount Mary can make lovely, rather brooding Pinot Noir, and De Bortoli Yarrinya Estate's Pinot can be beautifully plum-rich. Yet even if the Pinot always ripens here – it is warmer than Burgundy and only severe over-cropping should retard its ripening ability – there's still a lot of good fruit being turned into not very good wine.

Given that the temperature is a little cooler than Bordeaux, the Yarra does very well with the Bordeaux grapes. Merlot is not much planted but can be stunning. Bianchet is one of the few producers to release it on its own so far – a lovely fresh blackcurrant-leaf style. Otherwise Merlot is generally blended with Cabernet. If there is a general fault, it is an element of greenness in the fruit, but this is partly due to the youth of the vines in the valley, and partly due to over-cropping and unsuitable canopy management. The stunning blackcurrant intensity of a St Hubert's 1984 or 1988, or of the recent releases from De Bortoli Yarrinya Estate, the mint, gum and blackcurrant fragrance of Coldstream Hills, and the shocking richness of Yarra Yering show that great Cabernets are going to come out of this valley in at least as many vintages as they do in Bordeaux.

Fizzing with Confidence

Altogether there are some 80 vineyards now in the Valley, covering about 810 hectares (2000 acres). That's not bad going from 202 hectares (500 acres) in 1985, and just over 1.3 hectares (3 acres) at the end of the 1960s. But it isn't the Bordeaux or Burgundy look-alikes which have provided the confidence to plant on such a wide scale – it's the Champagne look-alike, the French/Australian operation Domaine Chandon. From a standing start in 1985, they have already outstripped their much longer-established Napa Valley counterpart as far as quality is concerned, and now contract to take around a third of the valley's grapes, as well as buying fruit from various other super-cool areas of Australia.

In this valley of smallholders, I'd have thought a multi-million dollar international investment on one of the original settlements might raise a few hackles. But I forgot how wily homesteaders can be. The city of Melbourne wants to re-zone the valley and allow it to be partitioned up into patchworks of one and two acre plots for tired Melbournites to flop down in. The only way to stop this 'unseemly' encroachment is for the inhabitants to prove its worth as an agricultural and viticultural jewel. Seven million French Champagne dollars say that's exactly what's going to happen.

Yarra Yering

I DON'T MIND AT ALL if one winery year after year produces a Cabernet Sauvignon of more startling intensity of flavour than any other winery in Australia. Commendable consistency, I'd call that. Laudable pursuit of excellence. But I don't then expect the same winery to match that by offering me Shiraz that is of peerless quality, wonderfully concentrated, magically achieving balance and delicacy within a massive frame – again just about every year. Well, perhaps that's not *too* much of a good thing. After all, good quality Cabernet and Shiraz have often gone hand-in-hand in Australia.

Then that same winery comes up with vintage after vintage of Chardonnay that bears an uncanny and irresistible resemblance to a great white Burgundy from Puligny-Montrachet or Corton. And the parade of brilliance still isn't finished. The owner then wheels out his Pinot Noir. The creator of the wine pours his 1987 and '89, and the '89 in particular has a wonderful untamed beauty, a flavour somewhere between the pungency of hops, the sensuous loveliness of lily and rose, and the sweet juice of a wild forest strawberry.

Damn the man! Too clever by half. But you can't damn Bailey Carrodus, standing there almost diffidently, his Alec Guinness face tidily framed by a whitening beard; dressed in a floppy cricket hat, khaki shirt and off-white jeans; his eyes twinkling with amusement as he quite candidly asserts that his wines may well be the finest of their type in Australia.

Carrodus does not disguise his impatience, verging on contempt, for those who hype the Yarra Valley and their various wines, yet signally fail to obey the simple rules of good wine-making. For Carrodus, everything comes down to one basic philosophy – 'the ultimate limit on quality is your fruit. You cannot make better wine than your fruit's quality. You can make worse . . .' This means careful choice of vineyard site, nurturing the vines – every vine, not just parcel by parcel – with a mixture of discipline and devotion, never attempting to exploit the plant's good nature by bumping up a crop – and striving for all the flavour those grapes possess. 'I don't think you can have too much flavour,' he says 'so long as there's no coarseness. Intensity is the hallmark of great wine, and it's difficult not to lose intensity if you overproduce.'

It was that intensity of flavour, married to a Bordeaux-like balance of tannins, fruit and acid, that made the Yarra Valley famous a century ago. That, and proximity to Melbourne with plenty of wine drinkers more than happy to drink the local produce. But being near Melbourne proved a mixed blessing. When public taste turned away from light-bodied table wines, landowners found they could make more money out of cows, or selling their land for housing. In 1921 the last commercial vintage in the Yarra Valley was harvested. And that was that – Yarra Valley wine was a wistful memory – until Bailey Carrodus, a research scientist in the physiology of wood at Melbourne university, decided in 1969 to kindle the Yarra tradition afresh.

Grapes were still being grown in the Yarra on a very small scale, but no one had set out to create a vineyard and a winery since nearby Yeringberg had ceased production in 1921. Carrodus, as well as possessing great expertise in plant physiology, had got himself a degree in wine-making from Australia's famous Roseworthy College back in the 1950s. He'd made wine too, on quite a grand scale in the Clare and Hunter Valleys. But he'd never made great wine. He wanted to. But he'd need the right land, and he took to driving out to the areas around Melbourne at the weekends, repeating to himself the maxim – go to a cool climate and choose a warm spot. Nothing looked quite right until one day he was tramping the grey clay soils streaked with bands of gravel about a mile south of the Yarra river. The plot on offer was much bigger than Carrodus wanted – 12 hectares (30 acres) – but he bought it anyway and between 1969 and 1970, he and a friend planted up every single acre.

Just Out of the Nursery

Although he was a plant expert, he didn't have much say in what he got to plant, or what clones to choose: it was a case of whatever the nursery stocked. He ended up with a fair amount of Cabernet Sauvignon, some Malbec, Merlot and Cabernet Franc, a chunk of Shiraz, a bit of Semillon – and ten Pinot Noir vines. He'd ordered a thousand but they'd only got ten, so he propagated as much as he could by taking cuttings from the original batch and built up his stock that way. Even so he discovered he had four different clones. Once he'd got these going, he added some Chardonnay, Sauvignon Blanc, Marsanne, Viognier, Petit Verdot and Mourvèdre. Each one has a place in his master plan.

He barrel-ferments his Chardonnay with the minimum of skin contact. At an average yield of not much more than two tons to the acre, he feels the fruit quality is quite powerful enough without more flavour from the skins, and I'm sure he's right. The wines have a fabulously forthright richness, a Burgundian richness of oatmeal and butter, hazelnuts and honey. There's no

The congenial, opinionated Bailey Carrodus with his new
Yarra Yering Pinot Noir – and his ever-present hat.

tropical fruit lushness there; it's all good old-fashioned low yield Burgundian power. The reds are picked into small plastic boxes that enable the grapes to arrive unbroken at the winery. Carrodus uses the gentlest of destemmer-crushers, 20 years old and still performing with the gentleness of a dove. And then he wheels out one of 35 square receptacles that reminded me of the kind of cupboards you'd expect to find full of dusty prayer books in a cathedral. Like large tea chests, lined with steel! Carrodus says these three-foot cubes are what he finds work best. He lets the wines ferment up to about 32° to 34°C (90° to 93°F) and then throws in bags of dry ice – still in the bag! – to cool the juice and skins down. Although he tried a little post-fermentation maceration on his 1989 Cabernet and produced an intensely spicy, excitingly dark batch, he usually prefers to run off the juice, tip out the mush of skins and run off any extra juice from that, and finally gently press more wine from the skins and pips.

He'll put his Cabernet into 100 per cent new wood nowadays, although it used to be nearer the 33 per cent the Shiraz still gets, and his Pinot Noir is mostly put into new barrels as well. And apart from a racking every three months, he'll do as little as possible to the wine

from then on. Minimum fining, no filtration, and bottling after 22 months for the Shiraz and Cabernet, 15 months for the Pinot.

Although the Pinot Noir is now his most expensive wine and attracts most attention from critics, I still fall silent with appreciation in the presence of his other reds. His Shiraz, labelled as 'Dry Red Wine No. 2', is always at least 85 per cent Shiraz, but has in the past been blended with either Pinot Noir or Mourvèdre. It now contains about five per cent Viognier and ten per cent Marsanne. The 1989 has a beautiful fresh sweetness, loganberries and raspberries, a lovely deep ripeness both perfumed and juicy. Wonderful now, it'll age to darker, more savage flavours in a few years – as a great French Côte-Rôtie would. The further back you go with vintages, the more unforgettable these 'Shirazes' become – and it's the bottle age, not any particular change in wine-making style, that is doing it. Gradually the dense richness of plum, blackcurrant, raspberry and pepper, liquorice, leather and chocolate builds over the years, until with vintages like 1982, 1981 and 1980, the concentration of luscious ripe fruit, the intensity of perfume and the increasingly exotic trails of leather, chocolate and liquorice make you think that surely there can't be a better Shiraz than this.

Can there be a better range of Cabernets than Carrodus' 1982, '84, '85, '87, '88, '89? And every other year from 1978 on was good to very good as well. You could find a thousand more subtle Cabernets in Australia. But if ever Cabernet was intended to demonstrate the sweetness of blackcurrant cassis fruit, at Yarra Yering they have distilled that particular sweet essence to the ultimate degree. It's almost overpowering in its intensity. Nowadays, particularly in the 1988 and '89 vintages, the soft spice of new oak is reasonably evident, and other fruits like plums and raspberries occasionally get a look in, but as they age, these wines too will begin to ooze with the thick juice of superripe blackcurrants sometimes splashed with a trace of perfumed balsamic vinegar. No, it isn't subtle. But yes, it *is* magnificent. And when Bailey Carrodus reminds you once again that intensity is the hallmark of great wine, for once you've got a winemaker putting his money where his mouth is.

NEW ZEALAND

*T*HE QUALITY OF NEW ZEALAND'S TRADITIONAL WINE INDUSTRY was so poor that I have yet to find a single defender of the old ways. I've tasted one or two venerable bottles of sweet 'hock' – or was it 'Moselle' – and I've heard people talk about the Cabernets that McDonald used to make at Hawke's Bay. But in general I've found more sympathy with the Royal Commission in the years after World War Two which found that much of the wine made in New Zealand would be 'classified as unfit for human consumption in other wine-producing countries'. When New Zealand producers made some efforts during the 1960s and 1970s to improve their wine, they took the advice of Dr Helmut Becker from the Rhine who decided the climate was ideal for producing light German-style wines. Just as California and Australia were dazzling themselves with visions of competing against the *grands crus* of Burgundy and the Classed Growths of Bordeaux, New Zealand was setting out to make a better 'Liebfraumilch'.

They succeeded. New Zealand Müller-Thurgau became the best in the world – at about the same time as Australia and California were challenging Corton-Charlemagne and Château Latour! But you can't start making decent wine until you know what decent wine tastes like. While the new visionaries of Australia, California, Oregon, Spain and Italy were setting off for France to discover what flavours were best and how they were created, New Zealand was only gradually loosening the puritanical colonial stays. The social revolution came late in New Zealand. Restaurants weren't allowed licences until 1960; the first wine bar was opened in 1979. Men with any international knowledge of fine wine (like John Buck of Te Mata) could be counted on the fingers of one hand.

New Zealand's development in the France-inspired styles of Cabernet Sauvignon, Pinot Noir and Chardonnay has not been an easy ride, and lack of a forum of internationally experienced wine people has not helped. But a past you wish to forget can sometimes be a better foundation for progress than one you cling to obsessively, so perhaps it's logical that the most notable New Zealand achievement has been the creation of a totally new style of wine from a totally new area – unoaked Sauvignon Blanc from Marlborough in the South Island. It owes little to the wines of Sancerre and Pouilly in France's Loire Valley which have always been praised as producing the quintessential Sauvignon style. This was a wine created by food technologists using a mixture of the common sense cold fermentation techniques learned from the German mentors, and a ruthlessly aseptic, almost sterile, hygienic approach learned from New Zealand's own dairy industry. The quintessential Sauvignon Blanc style is now made in New Zealand,

New Zealand is the youngest of the world's great wine countries, and much of its reputation is based on Sauvignon Blanc from vines like these in Marlborough, South Island.

not France, and is a rare example of an old classic being stripped of its crown by a new, rather than having to share the honours.

If Sauvignon was an immediate success, other grapes performed less well, untii they threw out the warm climate rule book, as taught to their young winemakers by the Australian wine schools. New Zealand Chardonnay grapes, for instance, can be unpalatably high in acid, so winemakers used to de-acidify by chemical means, stripping the wine of character along the way. Until it dawned on them that the winemakers of Burgundy and Champagne often faced searingly high acid levels in their grapes, and they used the malolactic fermentation that transforms green appley acid to creamy lactic acid, to reduce the acidity and actually add complexity. New Zealand is now making some of the world's most original Chardonnays.

Nobody in New Zealand pressed whole bunches of grapes because you could only process three to four tons at a time, whereas if you machine-picked and destemmed, as you were taught in South Australia, you could squelch 25 tons through in one go. But in Champagne and Burgundy they press whole bunches because the stems sieve out a lot of solid matter, and the juice runs out fast and clean – minimal skin contact, minimal oxidation, no need to add excessive sulphur.

And, whereas the hot, dry regions like California, Southern Europe and most of Australia have as their starting point nature's provision of lots of heat but very little rain, so that ripening is virtually guaranteed, New Zealand's climate and geology is very different. There is no problem with sunlight hours on the North or South Island, so long as you're trying to ripen the cooler climate grapes like Riesling, Chardonnay, Pinot Noir and, in some mesoclimates, Cabernet Sauvignon. The problems come in that most of the soils on the North Island are extremely fertile and the vines' vigour can be virtually uncontrollable. Wind sometimes has a positively beneficial effect, as at Marlborough on the South Island, where it is northerly and warm, but further south it can rip the crop from the vines.

Then there's rain. During the growing season you get a lot of rain from the west. Areas like Marlborough on South Island, and Hawke's Bay and Gisborne on North Island are fairly well protected by mountains. Areas like Nelson on South Island's west coast, and the vineyards to the north and south of Auckland on North Island, have no natural protection. At the end of the growing season the damage comes from the north-east. Again, Auckland suffers, as can Hawke's Bay, and Gisborne in particular often gets a real drenching before its harvest is completed.

So New Zealand has become a world leader in developing trellising and pruning systems that will make full use of sunlight but also protect the crop against wind and tackle the basic conundrum of grape growing on fertile soils. If you simply adopt a French rigorous pruning system the vine will go into a decreasing spiral of productivity, using all its energy on foliage growth. New Zealand wines *can* suffer from high acid, despite good potential alcohol levels, but exposing the fruit balances the acidity in a much more attractive way making it a positive, not a negative, factor. At Cloudy Bay they were able to reduce acid levels from 13g per litre to 9g per litre and maintain sugar levels in some of their best Chardonnay simply by re-trellising the vineyards.

New Zealand grape growers, especially in Gisborne, are used to very high yields, and new trellising systems will only be accepted if they keep yields up as well as facilitate ripeness. Here the growers can help themselves by improving their choice of plant material. In Marlborough especially, until they replant or re-graft hot

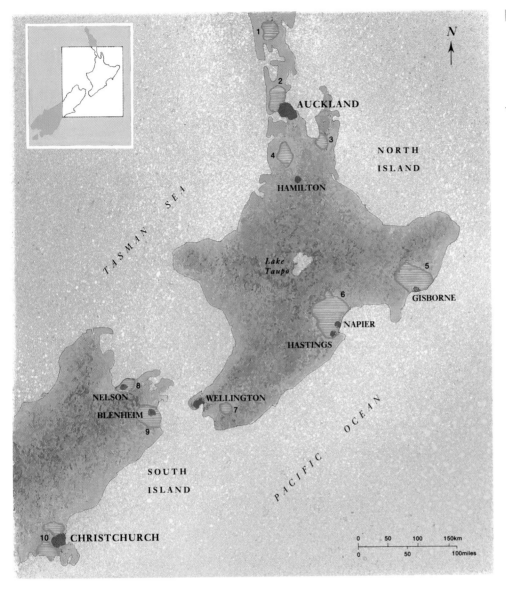

Wine producing areas
1 Northland
2 Auckland/Henderson
3 Bay of Plenty
4 Waikato
5 Gisborne
6 Hawke's Bay
7 Martinborough
8 Nelson
9 Marlborough
10 Canterbury

climate clones with strains like the MacRae – it does brilliantly at Te Mata and Ngatarawa – we won't know how good South Island Chardonnay can be. Pinot Noir from Canterbury, and from Waipara Springs between Marlborough and Christchurch will turn out to be some of the greatest in the world when they get good enough clonal material to make their wine from.

And she'll get there by revelling in the quality of her fruit, rather than by trying to stifle it. With Riesling, Sauvignon, and, bit by bit, Chardonnay, the results are already superb. Isolated Pinot Noirs, like Martinborough and St Helena, and Cabernets can be of world class too. But the red varieties do not ripen so easily in New Zealand, especially on the South Island, and most winemakers have yet to find a way of balancing the intensity of the fruit with the subtler nuances of an age-worthy red wine. It'll come, but at present, I still find too many of the Cabernets in particular tasting as though the producer had been slavishly following the instructions of a textbook on red wine-making written by a white wine producer.

Cloudy Bay

*I*T IS JUST CONCEIVABLE that New Zealand's most sought-after wine might have been labelled 'Farewell Spit'. After all, managing director and part-owner David Hohnen is renowned for possessing a sense of humour bordering on the eccentric which regularly surfaces in his own press releases and newsletters. And he did name his other winery in Western Australia's Margaret River region after the nearest geographical feature he could find – Cape Mentelle. In the flat Wairau river valley of Marlborough on South Island, the nearest promontory of any note is Farewell Spit.

Luckily there was one other geographical feature with much more tempting connotations. The Wairau river empties out its silt and sludge into a shallow bay. Captain Cook took one look at the turbid waters and dubbed them Cloudy Bay. Now that sounds much better, doesn't it? Though it actually refers to the murky estuary of a minor river, stop for a moment. Cloudy Bay. What about a romantic, rocky inlet? What about a razor-sharp mountain range ringing the shores? What about shafts of sunlight slanting on to the sandy beach, grape vines running down the gentle slopes, past waving pines and wispy clouds trailing like candy floss from the nearby peaks? And a *wine* made too in these idyllic conditions? David Hohnen was grateful to Captain Cook for the name, but the vision of *his* Cloudy Bay is altogether more exhilarating.

Hohnen's great strengths are his imagination and his ability to sell. He'd run Cape Mentelle in Western Australia with great flair and success since 1976. Excellent Cabernet, Shiraz and Zinfandel, of all things, as well as pretty good Chardonnay and Semillon. But no Sauvignon Blanc. Hohnen liked Sauvignon Blanc and looked around Australia for somewhere that might produce a Sancerre look-alike for him. No joy. But in 1984 he discovered more than a top Loire look-alike. Some New Zealand winemakers, headed by John Hancock of Morton Estate and Ross Spence of Matua Valley, poled up to Cape Mentelle to taste the Cabernet. In a spirit of trans-Tasman bonhomie they opened some of their New Zealand Sauvignon Blanc for the Australians to taste. Hohnen was dumbstruck. This wasn't a Sancerre look-alike: Sancerre should be lucky to taste half as good as this. If New Zealand could produce these flavours, he wanted to be involved too.

He was in New Zealand by November 1984, nosing about, looking at possible vineyard sites, tasting wines.

He ended up at the National Wine Show at the same time as another young Australian, Kevin Judd, winemaker for Selaks near Auckland since 1983. Hohnen loved Judd's wines and hired him on the spot. He hadn't got a vineyard yet, but he'd got a winemaker.

Judd's conversion to the cause of 'kiwi fruit' had been as immediate as David Hohnen's. After training at Roseworthy, South Australia's main winemaker's college, he'd worked at Hardy's Chateau Reynella as assistant winemaker. What he really wanted was a job as a chief winemaker, but it seemed that South Australia's big wine corporations were unwilling to take a gamble on too individual a style.

So when in 1983 Judd saw the advert for a job with Selaks, he didn't hesitate. He'd never tasted any New Zealand wine, but it was the only job on offer so he took it, and at least New Zealand was cool climate, as against the Southern Vales south of Adelaide, where Hardy's were based. Although it didn't seem so cool when he arrived in Auckland, palm trees shimmying in the warm breeze, soon followed by subtropical rainstorms and a suffocating humidity which made your shirt stick to your back like damp glue. My God, he thought, surely you can't grow grapes in *this* climate?

Alerted to the Potential

Judd wasn't even awake when the first juice arrived from Marlborough. Trucked up from South Island overnight, the Semillon arrived around dawn. He blearily asked the cellar hand for a sample and rolled over for a few more minutes shut-eye. But his eyes snapped wide open at the first taste. He couldn't believe the flavours – like fresh green peppers, almost a caricature of what cool climate Sauvignon Blanc should taste like – and this wasn't even Sauvignon Blanc. He remembers thinking he was crazy – he shouldn't just be *making* this wine. He should be *selling* it. To the Australians, who'd struggled for years to produce pungent, green-grass Sauvignon Blanc flavours without success. Funny. That's exactly what David Hohnen was thinking too. Hohnen and Judd were on the plane to Marlborough the moment the wine show was finished.

The two Australians arrived there to find that Marlborough was virtually a two-horse operation. Montana owned most of the vineyard land, in particular most of the Sauvignon Blanc, and processed the fruit at their vast local winery. When Hohnen enquired about buying some of the crop they politely showed him the door. In the public eye, Montana *was* Marlborough. But the real competition wasn't Hohnen, it was Corbans, New Zealand's other big wine company. They had planted a vineyard called Stoneleigh on the opposite

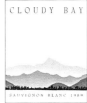

Kevin Judd – the quiet man who created New Zealand's most high profile wine without once raising his voice.

side of the Wairau valley from Montana in extremely stony, free-draining soil. But they had no winery. They were trucking their grapes over the Cook Strait to Gisborne, 563km (350 miles) away on the east coast of North Island. Hohnen struck a deal. Corbans were keen to develop Stoneleigh as a quality label. If they'd help him find a site, Hohnen would build a winery where they could make their Stoneleigh wines – so long as he could have some Sauvignon Blanc grapes in return.

And that's how Cloudy Bay all began. Well, not quite. Hohnen wanted to make a 1985 vintage. But he didn't have a winery yet. Judd had promised to make the 1985 wines for Selaks. So while producing a string of valedictory beauties at Selaks, he spent his meal breaks on the phone giving precise harvesting instructions to Hohnen who was down in the Corbans vineyard in Marlborough. Hohnen then took his grapes up to Corbans' Gisborne winery, and then got to a phone again for Judd's instructions on the vinification.

The phone lines must be good in New Zealand. This first attempt at gypsy wine-making by Judd and Hohnen won a gold medal at the 1986 Air New Zealand Export Wine Awards, and it topped a tasting of the world's best Sauvignon Blancs held in London by *WINE* magazine. Why? Fruit. Brilliant, piercing, lychee and apricot fruit shot through with gooseberry and lime acidity so that your mouth watered with excitement, but never puckered from aggression.

So the partnership was obviously going to work on Sauvignon Blanc. Judd's wine-making and Hohnen's

eye for marketing would ensure that. But the pair still needed a winery, a vineyard and someone to grow the grapes. Hohnen was finding that a chap called Hoare, the local Marlborough property agent, was being tremendously helpful in smoothing the way for the purchase of the Cloudy Bay winery site and the planning permissions the new winery would need. Purely by chance, Hoare had established a vineyard right next to the Cloudy Bay site. It grew Cabernet Sauvignon grapes rather than Sauvignon Blanc, but if Hohnen could see his way to making the wine . . . ? Of course Hohnen could. And a chap called Sutherland had been hired to manage the vineyard development. Purely by chance, Sutherland had a block of Merlot already planted. Now if Hohnen could see his way to . . . Yes, yes. Hohnen could. He'd already decided to have a go at Chardonnay, but, what the hell, he'd make a Cabernet-Merlot too – just so long as he got his winery built and his vineyard planted.

The winery was built at last in 1985. My first impression of the place was that Kevin Judd didn't care what it looked like, so long as the acoustics were right for his stereo system. It's a blockish, dull grey, concrete building, with corrugated iron roof and not an artistically-inspired bauble in sight. But the acoustics are great. Tall stainless steel tanks do wonders for Pink Floyd and Hound Dog Taylor; raucous heavy metal is graciously de-brutalized by the silently disapproving rows of new French oak.

Apart from good sounds, the other thing Judd cares about is winery hygiene. There is not the slightest whiff of anything vinegary or musty in the air; in fact the place smells actively clean, just stopping short of a hospital ward. Judd may be famous for his pretence that good wine 'just happens', but nothing, I reckon, 'just happens' at Cloudy Bay.

From 1985 to 1988 all the wines were made with bought-in fruit. In 1989 the first estate-grown Sauvignon Blanc was included as half of the blend, but, although there's Chardonnay already planted, and a great deal more land ready to plant, the Chardonnay and the Cabernet-Merlot still come from other growers' fruit. This doesn't bother Judd, as long as he can keep an eye on those grapes in the growing season.

The Sauvignon Blanc is the easiest variety to work with. Judd says it grows like a weed in Marlborough, and it is virtually impossible to find a local Sauvignon Blanc wine that isn't packed with flavour. His job is to get the right balance of flavour, not just the rush of gooseberry and green pepper and asparagus that first brought Marlborough to the world's attention. He achieves this partly by blending in about 20 per cent Semillon in the classic white Bordeaux manner, though he says he's not convinced the Graves producers would recognize the clone of Semillon planted in New

The pale grey mountains which feature on the label for Cloudy Bay's white wines.

Zealand. It never gets properly ripe, however long you leave it, and in a rare moment of deference to his South Australian past, Judd has planted some Barossa Valley Semillon to see if it will add the texture he likes.

Except that he can already achieve this with what he has. Most of the Sauvignon he uses is from free-draining, stony soil where control of vigour is less of a problem than water stress. He monitors his own soil humidity right up to veraison, when the grapes change colour, and his objective up to that moment is to give them not quite as much water as they want, but enough to keep them functioning. In 1989, on these stony soils, he was pumping on 16 litres (3.5 gallons) of water per vine per day, just to keep them in this state!

He aims to pick his Sauvignon Blanc in three phases, and he now does it on taste rather than a perfect set of ripeness figures. Some gets brought in early to give him the snappy green acidity Sauvignon is famous for. The bulk is then picked at the height of the harvest to give fruit strength to the wine. But Sauvignon Blanc's flavours change so dramatically in the last couple of weeks of ripening that he tries to leave some bunches hanging until the grapes reach peak sugar levels – and that's where he gains the wonderful, glyceriney, tropical richness of lychees and pineapples in syrup, of peaches

and apricots and cream that adds the extra layer of flavour marking out Cloudy Bay from other Marlborough Sauvignons.

With Chardonnay Judd's problem is high acidity, not sugar levels. The first Chardonnay in 1986 had such a sharp, green edge that they thought about blending it and pretending it hadn't happened – as he says, not only he but the whole of Marlborough were novices with Chardonnay to begin with. Now he's re-trellising his Chardonnay whenever possible with the Scott Henry system, pruning foliage away from the growing grapes, and he's still getting very high alcohol but lower acidity. Mix that with some Chardonnay from more fertile, loamy soil, and the acidity is mouthwatering, the richness undiluted.

He's been lucky with the Cabernet and Merlot vineyards, because they complement each other well and Hoare and Sutherland are both determined to prove that Marlborough can make great red wine. It can sometimes, and the hot 1989 vintage proved the point brilliantly. Sutherland's loamy fertile soil produced classic Merlot flavours of juicy blackcurrant and raspberry, streaked with grassy acidity. Hoare's Cabernet vineyard looks more like Châteauneuf-du-Pape in France's Rhône valley than anywhere else – all great big round stones and hardly a crumb of earth in sight. Those stones mean the water simply drains away however much you slosh on. But after every sunny day, they're packed with heat, warming the vines well into the night. In a cool area like Marlborough that can make all the difference, and the grapes ripen here two weeks ahead of neighbouring vineyards. In 1989, this Cabernet was almost black, as chewy and bitter-rich as the finest French black chocolate. With Sutherland's juicy-Lucy Merlot at its beck and call, the 1989 Cabernet-Merlot will soon challenge the North Island Cabernets for top honours, and it'll taste brilliantly different too.

Judd makes his red wines in a highly conventional Bordeaux manner. They're fermented in stainless steel at a maximum temperature of about 30°C (86°F) and the juice is macerated with the skins for three weeks. Then the wine is consigned to old-fashioned wooden upright vats for a year before spending the best part of another year in small oak barrels, half of them new.

Judd takes a rather more interventionist line on his whites. The Sauvignon Blanc grapes come in, are crushed, and then kept overnight to settle their juice. This skin contact has an important positive effect on flavour. Most of the juice is then fermented in stainless steel tanks at between 10° and 11°C (50° and 52°F). Semillon is added to the final blend to soften the wine, as is between 15 and 20 per cent of Sauvignon Blanc

which has been fermented in barrel and aged for several months in new wood. Unusually, Judd also sometimes likes to keep a little residual sugar in the wine, and the final effect is a wine of positively viscous richness, honey and lychees, blending with the floral sweetness of fresh peaches and apricots and stabbed through with nettles and gooseberry.

The Chardonnay doesn't get any skin contact and starts a slow, careful fermentation in tanks at 10° to 11°C (50° to 52°F) to preserve the fruit flavours, but halfway through most is transferred to barrels up to three years old to finish fermenting and develop richness. He leaves the wine in barrel on its lees for a year, not stirring if he can help it, and protecting the wine from air with a strict regime of sulphur additions. A proportion, up to 30 per cent, is kept in tank to go through malolactic fermentation, and if Judd feels the barrel portion is taking up wood flavours too enthusiastically, he'll put some of that back in stainless steel too. And despite putting all his whites through a sterile filter, the Chardonnay manages to combine a haunting floral fragrance like a crisp white peach, with a mouthfilling richness of coconut and butter.

French Connection

So far Cloudy Bay has managed to build up production (to 40,000 cases in 1990) while positively enhancing quality. They've done this partly by using fruit from their own vineyards, 45 hectares (110 acres) planted so far, but mainly by working with good contract growers, on whose fruit they built their reputation. 1990 changed all that. The year before, Veuve Clicquot, the French Champagne house, had bought 100 hectares (250 acres) of Marlborough land. In 1990 they took a 70 per cent share in Cloudy Bay (and in Cape Mentelle in Western Australia, where David Hohnen is still very much involved), and purchased another 100 hectares (250 acres) of land.

Clearly the suitcases-to-Champagne luxury goods outfit that controls Clicquot saw the need to add further 'de luxe' names to their range of wines, and Cloudy Bay's position as one of the world's most high-profile wines, a fame achieved from a standing start in 1985, was ideal for their expansion plans. Veuve Clicquot say they're going to raise production to 65,000 cases, but they'll have the grapes available for a far bigger increase than that if they so decide. Yet Kevin Judd came to New Zealand to gain freedom from the large corporations controlling South Australia's wine. Anyone interested in fine wine at an affordable price must hope his nerve doesn't fail him if the new owners decide to pump up the volume.

NORTH ISLAND

Kumeu River

'YOU CAN'T MAKE decent wine unless you know what decent wine tastes like.' That seems pretty obvious I'd have thought, but then I wasn't growing up in New Zealand in the 1970s. Michael Brajkovich was; on the family winery San Marino, perched by the roadside north of Auckland, doing a fast trade in dry red wine and Müller-Thurgau white, selling to passing holidaymakers and airfield personnel. I've tasted a few of those old San Marino wines and they were really quite nice – nothing spectacular, a bit light, but pleasant and easy to drink. As seventies New Zealand went, they were some of the best wines available. In fact, the New Zealanders got into Müller-Thurgau in such a big way that it wasn't long before they were patting themselves on the back and boasting they made the best Müller-Thurgau in the world.

Well, they possibly did. But, so what? was Michael's feeling. Müller-Thurgau is the main grape used for cheap Liebfraumilch in Germany, is virtually not planted at all in Australia or America, and the emerging rival to New Zealand for the crown of Müller-Thurgau king was England! For someone as bright and ambitious as Michael, the idea of being best at making wine from one of the world's dullest grapes felt like intellectual and spiritual suicide. So in 1979 he was the first of the now annual wave of New Zealanders to cross the Tasman Sea and begin to study at Roseworthy College in South Australia. He says he was like a sponge that first year, just soaking up knowledge. 'I went over there thinking I knew something about wine and after the first couple of weeks I realized I knew nothing. I realized just how far behind we were in New Zealand.' But he was soaking up more than book knowledge. He was soaking up wine.

Don't get me wrong. Certainly he threw himself wholeheartedly into the college drinking world, but he had a purpose. Having almost no experience of the world's wines away from New Zealand, he organized a group of similarly-minded students. Each week they would pool all their resources and then badger the local Adelaide merchants for special prices on all their finest wines – frequently from the other Australian states, but whenever possible from the great classic areas of Bordeaux and Burgundy, or the vintage ports of Portugal. And for a change, now and then, they'd line up Scotland's single malt whiskies too.

In 1981 Michael Brajkovich graduated at the top of his class. He went back to his family winery, re-named it Kumeu River, deciding that a radical change of direction and image was needed if it were to prosper in the rapidly changing international world, and began to apply the lessons he had learned. But he still wasn't

Michael Brajkovich in typically studious mood at Kumeu. In 1989 he became the first New Zealander to receive Britain's prestigious Master of Wine award.

satisfied. The grapes weren't good enough for a start. And what he had learned at Roseworthy seemed increasingly to be a formula relevant to South Australia but not to the humid, subtropical conditions of Kumeu.

The one teacher who had challenged and excited him at Roseworthy was Richard Smart, now an internationally famous vineyard expert. In 1983 Michael picked the Kumeu grapes, waited until they'd finished fermenting, then set off on a trip to California, Oregon and Washington with Smart. Hell, he was halfway around the world by then, he thought, so he might as well keep going. So he rang up the Moueix family in France, the people who run Château Pétrus and a cluster of other top properties. It's a good thing he didn't put off the call until he'd finished his coffee. The chief Moueix winemaker had just signed a letter offering the last place on his harvesting team to an American girl. Then Michael rang. The letter to America was never posted, and Michael turned up in Bordeaux instead of the girl, ready to work the 1983 vintage. (And no, he's never met the girl he replaced.)

As a trained winemaker, Michael had a major hand in the 1983 vintage, especially at Château Magdelaine in St-Émilion. Then he darted across to Burgundy, tasting Côte d'Or wines from north to south, before haring back to New Zealand to see how his Kumeu River 1983 Merlot was getting on. He tasted his barrels and remembers saying – God, why do we bother? Then he said – no; our fruit's good, we *can* do it, but we must do it properly, from the moment we plan the vineyard to the time we press the cork into the bottle.

Whereas other New Zealand winemakers may have adapted Australian methods to suit local conditions, or indeed developed wine styles without reference to anywhere else, Brajkovich has undoubtedly drawn heavily on Europe for ideas. Quietly, persistently, without seeming intrusive, almost without seeming inquisitive, Brajkovich is always probing behind the scenes – why is something done, what is its effect.

He cites a few examples. Barrel fermentation for his whites for instance. He'd asked his professor at Roseworthy about barrel-fermenting white wine and had been told that no-one would want to ferment in a barrel – you couldn't control the temperatures. Barrels were for ageing; stainless steel was for fermenting. Yet all the great white Burgundies are barrel-fermented. Michael started barrel-fermenting his white wines in 1984.

No-one in New Zealand knew much about malolactic fermentation. Growers got high acids in their grapes, so they chemically de-acidified, reducing the sharpness maybe, but frequently leaving a one-dimensional, stripped flavour instead. Michael reasoned that not only

did white Burgundies undergo malolactic fermentation, with a dramatic consequent improvement in the round, creamy character of the wine, but in cool Champagne where acids were screechingly high, it was normal wine-making practice. So encouraging the malolactic was introduced at Kumeu River. A lot of the locals scoffed, but since then the wonderfully creamy, nutty flavours of Kumeu River Chardonnays have had people making very complimentary Burgundian comparisons in Europe and elsewhere, and now, even in New Zealand itself.

Another thing – pressing whole bunches of grapes. It wasn't even considered in New Zealand in the 1970s. But in Burgundy and Champagne they did it – there had to be a reason – and of course there is. The stalks act as draining channels for the juice, as well as acting like sieves to filter off some of the grape flesh solids. The juice runs out clean and fast – so you get minimal skin contact and pick-up of unwanted flavour compounds, minimal oxidation, and you can reduce your sulphur dioxide to zero because of the speed.

French Polishing

Michael is certainly passionate about the techniques he has learnt in the classic French areas, but the humid climate and heavy clay soils of his 18 hectares (45 acres) of Kumeu land still produce very individual flavours that are merely moulded by classic French methods. His Sauvignon Blanc has an intense syrup and gooseberry richness despite its evident acidity. His Chardonnay is marvellous: toasty, with a spicy sweetness of vanilla and coconut, yet the unctuous syrupy fruit is recognizably different from a French Burgundy. And his Merlot-Cabernet has managed to catch the glycerine-soft, plum and strawberry earthiness of a St-Émilion, yet there's a pepperiness and promise of blackcurrant and liquorice as the wine ages, which once again marks it out as different from the French model. Brajkovich is an internationalist, yet his wines are memorably New Zealand. The natural intensity of good fruit isn't compromised, it's simply given a different cloak.

The turn of the decade confirmed Brajkovich's international credentials even further. Alain Moueix from Bordeaux came over to work the 1990 vintage in New Zealand and to learn from *him*. And Michael became a Master of Wine – the first New Zealander ever to achieve this honour. The MW courses and the exams are held in London. Michael couldn't take any time off for the courses, only managing to pop over to sit the exams between racking and bottling schedules at the winery. But his travels and his dogged determination to observe and then ask why seem to have been lessons enough.

Marlborough

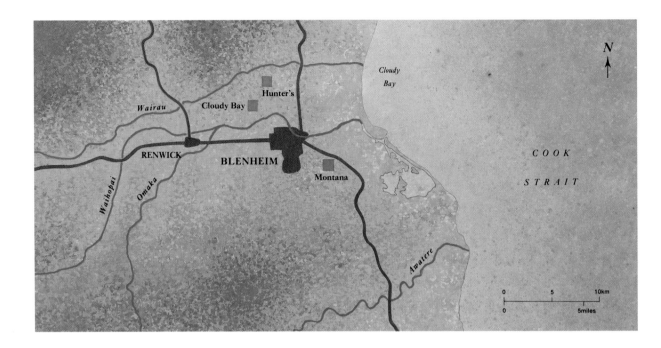

*J*OHN BUCK OF TE MATA reckons he found it first. In 1969 he was scouring New Zealand for a site where he could plant vines. There wasn't a single vine on the South Island, but Buck examined the soil and climate statistics of Marlborough, just across the Cook Strait from Wellington, and said this was silly – here was perfect vineyard land. He was billeted that night with the editor of the local newspaper. The next edition carried a banner headline extolling Marlborough's brilliant aptitude for quality vineyards. A week later Buck got a letter from Corbans, then the dominant force in New Zealand wine, telling him he didn't know what he was talking about.

But it's Corbans who got it wrong. Marlborough may have been vineless in 1969. A decade later it was already being hailed as a viticultural paradise in New Zealand's generally difficult climate. Corbans began planting in 1980. But Montana had done their homework and begun planting in 1973, and by the time Corbans released their first Marlborough wine, Montana had already established a worldwide reputation for their Marlborough Sauvignon Blanc which, ten years later, they look in no danger of losing.

By 1991 Marlborough had become New Zealand's biggest vineyard area with at least 1400 hectares (3500 acres) planted, but things move so fast down there, no one is sure of the exact figure. In 1990 alone 325 new hectares (800 acres) were planted.

What did John Buck see in these gusty, flat river-bed plains, which fan out eastward from the jagged Richmond mountains at the tip of South Island? Everything a white wine producer could want, with the exception of a ready market – the main town, Blenheim, is only a few thousand strong. Buck however had a passion to make classic *red* wines, so he ended up setting up vineyards in the warmer environs of Hawke's Bay on North Island. Every great Marlborough wine since the first vines were planted in 1973 has been white. And the majority of these have come from just one grape variety – the Sauvignon Blanc.

I'd put one factor above all others. Lack of rain. In particular, lack of the kind of autumn rain that can wreck crops all along New Zealand's north and east coasts. Marlborough doesn't have a particularly hot climate, but in most years the grapes can creep safely towards full maturity, and some varieties are picked, still healthy, as early winter snows begin to powder the nearby mountain ranges. March, the month before harvest starts, is the driest phase of the year, while in the February to April period Marlborough has a lower rainfall than any of New Zealand's other commercial vineyard regions. In 1990 there was no rain at all between January and March. Since most vine diseases develop when humidity and rainfall occur at the wrong times, this dry spell dramatically reduces the cost of anti-rot and mildew treatments and it gives you what every winemaker pines for – a reliable crop of healthy grapes.

The bad weather during the growing season in New Zealand generally comes in from the west, and Marlborough is well protected by mountains to the south and west. Autumn storms usually come from the Pacific to the east. Marlborough's eastern flank is protected by the northern end of the Southern Alps; and the south-east tip of the North Island (all these points of the compass, I *am* sorry) soaks up the tail of any cyclone pattern still active this far south.

Sun, Sea and Sauvignon

Lack of rain in itself is not enough: you need sunshine and warmth too to ripen grapes. Marlborough just hits the balance nicely. Sunshine hours are often the longest in New Zealand during the growing season, and these long sunny spells result in an average temperature which is pretty similar to Burgundy in France, generally warmer than Champagne, yet rarely as hot as Bordeaux in a top vintage. And this in spite of the fact that Marlborough is closer to the South Pole than any of New Zealand's other main wine regions.

Marlborough fruit is famous for its mouthwatering acidity. Too much daytime heat will soften that. Unless you have very cold nights. Marlborough does. The sea is just a few kilometres away, and every night the temperature drops, even if it has been sizzling at 32° to 33°C (89° to 91°F) during the day, and this keeps the acidity high in the grapes in all but the hottest years.

The other important factor is the wind. Usually cool climate vineyards need protection from heat-dissipating winds. But Marlborough is protected by mountains on three sides, and the prevailing winds are the warm northerlies. They're strong winds – you have to tuck everything on the vine under restraining wires or the gales will blow them to bits. But they're also warm. So long as your vines have enough water the winds will bolster the ripening process.

Which is where the soil comes in. With very low natural rainfall you might think that moisture-retaining soils are crucial for the success of vineyards. But the Marlborough plains exist as the result of the Wairau river pouring off the mountains into the Cook Strait over the millennia. Although there is fertile alluvial silt varying in depth from a metre or so to absolutely nothing, the basic soil in Marlborough is gravel, pebble or rock, going straight down for maybe six metres, to

aquifers where parts of the river still flow underground, providing an endless supply of water for the pumps.

Only on the southern side of the valley – where, interestingly, Montana have their main Sauvignon Blanc estate – may there be a water deficiency, which has to be handled by pumping supplies from the centre of the valley a couple of miles north. In partial recompense, the southern soils are more fertile and hold moisture better, but this advantage is offset by the soil's damp coolness, which retards ripening by as much as two weeks. This can be crucial in a late, cool area like Marlborough, though it also goes some way to explain how Montana's Sauvignon Blanc always keeps its appetizing green edge. All the successful vineyards are consequently drip-irrigated as a simple matter of routine for survival.

Like most great vineyard areas, Marlborough is on the cusp between managing and failing to ripen its grapes. Though almost all the white varieties will succeed to some degree, many Cabernet Sauvignons planted in the heavier, cooler soils in the centre of the valley, frequently fail to reach full maturity, resulting in what one visiting Australian described pretty aptly as 'red Sauvignon Blanc'. Cabernet is such a late season variety, it just runs out of time, or they have an early frost and the leaves drop off. Harvest is usually still in progress in mid-May, and when frost struck early in April 1990, Montana had yet to pick a single red berry. Only in scorchers like 1989 does Marlborough really do the business with Cabernet and Merlot.

Sauvignon Blanc, however, is at home on these soils, and the north and south sides of the valley provide two different, but complementary flavour styles. The gravelly, warmer soils of the north along the course of the Wairau river, ripen two weeks ahead of the southern side and can give ultra-ripe tropical fruit peach and apricot flavours to balance the greener, more asparagus-and-gooseberry flavours of the south.

The next most successful variety is Riesling, sometimes called Rhine Riesling in New Zealand, which also needs the long, dry autumns to ripen fully, yet which, if the weather does break, can be 'noble-rotted' to provide delicious sweet wine. Chardonnay so far remains a problem, partly because of widespread planting of unsuitable warm climate clones. Until the right clones are found, growers will have to work hard on their trellising and pruning techniques to restrict yields and expose fruit to the sun as much as possible.

(Overleaf) The sheep still share their pastures with vines in Marlborough, but every year more of the land is turned over to vineyards and fewer sheep graze.

Martinborough

*L*ARRY MCKENNA HAS GOT IT all worked out in easy stages. If he harvests the best fruit in the Martinborough district, he modestly reckons he's got more than an even chance of making the best wine. And if he can then prove that Martinborough district is producing the best fruit in the country, why, then, his aim will be to produce the best wine in the country, won't it? Amazingly, for an area which hardly boasted a vine ten years ago, the tiny area of Martinborough, at the south of New Zealand's North Island, has shot to prominence and now rivals the far larger and longer-established areas of Hawke's Bay and Marlborough. And it was McKenna who made the wines which have put Martinborough on the map.

Partner and winemaker at Martinborough Vineyards, McKenna startled the New Zealand wine hierarchy by gaining gold medals in three styles – Chardonnay, Pinot Noir and Fumé Blanc – with his very first vintage at the winery, 1986. Then, in the 1989 National Wine Competition, he did actually win the trophy for the best wine in New Zealand. All this in the space of five years.

Martinborough is a tiny town on the north-eastern side of a grazing valley known as the Wairarapa, an hour or so's drive north-east of Wellington. It once played an important part in providing food for the capital city. By the late 1970s however, the area was undergoing a discreet but prolonged decline, and the government instituted a project aimed at finding alternative uses for the land. Most of the soil is heavy clay loam, the sunlight hours are long and despite some problems with prevailing north-westerly gales, the rainfall over most of the valley is moderate to good. The governmental report recommended a whole range of crops to the beleaguered farmers – cherries, apples, kiwi fruit, an orchard mix. But there was one area, one isolated patch of land not covering much more than 245 hectares (600 acres), which had different soils, seriously deficient rainfall – and a suitability for growing only one thing – grapes.

The two biggest problems New Zealand faces in its long-established vineyards are an excess of rain – frequently at precisely the wrong time just as the grapes are trying to ripen in the autumn sun – and excessively fertile soil, which permits vines to throw out masses of vegetation and encourages them to support enormous crops. The soils around Martinborough, and the climate in this area are as different from the New Zealand norm as can be. The Wairarapa clay is thick and heavy, so

much so that the vine roots find it almost impossible to penetrate. Attempt to plant on this and you'd never get a half-decent yield of half-decent grapes. But as the river running down to the sea gradually shifted its course over the centuries towards the centre of the valley, it left a series of flat-topped river bank terraces to the north-east. These are as free-draining as any soil in New Zealand. The topsoil, strewn with chunky rocks and pebbles, is rarely very deep and below that it's almost pure gravel going down three or four metres as far as they can tell, and quite possibly more. The roots of the vine will stretch right down in their search for nutrients and water. They won't find much, but the deeper they go, the less vulnerable they are. Even in the hottest and driest summers, mature vines with deep roots will survive without too much stress.

They'll need all the strength they can muster at Martinborough, because this tiny mesoclimate is the driest in New Zealand's North Island. Martinborough has a normal, adequately wet winter, but the summer rains are all drawn off by mountains to the south-west, west and north-east. In March 1988 Cyclone Bola flooded Gisborne with over 500mm (20in) of rain. Martinborough got away with 50mm (2in); the vines quickly dried out, and Larry McKenna, for one, made a lovely ripe Chardonnay of 14 degrees alcohol that year.

The publication of the Wairarapa report on Martinborough in 1979 led to the immediate establishment of four small vineyards – the leading one being Martinborough Vineyards, a partnership between Derek Milne, who had published the report, and four others. By 1985 there were 20 hectares (50 acres) of vines around the town, and even a little wine. The fruit flavour of the grapes seemed excellent. It just needed someone to transform it into world class wine.

The Man Most Likely To

Larry McKenna was not an immediately obvious candidate. He hadn't even studied to be a winemaker, but, through a great friend at school in Adelaide, South Australia, he'd ended up making wine at Delegat's, a large Auckland winery. He's still very grateful for the chance Delegat's gave him, because he freely admits he didn't really have the paper qualifications for the job. But by 1985 he realized he wasn't cut out to be a corporate winemaker. He needed freedom to develop his own ideas and wine-making style, and he wasn't going to get that with an established winery, or in an established area, he reckoned.

When someone told him that there was a winery in Martinborough looking for a professional who would put quality above all else, he had yet to visit the area.

Larry McKenna normally jumps in and treads his vines by foot, but here he's gone high tech with a manual plunger.

But he knew that here was the chance to put his ideals into action. The parched summer grass of the Wairarapa reminded him of the conditions round the vineyards of South Australia where he grew up. And when he tasted the partners' efforts with the 1985 Pinot Noir, he says that despite its faults, he'd never tasted such beautiful underlying Pinot Noir fruit before in New Zealand.

And it's Pinot Noir that obsesses Larry McKenna. Although he makes Riesling, Gewürztraminer and Sauvignon Blanc, 70 per cent of his 5000-case production is based on the Burgundian brother and sister act – Pinot Noir and Chardonnay. His Chardonnay is good, veering to excellent. Trying to emulate Burgundian traditions he presses the bunches whole, ferments the juice in barrel, putting some through malolactic fermentation and giving the wine 11 months on lees in French oak barrels, of which around a third are new.

At the moment he sterile-filters the wine before bottling, chiefly because not all the wine goes through the second, malolactic fermentation, and he can't risk its starting to re-ferment in bottle. But his objective is to put all the wine through the malolactic and not filter at all. Larry insists on full ripeness, and since 1988 has

achieved about 14 degrees of alcohol every year. The softening, second fermentation adds a rich butterscotch lusciousness to the wine, yet leaves the lemon/lime acidity, the ripe apple fruit and the toasty oak.

But Pinot Noir – Larry admits he is captivated by it. He talks of Chambertin and Vosne-Romanée endlessly, wondering whether his 'Burgundian methods' are authentic enough to produce a South Seas Chambertin. I hope his sojourn with Domaine Dujac in Burgundy for the 1990 vintage bolstered rather than deflated his confidence, because his methods are actually far more traditional than the general techniques prevalent in Burgundy today.

Above all, he foot-crushes his grapes. 'I thought it was bullshit,' he said disarmingly, 'but then I decided – if that's the way the Burgundians do it, we'll do it too.' Oh, if only they did: I wonder what dusty old textbook he'd read. But the effect on McKenna's Pinot Noir is electric. The depth of colour, the intensity of fruit – all crushed raspberries and dark cherries, fragrant leather and gum and still-steaming tea-leaves – that marks out his 1990 is wonderfully exciting. The 1989 is lighter – one of the few times he couldn't quite get the ripeness he wanted – but the 1988 shows why he got so excited about Martinborough fruit in the first place – a rich, deep, most originally flavoured wine – like sloes long-steeped in gin, like cranberries boiled into sauce, like ripe loganberries in syrup, like herbs and plums and the breakfast toast of new oak barrels.

There's no doubt in my mind that Martinborough will take its place amongst the great Pinot Noirs of the world. It won't taste like Chambertin, it won't taste like Yarra Valley wine, or Carneros, or Santa Barbara Pinot Noir. It's an original, started from scratch by a guy who never meant to be a winemaker at all, but whose obsession with the grape, and whose single-minded doggedness of purpose should ensure that the fads and foibles and short-term ambitions which have bedevilled Burgundy, leave him unscathed. There are now 81 hectares (200 acres) planted in Martinborough. There'll be 162 (400) in five years' time. They're going to need a leader with a clear head and a passionate commitment if they are to avoid growing pains. Larry McKenna is the unlikely hero of the hour.

NORTH ISLAND

Matua Valley

I'VE HEARD ANY NUMBER of stories about house-hunters rounding a bend in the road after days of fruitless searching and – pow – there, perched on a hill right in front of them is the home of their dreams. So how does a house-hunting tale spiced with stampeding bulls and the elusive fluttering of a stray dollar bill strike you instead? Ross Spence had been searching long and hard for the right site for his winery in 1976 when he spied this old farm house perched on a rise, in the Waimauku valley just to the north of Auckland. He still wasn't certain about the site, though, so he popped out next day, and found himself standing at the bottom of the property's steepest slope, ruminating.

Not so the local cattle. Led by the bulls, they proceeded to charge headlong down the hill towards Spence. Most men would simply have leapt for safety over the nearest ditch. But Spence's beady eye had also caught sight of a dollar bill fluttering in the breeze – miles from anywhere. When you're trying to establish a winery, every dollar counts. So he sprang sideways, scooped up the dollar bill and was making a desperate dash for it . . . when the cattle for no apparent reason ground to a halt as Spence graphically illustrates: 'just this far away'.

Not being trampled to death and making a buck into the bargain was too good an omen to resist. Next day Ross bought the property, shaved several metres of clay off the top of the hill, to show the cattle who was boss around here – and with his brother Bill built what is now both a spectacular, and entirely practical winery for his Matua Valley wines.

The first winery they used had been neither spectacular, nor practical. And nor did they own it. Matua Valley Wines started life in 1974 in a rented tumbledown tin shack in a residential suburb west of Auckland. This Swanson Road base resembled, if anything, a bungalow for a particularly impoverished retired couple, and, as Ross Spence says, 'she was a bloody hard case place, I can tell you'. They bought some redundant shoulder-height dairy vats, stripped out the stirring mechanism in the middle, piled in some unfancied Seibel 5455 hybrid grapes – and proceeded to win the Champion Red Wine Trophy at the 1975 Royal Easter Show, much to the fury of the large companies who then dominated New Zealand wine.

Ross and Bill Spence, like many of New Zealand's new generation of winemakers, came from an old

Matua Valley's buildings have not kept pace with the winery's rapid expansion, and much wine is stored in the spare space of less successful neighbours.

traditional Dalmatian wine family. Their father had a winery making what one friendly critic called 'ports and sherries out of nothing mentionable . . . the real good old, bad old days', but the prospect of trying to apply life-support to a style of wine-making rapidly going out of fashion during the 1970s didn't appeal to the Spence boys. After university, and a spell working for big wineries, they took the plunge and decided to set up on their own in their dingy tin shack in Swanson Road.

In 1974 there really weren't many decent red *or* white wine grape varieties planted in New Zealand. German advice had been followed rather than any other, and Müller-Thurgau was by far the most common grape, followed by the sherry variety Palomino and the brandy variety Baco 22A. There was some Cabernet Sauvignon and a tiny bit of Chardonnay. But there was no Semillon. And remarkably, no Sauvignon Blanc. Today, Sauvignon Blanc is New Zealand's most famous wine. The very first Sauvignon Blanc in New Zealand was made by the Spences in their dairy vat in 1974, and the vast majority of today's plantings are direct descendants of the vines Ross Spence introduced to New Zealand for the first time.

Innovation, carefully tempered by acute awareness of market trends, is an enduring theme running through Matua Valley's development. Once they'd set up their new Waimauku winery they planted a wide variety of

grapes on the heavy clay soils, not really knowing what would work and what wouldn't. The humid, warm climate and excessive rainfall have forced them to cut back and back on varieties, until the 1990s will see merely a block of Cabernet Sauvignon, and some Pinot Noir and Chardonnay for early picking and transformation into sparkling wine. Even Sauvignon Blanc will have to go, because its tight-packed bunches can't cope with the humidity. Black rot, brown rot, sour rot (ugh!), botrytis – the conditions are perfect for all these diseases, and unless growers are really on top of their spraying programmes, one rain squall at vintage time can send rot rampaging through the vineyard. Estimates vary, but they say that you have to use between 5 and 20 times as many sprays in Auckland as you do in the drier regions like Hawke's Bay, or Marlborough in the South Island.

By 1979 they realized that although they might be able to grow decent fruit on their estate, it would be 'bloody hard work'. So they began a pattern that is now commonplace for all the Auckland wineries of any ambition (possibly excepting neighbours Kumeu River) – that of searching out grape supplies in New Zealand's natural vineyard regions, then trucking the grapes up to their centre of operations and sales around Auckland, to turn them into wine.

In particular, the Spences needed to pinpoint vineyards to supply them with top Chardonnay and top Cabernet Sauvignon. Since 1983, the Judd Estate, on high land above the Gisborne plains, has been providing the fruit for a single vineyard Chardonnay. The 1983

was so clinically fermented it tasted more like a snappy Sauvignon than a Chardonnay, but the Judd Estate style has gradually evolved into a beautifully balanced wine, with the apricot and toasty richness of barrel fermentation blended with some bright lemony, minty fruit from stainless steel fermentation. Today it is one of New Zealand's top Chardonnays.

The Cabernet Sauvignon from the shingle and loam soil of the Dartmoor-Smith vineyard, in a side valley just behind Hawke's Bay, has repeated the Spences' feat of 1975 by being voted New Zealand's top red wine. Both the 1985 and 1986 won trophies, the 1986 even winning a rare gold in England's International Wine Challenge. It deserves the honour. It has the depth of rich blackcurrant, damson and strawberry fruit, almost syrupy in its intensity, but streaked with a leafy, grassy, even peppery green acidity, uplifted by a perfume of wild strawberries and flowers that makes the Matua Valley Cabernet Sauvignon memorably good and uniquely New Zealand.

These grapes are trucked over the hills to the octagonal winery at Matua Valley. Up until 1985, capacity was more than enough for their needs, but by 1990 production had climbed to about 120,000 cases of wine a year, of which 25,000 are of the quality varietals like Chardonnay, Cabernet Sauvignon and Sauvignon Blanc, and 25 per cent are of cash flow Müller-Thurgau. They solved the volume crisis by hiring space in several of the local wineries and by indulging in some fascinating 'phone-line' wine-making.

John Belsham, once the winemaker at the Auckland base, now works down in Marlborough on the South Island, where Matua Valley regularly buy 300 tons of white grapes a year. The Spences don't see the wine until it's finished. They give Belsham very precise instructions as to wine style, he faxes them a detailed spec of how things are going daily, and they feel as close to the wine as if the tanks were in the next room.

The Spence brothers epitomise the best on New Zealand wine's entrepreneurial wing. Dramatic expansion, without dilution of quality. Fifteen years ago they were in a tin shack; now their wines are served at Buckingham Palace. And just to prove the sky's the limit for the Spence boys, in 1989 they got about as near as is possible without donning a space suit, when their wines were chosen for serving on Concorde.

SOUTH ISLAND

Montana

I'VE HAD THEM SPLUTTERING into their glasses. I've had them running sweepstakes on who can come up with the most bizarre tasting descriptions. I've had them cheering with unabashed excitement at the revelation of fruit after a drinking lifetime of lean, sharp, French dry whites. But I've never had a single wine drinker at any of my tastings who was bored by it, just hadn't noticed it, didn't have an opinion about it. Montana Sauvignon Blanc from Marlborough, in the South Island. The most argued about, rubbished or raved about, rejoiced in or rejected white wine in the world today.

Outside its native country, it is often the only New Zealand wine the majority of wine drinkers have ever encountered. And as volumes get higher and higher, the price stays relentlessly reasonable, and the latest releases, in particular the 1989, show a quality actually better now than when it was a newly-introduced special interest line back in the 1970s. I can think of no other mass market wine I could say that about.

Gooseberries. You know how disagreeably sharp and crunchy they are raw? But boil them for half an hour with some sugar syrup – the acidity hasn't budged but suddenly the green fruit seems ripe and mouthwatering, however acid it was. Peppers. Take a knife and slash into a fresh green pepper, and breathe in that cold, earthy fragrance before you take your first bite – then the crunch of the crisp flesh, the flow of cool rainwater.

And there's more. Think of the sharpness of just-picked blackcurrants, still smelling of the leaf rather than the juicy flesh. Think of grass fresh-mown on a spring morning, slightly damp and earthy, but fragrant in the drying sun. Think of new season asparagus – again the crunch, again the paradox of something vegetal but rich. And to sweeten out your thoughts – think of hints of honey, of apricots and apples and the spray of acid from a fresh lime. Think of all that and you've captured the heart of Montana Sauvignon Blanc.

In fact, Montana make every conceivable kind of wine, from low alcohol fizzy thirst-quenchers, through a whole gamut of reds, whites, rosés and sparkling wines to pretty decent so-called 'ports' and 'sherries'. In New Zealand itself, the Sauvignon Blanc is by no means the best-known wine. Their Chardonnay, from high-cropping Gisborne vineyards in the North Island, outsells its nearest Chardonnay rival by ten to one and is found on just about every restaurant list in the country. Blenheimer, a fruity, sweetish Gisborne

The aridity of Marlborough in late summer gives a stark futuristic backdrop to the Montana tank farm.

Müller-Thurgau sells six million bottles a year in New Zealand – two for every member of the population. And although Marlborough Sauvignon has captured the imagination of the rest of the world, it is the flowery, slightly grapefruit-fresh Rhine Riesling that most New Zealanders think of as Montana's best Marlborough wine. The only thing you can't disagree about is the fact that Montana dominates New Zealand wine, accounting for nearly half of the wines sold there, and controlling half the grape supply too.

And it all started with half an acre on the side of a mountain near Auckland. Ivan Yukich, like many of the founders of the modern New Zealand wine industry, was Dalmatian, and he settled in the Waitakere ranges in 1934 on land he named Montana. In the 1950s he and his son Frank instituted a remarkable period of growth. They planted 120 hectares (300 acres) of vines further south of Auckland in Waikato and in the late 1960s, Montana changed the face of New Zealand wine by setting up contract growers with vast holdings in the alluvial river plains of Gisborne, an area that is still the 'grape basket' for enormous quantities of grapes.

So far Montana had grown on the back of high volumes of low-priced wine, often fizzy, and not always based entirely on grapes for their flavours! But by 1973 Frank Yukich could see that this market would reach

saturation point and the only way up would be through better quality table wines. In his customary forthright manner he wanted to strike out in an entirely new direction. He couldn't have found a newer direction than Marlborough. Land given over to sheep, cherries, peas and garlic, cheap to buy, cheap to develop, it would enable Montana to establish a separate, quality-fruit identity. Marlborough was mentioned as a possible site for expansion in March 1973. By August 1973, the first vine was in the ground.

Frank Yukich left the company in 1974 and control passed first to the US distiller Seagram, then to a New Zealand consortium. By then the Marlborough venture had not only created for Montana a quality image it had up until then lacked, it had also given New Zealand its first world-class vineyard region on a grand scale. There are small sections of Hawke's Bay, patches of land in Gisborne and around Auckland, with growing reputations thanks to the efforts of individual growers and winemakers. But with Marlborough you could create something as new and thrilling as when they first drained the marshes of the Médoc hundreds of years ago, or first scaled the slaty slopes by the Mosel river. It was possible to create an entirely new wine style, which is precisely what Montana did with Sauvignon Blanc.

The rise of the small, quality-minded wineries in New Zealand, the praise accorded such names as Te Mata, Kumeu River and Cloudy Bay has also had an effect. As one of Montana's winemakers said, 'It's an attitude thing. We had the market to ourselves for a long time, and never cared about some little boutique winery, but they used to come around and show us what they were capable of and we began to think – hell, we've got the skills and the know-how. Let's go out and do it.'

Going out and doing it is easier said than done in a large national company with a head office a long way from its chief wineries, and with a team of winemakers more used to making up million litre blends of off-dry Müller-Thurgau. But they are having a go. I've tasted some of their new-look Chardonnays and Fumé Blancs. Suddenly the flavours of barrel fermentation, lees contact and malolactic jostle with the more familiar fruit-first Montana tastes.

There are still a couple more areas where Montana has to prove itself. They've just unveiled the results of their first joint venture in sparkling wine with the Champagne house Deutz. The package is stunning, but the power of the Marlborough grapes is such that the marriage between fizz and fruit intensity will not be achieved for a few vintages yet. And they've never really got it right with reds from frequently unripe Marlborough Cabernet. They've just bought 245 hectares (600 acres) of land in Hawke's Bay, along with the historic McDonald winery. Hawke's Bay is New Zealand's most famous Cabernet Sauvignon area. And a new joint venture with Cordier of Bordeaux shows they probably have the vision as well as the know-how to make the best of it.

Ngatarawa

GARY GLAZEBROOK'S INITIATION into the joys of wine-making was brutal. Thirty-six tons of crushed grapes arrived by tanker truck at nine o'clock on the Wednesday evening. The newly installed pumps failed, and, faced with the prospect of the entire load being wasted, his recently acquired business partner refused to allow him to go home for some kip until ten o'clock on Friday night, by which time they had literally shovelled and scooped all of the soupy gunge of juice and skins into a dozen second-hand dairy vats to begin their perilous fermentation. Glazebrook had spent 30 years trying to get involved in the wine-making business because he believed it would offer an unbeatable life style. Soaked in grape juice from head to toe, aching in every limb, and no sleep for two whole days and nights . . . it wasn't an auspicious start.

Still, he's glad he hung on in there. Although that first 1981 vintage of red wine has sunk without trace, the rest of the decade has seen Ngatarawa progress from tentative beginnings to producing some of the most authoritative and exciting wines in New Zealand today.

Not that he shovels grapes any more. He *is* in his sixties after all, although he's as sharp and energetic as a man many years younger. No, he leaves grape-shovelling to the wine-making half of the venture – the soft-spoken, solemn-eyed Alwyn Corban, nearly 30 years younger. What brought them together was the fact that Gary Glazebrook owned 2450 hectares (6000 acres) of grazing land to the west of the rich alluvial Hawke's Bay river-mouth land, where most of the region's vineyards are.

Alwyn Corban was making wine for McWilliams from these heavy-cropping vineyards, yet had noticed how, further inland, the soil changed dramatically, and was so free-draining that during the summer whole sections of it were parched and arid. He was convinced that the key to fine wine-making in New Zealand was to desert the traditional over-fertile vineyard sites and seek out poor, but well-drained soil. When a mutual friend introduced him to Glazebrook, in no time at all they were partners, roaming over the Glazebrook estate to find the precise conditions Corban knew would produce the grapes he wanted.

Gary is now so enthusiastic he says that the whole western part of Hawke's Bay should be cleared of sheep and planted with vines. Alwyn is a little more sanguine. The local soils are very variable, but there was one particular kind of soil he was after. Half a mile from the old stables that he has converted into a winery, there is a quarry, a deep quarry, 10 metres (30 feet) deep at least. Where the earth has been gouged out, there is a thin layer of fine sandy loam topsoil. Below that is a gravelly, pebbly, porous soil they call 'red metal'. Water goes through it like a sieve. All across the Glazebrook pasture lands are deep seams of this red metal soil, and that's where the Ngatarawa vines were planted.

The Meaning of It All

In case you're wondering, that's pronounced Na-ta-ra-wa – the 'g' is silent – and it is typical of Alwyn Corban that, though he acknowledges that such a name is not exactly a marketing man's delight, he decided if that's what the Maoris called this stretch of land (it means 'between the ridges'), he would too. He intended to make distinctive wines. No compromise on the wines. No compromise on the name.

As he saw it, the key to good grapes was control. Where the rainfall is too high and the land too fertile, it can be virtually impossible to control a vine's vigour, and both ripeness levels and yields become a lottery. But Corban felt that if he could install drip irrigation on this porous soil, he should be able to control yield, ripeness and acid levels. For a couple of years, 1984 and 1985, when he didn't irrigate enough, the vines became so stressed that after three weeks the leaves began falling off and the grapes never achieved ripeness, but since then, with the help of irrigation, he has regularly brought in crops of Chardonnay, Sauvignon Blanc and the Bordeaux red varieties at high sugar levels, but low acid levels, and crucially, a near-perfect pH acid balance. And the reds are remarkably free of the green harsh tannins that can afflict cool climate fruit. All he had to do now was work out how to make the wine.

Left to his own devices, he first fell back on the theories he had learned at wine school at Davis in California and during his years making wine for McWilliams. There they had attempted to make soft, fruity reds by fermenting the grapes in stainless steel for seven to ten days at cool temperatures. That's white wine-making, and by 1988 Alwyn was certain there must be better ways of keeping the softness yet getting more flavour from the grapes. So he began allowing the temperature to rise, all the while punching down the skins to extract colour and tannin. Then he allows the juice and skins to macerate for three to four weeks as the temperature gradually drops.

I've tasted his wines made by both methods and the difference is dramatic. The cool fermentation wines are quite good but earthy and slightly stringy. The warm fermentation styles are quite superb, with each Bordeaux varietal – Cabernet Sauvignon, Cabernet Franc, Merlot and Malbec – tasting as pure and mouthwateringly typical as any group of these grapes I have seen. After ageing in a mix of new and used French oaks, the effect, especially of the top 'Glazebrook' cuvée, is of a silky, deep, round red wine, without a trace of vegetal greenness.

The best reds from Ngatarawa are still to come. The whites are already showing tremendous style and individuality. In particular the Chardonnays and the sweet wines are hitting world class. They bear an uncanny resemblance to the other great example from Hawke's Bay – Elston, from Te Mata – and I was fascinated to see on the local geology map that the red metal gravel only appears twice in the valley – at Ngatarawa and at the Elston vineyard. Disregarding his technological experience, Alwyn now picks his grapes on taste whatever the figures tell him.

He has virtually given up adjusting acids upwards, simply because the books say he should. His palate says he shouldn't. Nor is he one to overshadow fruit with wood either, so he uses a mix of barrel sizes for his Chardonnays. When they're all blended together, the

Alwyn Corban checks the progress of his Ngatarawa Chardonnay as it completes its fermentation in oak barrel.

result is very Burgundian and very exciting. Equally good is Ngatarawa sweet wine. He now has four acres of Riesling outside the stables whose sole function is to try to get themselves infected with noble rot. Because of the drying winds and the free-draining soil (botrytis is happiest in damp, cool conditions), the vines won't always get infected enough, but some years the bunches do all wither and go to pulp. The result is a wonderful, golden orange wine, so thick and syrupy it plops out of the bottle like oil and swims lazily from side to side as you swirl your glass. In a land that is suddenly discovering its sweet wine potential, this is one of the finest efforts. Yet it is also one instance where Alwyn did listen to criticism. His first attempt in 1987 has a fabulous richness of raisins and granular honey, powder-sprinkled with sherbet. It also has a slight and, to my mind, entirely acceptable whiff of volatile acidity, which some people objected to. The 1988, though still wonderfully sweet and beautifully balanced with an earthy, lime peel acidity, is a safer wine.

He admits he changed his methods because of the criticism. To be honest, he's probably right. A young winery like Ngatarawa needs all the critical acclaim it can muster. But the quality and individuality he is building in his reds and whites is so impressive that in a few years' time the last thing that will worry him is a wine critic failing to see the wood for the trees.

Te Mata

*I*LOOKED UP THE SLOPE of the Coleraine vineyards to where John Buck's astonishing house sits like ice cream stalagmites plopped on to the grass. I said I'd never seen four acres look so tiny. 'Just like Romanée-Conti.' Did I hear John say that? I certainly did.

But he doesn't set out to rival the world's rarest red Burgundy; he sets his sights on Château Margaux, Le Montrachet and Les Monts Damnés in Sancerre instead, as the models he most wants to emulate in Cabernet Sauvignon, Chardonnay and Sauvignon Blanc. His chat is peppered with references to Paul Pontallier, the talented winemaker at Margaux, Leflaive of Burgundy fame, Jean-Marie Bourgeois in Sancerre, and it isn't idle chat. John Buck knows precisely what he wants. He's looked at what's best in Europe and he's now set about proving that their wines can be matched for quality and personality by wines from New Zealand, and in particular, wines from the scattered acres of vineyard land hugging the slopes of the Te Mata peak, on the eastern side of Hawke's Bay.

However he doesn't let his ambition outpace his realism. Unusually among New Zealand's tyros, John Buck understands the competition. Although trained as an accountant, he spent two years in the British wine trade with Stowells of Chelsea, from 1964 to 1966, and an indulgent managing director allowed him to taste all the French classics time and again. Buck toured all the major European regions, and then came back to New Zealand, firstly to a business partnership with TV chef the 'Galloping Gourmet' Graham Kerr of all people, and then to running a wine agency business, bringing in some of the best French Bordeaux and Burgundies.

Before he ever went to Europe, one of his responsibilities as an accountant had been to look after a small vineyard near Auckland, but his interest in owning a vineyard and making wine really stems from the time in 1966 when he visited Hawke's Bay's most famous winemaker, Tom McDonald and tasted some of his old Cabernets. Tom pointed over to the Te Mata peak and said 'that's the best Cabernet land you'll get in Hawke's Bay – frost-free, facing north, and free-draining.' John took the words to heart, tasted a few bottles of red wine from hybrid grapes grown on those slopes by Vidal, and reckoned that they showed great potential. So the search was on.

It was a long search. Eight years, 150 properties appraised, but always returning to the slopes of Te Mata, until in 1974, the old, semi-defunct Te Mata winery came on the market and Buck snapped it up. Te Mata was, and is, the oldest winery still operating in New Zealand, but by 1974 it had become what Buck calls 'the original Kiwi plonk' winery. 'Cream sherry' made on a Monday, sold on a Tuesday – never saw cream and never saw Spain – in fact it never even saw a barrel. 'Essence de Cream' did the tricksy stuff for you. Vines didn't enter into it.

It took Buck until 1980 to switch tack and begin to consolidate the vineyards around the winery. The Coleraine slope was planted with 70-year-old Pinot Noir and Shiraz before he replaced these with Cabernet Sauvignon (75 per cent), Merlot (22 per cent) and Cabernet Franc (3 per cent). Then one of those old Vidal vineyards became available, and it had some mature Cabernet Sauvignon vines. They only yielded small quantities of grapes but Buck took them, and that was enough to make a smashing 1980 Cabernet Sauvignon which immediately won the best red trophy at the 1981 National Wine Competition. My first wide-ranging tasting of New Zealand wines was in February 1982. Wine number 30 was that 1980 Te Mata Cabernet. 'I don't taste the grape variety, I taste the style,' I wrote. 'This is a very good young Bordeaux style.' With his first real vintage John Buck was already getting the classic comparisons he craved.

Training for the Top

With the arrival of full-time winemaker and partner Peter Cowley in 1984 it has been possible to hone the wine style further, but the power of that 1980 proved McDonald's point that it was the Te Mata soils which were the key. The east side of Hawke's Bay is dominated by upthrust volcanic limestone which, only 10,000 years ago, was covered with wind-blown volcanic loess dust from a massive explosion in the centre of the island. At the bottom of the slopes, centuries of water run-off have created virtually impenetrable cemented pans, but you can rip these away with a bulldozer to expose the limestone, and again, the quality is exceptional. And jutting out into the valley like a giant's thighs and knees are some of the old river edge terraces packed with free-draining 'red metal' gravel loam.

There are numerous vineyards on the valley floor, but the soil is really too rich, so the only valley fruit Te Mata uses is for its Castle Hill Sauvignon Blanc, and even this is from a long, thin bank of grey sandy loam rising above the flat alluvial plain. The wine isn't bad, but it has the least personality of any Te Mata wine by far. The Cape Crest Sauvignon vineyard, the Elston Chardonnay vineyards, which first cropped in 1984, and

I don't know what it's like to come home to each night, but John Buck's stunning house in his tiny Coleraine vineyard mirrors the Hawke's Bay pioneer's confidence.

the Coleraine and Awatea Cabernet vineyards are all on those eastern slopes and terraces.

Hawke's Bay gets really soaked with rain perhaps two years in ten, and seven years out of ten scarcely a drop falls in the harvesting month between March and April. In fact the annual rainfall figures are lower than Bordeaux's, while average temperatures are much the same, yet ultra-violet exposure is the highest in the world. With all those clear blue skies, the difference between day-time high temperatures and night-time lows is very marked. The result is that most years the grapes get fully ripe, are high in natural sugar, but also keep a tangy acidity in their juice.

All of which suits Cowley and Buck just fine. They have exhaustively examined wine-making techniques in France and then adapted them. The Cabernet juice is both pumped over and punched down during fermentation and maceration because the natural tannin and colour levels they're achieving with their Cabernet are less than in Bordeaux. After playing around with stainless steel fermentation, all their Elston Chardonnay has been barrel-fermented since 1989. They don't rouse the lees much, because they reckon the Burgundians only do it to keep fermentation and malolactic going in

their chilly cellars. And they usually only let about a fifth of the Chardonnay undergo the malolactic.

It works. Elston Chardonnay is the most Burgundian Chardonnay in New Zealand – 'in Australasia,' chips in John optimistically – with a syrupy richness and a coffee toast perfume sliced through with lemon and lime. The Sauvignons are less exciting, although Buck fooled the Sancerre growers one year when he slipped a bottle of his into the annual blind tasting at the Sancerre town hall. But it's on the Cabernet Sauvignons that Buck yearns to be judged. Originally two separate bottlings from the different Coleraine and Awatea vineyards, Coleraine is now the name for the top selection and Awatea the second label. How's he doing?

Well, they'd never slip unnoticed into a tasting of Classed Growths from Margaux, because the flavour and the texture of the wine is far too individual. With the exception of years like 1988 when the tail end of Cyclone Bola resulted in a harvest less than ideally ripe, they have a brilliant mixture of bitter cherry and blackcurrant sweetness, usually a hint of green grass, but grassiness never dominates Te Mata Cabernet as it does so many New Zealand Cabernets, and the wine finishes with a ripe luscious smoothness like raspberry sauce and plums and the perfume of fresh country earth. It's like Bordeaux with a Burgundy palate. More like Pomerol than Margaux, Buck wonders? The Château Pétrus of the southern seas . . . ?

EUROPE

*I*T MIGHT SEEM ODD to have included a mere handful of profiles from Europe, when it's the cradle of all the world's great wine styles, but the people and places featured here have been chosen to illustrate how grand new visions are possible everywhere, both in areas previously little regarded, and through new initiatives in the great old wine regions themselves.

France had to be goaded into wholeheartedly embracing the modern wine revolution. When you've spent a thousand years creating wine styles that are the envy of the rest of the world, it must be galling to realize that you've let some enthusiastic upstarts from overseas not only learn the techniques it has taken you all this time to perfect, but also improve upon them to such an extent that you have to learn from their success how to make necessary improvements to your own wine.

Italy, too, needed jolting into a new awareness both of native potential, and of the challenges and temptations offered in France and new regions like California. Tuscany and Piedmont are the two areas that have so far achieved most in radically altering Italian wine styles and expectations without in any way betraying their birthright. The new awareness is exciting; and that's what I look at here.

Spain is well behind these two leading nations, and only Torres and Raimat have regularly shown a sense of vision and purpose in their approach to wine. Other producers, in Catalonia, Navarra, Rioja and Ribera del Duero, fitfully burst out with exciting flavours, only to fade just as one starts getting interested. Portugal produces lots of excitement, but the wines have been inconsistent; I would have loved to include profiles in the book – in the future, I hope I shall. Germany, too, is beginning to look for new challenges, though things are still in a transitional phase, even for the most forward-looking producers. As for Lebanon, the influence of European culture still clings on, and just so long as Château Musar survives, there will always be a place for it here.

FRANCE

Bordeaux is France's most important wine area, and until recently the red wine producers of the Médoc Classed Growths have reigned supreme – so I've concentrated on Professor Peynaud, the man who quietly laid the foundations for the revolution in Bordeaux's red wines that served as the inspiration for so many other winemakers. I've also focussed on the small Pomerol region, which showed that there was a new, altogether more approachable style of red waiting to be made over the river from the Médoc. White Bordeaux production, until the advent of men like Denis Dubourdieu, André Lurton and the Australian Brian Croser, lacked

any sense of direction or vision. During the 1990s Bordeaux's white wines may overtake Burgundy's as the finest white wines in France. Burgundy's top producers had dwindled to a handful during the 1970s, a period when the local merchants ruthlessly dominated the trade. But during the 1980s, Burgundy became a place of pilgrimage for fans of Pinot Noir and Chardonnay from around the world, whose sole aim was to understand Burgundy's wines, then go home and improve upon them. And a gradually swelling minority of French producers took due note of the visitors' quality-first obsession and realized how much more they too could achieve through commitment to a vision of excellence. As the grip of the merchants was broken, even the previously despised co-operatives showed that excellence in Burgundy was not confined solely to the famous names of history.

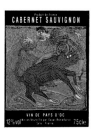

Further south, both in the production of world class wines like Mas de Daumas Gassac or Domaine de Trévallon, in areas never before recognized, or in the wholesale creation by Skalli of a new generation of high-quality, affordable wines in the often-dismissed Midi, new waves of imagination and daring are transforming the face of French wine.

These profiles are representative of the wind of change that is sweeping France. However, each vintage sees more areas, and more winemakers, embrace the new mood. The future for France is filled with possibilities. A new generation has come into its own in many regions: sons and daughters who have been to university to study wine science, who've met winemakers from other countries, tasted their wines, and visited their homelands, and have realized that the previous generation had in many cases signally failed to capitalize on the great inheritance France's classic regions possess.

In Alsace, young producers like Deiss, Zind-Humbrecht and Ostertag are going far beyond what was thought possible in producing great sweet wine, often employing methods not seen for a hundred years. A man like Didier Dagueneau in Pouilly-sur-Loire, with experience of California and New Zealand swimming around his mind, is striking out to prove that Loire Sauvignon Blanc can still be the world's best, so long as you ruthlessly reject compromise. Guigal has used non-traditional methods for the northern Rhône, introducing new oak barrels, to create intense rich reds that have catapulted Côte-Rôtie into superstar status. And in the byways of Gaillac, of Limoux, of Montravel and Bergerac, of Corbières and Roussillon, inspired young winemakers, assisted by overdue investment in stainless steel and new oak barrels, are using both traditional and non-local grape varieties to shake entrenched attitudes to the core.

GERMANY

The impossibility of ripening a wide range of interesting grape varieties makes options in Germany more limited than in any other leading wine nation. The ability to ripen the grape, and the chance to take control of the style of your wine by being able to exercise choice concerning ripeness, acid levels, and fruit maturity, constitute the most basic requirements for the forward-looking wine producer.

Germany has invested in generations of research dedicated to finding the best ways of adapting to the problems presented by a difficult climate, but the object of the research has largely been inward-looking rather than international. Research institutes have concentrated on developing strains of grapes that will give Riesling-like flavours without requiring so much sun, and, usually, at much higher yields.

I'm not worried about the vine variety, nor whether the cellar is clean or the wine any good – I'm just enjoying the sheer emotional pleasure of Provence in the springtime.

But it is taking a new generation, especially in the southern regions of the Rheinpfalz and Baden, traditionally dismissed as too warm for producing refined Riesling, to shock Germany's wine establishment into developing a wider perspective.

Lingenfelder and Philippi in the Rheinpfalz, the Gunderloch estate in the Rheinhessen, Johner in Baden and the original wild man of German wine, Armin Diel, in the Nahe, have all begun to throw over the traces of restrictive German wine laws, and have begun to experiment with fermentation and ageing in French oak barrels, sometimes brand new, the use of malolactic fermentation to soften and fatten the wine, the development of Chardonnay, Pinot Blanc, Pinot Gris and even Müller-Thurgau as varieties suitable for such treatment.

The most frustrating thing for Germany's ambitious winemakers has been the difficulty of creating decent red wine, but the Pinot Noir can ripen, if the yields are

kept reasonable, and in the south it can ripen very well. Better clones, more modern trellising and pruning systems to maximize ripeness, some use of good French oak and, above all, a more international outlook mean that Germany's new wave winemakers are beginning to make the Rhine an exciting wine region again after years of self-inflicted mediocrity. Philippi has even planted some Cabernet Sauvignon in the Rheinhessen. If warm vintages like 1989 and 1990 become the norm, we're really going to see some fireworks in Germany's sun-soaked south.

ITALY

Italy had to throw her mighty bulk behind the revolution in wine or die. The biggest producer of wine on earth had got so far out of step with the mood of the rest of the wine world by the 1970s, that she was in danger of drowning in a sea of unmemorable, sometimes undrinkable, and definitely unwanted wine. From top to

bottom, as the Italian economy strengthened, drinkers were using their new-found wealth to distance themselves from a wine-drinking image which seemed out of date and out of fashion. This was the breach into which the leading Tuscan wine producers leapt so gloriously in the late 1970s and 1980s and finally re-asserted the proud individuality that had been missing from too many Italian wine regions for generations. Almost forgotten wine traditions were at last linked with an acute sense of the international dimension.

Italian white wine had become, by the 1970s, a byword for tired, dull, oxidized rubbish. Here and there during the 1970s and nationwide during the 1980s, wineries adopted refrigerated stainless steel tanks, controlled fermentation, scrupulous hygiene and sterile filtration. New oak is appearing in more and more Tuscan cellars, usually to hold Chardonnay, but also on some estates Sauvignon Blanc or even the native Vernaccia. They have also succeeded in making the gutless Trebbiano into a decent drink – and that's a major achievement.

In the north-east, they've gone a lot further than that. Friuli makes Italy's most sharply-focussed whites. The Veneto is now able to supply enormous quantities of decent white wines, and bottles labelled Soave can nowadays approach the thrilling in the hands of someone like Pieropan or Anselmi. In the mid-1980s I could never have said that.

But if there is one area where the future holds the most potentially thrilling surprises it must be Piedmont. Along with Gaja's planting of Chardonnay and Sauvignon, and the increasing use of French oak barrels in many cellars for ageing and fermenting, the neglected local varieties are springing back to justified acclaim. The Moscato grape is being rediscovered, and varieties like Arneis, Favorita and Cortese only need modern production methods and some sensitive handling in order to shine – witness the wines of Deltetto and Castello di Neive.

And the same can be said of the reds. The Nebbiolo is used for Barolo and Barbaresco and is Italy's finest red grape – so far, that is: there may yet be undiscovered superstars in the forgotten hills and valleys not yet touched by progress. But in Barolo and Barbaresco, rigid tradition never allowed the variety to express itself in a way likely to impress an international clientele. Gradually during the 1980s, use of controlled fermentation, a reduction in the time the wine spent in barrel, earlier bottling and sometimes brief maturing in new French oak barrels are revealing the extent to which tradition was denying the world one of red wine's great taste experiences. And this openness of mind is now spreading to other local grapes like Dolcetto, Barbera, Freisa and Ruchè, from producers like Altare, Voerzio, Clerico, Vajra and Bava, with results ranging from the frivolously delightful to the seriously impressive. These may sound unfamiliar now – but just wait a year or two. If I had to choose one region in Europe that's going to be humming with excitement right the way through the 1990s – it would be Piedmont, with its old classics undergoing radical transformation, and a host of new classics joining them, brimfull of invention and sheer pleasure.

SPAIN

Creating really interesting modern wines in Spain is going to take a great deal of effort, and considerable investment in winery technology and barrels, if not in replanting and re-trellising the vineyards themselves – and it is going to take vision. Until accession to the European Community, Spain's domestic economy lagged well

behind other European wine nations, and there were few oases of quality in her table wines. Rioja was thought of as the best region for reds, and sometimes whites. Galician whites were sought-after. Cava sparkling wines sold well even if they were frequently made of less than top-quality grapes. And there were occasional brilliant maverick outfits like Torres, Leòn and Raimat in Catalonia, Vega Sicilia in Ribera del Duero and Marquès de Griñon in La Mancha.

Since joining the EC, Spain's economy has boomed and the drinking of *good* wine has become extremely chic. Yet few new visionaries have appeared. Torres, Raimat, Leòn, Vega Sicilia strive towards different goals; there are one or two other producers attempting to improve things in Catalonia, Rueda and Navarra; but few seem really prepared to take risks in the name of excellence. Most of Spain's own native grape varieties are rather dull. And most of the vineyard land is virtually unusable for any other form of agriculture.

Wine producers need to take more note of what is happening at the Raimat estate in the region of Catalonia, in the south of France, or in the Riverland in Australia and see that good wine can be created from unpromising natural materials. Until then, Spain's most exciting role in modern wine will be through the giant up-to-date wineries in the hinterland that can supply large amounts of attractive, undemanding reds, eminently enjoyable, eminently affordable, a vital, if unglamorous role in our modern world of wine.

PORTUGAL

Portugal has been very slow to take advantage of all the modern technological wizardry now available, mainly because there is a chronic shortage of money for investment in the wine industry and Portuguese rural society has proved unwilling to take risks in the mere hope of improved quality. Seventy per cent of wine production is in the hands of co-operatives, and in most cases these are fly-blown nests of neglect, rather than hotbeds of progressive fervour.

Yet I look forward to the wine revolution taking hold in Portugal more than in almost any other country. The exciting originality of her own grape varieties is only matched in Europe by Italy's. With reds like Ramisco, Vinhão, Baga, Touriga Nacional and Periquita; and whites like Loureiro, Alvarinho, Malvasia, Moscatel and the Madeira varieties, there is little reason to import international grape varieties, but a desperate need for the wholesale upgrading of wine-making practices and philosophies.

Already some southern co-operatives are beginning to realize that the only route to success is through using their excellent native grapes to better effect, and there are also two private companies in the south – João Pires and JM da Fonseca – who show considerable flair and a wider awareness of international wine markets.

EASTERN EUROPE

Much of the rest of Europe's progress depends on the political situation over the ensuing decade. Bulgaria's and Yugoslavia's progress has been temporarily halted by political uncertainty. Hungary, Czechoslovakia and Russia are all trying to establish free market systems which would require their wineries to respond to what the consumer wanted to drink rather than what the co-operatives felt like making. With that move will come investment, resources and ideas that may well make Eastern Europe into one of the great vineyard areas of the future.

Antinori

I WONDER WHAT THOUGHTS used to run through the young Piero Antinori's mind during the early 1960s as he headed west to the Tuscan coastline at Bolgheri to visit his uncle Mario? He had just left university and found himself immediately caught up in a growing crisis as the family firm, founded in 1385, faced a deeply uncertain future in a Tuscan wine world that had thrown aside its old traditional ways, and embraced an expansionist philosophy, financed by outsiders' money. The Chianti vineyard area was to increase five-fold during the decade, yet whatever quality reputation the region once possessed plummeted as production soared. The name Chianti was becoming a byword for cheap and cheerful. Or not so cheerful since most of the litre or two-litre wicker-covered Chianti flasks that found their way into every corner of the world contained stuff that was barely palatable.

And here was his eccentric uncle Mario, on a salty, windswept seaside estate in a zone notorious for the mediocrity of the wine, stubbornly planting the great grape of red Bordeaux – Cabernet Sauvignon – and making a wine which might be rustic but, my God, it had flavour, flavour from the grape variety, and, perhaps, flavour from the unusually small barrels which his uncle persisted in using to age his blood-red wine.

Cabernet Sauvignon. Small oak barrels. A Bordeaux from Bolgheri, called Sassicaia, and a good one too. The 1959 and 1961 vintages of the top Bordeaux wines were then renowned throughout Europe, and across the world were gaining high praise and high prices from connoisseurs. And here was the young Piero Antinori, faced with saving Italy's oldest wine dynasty with only the discredited tools of Sangiovese and Trebbiano grapes, a forest full of big, tired, old wooden barrels, and a mountain of wicker-covered flasks at his disposal. If there is one thing that marks out Piero Antinori's genius it is that he realized Italian resources alone could not lead Italy to the top table of world wine. That table was packed full of Frenchmen, and most of them were from Bordeaux.

Interestingly, it wasn't the first time that the Antinori family had turned to Bordeaux in their quest to improve on Tuscany's wine styles. Piero's great uncle had actually bought wines from Bordeaux to blend into his Chianti *riserva* in an effort to create a wine which would be acceptable to the international market. And Piero's father took a wide south-facing slope at the Antinori family estate of Santa Cristina, and planted it with Cabernet Sauvignon. The name of this slope was Tignanello. Although the vineyard fell into disrepair during the war, there was never any doubt as to its quality, and its fruit was to form the basis of a magnificent hybrid, part Bordeaux, part Chianti which was to transform Tuscan wine-making – Tignanello.

With production of Tignanello now at 20,000 cases a year, the wine now includes grapes bought in from a much wider area, but the principles haven't changed – to take the Bordeaux concept of wine-making and apply it to Tuscan grapes. Or rather, to grapes grown in Tuscany. Cabernet Sauvignon was a crucial part of the equation. Blending it with Sangiovese had worked before; it could work again.

Indeed it could work far better, for two reasons. Firstly, the malolactic fermentation, which transforms harsh malic acid into gentler lactic acid, was not at all well understood in Tuscany during the 1960s, and many wines never achieved it, with the result that red Chianti was frequently a harsh, rasping drink. As such, Piero Antinori's market-conscious mind realized it was unsaleable abroad for a decent price. Antinori's masterly winemaker, Giacomo Tachis, with some advice from the Bordeaux guru Émile Peynaud, was responsible for introducing the concept of controlled malolactic to Tuscany, and a smoother, more international style of wine became possible for the first time.

Reappraising the Cask

Tachis and Antinori next decided to reject Tuscan preconceptions about wood ageing and barrel size. Chianti was generally aged, often for an excessively long time, in large ancient casks made of chestnut or Slovenian oak. The object was to soften the astringency of the wine, but the result was that the wine lost whatever fruit it possessed and became stale and oxidized. Again, heeding Peynaud's advice, Antinori began importing small Bordeaux *barriques* made of French oak. These imparted a vanilla richness to the wine, and enabled it to be bottled, full of fruit at less than two years old.

The final piece of the jigsaw was the fruit. Antinori once said, 'Cabernet seems to have everything that Sangiovese lacks – the body, colour, aroma, plus the longevity', and he knew from Sassicaia what Cabernet could achieve in Tuscany. So he planted 20 per cent of the Tignanello vineyard in Cabernet Sauvignon, and set Tachis to work to produce an 'international' wine. Nowadays, Antinori is quick to leap to the defence of the 'Tuscanness' of many of his wines. But 'Tuscanness' wasn't the point in the 1960s and 1970s. Survival and

Vineyard workers look so reassuringly timeless in an old traditional area like Tuscany . . . even if they are driving a modern tractor for the go-ahead Piero Antinori.

economic stability were Antinori's aims. Certainly there is a certain sweet-sour cherryskin fruit to some of the Tignanello wines, but when people say it is more like a Classed Growth Bordeaux than a Chianti, they're absolutely right. At the 1990 International Wine Challenge in London the wonderfully smooth, ripe 1985 Tignanello won the red wine trophy. Everyone thought it was French.

Antinori's great skill is to see a trend before anyone else does and follow it. In so doing, he seems to be creating the trend itself. Tignanello inspired a flood of imitations, as producers saw the prizes and renown Antinori was garnering from his *barrique*-aged Sangiovese-Cabernet blend. So it was time to move on.

In the 1990s the 'estate' concept has become an increasingly effective marketing tool in Tuscany. The wine Santa Cristina, named after the estate where it was grown and made, became so successful the wine was downgraded in 1987 to *vino da tavola* to allow its production and wine style the expansion and flexibility the market could bear. In its place Antinori has bought two new estates – Peppoli, and Badia a Passignano, both in Chianti Classico. Without a single Cabernet vine.

Again, Antinori feels the pulse of the Tuscan wine world. The 1990s see a reaction against Cabernet Sauvignon, a proud Tuscan demand for a return to the traditions of the region – and the traditional grape variety – Sangiovese. Antinori is more than happy to

oblige. Peppoli is made by Tachis according to pretty traditional Chianti techniques – no Cabernet, and a short time in large, previously-used oak. But Tachis gives it virtually all of its statutory Chianti Classico ageing in stainless steel, and the result is a gorgeous easy drinking wine of exuberant strawberry fruit. The Badia a Passignano rides the current passion for *barrique*-aged 100 per cent Sangiovese wines, which are not entitled to the Chianti Classico title, yet sell for double the price.

The 'newest wave' in Italy is the creation of another type of 'international' wine – the *barrique*-aged white. Antinori has been there for years. Just over the Tuscan border in Umbria, the family have owned the Castello della Sala estate near Orvieto since 1940. On 100 hectares (247 acres) of perfect white grape vineyard, plantings of Chardonnay, Pinot Blanc, Sauvignon and Traminer can be seen mingling with the local varieties of Trebbiano, Grechetto and Drupeggio. The Cervaro della Sala has wonderful freshness and peachy fruit wrapped around with the cream and spice of oak.

But all Tuscans are red wine men at heart. Antinori certainly is. And his nose for a trend in the market is as sharp as ever. Just as Tuscans start to feel that perhaps they've strait-jacketed themselves a little too tightly with Sangiovese, and they think they need something different to play with – a little Pinot Noir, perhaps – Antinori is there already. He's had Pinot Noir since 1985, 500 metres (1640 feet) up at Castello della Sala. And there's another route open if it can't be turned into great wine. A world-wide boom in sparkling wine is gathering momentum as I write . . .

Buxy Co-op

*T*HE OLD MAN SEEMS nervous. The tractors hauling trailers full of grapes are queuing impatiently at the entrance to the winery, waiting to offload their cargo of plump black Pinot Noir grapes fresh from the vineyards. He's in the way. But as the growling queue edges forward, he determinedly keeps his place, his old Citroën lurching gracelessly as he puts it into gear. Why is he here, in a line of smart wagons, each carrying a couple of thousand kilos of grapes, their drivers eager to be away and back to the vineyards for more?

The trailer at the front now tips its load and a wash of squashy grapes slithers into the crusher to be weighed and tested for ripeness. They look dirty, they look a bit pale, and sure enough, within moments the digital sign lights up. 1580 kilograms. But only 10.7 degrees potential alcohol. The grower begins to remonstrate, but he knows his grapes aren't good, and the figures are there for all to see. 'Pas de sélection', 'No selection', he is told; his grapes are sidelined into the lowest category; he is paid just the basic rate.

The battered Citroën reaches the crusher. And in the gloom of the back seats I can now see two plastic trays of firm, tightly bunched purple grapes. The old man humps his trays to the yawning mouth of the crusher and tips his bunches in. They lie dwarfed by the giant archimedes screw at the bottom, and the technician in charge explains there's barely enough to register on the automatic measuring device.

The red light flashes at last, and the technician shouts at the same time, '102 kilograms. 12 degrees. Selection.' The old man's saggy face creases with pleasure and with pride. A sparkling new dumper truck is next. The Pinot Noir makes 13 degrees – and is creamed off for an 'Exceptionnelle' cuvée. But the old man made 12 degrees. He made 'sélection'.

Scenes like this are at the heart of the co-operative movement all over France. This is Buxy, in Burgundy's Côte Chalonnaise, dealing primarily with high quality Pinot Noir and Chardonnay grapes, from which the co-op will make *appellation contrôlée* wines that will command a good price. The scene could be repeated in a thousand other courtyards from the cold north-east to the arid southern plains. But there's a difference here.

Many co-ops are forces for conservatism and mediocrity in France's world of wine. Co-ownership by hundreds of peasant grape growers, few of whom possess enough vineyard land to make a decent living, has often meant that co-ops have had little incentive to concentrate on quality. Yet co-ops control almost half

the vineyard land of France. If French wine is not to be left behind in the rush to create the enjoyable and affordable drinking that marks out the efforts of New World countries, co-operatives must begin to find ways to persuade their members to take the quality line.

Buxy was founded in 1931 to service the vineyards of Montagny and the surrounding villages of the southern Côte Chalonnaise. In a depressed no-man's land, wedged in between the sought-after Côte d'Or and the Mâconnais, its vineyards in tatters, its wine of no reputation or quality, survival was the Buxy co-op's only objective. But during the 1960s and 1970s, as the wines of the Côte d'Or returned to fame and fortune and began to achieve high prices, it became clear to one man that Buxy's growers possessed one tremendous asset, if they could be persuaded to exploit it.

The man was Roger Rageot, appointed as director of the co-op in 1963. The asset was the name 'Burgundy'. The Côte Chalonnaise could either slump towards the mediocrity of the Mâconnais. Or it could set its sights on the famous Burgundies of Volnay and Beaune, Meursault and Puligny-Montrachet in the Côte d'Or to the north. The soils around Buxy were good, largely limestone and chalk; the grapes were substantially Pinot Noir and Chardonnay. What was needed was the will to improve, the consequent commitment of profits to investment in equipment to produce wines worthy of the ringing title 'Burgundy'.

Politics and Persuasion

Rageot was confident of his wine-making skills; it was his political skills that needed honing. It took him 17 years to persuade the 700-plus members with their 700 hectares (1730 acres) of vines, to let him invest in oak barrels and an air-conditioned cellar. This large, cool, silent chamber was opened in 1980, for red wines only. Yet the one superior *appellation* the co-op had access to was Montagny, a 100 per cent white Chardonnay appellation of which the co-op controlled 65 per cent. It had always been one of Burgundy's dullest whites, chalky and lean, almost stale in its flatness. But Rageot saw a potential for full, nutty whites, if he could persuade the growers to restrict yields and allow him to use oak to ferment and age the wines.

In 1984 he squeezed a handful of new barrels out of the reluctant growers and made a beautifully soft nutty white despite the difficult year. Rageot's British agent tasted it and went wild. He wanted a hundred barrels of

When the sun shines and the grapes are ripe, there is a sense of serenity during the Burgundy vintage. Here pickers harvest Pinot Noir at Chenevelles near Buxy.

it in 1985. Rageot went back to the growers, but they flatly refused to finance any more barrel purchases. At which point his wily British agent sent him a fax saying – buy them anyway, he would pay. Rageot told co-op members he was going ahead. 'But this Englishman isn't a member . . . we can't let him.' 'No,' said Rageot, 'You can't.' He got his barrels. The members paid. And the British agent heaved a huge sigh of relief.

Today Buxy is a model for co-ops in France. In the vineyard, quality selections are made during the season according to the number of bunches on the vine, and the grower is told candidly whether he can hope to make 'sélection' or not. Increasingly, individual sites are being sought. A 40-hectare (99-acre), south-facing 'Clos de Chenôves' is already producing the co-op's best red and white, the white in particular having all the smoky, toasty richness of a Meursault – at a quarter of the price. They have located a 70-hectare (173-acre) vineyard owned by the monks of Cluny, called, unbelievably, Mont-rachet (the name of Burgundy's most fabled white!). Around 7 hectares (17 acres) are already filled with Chardonnay, and more is planted each year as the maize is ripped out and vines return.

Roger Rageot is passionately against unnecessary interference in wine-making. He only uses natural yeasts, and he has invented a robot to gently punch down his red wine during fermentation, because he found that pumping over released too many hard tannins and obscured the lovely cherry perfume his Pinots naturally possess.

His whites start their fermentation in tanks, but are then transferred to oak barrels to continue fermenting at about 15°C (59°F) for three to four weeks. One special cuvée of white, made from old vines cropped at only two tons to the acre, is fermented for eight weeks at 10° to 12°C (50° to 54°F) in tanks, the yeast lees mixed continually to give the wine a magnificent fatness of melons and peaches, liquorice and cream, which is magically good.

The barrels of red and white then quietly slumber in the cool cellars for well over a year, and after bottling during their second winter, they are stored in bottle for another three to six months before release. So when someone tactlessly asked him, 'is the effort worth it for wines at this level', what must have gone through his mind? The excitement of ordinary wine lovers at last able to afford the flavours of fine Burgundy again through his beautifully fragrant wines? The present-day prosperity of those very same farmers who had spent 20 years blocking his every attempt at progress? Or maybe the pride of an old man whose two trays full of grapes had finally made 'Sélection'.

Maurizio Castelli

'SHOULD HAVE KNOWN BETTER than to put him near the door.' I could see the merchant's point. He'd hired this great big ballroom in a swish London hotel, shipped over, presumably at great expense, wine producers of all shapes and sizes from all around the world to titillate his customers – and here was this wild-eyed moustachio'd bandito stealing all the thunder. Perfectly good producers of Chablis and Sancerre, Bergerac and Beaujolais stood about twiddling their thumbs and pining for attention while a massive crowd pressed in upon Maurizio Castelli who responded with all the unabashed showmanship of a circus magician.

Magician he is. But his stage is far wider than a circus booth. His stage is the whole of central Italy, sometimes stretching as far north as the sub-alpine slopes of the Adige Valley just south of Austria, but mostly centred where the spotlights are fiercest and the critics most passionate – in the tumbling hills and valleys of Tuscany.

Castelli is one of a tiny band of roving magicians whose brief is to restore the tarnished glory of one of Europe's great wine regions. Consultant oenologist is his title. But you only have to feel the magnetism of his bear-like presence, his flashing eyes and his emphatic pronouncements against mediocrity and deceit, to realize that 'winemaker' is not all-embracing enough a title; he is also an unashamed promoter and image creator for his region and its wines.

It's difficult now to comprehend quite how low Chianti had fallen by the beginning of the 1980s, both in quality and in image, but Maurizio Castelli was in a better position to appreciate it than most – until 1980 he was a technical inspector for the Chianti Classico consortium. After Chianti's slump in popularity during the 1950s, there followed a decade when many outside interests bought up large tracts of Tuscan land. With no knowledge of local conditions or grape growing, the newcomers largely embraced the belief then current that, since France held all the high ground for quality in the international market, Italy would have to make its presence felt abroad by providing cheap bulk wine.

Yet all the best Tuscan wines had always come from the difficult, stony hillsides which were virtually impossible to mechanize. This didn't deter the new arrivals; during the 1970s vine plantings in Chianti increased by 500 per cent, mostly on unsuitably flat land. They also planted large amounts of strains of Sangiovese that produced massive crops of light red wine on the warm, fertile plains of Romagna. But they rarely ripened at all in the more demanding circumstances of Chianti! Add to this the permitted use of the high acid, neutral white Trebbiano, supposedly to soften the wine, and the legal addition of 15 per cent heavy concentrated grape must from the south of Italy to add body to what was by now a totally insipid brew, and the wave of bankruptcy and disaster which was sweeping the region by the early 1980s should have been easy to foresee. By the early 1980s the cost of production was 160 per cent of the price a merchant would pay a grower for his Chianti wine.

This was the situation which confronted Castelli in 1980. There was only so much he could do as an employee of the Chianti Classico consortium. Castelli saw that the entirely unsuitable wine laws which condoned bad clones of Sangiovese, enforced dilution of the wine with other inferior grape varieties and encouraged hopelessly outmoded wine-making practices, would cause endless conflicts of interest between himself and his employers. So he went freelance and signed up with four Chianti Classico estates whose wines he had already been instrumental in improving, later adding estates in Montepulciano, Montalcino and Orvieto, to the south of the Chianti Classico zone.

Will the Real Sangiovese Stand Up?

Since then he has adopted a fascinating two-pronged attack. The estates he deals with possess some of the best vineyard sites in Tuscany, and Castelli has made an absolute religion of respecting vineyard character. He is no enemy of Cabernet Sauvignon, but feels that no one has yet made enough effort to understand the indigenous Sangiovese – or Sangioveto, as he prefers to call it – and he intends to do so rather than rely on the easy option of loading his wines with the internationally popular flavours of Cabernet. All his red wines are based largely or wholly on Sangioveto, with the exception of an occasional 'Super Tuscan' *vino da tavola* like the Balifico of Castello di Volpaia, where he includes some Cabernet to stunning effect, though he seems almost apologetic for messing around with the flavour of the majority Sangioveto.

However, Castelli is not at all averse to developing international varietal styles where no local alternatives exist. The main indigenous whites in Tuscany are the undistinguished Trebbiano and Malvasia. So he has replanted areas suitable for white wine production with Chardonnay and Sauvignon Blanc. He has honed his white wine-making skills on a blend called Vinattieri Bianco, largely based on Chardonnay from the Alto

The setting sun casts a crimson glow over the Volpaia estate, one of Castelli's greatest success stories in Tuscany.

Adige in the far north. But even here, he would like to find sources for his wine in future in Tuscany. He firmly believes the northern part of Chianti Classico can make great Chardonnay and Sauvignon Blanc, full of the ripe richness of a warm climate, yet able to preserve perfume because of the great variation in temperature between the warm days and the cold nights.

Today Castelli is in the vanguard of the emotional 'back to tradition' move among Tuscan red wine producers, as well as being in a position to capitalize on the world's insatiable demand for high quality *barrique*-fermented whites.

Re-reading the Classics

Yet his reds don't just go 'back to tradition'. They are creating the tradition. Traditionally, Tuscan reds have been lean and dry, astringent rather than fruity, the result of fermenting the grapes with their stalks at uncontrolled temperatures. He controls fermentation temperatures carefully, punching down the cap of skins, rather than using the traditional and rougher method of pumping the juice over the cap, and often macerating the skins and wine together for 10 to 15 days after fermentation. After which the wine may go into *barrique*, but is just as likely to go into barrels twice the size so that the flavour of oak doesn't predominate.

The result is wines bursting with fruit. He says he does want structure, seriousness, in his wines, but that the first impression should be an explosion of fruit in the mouth. He believes that wines with a richness of fruit are the ones which age, and that a red wine need not be fiercely tannic in its youth. After five years his 1985s were exhibiting a quite brilliantly original flavour of fruit. Sometimes it's chocolate and plum seemingly mixed with sour cherries in brandy, as in Elegia from the Poliziano estate in Montepulciano. Sometimes, as in his Cetinaia from Castello di San Polo in Rosso in Chianti Classico, it is wonderfully rich with flavours of blackberry, plum juice and black treacle laced with lime. Sometimes, as in his I Sodi di San Niccolò from the Castellare estate in Chianti Classico, there's a fabulous stewy sweet blackcurrant fruit made almost bitter but beautiful with the rasp of pepper and minerals. But there's always structure, and there's always fruit quite unlike any other in the world.

Despite all his flamboyance and passion, Castelli does not feel he has presided over a revolution; rather he feels he is merely rediscovering the essence of the vineyards now planted with the best possible grapevines. Even in his wine-making decisions he says he follows his intuition first, and then rationalizes after he's seen how it turns out. There has been an understandable reaction to the decay of Tuscan viticulture and wine-making. Many winemakers and grape growers naturally wished to go against the grain to prove they were making a real effort to change. Castelli's decision was braver. Everyone knew what Cabernet could do. No one knew what Sangioveto could achieve. Now we are finding out. As Castelli said, with another theatrical waggle of his bushy eyebrows, 'I go with the grain; it's just a case of working out which way the grain's going.'

Château Musar

*E*VERY TIME I TASTE Château Musar, one flavour consistently outweighs all the others put together. Courage. The rest pales into insignificance when you realize that as every vintage comes around, Serge Hochar, the Maronite Christian owner of Château Musar, must brave shells and rockets, as well as the unpredictable attentions of the various local militias marauding the region – if he is to have any chance of turning his grapes into wine.

Château Musar is in the Lebanon. The vineyards are in the hauntingly beautiful Bekaa Valley, up beyond the opium fields, straddling the front line between the Syrian and Israeli forces. The winery is 20km (12 miles) north of Beirut, in a Christian enclave just below Mount Lebanon. Hochar thought that here at least he would be safe from the ravages of Beirut's civil war. But from February to October in 1989, the fighting became ever more furious. Hochar's house, and his brother's house, were hit and in May a couple of direct hits on the winery itself turned the subterranean wine cellars into bomb shelters.

So why does he stay? For the oldest, the truest reason in the world. Because Lebanon is his home. Lebanon is his passion. A dangerous passion, a wild passion, one fuelling what he calls 'his own personal battle'. He spent ten years looking for other estates in Europe and America, but in 1988 realized he must brave it out in Lebanon.

The terrifying circumstances in which he makes his wine have affected his way of describing it too. Most winemakers, especially those who, like Hochar, had a positively classical training under Professor Peynaud in Bordeaux, and then at the ultra-classic Château Léoville-Barton in St-Julien, use rather refined, reserved language when talking about their wines. But when I've tasted Musar with Hochar, I've realized that it is not just the taste that matters to him, it's the spirit and soul of the vintage that's at least as important. 'Great wine should be dangerously attractive rather than simply enjoyable', he says. 'What I want is a wine that troubles me.' His favourite, the 1964, excites him because it is so 'animal, so wild'.

I couldn't agree more. Since the Musar wines first shocked an unsuspecting wine world at England's Bristol Wine Fair in 1979, many experts have struggled to catch the essence of Musar by describing it as a cross between Bordeaux and Burgundy. It is nothing of the sort. It is far too wild, far too exotic for Bordeaux – although 70 per cent of the wine in most years is from Cabernet Sauvignon grapes – and it has none of the fragrant delicacy which marks out Burgundy. It is proudly Lebanese.

The smell of a mature Musar seems deep and old and sweet, sometimes as intense as burnt raspberry sauce scraped from the pan, sometimes thick with dark syrup of black cherries steeped in brandy, sometimes with the sweet sourness of sublime vinegars, sometimes a yeastiness as heady as fresh brioche, and often wafted through with the scent of cedar. The flavour generally seems oxidized at first, and paradoxically, if you taste Musar too young, you're certain it can't last. But that's part of the magic. The young wines show too much age. The old wines show too much fruit. They all throw a sediment in their seventh year, and between eight and ten years old, just as you think they can only slip downhill, they break out into their unique maturity.

I look back at my notes on the 1981, for instance. Consistently I described it as disappointing. Until 1990. I couldn't believe the change, but it shouldn't really have been a surprise: Serge Hochar had told me to be patient often enough. Now the wine has kept its oxidized decay, but added to it a most unlikely fresh red fruit sweetness, almost as though it *is* actually sweet. The cedar which was missing has now returned, and it is fresh cedar, wafted on sea breezes from the Bay of Jounieh. But then again, it *is* oxidized – the rich fruit reminds me of shrivelled berries dusty with the parched earth of high summer. Yet it *isn't* oxidized. The freshness comes back, a bitter cherry roughness, the cedar now turned to cured leaves of tobacco in a warm loft, the sweet decay of balsamic vinegar seeming to gnaw at the richness, turning the candy of sugared almonds into the tangy intensity of sloes. And I thought this wine was a disappointment?

Hardly a New Idea

There's every reason to believe that the Bekaa Valley, which runs parallel to the Mediterranean between Damascus and Beirut, is one of the earliest sites in the world for developed vineyards. The Phoenicians actively traded the wines of Lebanon, and at Baalbek, in the north of the Bekaa Valley, the Romans built one of their greatest temples in homage to Bacchus, the god of wine. Serge Hochar's father established a winery in the eighteenth-century Castle of Mzar north of Beirut in 1930, and it was to the Bekaa Valley 50km (31 miles) east that he looked for his grapes. The east-facing Bekaa slopes are mostly gravel on a limestone base, virtually frost-free at 1006 metres (3300 feet) above sea level, and despite 300 days of sunshine every year, the altitude tends to keep the average summer temperature down to about 25°C (77°F).

Serge Hochar took over the winery in 1959, and the Hochar vineyards now total 145 hectares (358 acres), a mix of Cabernet Sauvignon, Cinsaut, Syrah and various whites including Chardonnay. The white wines have never appealed to me – perhaps the journey from vineyard to winery is too much for the grapes. With the exception of 1976 and 1984, however, years when the whole vintage was lost, the red grapes have survived the often tortuous trip. Usually the final blend is about two-thirds Cabernet and one-third Cinsaut with Syrah playing a small part. The Cinsaut plays a crucial role, because its acidity and simple fresh fruit dilutes and tempers the rich concentration of the Cabernet.

Although Hochar uses oak to age the wine, he does so cautiously. After fermentation in concrete which may

Château Musar's vines look somewhat unkempt – hardly surprising when war rages all around – but the wines remain wonderfully consistent.

last four or five weeks, the wine is racked into big vats for a year, and only then given up to a year's ageing, primarily in French Nevers oak. And then it goes back to vats again for as long as three years, though one year is usual. During this period Hochar begins to work on the blend of his Château Musar – the lesser wines are sold as Cuvée Musar – and he blends according to the emotional and personal perception he has of the vintage, not according to the technical figures.

With no fining, and the minimum of filtering, it isn't too fanciful to believe that you actually can taste the passion and the pain in the wine, rather than any set amount of Cabernet or Cinsaut, any particular percentage of old oak or new, Nevers or Vosges. And you do taste the courage. When you taste the 1983, remember the battle for the Chouf mountains began around the vineyards on 1 September and Serge Hochar had to be smuggled into the country by boat to make the wine. As you taste the 1988 and 1989, remember the wine had to share its vaulted cellars, a dozen metres underground, with refugees from the shells and rockets of a nation tearing itself apart.

Domaine de Trévallon

*D*ID I WANT TO smell white truffles? Did I want to taste them? Of course I did. I'd spent years hearing about the mythical paradox of seemingly incompatible flavours that sent gourmets wild with desire the world over. But I'd never smelled anything more than damp cardboard by the time the truffles got to me. And here was this tall, bearded Frenchman, eyes blazing, dragging me by the arm through a crowded Paris hall. But not a truffle stand in sight.

As we elbowed and shoved our way through the throng, he explained. His name was Jean Lenoir, and he had invented a product called Le Nez du Vin – the nose of wine. He had isolated dozens of the most common flavours in wine and bottled essences of them all which he sold as a pack, along with a little book. The one of which he was most proud, the aroma which was supposed to be the hallmark of Château Pétrus, the world's most expensive red wine, was white truffles. And now he had found this disturbing and erotic perfume in an unknown red wine from the south of France that couldn't even boast an *appellation contrôlée*. And it was on display just down the hall.

So I was finally hauled face to face with one of the most remarkable wines in France, from one of the least known but most promising regions – the wine was Domaine de Trévallon, the region was Coteaux des Baux en Provence, at that time an insignificant, sparsely farmed *vin délimité de qualité supérieure* – the rank below *appellation contrôlée*. And as the owner, Eloi Dürrbach, explained exactly where his region was, on north-facing slopes of a distinctly minor mountain range called Les Alpilles, north-west of Marseilles, I vaguely remembered taking a pretty unsuccessful short cut towards Arles through those mountains years before. I also remembered gazing enviously but impecuniously at the famous Michelin three-star restaurant L'Oustau de Baumanière on the way, and thinking what a magnificently desolate region it was. 'My wine is the house wine there,' said Dürrbach, not boasting, just matter of fact. By the way, he added, if you think it's wild there, wait till you see the Domaine de Trévallon.

Well, I'm not *sure* that I found the white truffles in the end, but I found one hell of a wine. Dürrbach had opened his 1980 and 1981. The 1980 had a deep red colour, a wonderfully unctuous rich fruit nose simply oozing figs and blackcurrants, and the flavour was a wild Mediterranean mix of tastes, perhaps there was a

little truffly decay lurking amongst the herbs, but mostly it was blackcurrant jam, raspberry jam, blackberry too – was it like Bordeaux, was it Rhône? The 1981 seemed twice as deep, the leather and smoke perfume of the northern Rhône reds steeped in blackberry jam and the sweet chewiness of ripe grape skins, and all of it in perfect balance. Was *this* one Rhône? Or Bordeaux?

In a way, Trévallon is both. 60 per cent Cabernet Sauvignon, 40 per cent Syrah. As such it breaks the law of the local wine authorities, but Eloi Dürrbach was not the kind of man to let a few parochial diktats stand in the way of his vision. And one look at Domaine de Trévallon will show you that he's not interested in anything remotely cosy.

The domaine is not quite as thrilling in its setting as the outcrop of Les Baux, where the town looks from a distance as though it was hewn from the rock at the birth of civilization. But when you look at the Trévallon soil it seems impossible that anyone could conceive of planting vines here. Les Baux gave its name to bauxite, the mineral used in the refining of aluminium. You have to dynamite the rocks simply to create enough fissures among the rubble to plant your vines at all. And there would be nothing to nourish vines in such a place, if underneath the chaos of surface rock there were not a crucial, moisture-retaining bed of limestone. This is one of the hottest parts of France. Even on north-facing slopes as at Trévallon, in the non-irrigated world of French viticulture, the water supply is so limited, that without the limestone, no vine could survive. As it is, two tons to the acre is regarded as a bounteous crop.

Stained Glass to Wine Glass

Dürrbach comes from a visionary family. His father had bought an extensive property below the Alpilles in 1950. He was a renowned painter and sculptor and concentrated his efforts on sculpture, tapestry and the reconstruction of stained glass windows destroyed in the World War Two. But he did muse on the fact that his land, with its rocky surface and limestone subsoil could produce great wine. It was necessary for his son Eloi to grow fatigued with a life studying mathematics and architecture in Paris for the musings to take form. In 1974, Eloi came home, and took over a dilapidated farm of his mother's on the family estate and began to blast the rock apart and plant vines.

In the meantime he took a job at Château Vignelaure in the nearby Coteaux d'Aix en Provence, to gain confidence, he says, for his ideas. To gain grapevines too. The cuttings of Cabernet Sauvignon he took from Vignelaure formed the core of his first plantings at

This is actually one of the less forbidding parts of the Domaine de Trévallon vineyard, but the soil still looks like chunks of rock – and that's exactly what it is.

Trévallon. Georges Brunet, the owner of Vignelaure, had come from Bordeaux in 1964 (he had been the proprietor there of the Classed Growth Château La Lagune). And he hadn't lost his Bordeaux tastes. A certain Dr Guyot, in the 1860s, had produced a classic French work called *Study of the Vineyards of France* which had suggested that you could produce superb wine from Bordeaux's Cabernet Sauvignon and Syrah – the Rhône grape – in the area around Aix. One hundred years later, Brunet planted Cabernet and Syrah and set out to prove Guyot right. He also included a little Grenache as a sop to local tradition. Dürrbach decided that tradition wasn't worth the sop, and, despite threats from the authorities to ban him from the appellation for refusing to include local grapes when Les Baux became an AC in 1985, he has stuck to the Guyot formula of 60 per cent Cabernet and 40 per cent Syrah. He now has 16 hectares (39 acres) planted, although he is thinking of planting some more land with Cabernet and Syrah, and has already begun to toy with the idea of a white, initially of Chardonnay and Roussanne, maybe later with a little of the star Rhône grape Viognier.

But he has surely made the right decision, and the fact that Domaine de Trévallon is now the most sought-after wine in Provence – just because its flavour is the best *flavour* in the whole of Provence – is giving courage to winemakers of ambition right across the south.

Above all, Dürrbach wants to allow the fruit of this remarkable vineyard to express itself. In such a dry climate, disease is not much of a problem, and he is able to follow an organic approach to viticulture. He does periodically add a little sheep manure to his 'soil', and he chops up vine prunings and digs them in between the rows to provide a little organic matter, but otherwise he uses no fertilizer, and his only chemical spray is the organically accepted copper sulphate; his only insecticide is a spray he makes up of essence of lavender and rosemary, which sounds heavenly but seems to overpower all but the most determined insect pests.

Dürrbach's wine-making too, is solely based on drawing out his fruit's personality. He tried new oak, but swiftly rejected it because of the influence on the fruit. Now he simply ferments his two grape varieties separately, at high temperature, and allows the wine to macerate with the skins for up to five weeks. Then the wine goes straight into old wooden barrels, where it lingers, without any fining or filtration, for 18 months before bottling. Nothing added. Nothing taken out.

I haven't tasted his first vintage – he made a mere 50 hectolitres (1100 gallons) in 1976 – but have kept close tabs on each release since that revelation of the 1980 and 1981 in Paris. The Syrah usually dominates the young wine, a leathery, sometimes smoky mix of deep blackcurrant and blackberry fruit, often sweetened and spiced with a lick of *garrigue* honey. But as the different components age, a perfume of cedarwood and Havana tobacco slowly unfurls and the wine becomes quite absurdly Bordeaux-like at about ten years old. But the delicate cedar fragrance never quite overpowers the feeling of a passionate fruit that has clawed desperately for nourishment and survival in this unlikely birthplace. Delicacy, fragrance and balance are all very well. But it's passion that I still taste in every glass of Trévallon, however mellow and mature the wine has grown.

Angelo Gaja

*P*RIDE IS A TWO-EDGED SWORD when it comes to wine-making. Local pride can make a producer close his eyes to progress, cling resolutely to the methods of his ancestors, and the flavours of wines unchanged through generations, refusing to accept that the world around him is moving on.

But pride can also make a producer look at his region and its wines, look at the history, the glory of the past contrasted with the stagnation of the present day and feel the blood surge to his temples, feel the bitterness as the efforts of his predecessors are casually dismissed and other countries and other wines reap the rewards. This pride can fill a man with a single-minded, fanatical ambition, making him seethe with chill passion to place his family name among the elite band at the very top of the world aristocracy of wine.

Angelo Gaja is a controversial figure. Coming into his family business in 1961 at the age of 21, he was remarkably quick to see that Piedmont was resting on its laurels as Italy's greatest red wine area. He was also quick to discover far-reaching solutions to Piedmont's problems, completely at odds with anything that had occurred in Piedmont until then.

The chief problems that Gaja found when he assumed the reins of the family business were the quality of the grapes and the standards of wine-making in Piedmont. Gaja's father had built up a considerable reputation for the company's wines selling a much respected Barolo, made from bought-in grapes, and a Barbaresco that was already the most expensive one around. But young Gaja showed great foresight in deciding that the only way to control your fundamental wine quality was to own your vines, since a contract grower merely wants a large crop of saleable grapes, whereas the winemaker craves a much smaller crop of much more concentrated grapes.

Piedmont's top quality grape – the Nebbiolo – is a very late-ripening variety, and yields had been gradually creeping up, making it impossible to ripen the grapes in many years. So Gaja instructed his vineyard workers in 1962 to leave barely half the usual number of buds on the vine, reducing the yield and thereby producing a good wine in an undistinguished vintage. And he also decreed that the company would make no more Barolo, because they owned no Barolo vines. He's still in two minds about that decision because his father's Barolo had been good, and without Barolo to lead the way,

Gaja found it much more difficult to get people to accept his increasingly expensive Barbaresco. But at the same time, the name Barolo was being debased by large concerns selling wines labelled Barolo for low prices, which had little if anything to do with the real thing.

So Gaja turned back to his roots, to his Barbaresco vineyard holdings, reducing yields, improving the chemical composition of his soils, and searching out the best microclimates. During this time he was a frequent visitor to France. He studied at Montpellier wine school, but in particular, he worked in Burgundy. He saw how, with a fickle grape variety like Pinot Noir, grown at the limit of its ability to ripen, microclimate and soil variation made dramatic differences. In Burgundy, the best plots were kept separate and sold under their own name. In Piedmont the Nebbiolo was just such a grape, grown in just such conditions, yet the wines were all lumped together.

Divide and Rule

Back in Barbaresco, Gaja set about pinpointing his best pieces of Barbaresco land and from 14 different plots, he chose three. He made his first single-vineyard wine – Sorì San Lorenzo in 1967, followed by Sorì Tildin in 1970 and Costa Russi in 1978. And he charged more, just as a good domaine would do in Burgundy.

He also took a careful look at French wine-making techniques, and in particular at the use of the small 225-litre (50-gallon) oak barrel to age the wine. In Piedmont, wines were traditionally matured for years in vast old wooden barrels or vats. The object was to soften the wine, but all too often the fruit disappeared, and the volatile acid level went soaring skyward, long before the tannins gave way – if they ever did. And whereas the big old barrels gave no flavour of their own to the wine, new oak barrels gave a strong, sweet vanilla richness, a taste equated increasingly with quality.

In 1969, Gaja started experimenting with new oak, but quickly found that, although oak gave a rich vanilla sweetness to the wine, it also gave harsh wood tannin. Nebbiolo had quite enough tannin of its own, and it took Gaja a number of years to develop a method that he was happy with. He orders wood from France and elsewhere in Europe which he seasons himself for three years, and then has made up by a local cooper. The barrels are then treated with steam and hot water for an hour to remove about half the wood tannins, but not destroy the sweet vanillins. He didn't release a *barrique*-aged wine until 1978, and only now feels he has the techniques right. The 1978 release created a furore; now every forward-looking Piedmont winemaker has a few barrels in the cellar. And the Gaja prices rose as

Angelo Gaja is probably Italy's highest-profile wine producer and his single-minded pursuit of international acclaim has done much to boost Piedmont's reputation.

demand rose. Gaja travelled ceaselessly promoting his wines, and drew himself closer to the French wine superstars by forming a distribution company to import many of the top Bordeaux and Burgundy wines. The general feeling worldwide still was that France was not only the producer of the greatest wines, but it also offered role models. No-one was trying to produce a great Barolo in California or Australia; they were all trying to produce a white Burgundy like Montrachet or a red Bordeaux like Mouton-Rothschild. So. Gaja decided he would too.

He had begun experimenting privately with Chardonnay as long ago as 1970 and with Cabernet Sauvignon in 1971, and in 1978 he went public by planting a Cabernet Sauvignon vineyard in the heart of Barbaresco. In 1979 he planted Chardonnay, followed by Sauvignon Blanc in 1983 and more Chardonnay in 1984. Although there had been some Cabernet in Piedmont in the nineteenth century, this defiance of tradition brought a massive reaction in Piedmont. But it was precisely by use of *barrique* and the planting of Cabernet Sauvignon that Tuscany had transformed itself during the 1970s. Gaja intended to follow the same path, but even more singlemindedly.

He reasoned that the world was increasingly becoming obsessed by Chardonnay and Cabernet Sauvignon. International acceptance was being achieved by winning competitions and awards with these varieties, but there was no way you could put a Barbaresco into these events. Gaja felt if he grew the right fashionable grapes, and applied his usual sense of purpose to the exercise, his achievements would then be judged alongside the established French classics or the new pretenders from California and Australia. Suddenly the name Gaja would become internationally known and doors which were still closed to Barbaresco would open to a medal-winning Chardonnay from Gaja.

Proof of the success of his strategy came in 1989 when the American wine magazine *The Wine Spectator* awarded two vintages of his Chardonnay Gaia e Rey near-perfect scores. Demand for Gaja Chardonnay and Gaja Cabernet today far outweighs supply. Gaja says this has proved two things to the world. Firstly – the land on which he grew the Cabernet was prime Barbaresco land. The customer liked the Cabernet, therefore he liked the 'attitude' of the land. If he now had confidence in this land, he should be ready to try what it traditionally produced – Barbaresco from the Nebbiolo grape. Secondly, Piedmont was seen as a red wine fiefdom, apart from the production of sweet Asti Spumante. The Chardonnay proved that Piedmont could make world class white, and sell it for world class prices. Now Gaja could get back to basics.

He installed stainless steel tanks with computerized temperature control and eased back the skin contact period for his Barbaresco, from the traditional two months or so to between three and four weeks.

The Barbarescos are still tannic, and they'll still take a dozen or more years to develop the magical perfume of fruit and flowers, chocolate and tar which marks out the best Nebbiolo wines, but they have become comprehensible to the international palate, something that traditional Piedmont reds never were. He has also made his wines some of the most sought-after anywhere. The prices for Gaja's single vineyard Barbarescos now outstrip all the Bordeaux First Growths except Château Pétrus. That really *is* international acceptance. But he has one more hill to climb. I don't believe Gaja's Barbaresco vineyards will ever produce Piedmont's greatest red wines. In 1988 Angelo Gaja bought the Barolo vineyard his father used to purchase from before 1961. I think perhaps this vineyard will.

Isole e Olena

*W*ELL, HE COULD HAVE replanted with 'priest strangler' and saved everyone a lot of fuss. A few rows of 'wet-the-bed' to provide a nice domestic feel to the wine and Paolo de Marchi would have struck a major blow for the preservation of traditional grape varieties in Chianti, because these are just two of the 270 different native strains so far identified in the Chianti vineyards which stretch into the hills and valleys around Florence and Siena.

He might have found gold, because no-one has got as far as vinifying these curiosities separately yet. That day may yet come, but for the time being Paolo de Marchi has his work cut out improving the Sangiovese selections on his Isole e Olena estate. When de Marchi returned from a trip to California in 1976, to find his family's Chianti Classico winery becoming increasingly unprofitable, he was one of the first Tuscan producers to see that an innovative, quality-first approach was the only way to survive.

The Isole e Olena estate had previously only made wine in bulk. One of de Marchi's first decisions was that some of the estate's wine should henceforth be kept back for ageing. At the same time he ripped out all the rotting chestnut and oak vats, and began to install new wood, some of it the small French oak barrel size of

225 litres (50 gallons) then almost unheard of in Chianti. And he cut production on the estate by half.

Paolo de Marchi also planted the fashionable Cabernet, but he never regarded its use as anything more than one possible route to explore. Indeed, by the early 1980s he'd already realized that Cabernet grew well in his vineyards, and that five to ten per cent added to his Chianti made excellent wine. But he felt it wasn't Chianti any more, the Cabernet was simply too strong a taste for the Sangiovese, and as the wine aged he felt the two varieties seemed to mature at different rates, to the detriment of the flavour balance.

And ageability was one of his passions. 'Every region must have a wine capable of very long life, because the reputation of an area's red wines is built by fine old wines.' Brunello di Montalcino, just to the south, was regarded as far finer wine than Chianti because the most important producer, Biondi-Santi, had gone out of his way to create a wine which had to be aged for decades before becoming drinkable.

De Marchi was too much of a modernist to force his wines through years of fruit-shrivelling wood-ageing. He realized that if he kept separate the grapes from his older vines, cut their yield to about 40 hectolitres per hectare, and picked as late as he dared, he could get far more structure and fruit in his Sangiovese than was considered possible by other producers. If he then fermented the juice on the skins for up to 20 days, as against the usual period of 10 to 12 days and then aged the wine for a year in small wood, he could get all the

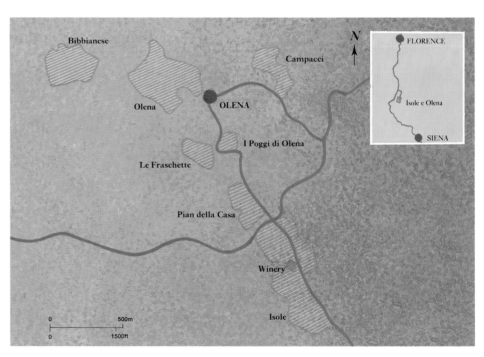

Vineyards

Bibbianese
Cabernet Sauvignon
Sangiovese
Syrah

Olena
Canaiolo
Sangiovese

Campacci
Chardonnay

Le Fraschette
Sangiovese

I Poggi di Olena
Sangiovese

Pian della Casa
Canaiolo
Sangiovese

Isole
Cabernet Sauvignon
Canaiolo
Chardonnay
Malvasia
Sangiovese
Syrah
Trebbiano

depth and structure he needed. By only using 20 to 30 per cent new wood, and including 30 per cent chestnut barrels – which have less aroma than oak and so allow the flavour of the fruit to sing out, he'd also find out whether the Sangiovese really has what it takes to make exciting wine on its own.

It obviously does. He makes a 100 per cent Sangiovese wine called Cepparello, and it has all the deep, slightly bitter cherry stone and cooked plums fruit with some mint and pine resin perfume, sometimes softened by a whiff of vanilla and coconut from the wood, that marks out high quality Sangiovese. Except that he can't call it Chianti. One of the enduring idiocies of the wine laws in Chianti is that a wine made to tip-top quality, out of Chianti's finest indigenous variety, not blended with inferior varieties to increase yield – is refused the Chianti DOCG. De Marchi does make extremely good Chianti Classico as well, which complies with the DOCG regulations, but he is the first to realize the absurdity of the situation.

The Rhône Meets Tuscany

He blends Syrah into his Chianti! Not just for devilment; he's put serious thought into it. Although he has come full circle and now feels that the Sangiovese can be good enough on its own, provided the clones and growing habits are well enough understood, he is too much of an internationalist simply to sit still working on one grape variety. Most of the Sangiovese at Isole e Olena was still producing relatively light wine in the early 1980s, the result of replanting with high yielding clones in the 1960s. It had to be boosted; Cabernet Sauvignon was fashionable but too dominant for him. Syrah was the other classic full-bodied French variety, so he went straight to the king – Etienne Guigal, the superstar of Côte-Rôtie in the northern Rhône and said – what do you use? Guigal told him, and directed him to the nursery that would supply him with the right material.

It works brilliantly. Up to 1986 the Isole Chianti Classico was good, but not memorable. In 1986 de Marchi blended a small percentage of Syrah into the wine. Ally this with a vintage of aromatic grapes, the result of warm days and cool nights, and the flavour is a mix of beautiful blackcurrant fruit, an earthiness which is positively perfumed, like fresh earth after rain, and an aroma like a celestial balm of cedar and pine. In 1987, a less than ideal year, de Marchi added a splash of Syrah to the blend, and there is a beautiful breeze-blown pine resin perfume to a soft damson-fruited wine. And the 1988 is so far developing these same damson and seaside pine forest flavours, in a most delicious way. How much

is that due to Syrah just providing the catalyst needed for the Sangiovese to flower? De Marchi will give it no more credit than that, not yet totally happy about the Syrah's fundamental personality when grown in Tuscan vineyards. Well, I hate to disagree; but I think Isole e Olena Syrah is simply stunning – and like their Cabernet, it is a brilliant example of the variety, yet very different from the French model.

It again brings me back to the point – what is a Tuscan taste? Cabernet grown in Tuscany gives quite different flavours compared with Cabernet from Bordeaux. Syrah, in de Marchi's case, gives a most original and exciting sweetness of blueberries, of mulberries, of greengage and nettles, perfumed cherries and angelica, and is blindingly original in its own right.

And he's got Chardonnay. What iconoclast could resist a few rows? But he didn't plan it on purpose. He asked a neighbouring Chianti grower for some Cabernet Sauvignon wood and it turned out to be Chardonnay! 1985 was his first crop, 1986 his first bottling, but he wasn't happy with it. He's so self-critical it might have been like a very decent Meursault and he'd still say it tastes of nothing. In fact his latest vintages have a lot of the buttered brazils and toffee creaminess of good Meursault, allied with surprisingly good acidity. The acidity is a struggle, because he freely admits Chianti can be too warm a region for Chardonnay. So he unashamedly goes for a full, primarily barrel-fermented style to make fragrant white wines. He has in fact now planted a shaded two-hectare (5-acre) plot with Chardonnay, to give himself more blending options.

The image de Marchi gives is relentlessly modern and forward-looking, so it comes as a delightful surprise that he is also an assiduous supporter of one of Tuscany's oldest wine traditions – production of the sweet, late harvested Vin Santo. There are few decent or honest Vin Santi left, but de Marchi's is beautiful stuff – with a sour richness of balsam, raisin and nuts, and the thick, mouth-coating weight of a good Sauternes. He attributes the wine's quality to his retention each year of the thick syrupy sludge at the bottom of the barrel which he then uses to re-start each new vintage's fermentation. His 'mother' he calls this. So he douses his mother with grape juice, seals up the barrel with wax and leaves her there for up to five years. And he seemed such a nice man.

Mas de Daumas Gassac

MICHAEL BROADBENT, THE HEAD of Christie's Wine Department, is one of the world's most famous wine tasters, and tales abound of his ability to pick out the precise vintage, and identity, of fabled wines from Bordeaux and Burgundy at the tables of the rich and famous. But the coup of which he is most proud didn't concern a famous wine at all. In fact he'd only heard of the estate once before. But when Hugh Johnson ceremoniously wheeled in the unmarked decanter murmuring ominously, 'You'll never get this one, old bean', and began to pour the thick, dark liquid into Michael's glass, the great taster didn't sniff it or swirl it around his mouth in pensive evaluation. He didn't need to; the very sight of it was enough. 'Mas de Daumas Gassac 1982,' he pronounced, and so it was. It quite spoiled Hugh's weekend, but Michael has been dining out on the story ever since.

I know that wine, and I believe its consistency gets more gooey and its colour darker year by year. I can see why Michael had this flash of recognition because the liquid uncoils from the bottle like treacle of rubies, and the syrup smothers your mouth with an essence of the hot fruit flavours of the south – blackberries and plums and the dry, wind-blown dust of the high barren hills of France's Hérault, all bound together with the bitter-black sweetness of molasses. Yes. Memorable stuff, that 1982. Yet barely five years previously, the vineyards of Mas de Daumas Gassac had not yet yielded up their first bottle of wine, and Aimé Guibert, the owner, had never in his life harvested or fermented one drop of grape juice.

In 1971 he had no intention of doing so, either. He was a successful glove manufacturer and leather processor at Millau, way up in France's lost kingdom, the Massif Central. But his wife Véronique is an ethnologist (indeed an expert in Irish peasant customs, of all things!) and had landed a teaching job at Montpellier university. It's not *that* far from Millau to Montpellier, but the roads are terrible, and since they both hankered after a back-to-the-soil country existence, this was the chance to up sticks and build a family life in the wild. But, unlike many other 1970s pioneers in Australia and California, the Guiberts were most definitely *not* looking to start a vineyard.

They certainly wouldn't have been prospecting round Montpellier if fine wine was their objective. Montpellier is bang in the middle of the flat, featureless swathe of land known as France's Midi. Endless forlorn rows of vines produce oceans of mediocre wine, which goes straight into Europe's wine lake without anyone even bothering to taste it. North of Montpellier are the tumbling hills and valleys which make up the Coteaux du Languedoc – an appellation where growers are struggling to improve the wines of the region – yet no-one had ever planted vines up the tiny Gassac valley. Hardly anyone had even lived there; but the Guiberts found an ancient farmhouse next to a flour mill which last ground corn in 1924, a mile or so off the Aniane to Gignac highway. Tidy the house up, cut a decent road through the rocks to the house – and they could soon invite their friends to stay. Harmless enough, unless one of your best friends happens to be Henri Enjalbert, one of the world's greatest experts on the geology of vineyards and a professor at the University of Bordeaux. And then you happen to have cut your road through a soil formation which almost sends the renowned professor into paroxysms as soon as he sees it, and which he then describes in passionate terms as a 'geological miracle'.

The Science of the Soil

It seems that over the last million years or so, the earth has enjoyed three short periods of warmth – the rest of the time being basically ice age. When the warming occurs, the glacial rocks literally explode in tiny fragments of dust which are then blown or washed away – the Médoc in Bordeaux and the Côte d'Or in Burgundy have both benefitted from the settling of this dust, but Enjalbert found himself staring at the purest wind-blown pinky-red glacial deposits he had ever seen. And they were deep, sometimes going down as much as 6 metres (20 feet).

Such soil is almost completely porous, and by itself wouldn't be much use for vines since it could never hold water long enough for the vines to refresh themselves. But the soil at Mas de Daumas Gassac was deposited on a bed of water-retentive humus and limestone, so that the vines could push their roots way down below the surface, away from the dangers of drought or flood, and settle deep in the earth in the damp, cool humus. It was the kind of soil structure that any *grand cru* owner in Bordeaux or Burgundy would give their eye teeth for, and Enjalbert told Guibert that if he was prepared to be 'completely crazy', to invest enormous sums of money and work himself to a frazzle,

The wild beauty of this Mediterranean terrain drew Aimé Guibert to Mas de Daumas Gassac long before he thought of starting a vineyard.

he could make Mas de Daumas Gassac into one of France's greatest vineyards – and Enjalbert meant *greatest* – Chambertin, Romanée-Conti, Latour and Lafite – that's what he meant by great.

Well, he certainly chose the right people to tantalize with a vision of immortality. The Guiberts couldn't resist the challenge and they set about the creation of France's newest *grand cru* with furious determination. They knew nothing about wine-making, even less about vines, but both knew about striving for perfection. The factory in Millau produced hides and skins in demand worldwide by the top fashion houses.

So Guibert simply went to the top man – Professor Émile Peynaud of Bordeaux university, the man responsible more than any other for the dramatic rise in quality of Bordeaux's wines during the 1970s and 1980s.

Peynaud actually made the first two vintages at Mas de Daumas Gassac – the 1978 and 1979 – and has been in close consultation ever since. As for vines – Guibert *did* want to make an attempt on a new Bordeaux-type *grand cru* – his chief advisers were after all, two of Bordeaux's leading experts, but he had a wonderfully open mind about precisely how to achieve it, and because his vineyard was in the Hérault mountains, outside any recognized *appellation d'origine contrôlée*, he could plant whatever he pleased.

Guibert says that right from the start it wasn't recommended modern clones with all the correct scientific pedigree he was in search of, but vines whose personalities excited him. He planted Cabernet Sauvignon – his red wine is three-quarters Cabernet Sauvignon – seeking out pre-war vines from Bordeaux's

top properties as his core material. He wanted Pinot Noir too, so he tracked down some 80-year-old vines in Clos Vougeot and took cuttings from those. Malbec, Merlot, Syrah and Tannat were planted as well, to add complexity. His passion for excellence shows up just as much in the little parcels of white vines. He put in Chardonnay, Muscat, Bourboulenc and Chenin, reserving his special efforts for two of the world's rarest but most exciting grapes – Viognier, cuttings of which he obtained from Condrieu's top producer, Georges Vernay, and Petit Manseng, the grape of Jurançon, the heady, fragrant wine of the Pyrenees. Clos Uroulat has the oldest vines; that's where Guibert got his cuttings.

Rarer still are the plantings of the Swiss Petite Arvine and an extraordinary beast called Neher Leschol, a Middle Eastern vine variety which is mentioned in the Bible and which yields enormous quantities of grapes. The vines came from an Israeli student of oenology at Montpellier and give Aimé Guibert tremendous pleasure, for their history and antiquity rather than their epicurean potential. There are too many people working for today and tomorrow, he says, and all too few look at what we can learn from the past.

Guibert now has 25 hectares (62 acres) – just under half of them Cabernet Sauvignon. But he hasn't planted in a single block; he's followed the changes in soil structure closely – for instance using outcrops of limestone for his Viognier – and he's also followed the patterns of the natural habitat. He was serious about wanting to establish a pure, clean country environment in which to raise his family – he's got five sons – and has insisted on a totally organic regime right from the very beginning.

He uses no chemical fertilizers, with the result that his already low-yielding vines only produce a maximum of 40 hectolitres per hectare and often less. He actually employs someone to weed the vines by hand, and he uses no pesticides. Whenever possible, he's retained the original Hérault *garrigue* – that marvellous wild tangle of thyme, rosemary, lavender, laurel and mint that carpets these hills, providing a habitat for the natural predators of any vineyard pests. He also says in moments of reflection that he believes the savage aroma of the hills will somehow infiltrate the flavours of his wine. And it may. It just may. There is a raw, herby quality to his red wines, like the rasping yet heady sensation you get biting into leaves of fresh rosemary or thyme.

There's a further reason for preserving the natural scrub vegetation – it serves as a guardian of Mas de Daumas Gassac's particular climate. The Gassac Valley here is about 90 metres (300 feet) above sea level, yet temperatures are those of a valley 300 metres (1000 feet)

The magic soil that gives such perfect growing conditions for grapes at Mas de Daumas Gassac.

up. Despite being within sight of the sweltering Midi flatlands where the overnight temperature in summer rarely drops below 27°C (80°F), and daytime temperatures regularly soar into the high 30°s (100°s), the Gassac temperatures average 5° to 10°C (9° to 18°F) less. The grapes don't broil in the sun, and during the night they can rest rather than go on building up sugar levels and losing acidity. The result is relatively late flowering and a very late harvest – often it doesn't start until October, a month later than the Midi vines a few miles to the south. Consequently the grapes' physiological ripeness is much more complete – crucial for the *flavour* of the wine – and the harvest can take place in cool conditions.

The interior of the winery is itself naturally positively chilly. That's another slice of Guibert luck. The ancient mill was water-driven. The Gassac river bubbles up from underground, emerging just above the mill and the ice-cold water tumbles down, literally, underneath the buildings. Guibert has built his winery in these old buildings, and even in the height of summer, the spring water keeps his vats and his bottle store chilly and damp.

Guibert had remarkable luck in finding Mas de Daumas Gassac. Since then, however, he has single-mindedly pursued his goal. He waited seven years before releasing a first vintage red, the 1978, and although Professor Peynaud made the 1978 and 1979, Guibert has made the wine himself since then – with a fair amount of Peynaud telephonic advice when crises occur. Guibert still takes the Bordeaux wine-making style as his model. He loads the picked grapes into small, 20kg (44lb) plastic trays and pulls out any unhealthy grapes at the winery. He destems the red

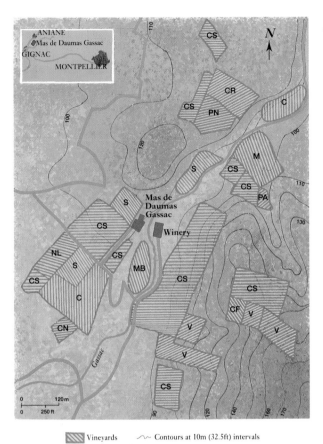

C Chardonnay CS Cabernet Sauvignon PA Petite Arvine
CF Cabernet Franc M Merlot PN Pinot Noir
CN Cinsault MB Malbec S Syrah
CR Carignan NL Neher Leschol V Viognier

Vineyards   Contours at 10m (32.5ft) intervals

phenomenon. Indeed, it was Professor Peynaud in the 1970s and 1980s who changed the whole direction of Bordeaux towards fruitier wine, and wine more suffused with the sweetness of new wood.

It is as though Guibert decided to go back to a pre-Peynaud world first – to try to discover the heart of the old-style Bordeaux wines which often needed 30 years to show their full personality – before inching his way into the style of today. The 1978 and '79 are more in the mould of a firm, unyielding Italian Nebbiolo. The first wines of the 1980s show a little more fruit, a hint of rich, dark sweetness, still too shy to uncover itself in the bright daylight glare, yet slowly gaining confidence and complexity as the wine ages. Blackcurrant, blackberry, liquorice and black treacle flavours lurk in there in black richness, still coated with tannin, and swished with a few sprigs of thyme and rosemary.

It isn't until you taste the 1987 that a genuinely more modern style becomes apparent. The wine is lighter – 1987 was a cool year even down in the Hérault – but the oak sweetness is more marked here, and the spice of cinnamon, the fresh smoky toast, the sweetness of plums – and the tannin too– make this the best Guibert wine yet. Paradoxically, the wine from the very hot year of 1989, with its early harvest, shows every sign of developing in the same way. It does look as though, with mature vines and a decade of apprenticeship, we really could see a major *grand cru* rising out of a lost valley in France's far south.

Indeed, we could see two *grands crus*. His white, usually Viognier-dominated, is absolutely stunning, already far more exciting than most of the Condrieus on offer. The 1988 (60 per cent Viognier) is so rich, so creamy, with fabulous mouth-coating fruit and a fragrance which is at once all dried apricots intensity, quickly soothed out into the wispy fluffy sweetness of spun sugar and candyfloss and leaving a heavenly aftertaste like the magic dust on Turkish Delight or marshmallows. The 1990 promises to be even better. On the wall of Aimé Guibert's office there is a newspaper headline plastered up – 'Château Lafite Languedocien' – the Château Lafite of the Midi. I wouldn't mind betting that his white, which he first made only in 1986, is next for the headline treatment. Le Condrieu du Midi? I wouldn't disagree.

grapes completely and ferments in various small stainless steel vats at a fairly traditional 28° to 30°C (82° to 86°F), pumping over twice a day for about half an hour, firstly in the presence of air, then, after about three to five days, anaerobically to reduce oxygen contact, in accordance with the Peynaud style. The barrels he uses are about ten per cent new and the wines will spend 15 to 18 months in wood before being blended in a large stainless steel tank for three months – 'to digest the wood' – and then bottled in their second spring. Throughout this process, all the wine is moved by gravity rather than being pumped, and though he fines with egg whites, he doesn't filter his red wines.

The result is a wine as deeply, densely coloured as blackstrap molasses, old-fashioned in structure; yet each new vintage shows that Guibert is working towards a more approachable style – albeit very slowly. He agrees that the considerable tannins are a problem, and since 1982 he has blended in his other red varieties to increase perfume and richness. Yet the desire to make an ebulliently fruity wine is a relatively modern

Émile Peynaud

*T*HEY SHOULD ERECT a commemorative plaque at Château Duplessis-Hauchecorne. This property in the quiet Bordeaux appellation of Moulis is verging on the obscure, I do agree, but without the foresight of its owner in the 1940s, all those majestic Napa Cabernet Sauvignons we like to swoon over, or those Coonawarra Cabernets they boast of down under as the Médocs of Australia just wouldn't exist. Because Duplessis-Hauchecorne was the very first wine to be vinified by Professor Émile Peynaud, the father of modern Bordeaux, the creator of the red wine style which has served as the model for any modern producer of Cabernet Sauvignon who wasn't content just to sell wine by the half-gallon jug or five-litre bag-in-box.

Peynaud is in his late 70s and semi-retired. But in a way, we all now benefit from the work he did in the later part of his professional life. The Bordeaux Classed Growths did not achieve the astonishingly impressive standard of rich, ripe fruit combined with the sweet influence of new wood which are Peynaud hallmarks, until the late 1970s. Since the 1940s, however, Peynaud's work at the University of Bordeaux has served to revolutionize the understanding of how to make good wine in very fundamental ways. It's not simply a matter of using new French oak barrels for maturing the wine and practising the rigid exclusion of the less impressive vats from the final blend of a château. These techniques have been copied worldwide, but such refinements of quality were only possible because Peynaud and his equally distinguished senior colleague Professor Ribéreau-Gayon had turned inside out the principles of fermentation and wine-making which had held firm since Pasteur's time, and with them the concept of how a good wine could and should taste.

Great Bordeaux wines have been made for 200 years – or perhaps I'll rephrase that. Great Bordeaux wines have *occurred* for 200 years. But as Peynaud says, these wines basically made themselves. In great years a good number of memorable wines were made because the grapes were ripe and healthy and the wines had sufficient structure and richness not to be ruined by antediluvian practices in the cellars. But in lesser years, few decent wines were made, sometimes none at all. Peynaud's first task was to learn how to stop this wanton spoilage, both in the vineyard and in the winery. He instigated the methodical sampling of grapes to assess their ripening rates and predict the best times to

harvest and the likely style of the resulting wines, and he routinely lectured growers on why rotten grapes should not be included in the fermentation. Also, since different grape varieties ripened at different speeds, depending on the age of the vines, the soils and the microclimate, it was important to ferment the grapes from individual parcels separately.

This may seem obvious to us now, but it wasn't 50 years ago. Peynaud says that before and after World War Two, virtually all wines of whatever quality suffered to some extent from excess of vinegary volatile acidity. This was because the wooden vats and casks used for fermenting and maturing wines were old and infected with bacteria and because no one knew how to control the heat of fermentation efficiently. I've tasted wines from the 1920s, the 1930s and the 1940s – and even the best have a distinct acetic tang to them. Peynaud persuaded growers to turn from wood to cement for their vats, and even today says he prefers clean cement to dirty oak barrels for maturing wine, although at the wealthy properties his preference now is for ultra-clean stainless steel for fermentation and a French oak barrel for maturation.

The malolactic fermentation, during which a wine's green, raw malic acid transforms into the softer, milky lactic acid, simply wasn't understood before Peynaud. Professor Winkler at UC Berkeley in California carried out research on the process in 1948, but since California's warm climate was conducive to malolactic's spontaneous occurrence almost every year, no-one had given his work due credit. In Bordeaux, however, the malolactic did not always occur, often as a result of high acidity in the grapes and cold climatic conditions.

The Broader Picture

Bordeaux in the 1940s and 1950s, with a string of fine vintages, was looking to re-establish crucial exports in fine wine after the war, yet far too many wines would seem to re-ferment and spoil in bottle by the time they reached clients. The reason was the malolactic fermentation haphazardly occurring inside the bottle. It took Peynaud's efforts to isolate the bacteria responsible and learn how to control them. Peynaud is sometimes criticized for advocating a softer, gentler style of wine. Those critics should taste the harsh, pricked red wines which were the norm before Peynaud unravelled the mystery of the second fermentation's softening, stabilizing effect on red wine.

Throughout the 1950s and 1960s, the work of Peynaud and his colleagues in Bordeaux resulted in increased understanding of the behaviour of yeasts and bacteria, and of the composition and structure of

With his deep understanding of wine chemistry allied to a great passion for the soil, Peynaud has done more to lay the foundations of modern fine red wine than anyone else.

Bordeaux's different grape varieties. The ability to analyse wines enabled winemakers to prescribe treatments for any problems they might have. And Peynaud became known as the 'flying doctor' of Bordeaux, tearing from one property to another, checking out fermentations, giving on-the-spot advice and encouragement before rushing on to the next château. He reckoned to visit 15 properties per day, seven days a week at fermentation time, and he has acted as the adviser to no fewer than 35 of the Classed Growths in the Médoc.

However, it was only in the 1970s, as the proprietors began to achieve viable prices for their wines, that the two legacies for which we now know Peynaud best became possible – the widespread use of new French oak barrels for maturing the wine, and the ruthless selection of the best lots of wine for the final blend under the château label. A new oak barrel costs in excess of 3000 francs and the contents would fill about 288 bottles of wine. A proprietor needs to be able to

charge at least ten francs a bottle more for his wine to pay for the investment. In the enormous vintages which became common during the 1980s, top properties might be persuaded by Peynaud to remove as much as 40 to 50 per cent of their wine from the final blend, to be released under a subsidiary label at a much lower price. The financial sacrifice can easily run into hundreds of thousands of francs, but is crucial for any property wishing to be taken seriously. It is the ripe, concentrated fruit of these wines, their immediate appeal, but their undoubted ability to age, which has provided the benchmark for top Cabernet creators around the world.

Before Peynaud there was no history of rigid selection and small French oak *barrique* ageing at all in California. There was no history of such wine-making in Australia, New Zealand, South Africa or Chile before Peynaud took the basic traditional practices of Bordeaux, isolated their most important facets, and then persuaded a generation of proprietors to put his advice into action. He has transformed the red wines of Bordeaux in the last 30 years, and has inspired a host of emulators across the world, whose red wines can now equal and even surpass those of his beloved Bordeaux.

Pomerol

*P*OMEROL? EXCUSE ME, BUT why on earth is there a section on Pomerol in this book? This is supposed to be a book about areas and people and wineries that have created something new, something which breaks the mould, something which points the way forward to a new age of wine. And surely Pomerol is one of the most sought-after *appellation* names in Bordeaux, the bedrock of conservatism and tradition in the world of red wine, and Château Pétrus, the most expensive red wine in the world, is a Pomerol.

I accept all those points, they're all true. But they weren't true a century ago, they weren't true after World War Two, they weren't even true during the boom-bust days of the 1970s when Bordeaux and its speculative indulgences and political intrigues were splattered all over the front pages of the world's newspapers. Château Pétrus wasn't the world's most expensive red wine *then*. Pomerol wasn't the most sought-after name in Bordeaux *then*, any more than Coonawarra or the Yarra Valley were regarded as Australia's leading quality wine regions; any more than Carneros, or the Santa Maria Valley in California were the objects of land grabbing and exploitation then.

But Pomerol has just as much right as these to be regarded as a *new* classic area, not because it didn't exist before – it did; it was producing wine 600 years before the first settlers arrived in Australia – but because Pomerol has only during the last generation proved its quality is as high as any region in Bordeaux. And its style is uniquely suited to the modern mood, offering immediate appeal plus ageability through its wonderful ripe plummy fruit, dripping with the sweet treacle of a hundred sunny summers' days, and its texture, smooth as cream and flowing as silk.

The experience of Pomerol is entirely in the wine itself; none of the experience is in the atmosphere of the place. Pomerol is more featureless and monocultural than any quality vineyard area in France. There is no village of Pomerol, just a massive church totally out of proportion to its surroundings. And there's no slope, not one that you'd notice, although Château Pétrus' vineyard is at the top of a plateau all of several metres higher than its neighbours.

As for grand châteaux of the kind that enliven the monotonous landscape of the Médoc – no, just some sturdy farmers' houses, nothing fancy, and nothing which would take up valuable vineyard land. Pomerol

only totals 729 hectares (1800 acres) – it's the smallest of Bordeaux's leading appellations, and the vineyards are divided between about 180 owners. In the Médoc 40 hectares (100 acres) would be regarded as an average size for a Classed Growth, here the average is nearer four hectares (ten acres). And Pomerol relies traditionally on the town of Libourne, 32km (20 miles) to the east of Bordeaux, to sell its crop.

These two factors have kept Pomerol almost invisible in the Bordeaux hierarchy for centuries, because there were no properties big enough and powerful enough to create a marketing proposition for an ambitious merchant, and in any case the traditional merchants of Bordeaux were those clustered along the quays of the city of Bordeaux. They had built their profitable trade on the Graves and the Médoc and ran a rigorously protectionist system designed to keep the export trade in particular in their hands. Libourne traders were excluded from this incestuous group.

That meant they were also excluded from the ability to attract the writers and commentators who trooped in annual pilgrimage to Bordeaux. Until the 1970s almost the only authors with any international readership were English, and they seemed as captivated by the Médoc and its Classed Growths as rabbits caught in the headlights of a car. Even the historic and widespread St-Émilion area, next to Pomerol, and also dependent on Libourne, was afforded merely a cursory nod.

Stirred but Unshaken

But Pomerol's luck was beginning to turn. Firstly, in 1974 a wine adulteration scandal since dubbed 'Winegate' rocked the quays of Bordeaux but left Libourne unscathed. The oil crisis in 1973 following upon a mad surge in prices between 1970 and 1972 and a consequent collapse with the mediocre 1973 and 1974 vintages had stripped the old Bordeaux merchants of their financial stability. The Médoc proprietors were left with cellars full of unwanted wine needing to be financed at crippling interest rates.

Through all this, the Libourne merchants were quietly getting on with selling their Pomerol wines without fuss to their regular clients in northern France, Belgium and Holland, people who bought the wine every year, on personal contact, to drink rather than store for speculation. The fact that the wine books of the nineteenth century didn't even mention Pomerol didn't worry them. The fact that even after World War Two leading wine writers could list Pomerol as a subdistrict of St-Émilion didn't bother them. But it did bother one man, Jean-Pierre Moueix. Moueix had become a merchant in Libourne during the 1930s in a

Pomerol has few fine buildings or landmarks, but great wines are produced here in homely surroundings. This little clutch of buildings contains the famed Château Pétrus.

desperate attempt to sell the wine from his own St-Émilion property – Château Fonroque. Succeeding in selling his own wines, he set about minutely examining the numerous small producers of the Pomerol vineyards which spread out from the Libourne suburbs. Over the next 30 years he sorted the great from the merely good and either bought many of these properties, contracted to farm them and make the wine, or undertook exclusive arrangements to sell their wines. In particular he befriended Madame Loubat of Château Pétrus, who has been described as never making the mistake of underestimating the value of her wine. Even when no-one wanted it, in the 1940s and 1950s, she refused to sell it at anything but a top price. For Moueix, Pétrus was the flagship he needed. For Pomerol, Moueix was the visionary *it* needed.

Until his arrival, Pomerol's small size, its lack of grand properties, and its reliance on the unfashionable Merlot grape rather than the Cabernet Sauvignon had all been disadvantages. Moueix turned them all to his advantage. Pomerol's compactness allowed him to discover the possibilities in every patch of soil and the ambitions and capabilities of every proprietor in a way that the merchants involved in Médoc wines could never do. The lack of grand properties made it easier for him to take estates under his wing, convince the owners of his vision and then show them, through vineyard practices and wine-making improvements, how to maximize their potential. And the soft, fruity, juicy-flavoured Merlot grape imparted a homogeneity to the

wines that meant he could begin to market Pomerol as a concept in itself.

It was the 1970 and 1971 vintages that first saw a leap in prices in Pomerol, largely because Moueix had decided on another move of enormous importance. The Americans were finally becoming interested in Bordeaux wines. Though the famous *names* of the Médoc might appeal to them, he felt the suppler, richer, more immediately approachable *flavours* of Pomerol would be far more to their liking. He was right. Even though the northern French and Belgian trade provided the bread and butter during the difficult 1970s, it was America which would catapult Pomerol ahead of the Médoc, just so long as a fine vintage and a strong dollar coincided.

It happened in 1982. A long, hot summer produced a large crop of superbly ripe wines across Bordeaux, and the Pomerols just oozed richness. Château Pétrus 1982 remains to this day the most astonishing young wine I have ever tasted. 'A Californian vintage' was what everyone lightheartedly called 1982, but in the end it was Maryland not California that anointed Pomerol's rapid rise to stardom.

There, an American lawyer called Robert Parker was publishing a consumer guide called *The Wine Advocate*. One of America's leading wine writers had just panned the 1982 vintage in Bordeaux. Parker proclaimed 1982 one of the greatest vintages of the century, showering praise on Pomerol for producing almost twice as many outstanding wines as any other Bordeaux *appellation*. It made Parker's reputation. And it made Pomerol's reputation. From being sold in quarter barrels to the doctors and dentists of Belgium for bottling in their garages, Pomerols are now the most sought-after red wines in the world.

Raimat

PAIN IS A LAND full of unpromising sites for high quality vineyards, but there can be few more miserable propositions than the scrubby, arid flatlands to the north-west of Lérida in Catalonia's interior. On my first visit to the area it seemed as though nothing of any value could possibly grow on such parched infertile land. But that was before I'd been to California and to Australia and seen how modern methods of viticulture and irrigation can transform deserts into verdant orchards and vineyards. If any part of Europe needed the 'New World' treatment, I thought, it was the vast arid acres inland from Spain's coastline.

On my next visit to Lérida, I realized I wasn't so smart. The owners of the Raimat estate had been trying to adopt modern techniques since 1914. It says a lot for the conditions they were working under – but also for the determination of the Raventos family – that it wasn't until the 1980s that Raimat finally began to turn out what are now among Spain's most modern, most affordable, and most delicious wines.

It is difficult to know what inspires visions in men, but Manuel Raventos must have been inspired by a Utopian vision in 1914. The 3240 hectares (8000 acres) of land he bought, with money from his family company Codorníu, Spain's largest sparkling wine manufacturers, had been barren for generations. Rainfall was negligible, sunshine and heat almost intolerable, and the soil itself uncultivable, being liberally laced with mineral salt deposits which killed any plant life that attempted to establish itself there.

I wonder if he knew that the Catalonia and Aragon canal was about to be built and that this, fortuitously, would provide him with a reliable source of Pyrenean water that he would then be able to siphon off to irrigate his acres. In any case he built a whole village for the workers he intended to employ, as well as a railway station, a school, a church, post office, sports fields and shops. But if he thought the irrigation waters would buy him instant success, he'd failed to reckon with how stubbornly the desert would resist his attempts to tame it. It took him and his successors 60 years to create the modern Raimat estate and produce Spanish wine of international quality.

He began by planting alfalfa grass to de-salinate the soil. Then he planted 35 million pine trees. By the time these had matured, and the land had been extensively treated with fertilizers and minerals, Raimat seemed ready for its vines. The trees were ripped out, and as much as 90cm (35in) of topsoil was added to the land from nearby. To no avail. The soil was infected with virus. The vines died.

It really wasn't until 1975 that the founder's grandson – also called Don Manuel Raventos – finally

began to crack it. He and another grandson, Don Daniel Pages Raventos, had established a relationship in the 1960s with Davis and Fresno wine schools in California to try to find a way of making the estate viable. They greatly improved the irrigation system, building 12 reservoirs and pumping stations, and initiating a programme of rootstock propagation and clonal selection to pinpoint exactly how they could combat the viral diseases in the soil and make this troublesome land fertile. On Californian advice, they planted the classic 'foreign' varieties; Cabernet Sauvignon and Chardonnay, followed by Merlot, Pinot Noir, Sauvignon Blanc, and Spain's best red grape, Tempranillo. Once the suitable rootstocks had been identified, plantings of Cabernet Sauvignon and Chardonnay were undertaken at such a pace that there are now about 400 hectares (1000 acres) of Cabernet and nearly that much of Chardonnay. No-one else in Spain gets close. Indeed, hardly anyone else in Europe has such an acreage.

And they have been planted in a way which is very 'New World' in style, and quite alien to Spain. Most Spanish vines are planted on dry soil and have to survive torrid summers without irrigation. Consequently the traditional practice has been to plant vines extremely sparsely over large acreages, and to allow foliage to flop over like a bush. This was supposed to minimize loss of moisture and keep the grapes cool. The yields from such scattered, water-starved plants are the lowest in Europe. But such unproductive methods are positively encouraged by the bureaucrats in Brussels, simply *because* they are so inefficient. The Raventos clan hadn't made millions by running an inefficient sparkling wine operation at Codorníu – and they didn't propose to waste their millions on inefficiency now.

So the vines are trained along tautened wires between 90cm (35.4in) and 110cm (43in) high and the foliage is neatly hedged. The spacing between vines is much closer than is usual in Spain, though still not as tightly packed as in northern France and Germany. Typically the Cabernet Sauvignon is planted at 3.2 metres (10.5 feet) by 2.1 metres (6.9 feet), and on the lower wires so that the warmth of the soil is better conserved. Chardonnay, which ripens more easily, is on the higher wires to maximize freedom of air movement and so avoid rot and the plantings are at 3.2 metres by 1.7 metres. Such bald figures cannot convey how revolutionary such controlled vineyard planting is in Spain. You have to see the struggling chaos of a typical

Raimat has always pursued an enthusiastically avant garde line in its buildings. This new bodega, all shining glass and marble pillars, keeps up the image.

Spanish vineyard to appreciate the difference. For Raimat the result is far better yields and much better fruit flavour in the grapes.

The vines survive entirely on irrigation. They have both drip irrigation and overhead sprinklers. You can turn the sprinklers on to create a protective mist when the temperature falls too low – as it can on spring mornings, though frankly the danger should be past soon after dawn. And, of course you *could* leave the sprinklers on to cool the vines in the midday heat. Irrigation is forbidden throughout Spain except for 'experimental' plots, and temperature control. Raimat classify their vineyards as 'experimental', in need of temperature control.

Well, to be honest, the more Raimat work their way around the regulations the better, because Spain is desperately short of top class wine and Raimat are providing it in increasing quantities. Talking of which, the quantities *are* increasing. Raimat are planting more vines. They've got around the new vineyard planting ban throughout the EC. Must be that 'experimental' status again. But should an 'experimental' vineyard be granted a Denominación de Origen? That rather implies that your experimental days are over. Yet since 1988 there has been a new DO – Costers del Segre – for the land around Lérida. It means recognition of what the Raventos family has achieved, but it doesn't place any curbs on their originality; the DO even has a provision for the future inclusion of any grape variety that might prove itself 'capable of producing prestigious, quality wines'. Most wine regulations end up stifling originality and innovation. If they can *enshrine* them in their regulations, that's brilliant!

Aiming to Please

Just so long as the wines keep coming. Although the whites and the sparkling wines can exhibit a certain faddishness that doesn't always work, the reds have a crowd-pleasing personality based on maximum ripe fruit flavour and ageing in Virginian oak barrels from America. The Abadia is usually a mix of Tempranillo, Cabernet Sauvignon and maybe Merlot, while the Cabernet Sauvignon just blends in a little Merlot. Both have a wonderful warm toasty oak spice and delicious sweet fruit – the blackcurrants in the Cabernet Sauvignon are brilliantly unsubtle and delicious. And their Pinot Noir is marvellous, with a mouthfilling fruit soup of plums and cherries and the perfume of flowers. Yet another sign that all over the world, committed winemakers are at last breaking the Pinot Noir's secret code – even somewhere as unlikely as an irrigated windswept desert in the parched Catalonian wilderness.

Sassicaia

I DISCOVERED THE JOYS of Sassicaia about a year before the rest of the English-speaking world. It was 1977, and I have to admit I was in bed. Well, it was Saturday, and it was springtime, and I was feeling unforgivably self-indulgent that warm sunny morning. I'd been given this bottle by a friend – a deep royal blue lead capsule around the top, a simple white label embossed with an ocean-dark circle of blue holding an eight-pointed golden star. And the single name 'Sassicaia', with the vintage, 1968. I had no high expectations and I didn't even use a proper wine glass.

Not for the first mouthful, anyway. But I did for the second because a flavour of such thrilling purity, such piercingly beautiful blackcurrant fruit spread across my palate, that I was instantly wide awake. This was First Growth Bordeaux, wrongly labelled, surely.

It wasn't. This was one of 7300 bottles of Cabernet Sauvignon produced from an experimental vineyard plot on the Tuscan coast where, in all the region's long vinous history, no-one had ever produced a decent bottle of *anything*, let alone world-class red. A year later, in 1978, London's *Decanter* magazine held a tasting of the world's greatest Cabernet Sauvignons, including the top wines of Bordeaux, America and Australia. Someone slipped in a bottle of Sassicaia 1972. And it won. Two of the five judges gave it a perfect score. Since that moment Sassicaia has been a world-famous classic.

Although Cabernet has been grown in Tuscany, sometimes with considerable success, for generations, no-one had ever focussed on the full potential of the great Bordeaux red grape. But a Piedmont-born marquis, Mario Incisa della Rochetta, had begun to develop a liking for the red wines of Bordeaux during his student days at Pisa. He married a Tuscan heiress and settled on her family estate, Tenuta San Guido, at Bolgheri on the coastal flats south of Livorno.

The locals said that the wines made in the Bolgheri zone tasted of salt, which, perhaps, given the location by the sea wasn't surprising, and he stuck to Bordeaux for his drinking pleasures. But in the back of his mind he'd long nursed the idea of producing a Tuscan 'Bordeaux', and when World War Two put paid to his supplies of French wine, it seemed like the time to translate his musings into practice.

It was 1943 when he chose to clear a 1-hectare (2.5-acre) patch of the rock-strewn Castiglioncello hill and plant Cabernet Sauvignon vines. He knew the nutrient-poor gravel banks of Bordeaux's Médoc produced pitifully low yields in the best years and he wanted to do the same. He also obtained some small Bordeaux-style barrels of new Yugoslavian oak as against the massive and ancient barrels favoured throughout Italy, and from 1948 he began to produce small amounts of thick, tarry, bitter red wine which every one of his friends and family were united in agreeing was undrinkable. But since no-one else was making a pure Cabernet Sauvignon in Tuscany, and since most Chianti wines were light and designed for quaffing there was no reason why the local wine drinkers should have foreseen any glimmers of pleasure in this viscous black fluid they spat out so ferociously in the Marchese's parlour. The Marchese spat with the best of them and began stocking up on Bordeaux again. But he carried on making about 300 bottles a year, and when his family refused to drink it, he'd put the remaining cases in the cellar and, to the relief of all, crack open some more claret.

In hindsight, one can see that tasting a six-month-old First Growth Pauillac can often be a similarly unpleasant experience, and you need considerable foresight to see that, 15 or 20 years down the track, all the bitterness will have fallen away and you will be left with the heavenly aroma of cedar and the luscious sweet fruit of blackcurrant.

Sleeping Beauties

During the 1950s, one by one, the wines began to come round. They were unsubtle to say the least, often volatile, usually thick with sediment, but they did show the magical sweetness of blackcurrant fruit that marks out the best Cabernet Sauvignons. This vindication of his dream of making fine Cabernet wine must have given the Marchese a great deal of pleasure, but until the mid 1960s, wine-making remained very much a hobby for him. It was Piero Antinori, his nephew and now head of what has become one of Italy's most influential and successful wine companies, who eventually persuaded him the wine was potentially too great not to find a wider market.

Antinori began by tidying up the wine-making – the great Bordeaux guru Professor Émile Peynaud gave advice, as did Antinori's talented winemaker, Giacomo Tachis. They found a source of oak barrels which did not leak and installed a proper modern press. Then they looked for more vineyard land, and found two sites, one called Aianova, and the other, with a pebbly soil very similar to the Graves in Bordeaux, called 'the place of many stones', in Italian, Sassicaia. In 1965 the two sites were planted and Sassicaia's transition from home winemaker's hobby to international superstar had begun.

The Marchese Incisa della Rochetta resolutely continues the tradition of making great red wine at the family estate at Sassicaia, which his father began as a hobby in 1942.

They did sell a little 1967 through the farm shop at Tenuta San Guido, but it was the 1968 which catapulted Sassicaia into the limelight. Antinori sent a bottle to Italy's leading wine critic, Luigi Veronelli, who immediately hailed it as Italy's new 'First Growth'. The 1968 was stupendous, so was the 1970. 1972 was magnificent in a tricky year. 1975 was another knockout, as was 1976. By the time the 1976 was released in 1979 Sassicaia had become world-famous, even though the wine had been worthy of the accolade since that 1968.

Purists often say that only indigenous Italian grape types should be used for Italian wine, and in some sectors there's a tendency to decry Sassicaia as 'too French'. I strongly disagree. If you can make a wine which is genuinely as fine as a Bordeaux First Growth – for goodness' sake make it. There is never too much wine of that quality. The importance of the Marchese lies in the fact that although he was not even primarily a wine producer, he was fired by a vision of excellence far beyond the boundaries of Italy's traditions, and against all the odds, he did doggedly set about achieving it.

He had realized that his wine would not qualify for any DOC, so he unashamedly labelled it *vino da tavola* – table wine – the lowest quality rating on the Italian scale. His brilliant success outside the rules encouraged, first Antinori, and then a whole army of others, to act upon their beliefs, to pursue ambitions far beyond the stifling constraints of Italy's regulations and traditions.

The Marchese died in 1983 and his son Niccolò now manages affairs in the cellar. The fermentation tanks are now stainless steel and most of the barrels are now of French Tronçais and Allier wood, although a proportion of Slovenian wood is still used. Over half these barrels are new each vintage and the wine, which is usually three-quarters Cabernet Sauvignon, the remainder Cabernet Franc, ages for between 18 and 22 months in wood. The estate can now yield up to 10,000 bottles.

But remarkably the character of the wine is still the same and I'm not sure the quality isn't actually better, despite the ten-fold increase in production. Tasting a decade of Sassicaia vintages, from 1978 to '87, every wine was fine, even from the lesser years like 1983, '84 and '87, when sweet oak tends to enrich the slightly leaner fruit. But the great years were truly majestic. The 1978 – ah, that wonderful cedar smell of old caskets and cigar boxes, mingling with a deep ripe blackcurrant richness, just now touched by moist, dark honey.

The 1981 – still a little tannic, but it's the tannin of chewy blackcurrant skins, of damson skins, showing a first flicker of sour acidity easily overcome by the sweetness of the fruit, and that honey comes again, this time with all the smokiness of Mount Hymettus.

The 1982 is more like the 1978, the tannins still a bit leathery, but the sweetness of the blackcurrant and the vanilla cream of the oak easily pushes past the toughness, the cedar scent is still a little raw, and the first sign of the delicious decay of honey waits, far to the back of the palate.

As for the 1985, I think it might even be the greatest Sassicaia yet. Its dark red mirrors the deep, concentrated richness of its fruit. There's a passionate richness there – an essence of blackcurrant still wrestling with lean acidity, and through all the turmoil flows the perfume of mint, the fascinating cream of *marron glacé* and blackberry, plums and hazelnuts, blackened by liquorice, uplifted by wafting cedar.

Not only Italy, but the whole wine-drinking world has a lot to thank this home winemaker for.

Skalli

*T*HEY'RE INCLINED TO REFER to the Midi as France's equivalent of the Central Valley in California, or the irrigated Riverlands of South Australia. Or rather they're likely to say the Midi has the potential to become as good as these places; the reliable jug-wine grape basket of France.

Yet surely the Midi, those hills and coastal flats that spread from Marseilles right round to the Pyrenees in the far south, is the cradle of French wine civilization? The Greeks were making wine at Agde on the coast in the fifth century BC. And the Romans were cultivating vineyards at Narbonne before the birth of Christ – Cicero thought the wines were rather good.

Well, the south did spawn France's great wine regions, certainly, but only because that's where the Greek and Roman galleys landed. Although a few villages did create a localized reputation for themselves, the first time the Midi wines achieved any national renown was in 1710. Most of France had been devastated by frost the previous year, and most of the vineyards further north were destroyed. Suddenly everyone clamoured for Midi wine. Quality wasn't the point. Availability was.

Until the 1980s, that was the continuing story of the Midi. The only 'tradition' in the Midi was having generations of grape growers growing as many grapes as possible to turn into as many litres of wine as possible – regardless of taste. Until then, 'le gros rouge' – the gross red – was France's staple drink. The grape varieties which sprawled all over the Midi became dominated by the Carignan and Aramon – planted solely for their ability to produce massive yields, often more than 20 tons to the acre. And the wine produced was reedy stuff, needing beefing up with thicker brews from Italy or North Africa. It wasn't a glamorous business, wine in the Midi, but everyone was making money.

Things began to change in the 1960s. With the independence of Algeria in 1963, the source of the rich, heady red blending wines dried up. But more importantly – the French were starting to drink less wine. During the 1970s and 1980s, national consumption continued to tumble, as French people saw 'le gros rouge' as a hangover from a pre-prosperous era they wished to forget. Only *appellation contrôlée* wine sales were healthy – wines that could extol their history, their uniqueness, their special soils. The Midi had spent two and a half centuries supplying bulk wine to the nation, while other less agriculturally fecund areas had to justify their higher prices by recourse to mystique and tradition. Suddenly the Midi needed to discover a mystique and tradition of its own. And it found its cupboard pretty bare. The Midi appellations of Coteaux du Languedoc, Minervois and Corbières are all trying to play the quality card, but they are hamstrung by the ban imposed by the *appellation contrôlée* authorities on replacing 'traditional' vines, with varieties more in tune with modern tastes.

Still, the last thing Robert Skalli wants is to call his wines by *appellation contrôlée* names. He prefers names like Chardonnay, Sauvignon Blanc, Cabernet Sauvignon, Merlot and Syrah. And he doesn't mind if you compare the Midi with California's Central Valley – that's where he got his ideas from in several trips to America during the 1970s. Except that he intends his French 'Central Valley' to be far superior to the Californian one. And he intends to do it on the very modern model of 'varietal' wines.

Simplicity is the Answer

Skalli had seen that the grape variety alone, without any detailed geographic provenance, conveyed a powerful message to the wine buyer. Californians had come to Europe and decided what were France's best wines, and had filled their vineyards with the grape varieties used to create France's masterpieces, reasoning that if they used the same grape variety at least they'd be starting out with the same kind of fruit flavour. Then, since they couldn't label their efforts as 'Le Montrachet', or 'Château Mouton-Rothschild', they'd taken the blindingly simple decision to call the wine after its grape variety. With one stroke, most of the complications which bedevil European wine names were removed. And people lapped it up. because suddenly good wine, great wine, even, had become something simple.

Robert Skalli was just as interested in North America's marketing ideas as in its vineyards. So when he was faced with inheriting a wine company in Sète – France's biggest wine blending and shipping centre – Skalli could see that with the bulk wine market shrinking, he had to take a quality approach. He also saw he'd need an entirely new marketing concept. America had convinced him that the new wine drinker would eagerly embrace the 'varietal' concept. In 1983 he created his own 'Fortant' brand of varietal wines, hardly mentioning the Midi on the label, and within five years he had built production to 450,000 cases a year.

The reason no-one had developed the varietal philosophy before was simple. All the good grape varieties were tied up in the *appellation contrôlée* system.

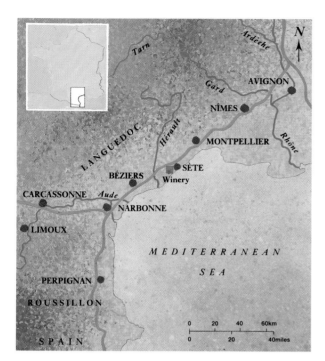

Midi vineyards weren't subject to any appellation law, so long as he could choose the varieties, and the clones, then choose the methods of pruning, the trellising, the yield per vine, he could really fly. There was no regulatory body to stop him. The only things standing in his way were the notoriously conservative grape growers of the Midi.

Skalli's eventual aim is 'maximum interference' in their vineyards, but it's a long, slow haul. In the early 1980s, having assembled a strong wine-making team at Sète for the first time, he sent out a questionnaire to all the local growers of any consequence – asking questions about replacing grape varieties and so on. He finally chose about 150 of the growers, primarily selected for their evident willingness to improve their vineyards. He developed a system of contracts lasting three, five, seven or nine years, based on production of Sauvignon Blanc, Chardonnay, Cabernet Sauvignon, Merlot and Syrah, the most popular varieties. He gave them no cash incentives to replant, or install irrigation. He simply showed them the figures. If they agreed to replant in the right varieties, he would pay a premium for all their grapes, and any bank would lend them the replanting costs against a nine-year contract offering far higher prices than the current Midi rate. With Chardonnay, a return of between two and three times the average earning was guaranteed. The word even got to the *appellation contrôlée* producers on the fringes of the Midi. Apart from in Fitou, basic prices hadn't changed in ten years. In 1989, for the first time, Skalli found growers coming to him, willing to forego their AC and stake their future on the varietal bandwagon.

Skalli now employs a team of vineyard experts, each with responsibility for a group of estates. Their job as much as anything is to gain the trust of the growers because the habits of generations may need overturning. In equivalent parts of Australia and California, for instance, the entire crop would be irrigated and machine-harvested. These growers have always dry-farmed. But if you want to benefit from Chardonnay prices, you've got to install irrigation – the vines won't set a crop in the Midi without it. And machine-picking requires special trellising systems to hold the fruit. But these growers aren't using wires at all yet. The vines

And throughout France growers of AC wines jealously guarded their sites, their tradition, all that – and had nothing to gain by selling, for instance, Bourgogne Blanc labelled as Chardonnay. Many appellations even forbade the use of the varietal names with the appellation title. The only part of France not tightly controlled by *appellation contrôlée* was the Midi – simply because no-one had thought it was worth the effort.

The Midi was producing ten per cent of all the world's wine. The area was producing twice as much as all of California, eight times as much as Australia – yet the varieties that were fuelling the rise in popularity of those wines were virtually unknown in the south of France. Chardonnay, the world's most sought-after quality grape, occupied less than two per cent of France's total acreage, and the few experimental plots round the Midi's Limoux didn't even merit a percentage point in the statistics. There was a bit of Cabernet on the sand bars of the Rhône delta, some Syrah in the stony soil to the east, that's all. The plus side was that neither was there any barrier to planting these varieties, because no-one had thought it necessary to formulate restrictions. Now, if someone realized that, this open house could be a gold mine in the making . . .

So that's exactly what Skalli did. He checked the climate and soil conditions in the Midi against different parts of California and Australia and found major similarities rather than crucial differences. He wanted to buy grapes, rather than own vineyards, but so long as he could use irrigation – which he could because most just sit there like bushes – as they have done ever since the Romans left.

Skalli's 'interference' still primarily takes the form of advice, though he feels that when contracts are re-negotiated and growers have already felt the benefit of the relationship, more 'interference' must be built in to the terms. He must be able to lay down the pruning required, the yield, the potential alcohol level – just as he could if he were dealing with contract growers in a place like California.

The chief problem in the Midi is to give the growers some sense of ambition. This gets to be critical in the month before harvest, and in the final week, the viticultural team closely controls every estate – particularly those with Chardonnay. It's not all plain sailing because growers have learned that people will pay for a lean, simple 11-degree Chardonnay – and they'll send in the pickers, sure of a quick sale despite pleas from the Skalli team to hold off for something richer and riper. In times of shortage of Chardonnay – that is, just about every year – they'd see the price of Chardonnay rocketing on the open market, so they'd maximize their yields, regardless of ripeness, to cash in on the boom. The contracts for the top estates now guarantee a minimum earning per hectare to take the speculation out of the hands of the growers. Skalli gives them the money early in the season and says – right, you've got your money, now we're in charge, so prune like this, thin those bunches . . .

Varying the Pitch

Another of the Midi's problems is that people, especially in France itself, think of it as one boring uniform mass. But Skalli's viticulturalists know there are wide variations in soil and climate. Limoux, high up to the west where the climate begins to take on the Atlantic influence, has reasonable rainfall and a lot of hard gravel, sandstone and limestone soils. These produce light, very fruity Chardonnays but also, to the confusion of the traditionalists, remarkably well-structured and perfumed reds from Cabernet and Merlot. The flatlands near the A9 autoroute running from Narbonne past Béziers and up to Nîmes are thought of as the most lifeless examples of low quality vineyards in France. Yet by applying a modern viticultural approach, these alluvial plains are yielding fruity, ripe, exciting Chardonnays, heady with the scent of peaches and passionfruit. Ally this to contract growers as far south as Perpignan, a string in the hills of the Coteaux du Languedoc, and some in the wild highlands of the Ardèche well to the north, and Skalli's winemakers can choose from as wide a variety of fruit as

any efficiently organized Australian outfit. With Chardonnay, for instance, they can find high acid, ten-degree potential alcohol fruit for sparkling wine, as well as fat, ripe fruit at 14 degrees potential alcohol. And they can blend any style desired between these two.

Against the figures for the average Midi crop – 28 million hectolitres – Skalli's output is still a mere drop in the ocean as yet. But that drop will become a puddle and that puddle a sea if current trends towards lower levels of consumption but higher quality expectations continue. Skalli has created a futurist's dream of a winery at Sète, combining state-of-the-art equipment with exhibitions of surrealist painting and sculpture. They've also taken over one of the long high white barns that used to serve the traditional merchants' trade in Sète. This is their barrel-ageing centre – a concept unthinkable only a few years ago. From not possessing a single new barrel in 1988, by the 1990 vintage they had 1500, with 600 being used to barrel-ferment the 1990 Chardonnay. By 1992 they'll have 3000. And as relationships develop with growers, Skalli intends to establish vinification centres in other areas. At the moment the red wines generally undergo their initial fermentation at the estates. Soon they'll be trucking their grapes to a local Skalli winery – just like growers do in Australia.

Australia and California. In the heady days of 1982, as well as starting their grape contract scheme in the Midi, Skalli bought the Saint Supéry winery in California's Napa Valley. So far the Americans have shown no signs of investing in France's Midi. But the Australians have. Thomas Hardy of South Australia have set up near Béziers. Mark Swann was Skalli's agent in Australia. He saw the potential of the Midi and the inexplicable lack of Chardonnay plantings throughout the south. Along with his Australian partner Robert Hesketh and a Briton named James Herrick, they've planted 100 hectares (250 acres) of Chardonnay on the flat alluvial land near Narbonne. And Skalli can't wait to take those grapes.

Herrick's view is that in 10 to 20 years' time, all the serious wineries in the world will be making good wine from the leading varietals as a matter of course and then in a worldwide market, the magic words 'Produce of France' on the label will once again become a desired symbol. The modern wine revolution will eventually bolster France more than any other country. And the Midi more than any other vineyard region.

It is from the wild and beautiful hinterland of Languedoc and Roussillon that many of the fine wines of the future are going to appear.

Torres

'IT MAY BE ALRIGHT for a bawdy night out, but hardly for an elegant luncheon.' The French do hate it so when they have to take one full on the chin, especially when the whole exercise is intended as a re-confirmation of France's traditional supremacy in the wine stakes, yet some rank outsider sneaks in and lifts the trophy. That was what happened in 1979 when France's Gault Millau magazine organized a wine Olympics and persuaded top producers like La Mission Haut Brion with their 1961, and Latour with their 1970, to enter what they were sure would be simply a contest between the leading Classed Growths of Bordeaux.

But south of Barcelona a Spaniard had been beavering away with Bordeaux's Cabernet Sauvignon grape. In 1970 he felt ready to make it into an experimental wine which he called Black Label, simply because the label was black instead of his family firm's more usual sepia and gold. This young Spaniard's name was Miguel Torres. And Torres Black Label 1970 was the wine described as more fit for the bordello than the lunch table. But then it would be by certain people, wouldn't it; especially by the manager of Château Latour. Torres Black Label 1970 had just beaten Latour 1970 in the taste-off to win first prize. I don't know how long it took him to recover his sense of propriety. But Spanish table wine had arrived on the international scene with a grand 'olé'.

Of all the leading European countries, Spain is still the one that is finding the struggle to create top quality, internationally admired wines the most difficult. There are several reasons. Until Spain's recent accession to the EC, rural conservatism tended to act like a tourniquet on the flow of new ideas; the Spanish climate is generally hot and dry and not always conducive to the production of wines of fragrance and balance and ageability; and the native grape varieties are by and large pretty unpromising.

It is this dearth of decent grape material allied to an unwillingness on the part of proprietors to uproot and replant – which was and is at the root of Spain's problems. And it took a young wine man, whose family company owned no vines at all in the early 1960s, to see the way forward and virtually single-handedly prove that Spain can make world-class wines. But to bring Spain centre-stage, the great grape varieties of France and Germany would have to be employed. And of all these Cabernet Sauvignon, Chardonnay and Pinot Noir provide the biggest challenges and the biggest rewards.

The Torres story is one of two generations. The late Miguel Torres and his son – also Miguel – had similar personalities – proud, single-minded in pursuit of their goals, eyes glittering with passion and commitment. Yet the goals of father and son were different, and so was the passion.

Torres senior took over the family company in 1932 at the age of 23. Life was never easy. The company was expropriated during the Spanish Civil War, and the sweetness of regaining control was soured by a stray bomb making a direct hit on all his wine vats in the last days of the war. But today the company sells 17 million bottles of table wine and another 7 million of brandy.

'Sells'. That word is the key to how Miguel senior made Torres such a force worldwide. But the second chapter of the Torres story increasingly hinges on Miguel junior, and the key to his personality is creativity. He went to Dijon in Burgundy to study oenology in 1959 and in 1962 on his return to Penedes says he only had one objective – to try to create some decent red wine of his own. But the local Spanish grapes just weren't up to it, so he assembled 30 different varieties from other sources and planted a few rows of each on the old Torres farm. By 1967 he was already excited by one variety in particular – the Cabernet Sauvignon. He'd just bought a new estate near Vilafranca at Pachs – and he set to planting Cabernet Sauvignon with a vengeance. The resulting grapes formed the base for his Bordeaux-beating 1970 Black Label, and now produce 12,000 to 14,000 cases of that wine each year. Although just down the road a producer named Jean Leòn was planting Cabernet Sauvignon at the same time, Torres Black Label was the wine which broke the mould.

Reasoning and Results

But it wasn't just a matter of the grape variety. Miguel Junior is a most analytical, scientifically correct man. You feel that he never makes a decision in wine without working out every possible angle first. At the same time as planting Cabernet Sauvignon on the vineyard at Pachs he now calls Mas La Plana, he was setting up a state-of-the-art laboratory, introducing underground ageing cellars to combat the fierce Catalonian heat, stainless steel temperature-controlled vats to try to preserve whatever fruit and freshness there was in the grapes – and, crucially for his red wines, insisting on early bottling after a period of ageing in small Bordeaux-style oak barrels. One of the reasons no-one in Spain had cared too much about grape varieties was that traditionally wine was left so long in barrel you

Miguel Torres is Spain's most indefatigable winemakers –
he also makes wine in Chile and California!

couldn't tell which grape was the starting point in any case. Between 14 and 18 months maximum, in a mix of new and slightly used barrels, some American, but some French, is what Torres had seen producing great results in France and, increasingly, in California.

Black Label – now labelled as Mas La Plana – is wonderful wine. It's not subtle, I agree, but it's rich in blackcurrant and strawberry fruit, frequently ending up like an autumn fruit stew with sweet blueberries, plums, mint, liquorice added in for good measure, and as Miguel's 20 years of experimentation finally bear fruit, a smoky streak of cedar which does begin to knock at the castle gates of the great Bordeaux styles. But it will never achieve true Bordeaux style, because it is basically warm climate wine. So Miguel has turned his attention to the two other world-class grape varieties among the 70-plus he is currently experimenting with – to satisfy his craving for a wine which really does equal the French classics in style as well as quality – Chardonnay and Pinot Noir.

He knew straight away that the traditional Penedes areas down by the sea and even in the central valley a few miles inland were always going to be too hot for really elegant wines. But in the Upper Penedes, back in the high hill country towards the very borders of Penedes, and in the case of the Milmanda Chardonnay vineyard, just outside the boundaries, Torres found

deep, well-drained soils at heights of up to 500 metres (1640 feet), the heat tempered by the altitude, and the air cooled by sea breezes during the day, and in Milmanda's case, inland mountain breezes at night. At Milmanda he has pinpointed three small sections of land totalling 10 hectares (25 acres) which are now producing low yields – around 30 hectolitres per hectare – of Chardonnay, and further north and a little lower in altitude, at Mas Borras, he has 20 hectares (50 acres) planted with Pinot Noir, also producing tiny yields.

Every last detail of the reaction of the vines to each different plot of land in the vineyards is scrutinized minutely, and every possible nuance of wine-making technique is tested with every vintage in the little separate cellars each single vineyard or 'pago' wine now inhabits. Milmanda is a marvellously toasty, beautifully balanced Chardonnay quite unlike anything Spain has ever produced before, and very like indeed the wines which have made Puligny-Montrachet famous for generations. Mas Borras is a gently fragrant Pinot, lightly dusted with toasty oak and with a heavenly scent of violets. When they did a re-run of the Gault Millau Olympics in 1986, Torres put in his 'experimental' Milmanda and Mas Borras 1985s. They came fifth and third respectively. Yet these are just 'experimental' wines still, because Miguel reckons it takes him 20 years to really get to grips with each vineyard and variety. Mind, the Torres 1970 trounced classics which had centuries of breeding to fall back on. That was an 'experimental' wine too.

White Bordeaux

Château La Louvière was one of the first to use stainless steel and new oak barrels for white wines and its wines get better and more widely known with every vintage.

So who started the revolution in white Bordeaux? André Lurton, owner of Château La Louvière in the Graves, reckons it started in the 1950s when he started wrapping cloth around his fermenting vats and pouring water down the sides to help chill them. He got the idea from soldiers who kept their water bottles cold that way.

Denis Dubourdieu, who makes Château Reynon in the Entre-Deux-Mers, says it was when he started chewing the grapes in the vineyard at the beginning of the 1980s. This was regarded as a most un-French habit but it led to him giving the crushed grapes and their juice a period of contact before fermentation began so that the flavours you can taste beneath the skins would permeate the wine. He got the idea from wine producers in California.

Michel Dupuy at Château de Fieuzal in Pessac-Léognan reckons he was the first. In 1985 he fermented all this property's white wine in new oak barrels – and the owner not only more than doubled the price for the wine, he sold it with the greatest of ease to great critical acclaim. He got the idea from Burgundy.

Or perhaps it was Brian Croser, Australia's leading innovator and wine-making consultant since the 1970s. Château Rahoul in the Graves called him in to try to make something drinkable out of their white grapes. Croser wanted to introduce cultured yeasts for fermentation. The winemaker there had a fit. So Croser went into the vineyard and collected a couple of hundred yeast and bacteria colonies from the fruit he gathered. He finally selected a single, highly efficient and unobtrusive yeast which dramatically pointed up the actual fruit flavour of the grape. Croser called his yeast R2 or Rahoul 2. During the 1980s it was so successful that it became Australia's most widely-used quality yeast. So it was brought back to Bordeaux and is now a crucial element in the creation of the new wave of fruit-dominant, fresh-flavoured, white Bordeaux wines.

Or did it start in the vineyard? In the Graves whites are traditionally grown on sandy clays rather than the gravelly soils better suited to its reds. However, the bulk of white Bordeaux comes from the far-flung Entre-Deux-Mers region stretching between the Dordogne and Garonne rivers where the chief soil is tightly compacted and sand-based capable of squeezing the life out of vine roots. During the 1950s and 1960s the more forward-looking growers restructured their vineyards by ripping out every alternate row of vines, so that the soil could be cultivated and broken up, and developing a high-trained trellis system designed to produce not only a decent crop but also a fully ripe one.

The result of all this is that Bordeaux in the 1990s is leading the new white wine charge on two fronts. It is now the chief producer of marvellously crisp, green-edged, nettle and gooseberry dry whites, very much Sauvignon Blanc in their snappy, mouthwatering style, but usually based on Sauvignon with Sémillon grapes, sometimes spiced up with a little Muscadelle.

At the same time, thanks to the Graves and Pessac-Léognan region, and increasingly, the top properties in the Entre-Deux-Mers, Bordeaux has wrested from the Burgundian Côte d'Or the role of leading the way in the promotion of tip-top quality whites fermented and matured in new oak barrels. Such wines are thrilling to drink when young, positively drooling with the richness of apricot and spice and cream just streaked with nettle green, yet capable of ageing to a deep, thoughtful nutty maturity, more majestic than all but the very top Burgundies. The leading Pessac-Léognan properties, like Fieuzal, demand the same kind of prices as top Burgundies – but offer a guarantee of excitement almost unheard of in the often high-yielding vineyards of modern-day Burgundy.

White Bordeaux was generally a thoroughly dispiriting and occasionally repulsive drink as recently

as the early 1980s, usually sugared and always over-sulphured insensitively. Until 1970, more Bordeaux white was produced than Bordeaux red, but except for a few oases of quality in Sauternes and the Graves, the product was largely terrible muck, anonymously blended under various merchants' names. Entre-Deux-Mers was the only wine my grandfather allowed my mother to drink – presumably because he knew it was so filthy it might put her off drink for life and at very least keep her a sober step or two ahead of the liquorous lunges of her ardent suitors.

While the growers just about managed to scratch a living, this state of affairs persisted. But in the 1970s, costs of production began to outweigh income, as people got so used to the name 'Bordeaux' standing for a cheap, mediocre liquid that they refused to pay much for it. Matters were exacerbated in the 1970s by an increasing swing in taste to dry white wines. Burgundy and the Loire took full advantage, Bordeaux was stuck in its medium-sweet rut. So the authorities decreed that Entre-Deux-Mers and Graves had to be totally dry wines. In a fit of revolutionary zeal, the supposedly trendy Sauvignon was planted instead of the suppler, rounder Sémillon, the grapes were picked green, the resulting wines were fruitless, searingly sharp – and, often, still marred by unacceptable clouds of sulphur.

That's the point when Brian Croser began to exert his influence on Château Rahoul. He had a vision of the final flavours he wanted to produce and he knew that the grapes were potentially good. Sémillon, in particular, had made great wine in Australia for more than a century. Sauvignon regularly did so in France in

the Loire. Denis Dubourdieu also stopped just chewing the grapes, and began to put into action the ideas which were increasingly filtering in from elsewhere in France and California. Burgundy was pricing itself out of reach; so were Sancerre and Pouilly-Fumé in the Loire. There was a shortage of dry white wine developing, because these vineyard areas were restricted by appellation limits. Yet here was Bordeaux, extensively planted with two classic white varieties – Sémillon and Sauvignon Blanc – producing two million hectolitres of wine a year, most of it needlessly undrinkable because of lack of care in vineyard and winery. Dubourdieu, aided and abetted by such winemakers as André Lurton in the Graves and Entre-Deux-Mers, and Peter Vinding-Diers and Pierre Coste in the Graves, finally brought Bordeaux into the modern white wine world.

Firstly, grapes had to be healthy and ripe, so that 12 to 24 hours of gentle steeping would bring out all that aroma which was so appealing in Australian and Californian whites. Then stainless steel tanks with temperature control were needed. Wines were being allowed to ferment at up to 28°C (82°F). Dubourdieu stipulated 18°C (64°F) as the optimum temperature to conserve aroma yet draw out the full flavour from the grapes. Then you store the wine cool and protect it from oxygen, filter it and bottle it fresh. The revolution in basic white Bordeaux was just a case of doing the simple things well, with the aid of the technology available.

The revolution at the top end of Bordeaux, which has turned Graves and Pessac-Léognan into two of the most exciting white wine regions in the world, revolves around new oak, preferably Allier. Bordeaux properties had become lazy after the war, even at the Classed Growth end, and virtually all wine was made and stored in concrete until the 1980s. Then tentative moves had been made towards ageing whites in oak after fermenting in stainless steel, but Dubourdieu and Dupuy at Fieuzal noted the ease with which Haut Brion and Domaine de Chevalier produced tiny amounts of peerless, barrel-fermented whites every year. Secondly, their own scientific studies had shown that the old, old Burgundian way *was* the only way to recreate the level of excellence they were after. Except for the fact that the barrels would be new, the techniques really weren't that different from those of good Graves 50 years ago. Ferment in the barrel at a reasonably warm temperature, leave the wine on the lees, mixing lees and wine together to give a rich creamy texture to the wine, minimize sulphur and maximize richness and fruit. Good wood, careful hygiene, and the effort required to make wine barrel by barrel. Simple, really.

WINE 2000

*L*ET'S LOOK THE NEW MILLENNIUM in the face. Let's look it in the face right now. What do we want our wine world to look like in the year 2000? Do we want to see the end of bad wine and the proliferation of good quality vineyards growing the grape varieties people actually want, regardless of historical precedent? Will we make triumphant use of the exciting progress achieved in the world's wineries during the 1980s and the world's vineyards during the 1990s, to ensure that good wine can be a joyous part of our modern civilization, affordable by all, available to all?

As the 1990s progress, the wine world is moving at a hectic pace. Labelling wine according to grape variety has been one of the most important recent developments. Wine was simplified at a stroke. Indeed Chardonnay has virtually become the universal word for decent dry white, usually with a nice soft texture. Cabernet is shorthand for decent, full-flavoured red, often quite tough but with gutsy blackcurranty fruit to make up for that.

By the year 2000, other varieties will have come into vogue, and sometimes, faded from view. With reds, Cabernet's Bordeaux stablemate Merlot will gain in popularity because it makes a fairly soft wine, and Burgundy's Pinot Noir will be making a substantial number of thrilling reds by the end of the century. Syrah, or Shiraz in Australia, will have shown that it more closely resembles a richer, even more sensuous version of Pinot Noir than a beefier Cabernet Sauvignon. California is already realizing that her climate is wonderfully suited to Syrah and the other Rhône varieties. As the Cabernet craze fades, as palates get bored by monochrome Cabernet styles, Syrah, Mourvèdre and Grenache will take up the slack.

In fad-conscious California, the 1990s show every sign of being the Italian decade, and Italian grape varieties will make their first bid for international attention on the West Coast. Barbera is already extensively planted, it's just a case of creating a few chic labels for this excellent low tannin, high acid grape. Nebbiolo and Dolcetto will prove more exciting, as the red Bordeaux varieties' stranglehold on California's vineyards slowly weakens.

Most of the white varieties to grow in popularity will still be French. The Viognier of the northern Rhône is sufficiently esoteric to become a fad California grape in no time at all, and Roussanne and Marsanne will follow. Australia already has two great grapes apart from Chardonnay just waiting for the call – Semillon and Riesling. New Zealand's whirlwind contribution has been Sauvignon Blanc. Semillon and Sauvignon will gather momentum, and if ever Riesling is to make a comeback, it'll be with wine made in New Zealand or Australia, not Germany.

Are other countries going to get in on the act too? There are three areas of the world certain to make their mark during the 1990s. How far they progress will depend upon whether their political situations deteriorate or improve during the decade. South America has already shown signs of sputtering to life, principally in the long-established vineyards of Chile and Argentina (though recent developments way to the north in Mexico are hopeful too). Investment is now being made in Chilean wineries, but results are still patchy, thanks to a combination of lack of internationally experienced winemakers, and exceedingly high yields from the heavily-irrigated vineyards. Even so, Cabernet, Merlot, Chardonnay and Sauvignon have all shown how good, and how fairly priced, they can be.

The vineyard potential in the Argentinian regions of Mendoza, Rio Negro and Salta is enormous and the range of varieties grown is much wider than in Chile. The Torrontes makes a deliciously floral style of white, and local experiments with hybridization have produced absolutely massive crops of well-flavoured grapes that would make far better wine than most of the basic varieties in Europe.

South Africa has slipped from being on a par at least with California, and ahead of Australia and New Zealand, to being well behind all three but reforms continue apace. There are some fine winemakers in South Africa, but they are frequently working in a vacuum, excluded from the international flow of ideas and experience now taken for granted in the rest of the New World. This will change, and if the seriously debilitated vineyards can be revitalized, we will all benefit.

In Eastern Europe, Hungary and Romania both possess marvellous potential, while Bulgaria's vineyards have already provided quantities of gluggable Cabernet. Russia probably has the greatest potential of all, and in grapes like the Saperavi, some true originals which, with encouragement and investment, could yield great wine. Australian, French and even English wine consultants have been spotted in the cellars of the Crimea and Moldavia dispensing advice.

The battles of the developed wine countries will be in the vineyard. Although the top vineyard sites in France, Italy, Germany and Portugal may benefit from systems of controlled appellation of origin, in other cases these systems stifle progress and protect privilege. Italy led the way in refusing to accept the restrictions of its system, and Southern France is rapidly showing that quality should be judged by what is in the bottle, not by a place name of origin on the label. As other countries, in particular North America and Australia, try to put in position systems of controlled appellation, they should reflect upon the freedom they were able to exploit so brilliantly when they first hit the world stage 20 years ago.

In any case, such arguments about appellation may prove to be futile. Not only is phylloxera on the warpath again, and not only is fungal disease destroying significant portions of Europe's great vineyards, but there is a threat far greater than either of these. Global warming. The average temperature in the main temperate areas of the northern and southern hemispheres could rise by one degree Centigrade every 15 years from now on. Although this would mean that countries like Germany, Belgium, Holland, England and Canada would benefit and could become important wine producers during the next century, it would completely wreck the appellation systems of Europe. In France, 2000 years of experience as to which grape variety ripens best where, would be proved worthless in the face of such dramatic climatic change. Today's courageous experiments outside the *appellation contrôlée* system may yet prove to be the classic models of the future.

Index

Acknowledgements

The author and publishers would like to thank all the wine producers profiled in the book, as well as their UK agents, who provided information, wine labels, pictures and bottles for photography. Special thanks go to those who went to so much trouble to help us with maps. Abundant information and assistance was also provided by Hazel Murphy and the Australian Wine Bureau, as well as the California Wine Institute, Dr Rebecca Renner, Alastair Mackenzie and the staff at Bibendum.

Photographs supplied by Ted Stefan/Cephas *1*, Mick Rock/Cephas *2*, Mick Rock/Cephas *10/11*, Michael Busselle *13*, Michael Busselle *15*, Michael Busselle *16*, Mick Rock/Cephas *19*, Michael Busselle *21*, Mick Rock/Cephas *22/23*, Mick Rock/Cephas *25*, Mick Rock/Cephas *26/27*, Mick Rock/Cephas *29*, Mick Rock/Cephas *31*, Mick Rock/Cephas *33*, Mick Rock/Cephas *34*, Mick Rock/Cephas *37*, Mick Rock/Cephas *39*, Mick Rock/Cephas *41*, Mick Rock/Cephas *43*, Mick Rock/Cephas *44/45*, Mick Rock/Cephas *47*, Mick Rock/Cephas *51*, Mick Rock/Cephas *55*, Mick Rock/Cephas *56/57*, R & K Muschenetz/Cephas *59*, R & K Muschenetz/Cephas *60/61*, Mick Rock/Cephas *62/63*, Mick Rock/Cephas *65*, R & K Muschenetz/Cephas *66/67*, Shmuel Thaler *69*, Mick Rock/Cephas *75*, Mick Rock/Cephas *77*, Mick Rock/Cephas *78/79*, Mick Rock/Cephas *81*, R & K Muschenetz/Cephas *82*, R & K Muschenetz/Cephas *85*, Mick Rock/Cephas *87*, Mick Rock/Cephas *88/89*, Mick Rock/Cephas *91*, R & K Muschenetz/Cephas *92*, Mick Rock/Cephas *94*, Mick Rock/Cephas *96*, Robert Mondavi Winery *99*, Mick Rock/Cephas *100*, Ted Stefan/Cephas *104/105*, Dr Su Hua Newton *107*, Dr Su Hua Newton *108/109*, R & K Muschenetz/Cephas *111*, R & K Muschenetz/Cephas *112/113*, Mick Rock/Cephas *117*, Mick Rock/Cephas *119*, Mick Rock/Cephas *123*, Mick Rock/Cephas *125*, Mick Rock/Cephas *127*, Mick Rock/Cephas *129*, Patrick Eagar *137*, Patrick Eagar *139*, Mick Rock/Cephas *141*, Mick Rock/Cephas *142*, Mick Rock/Cephas *144/145*, Mick Rock/Cephas *147*, Mick Rock/Cephas *148*, Mick Rock/Cephas *151*, Mick Rock/Cephas *152/153*, Mick Rock/Cephas *155*, Mick Rock/Cephas *159*, Mick Rock/Cephas *160*, Lake's Folly/Stephen Lake *164/165*, Mick Rock/Cephas *166*, Mick Rock/Cephas *169*, Mick Rock/Cephas *171*, Mick Rock/Cephas *174/175*, Mick Rock/Cephas *178*, Milton Wordley/Petaluma *180*, Milton Wordley/Petaluma *182/183*, Mick Rock/Cephas *184/185*, Patrick Eagar *187*, Mick Rock/Cephas *189*, Mick Rock/Cephas *190*, Mick Rock/Cephas *193*, Mick Rock/Cephas *197*, Mick Rock/Cephas *201*, Mick Rock/Cephas *203*, Patrick Eagar *207*, Patrick Eagar *208*, Mick Rock/Cephas *210*, Mick Rock/Cephas *214/215*, Mick Rock/Cephas *217*, Mick Rock/Cephas *218/219*, Mick Rock/Cephas *220/221*, Mick Rock/Cephas *223*, Mick Rock/Cephas *225*, Michael Busselle *228/229*, Mike Newton *233*, Mick Rock/Cephas *234*, Alan Williams *237*, Francis Jalain/Explorer *239*, Patrick Eagar *241*, Alan Williams *243*, Emil Perauer/Daumas Gassac *247*, Daniel Kuentz/Daumas Gassac *248*, Michel Guillard/Scope *251*, Nigel Blythe/Cephas *253*, Mick Rock/Cephas *254*, Alan Williams *257*, Michael Busselle *261*, Jon Wyand *263*, Janet Price *264/265*.